Voice of Justice

Voice of Justice

Dr. Justice AR. Lakshmanan
Judge, Supreme Court of India

Foreword by
Dr. Manmohan Singh
Prime Minister of India
and
Justice Y.K. Sabharwal
Chief Justice of India

Universal
Law Publishing Co. Pvt. Ltd.

2006 Edition
Reprint 2007

ISBN : 978-81-7534-560-2

Published by
UNIVERSAL LAW PUBLISHING CO. PVT. LTD.
C-FF-1A, Dilkhush Industrial Estate,
(Opp. Hans Cinema, Azadpur) G.T. Karnal Road,
Delhi-110 033
Tel : 011-27438103, 27215334, 42381334
Fax : 011-27458529
E-mail *(For sales inquiries)* : sales@unilawbooks.com
E-mail *(For editorial inquiries)* : edit@unilawbooks.com
Website : www.unilawbooks.com

Recommended citation: *Voice of Justice*, Justice AR. Lakshamanan, (New Delhi: Universal Law Publishing Co. Pvt. Ltd., 2006)

Computer Typeset at ULPC & *Printed* at Sita Fine Arts, New Delhi.

Dr. Manmohan Singh, Prime Minister of India and
Dr. Justice AR. Lakshmanan, Judge Supreme Court of India on
the occasion of handing over the Foreword for this book.

Dr. Manmohan Singh
PRIME MINISTER

सत्यमेव जयते

FOREWORD

Our judiciary is one of the four corner stones of our democracy, along with the executive, legislature and the media. India has been blessed by a proud tradition of jurisprudence and our people have benefited from the wisdom and sense of fair play of successive generations of legal luminaries. Dr. Justice AR. Lakshmanan comes from a proud lineage of judicial scholarship and erudition that we have been so fortunate to have.

I am delighted that Justice Lakshmanan has found the time to put pen to paper and write down his thoughts on a wide range of issues that are of direct concern to our people and the legal profession. The essays collected in this volume cover a wide range of issues that will be of interest to a large cross-section of students, scholars, lawyers, political leaders, journalists and others in public life. The range of writing here spans all the way from philosophical tracts on jurisprudence and law to very practical essays on specific aspects of Indian law and its application. These essays will, therefore, appeal both to the legal profession and to those who deal with it.

What I find truly inspiring about Justice Lakshmanan's writings is that they are firmly embedded in our traditional and ancient wisdom and scholarship. He begins with quotations from the Thirukkural that ring true even today and shows their practical relevance in matters of day-to-day delivery of justice.

Books like these should help in educating public opinion on legal issues and judicial pronouncements so that we have a more informed and empowered civil society. I do believe that our Constitutional commitment to the Rule of Law becomes an empty dream when it is beyond the grasp of the common man. Democracy can effectively flourish only when people know their rights and privileges and also their duties and responsibilities. However, all the fundamental rights enshrined in our Constitution become illusory rights for those who do not understand them and are not aware of them.

v

Equality in law requires equal access to law for this noble principle to translate into reality. I do believe that while low rates of literacy have not come in the way of a high rate of political awareness in our country, they are an important impediment in securing legal rights. The ability of our people to assert their political rights is not balanced by an equal ability to secure their legal rights. This makes it necessary for all of us to increase the citizen's legal literacy. This is why we have launched the National Legal Literacy Mission. I hope books such as these, written by our eminent jurists, will also contribute to this national effort.

I compliment Dr. Justice AR. Lakshmanan for publishing this volume. I am sure its readers will benefit from it.

New Delhi
July 25, 2006

(Manmohan Singh)

Y.K. Sabharwal

Chief Justice of India

5, *Krishna Menon Marg*,

New Delhi – 110011

July 18, 2006

FOREWORD

I have perused the compilation of 116 selected speeches of Dr. Justice AR. Lakshmanan, which is being published under the title **Voice of Justice**.

Democracy thrives on a number of freedoms that have been guaranteed by our Constitution, one of which is the "freedom of speech and expression". Public discussion and debates, of which speech is a specie, result in dissemination of information, exchange of ideas, creation of public opinion and opening the door for possible consensus in areas where there may be conflict of interests.

Public speech, indeed, is an art that has at its core the object of service to humanity. It is important that words of wisdom that befall from men who have attained excellence in their respective fields are preserved for posterity, so that benefit can be derived there from even by those who did not have the good fortune of being present when they were actually spoken.

Brother Dr. Justice AR. Lakshmanan possesses a wealth for knowledge and wisdom acquired by dint of hard work and commitment in the cause of justice in various capacities. Eversince he joined Bar, he has held many public offices, served the society in different capacities and has been associated with various public spirited organisations. His interests are not restricted only to the field of law. He possesses a clear analytical mind and is gifted with power of erudition, lucid exposition and uninhibited style.

The speeches included in this collection are couched in language that even a common man would relate to and find it easy to comprehend. The speeches cover a variety of subjects and provide an insight into the mind of someone who is an independent thinker and is ready to speak his mind fearlessly on issues that are of contemporary relevance. I am confident this collection would prove to be of immense utility for a long time to come.

While exhorting Dr. Justice AR. Lakshmanan to continue in his quest for justice, I wish the publication a great success.

Y.K. SABHARWAL

PREFACE

I was born in Devakottai a town in the southern most part of Tamil Nadu known for its munificent contributions to the cause of religion, culture, education and health care. I had the inclination to study Tamil Literature encouraged by my father and his elder brother. They inculcated in me a taste to study the works of the saivite saints which were called *Thevaram & Thiruvasagam*. I had great interest in Thirukkural a treatise on human ethics which was translated into English by G.U. Pope.

I did my schooling in my home town and I am proud to say that five students of that school in Devakottai rose to the position of High Court judges.

My taste for literature grew still further when I studied my pre-university course in Thiagarajar College, Madurai. The founder of the college was Thiru Karumumuthu Thiagaraja Chettiar. He was not only one of the great industrialists of Tamil Nadu but also a great visionary who had un-quenching interest in the studies and propagation of arts, culture, language and literature. He had established schools and colleges in and around Madurai.

By the grace of the Almighty I had the opportunity of serving in four High Courts of our country from the years 1990 to 2002 before I was elevated to the position of a judge in the Supreme Court of India. During these years while I was in Tamil Nadu, Kerala, Rajasthan and Andhra Pradesh both as the Judge and as the Chief Justice of the States I was invited by many forums to preside over and deliver lectures on varied subjects. I fully utilized these occasions into useful opportunities.

In-depth studies in various subjects as the occasions warranted were necessary. I made thorough studies of the subjects and delivered these speeches. They are on various fields like Law, Spiritualism, Art, Education, Social, Feminism, Environment Protection, Patriotism, etc. They were in Tamil and English as well.

Not only did I take pre-operative care but also took much post-operative care in preserving these speeches all these years. With modesty let me claim that the number of speeches delivered by me may be more than 400.

Some of my friends insisted the need of preserving these speeches in a book form so that it may be permanent and also useful for the society and as a result this book is now in your hands. Amongst them a special mention must be made about Prof. K.N. Chitsabesan who taught me Tamil literature in Thiagarajar College, Madurai, who not only insisted the importance of such a publication but also chose the speeches for this book. It is his vision that has given the apt and catchy titles for these essays.

My next job was to choose a publisher. The name that struck to me first was Universal Law Publishing Co. Pvt. Ltd., one of the leading publishers of law books. Mr. Manish Arora, Director, Universal, deserves appreciation for getting this collection organised into a presentable and publishable book.

I wish to record my sincere thanks to the Hon'ble Prime Minister of India and the Hon'ble Chief Justice of India for snatching time out of their busy schedule to go through this book and blessing it by writing Foreword.

August, 2006   **Dr. JUSTICE AR. LAKSHAMANAN**

CONTENTS

PART IV
GENDER JUSTICE

PART V
LAW AND SCIENCE

PART VI
LAW AND ENVIRONMENT

PART VII
CYBER LAW & IPR

PART VIII
CRIMINAL LAW

PART IX
ALTERNATIVE DISPUTE RESOLUTION & SPEEDY JUSTICE

PART X

HUMAN RESOURCE AND DISPUTE RESOLUTION

PART XI

TAXATION

PART XII

SPIRITUALISM

PART XIII

ACADEMIC ENLIGHTENMENT

PART XIV

MEN AND MATTERS

PART XV

MODERN INDIA

PART XVI

MISCELLANEOUS

PART I

VOICE OF JUSTICE

VOICE OF JUSTICE

VOICE OF JUSTICE had been raised and heard from the early days of history. It was well articulated from those days after mankind had learnt civilization. They were recorded by the great men of history. These men were called sages in India, Seers in other countries, teachers in some other part of the world, Saints in some. Generally they are venerated by the term *philosopher*. The term *philosophy* means love of wisdom. While knowledge makes man know things wisdom helps him to understand them.

Understanding a thing is a difficult process. One has to understand the nature of a thing he studies, the components it is made of, the qualities it has, the effect of it on other things, its relativity in its setting etc. This is what physics does. But physics helps us study and understand the external nature of any object. Whereas philosophy helps us study deep into the inner nature of any object, their relativity to our life. It is more difficult a study.

Therefore, the philosophers of olden days wanted to study the meaning of human life and record the results of their studies. Their works are called treaties. During the course of their studies they found that the human society had to be regulated and every man and woman of worthy of their names should behave in a regulated pattern. They had to curtail their free wills and acts in order not to interfere with those of others. This they found could be achieved by self restraint. They codified the code of conduct for men and women living in a society. Then only the society, they were destined to live would be an organised one

The self restraint was possible only to those men and women of higher plane and not to those living in lower base. Philosophers' words of wisdom and counseling would not work with them. There came the kings of those olden days to pronounce punishments to those who were found violating the normal order causing injury to the social fabric by their misdeeds. These kings had to set some patterns to these punishments. These forms of patterns were given the name *law*. If the teachings are called *tenets* the regulations put forth by the kings are called *laws*.

In those olden days kings were having the onerous duties of both law giving and law enforcing. There were no separate systems to frame these laws on one side and promulgate them on the other.

3

IN INDIA:

Vedas scripted in *Sanskrit* by sages unknown in India and the teachings of the Sakhya Muni popularly known as the Buddha in *Pali* language in the North and *Tholkappiyam* and *Thirukkural* in *Tamil* language in the south are scriptures codifying the conduct of not only men and women but also of the rulers, traders and all the people thus encompassing the entire society.

Bagavat Geetha: It is an accepted fact that Geetha is the essence of the Vedas. It is believed that the Supreme Lord Krishna himself preached the Geetha.

There are striking similarities amongst all these works because they deal with the common subject of improving humanism.

e.g.: There is couplet in the Tamil didactic work *Tirukkural* which says that

It is only the pleasure that is derived by virtuous means is pleasure All others are not only displeasure but also will earn infamy.

The entire work Tirukkural stands on the edifice of virtue. It has three parts the first part called "Virtue" dealing with the ways of leading good family life. The things that are to be adopted and those to be totally avoided by men and women in a healthy society are codified in this first part.

The qualities of a husband, wife and even the children are narrated in a most disciplined way. So also the social obligations of a family men and women are also given here.

On the negative side the evils like envy, back-biting, prostitution, lying, are also narrated. So also the codes of conduct for the ascetics are given in this part. Some of them are vegetarianism, compassion, penance, casting away anger, desirelessness.

Part two deals with the codes for the monarch for good governance. The first and foremost quality of a ruler is wisdom which he should acquire by reading, by listening to good people and by applying his own reason.

He, the king should be a benevolent ruler. He should on the one hand protect his subjects from internal dangers like famine, diseases, robbery etc. and from the external dangers like war on the other.

The qualities of the ministers are also given in this great work.

We are wonder-struck when we read Plato's *Republic* which also emphasizes wisdom for a good ruler. Plato calls these rulers as *Philosopher Kings*.

There is another couplet in the same book which speaks about the delivery of justice

It speaks thus:

The judge-the noble one, should be like a balance

When it weighs without leaning on one side.

He has to weigh both the sides equally and finally decide on the merit of truth

as the scales of balance equal and stand straight when the weights are equal. He should not be biased or lenient. He should not take sides.

In another couplet the poet says

It is not wrong for king to execute a wicked one by death sentence

It is but his duty like removing the weeds from the field to protect the crops

In Geetha also it is said that one who performs righteous deeds with calm and composed intellect becomes Soul Supreme and be the beloved one to God

IN GREEK:

The works of the great men born in Greece are claimed to be the basis of entire knowledge of the western world in all branches of learning. The three great men were Socrates, Plato and Aristotle. We are struck by wonder and exclaim how these great men thought of the codified principles of good and noble life of the people on one side and good and just governance on the other at such an early age of history.

It was Socrates who defined the qualities of a good judge:

A judge should hear courteously

Answer wisely

Consider soberly and

Decide impartially

IN CHINA:

China is one of the countries in the world which has contributed to the welfare of good society. Even before the dawn of the Christian era China had people like the great Confucius who was a great mentor of both men and kings. He had founded a core formula which he called *'harmony'*. According to him *harmony* should be the central theme around which every thing should evolve. There should be perfect harmony in a man's body, in his mind, in his family, in the society and finally in the governance.

He had codified rules for individual well being and good kingship.

He says "A wise man lives with the moderns but studies ancients". His five famous principles are relevant even today. They are: 1. Politics and ethics; 2. Rationalised Social Order; 3. Humanism; 4. Personal Cultivation; and 5. The Intellectual Upper Class. He was of the firm view that the measure of man is man himself and every other order should begin with the improvement of the self. Three qualities that are necessary to an individual are wisdom, compassion and courage.

RELIGIOUS WORKS:

Old Testament and new Testament are but law books which speaks about the conduct of men and women.

Lord Jesus was the fountain head of many reforms. His main aim was to establish the heaven on this earth here and now.

He says:

"As a man thinketh in his mind

So he becomes."

We can compare a couplet of Thirukkural here which says

The length of the stem of lotus floating on a pond is but the water level So also the moral being of a man is decided by the virtue of his mind.

KORAN:

So also the *Koran* codifies the principles of good and noble life of men and women. It is heartening to note that the meaning of the Arabic word Islam is submission and obedience to God. *Koran* defines the duties of a real muslim. Islam is a way of life of peace and harmony. It teaches men to obey the law of Allah. He points to us the harmony that is found in the working of the nature which has been created by Allah. Don't we see perfect order and harmony in the system of nature. Islam teaches good conduct for men and women by saying that good deeds will be rewarded and the bad ones will be punished. It narrates various duties for a good muslim. The duty towards one's parents. Koran states that one should speak kindly to one's parents, relatives and orphans and the needy.

Kindness, Politeness, Mercy, Patience. Trustworthiness, Forgiveness, Generosity even Punctuality, are some of the positive qualities a muslim is expected to cultivate. One good quality that is stressed is Justice, Allah commands justice and fairness.

ROMAN LAW:

Ancient codes were the ones which were formulated in the Greek City States around 7th Century B.C. This is called Roman Law. Around the same period the Hindu Codes of Manu in India and the Codes of the Chinese Tang dynasty were formulated.

We can find Roman Law influencing the growth and development of modern law in the western world. During modern times Spanish Law was formulated in the 13th century. In France Napoleon planned the civil law of France and first named it as *Code Civil des. Francais but* later renamed it as *Code Napoleon*. It is to the credit of the great emperor Napoleon that his code formed the basis for the legal systems of various countries like Belgium, Netherland, Romania, Portugal and a number of Latin American countries.

So were the law codes formulated in Denmark, Norway, Germany during the 17th and the 18th centuries.

In the United Kingdom the legal system is based on common law. The pioneer in the field of codification was the British philosopher Jeremy Bentham. His work influenced the later codes adopted by the British government in India.

Now we have a fully developed legal system and an enviable justice delivery mechanism in India.

The word jurisprudence means science and philosophy of human law.

Therefore, the *voice of justice* will always ring the glory of human law. But our ultimate goal and aim should be to make the *voice of justice* ring more from within than without, so that man would be free from the jaws of litigations and courts from cases.

PART II
LAW & JUSTICE

CONSTITUTION OF INDIA

Regarding the working of the Constitution, Dr. Ambedkar had observed with a visionary zeal that *"I feel that it is workable, it is flexible and it is strong enough to hold the country together both in peace time and war time. Indeed, if I may say so, if things go wrong under the new Constitution, the reason will not be that we had a bad constitution. What we will have to say is that man was vile."*

What is a Constitution? It is a collective declaration of the determination of the people of a nation, to live in an orderly fashion for the common good and well-being of the whole nation. The constitution should be alive and responding document to meet the needs, necessities and exigencies of changing socio, economic and political environment, not only of the nation but of the entire globe. If the Constitution does not admit the changing concepts of human ecological conditions, it shall not only retard the march of the nation towards its logical goal but also generate socio-economic-political tension and which shall eventually pave way for the undoing of the Constitution.

The higher judiciary of our land which are entrusted with the onerous task of protecting, preserving and enforcing the Constitution cannot and should not be unaware of and unmindful of marching trends of human aspirations and the fall outs of conflicting rights and equalities. The success of the constitution also rest, with the Bar and the Judiciary in a very large measure. Wooden interpretation and technical enforcement of the Constitution just by its words and not by its spirit shall prove to be destructive of the Constitution. The Law should march in parallel line with the aspirations of the people of the nation. The march of law is largely controlled by the Judiciary. When law is unable to keep pace with the march of the nation, resort to amendment of law, be it constitutional law or ordinary law becomes inescapable. It is true, the Courts interpret the law as it is and the Legislature amend the law as it ought to be.

As Indians, we are justly entitled to be proud of our nation and its endearing and enduring democratic institutions. Needless for me to state that almost all nations which had attained independence from the colonial rule of British,

---

Speech delivered on the occasion of Golden Jubilee Celebrations of the 'Adoption of the Constitution of India' at Kerala on 26th November, 1999.

French and Portugese, Asia, Africa, Middle and Far East have lost their independence to dictators and usurpers of powers of all sorts. In the dark sky of anti-democratic forces, our India, shines like a bright star emitting rays of light of Freedom, Democracy and Rule of Law. But for our Constitution, this unique place held by us in the comity of nations would not have been possible.

It is the duty of every citizen to address himself as to how and what he could contribute to the efficient and improved working of our Constitution and Institutions created under the sacred document.

The evils of casteism, communalism, criminalisation and corruption have stood in our way to progress and development. It is time to garner strength, both moral and intellectual, to combat these cankers. To achieve the lofty ideals enshrined in our Constitution, we cannot adopt a process involving violence and blood shed but a gentle process, not of revolution, but of reformation.

The basic, cultural, religious and social diversities of Indian people have been the foundation of our national stamina and strength. We cannot afford to lose this strength at any cost.

To emphasize, that some of our greatest fighter for Independence were legal luminaries. Hence, the members of the legal fraternity should come forward and fight the divisive forces and work for the preservation of the fundamental values upheld by the Constitution. In the words of Chief Justice Earl Warren of the Supreme Court of America, *"the preservation of a democratic society needs a militant Bar, for there can be no compromise or surrender where the basic rights of a citizen are in jeopardy"*.

As the guardians of law, let us resolve to rededicate ourselves to preserve and protect the constitution and its institutions from the onslaught of individual and group misdemeanours, so that, we ourselves and our posterity may live in a civilised state of democracy.

ಐ ಐ ಐ

CHALLENGES AHEAD IN INDUSTRIAL JURISPRUDENCE

It is needless to say that the industrial law occupies a pivotal place in the legal system of our country, for it affects a large section of the population of India. The industry is also contributing for the economic well-being of the nation, and the progress of the country depends upon the industrial growth. This branch of law itself is novel in its origin, purpose, theory and in its application. It is better to quote Ludwig Teller, who in his monumental treatise "*Labour Disputes and collective bargaining*" said "Industrial arbitration may involve the extension of an existing agreement, or the making of the new one or in general, the creation of obligation are modification of old ones".

This new obligation would come into existence notwithstanding the fact that one of the parties may be entirely opposed to the arrangement. Instead of the parties making a contract; the Industrial Tribunal superimposes a contract on the employer and the workmen. This idea of an independent authority making a contract and superimposing it on the employer as well as the workmen is a strange and a novel idea. Ordinary civil courts can only enforce the terms and conditions of a contract entered into between two legally competent persons and such courts cannot under the system of law superimpose a contract on the parties. No doubt, this noble ideal of Industrial law would have shocked many who were holding the notion that contract can arise only out of free will of the parties. Thus, under the industrial law, in the absence of collective agreement between the employer and workmen, a labour court or tribunal is entitled to make a contract for them and this contract can be enforced against both parties. Thus, industrial jurisprudence reverses the old accepted concept of contract.

An industry is a dynamic socio-economic institution in which capital and labour are both equal partners, and without the co-operation and co-ordination of both the labour and the capital, the industry cannot aspire to move forward. What is produced in an industry is a result of joint contribution of both labour and capital. It is the labour who invest their sweat and toil for the industry and

Speech delivered on the occasion of Southern Regional Conference on "Winds of Challenges in Managing Human Resources" conducted by NIPM, Madras on 24th September, 1994.

11

undoubtedly the capital contribute their own might in terms of financial investment in the company.

Our Constitution has shown great concern for the working class and given them a place of pride in the new socio-economic order envisaged in the Preamble and the Directive Principles of State Policy.

It has been recognised that workmen are entitled to come together and form themselves into a union which will deal with employers collectively because the individual workmen are not in a position economically and otherwise to do so by themselves. The State or the government cannot leave the workmen to the tender mercies of the employers. It is the primary obligation of the government to intervene by bringing its influence and good offices to bear on the parties with a view to conciliate their differences and failing which it is the duty of the Government to entrust the matter to an independent tribunal to adjudicate upon the dispute. The decision of the Tribunal is made binding on the parties as if it is a statutory contract made by the parties. The tribunal and the labour courts have the right to ignore "Private Rights" and do social justice. Social justice is not based on contractual relationship and it is something which is invoked to do justice without contract to back it.

The Industrial Disputes Act, 1947, is drafted on the lines of analogous provisions of law prevalent in Britain, Australia and other countries. This act was drafted when the interim government formed by the then British Government was in power. At that time, India was on the threshold of freedom.

Articles 37 to 39, 41 to 43, 46 and 47 of Chapter IV of our Constitution amplify and elaborate the idea of social justice set out in the Preamble.

In its quest to do social justice, the courts of law interpret the definition of industry and workmen to meet the changing times. It has been recognised by the courts of law that workmen play predominant role like capital. Irrigation department of state is held to be an industry. Charitable and religious institutions have been brought within the preview of Industrial Disputes Act. Hospitals are held to be industries. The right of workers to intervene in winding up proceeding has been recognised by courts. The industrial jurisprudence has undergone a great change during the past two decades. What was held to be not an industry in 1960s, is held to be an industry in late 1970s. There cannot be any doubt that the industrial jurisprudence will suitably adjust itself to meet the challenges ahead.

There should be a simple and well planned labour enactment which would be of very great help to the citizens to observe law, lawyers to understand and to the Law Courts, in applying it. Our Indian Penal Code drafted by Macaulay before 1837 and enacted in 1860, even today remains largely un-amended. It has stood on the statute book for all these decades declaring in language which is as simple as possible and with unequalled precision what the law is on every subject that can come within the scope of the Penal Law.

According to me, the Industrial Law, which governs the rights and obligations of workmen, should be simple and precise. The Industrial Disputes

Act has undergone innumerable amendments by Ordinances and Amending Acts.

Labour Relations Bill, which was placed before the legislature during 1950, was allowed to lapse though the same provided a comprehensive law superceding the Industrial Disputes Act and similar legislation obtaining in some states. Similarly, the subsequent Industrial Relations Bill has not seen the light of the day. Amended definition like 'Industry' has not been brought into force till date.

I am confident that the Industrial Jurisprudence will speak in a language which would meet the challenges ahead.

సహసహస

ROLE OF OMBUDSMAN

"Insurance" is the greatest blessing that modern times have bestowed upon mankind. It enables man to overlap the barrier of death to overcome the grim fear, that his loved ones may some day become dependants upon the charity of others. It enables him to project himself into the future and in a real sense even if he dies to live again. The immortality that comes to a man who has insured his life for the protection of his or her dependants is certain evidence of a mental and spiritual development that ought to make man rank high in the future world. The institutions furnishing this great social service to the masses of people are encouraging prudence, removing anxiety, destroying fear of the future, creating self respect and bringing about co-operation for social uplift that has never seen its precedent in any time in the history of the world.

Of course, there may be some procedural and administrative wrongs, knowingly or unknowingly committed by the companies in the settlement of claims, repudiation of claims, non-issue of insurance documents after receipt of the premium etc. To resolve such complaints on the part of the insurance companies in a cost effective, efficient and impartial manner, a mechanism was felt needed and required.

As far as Judiciary is concerned, after Independence, the legal aid concept was on the agenda of our Central Government. Various committees and commissions examined the issue but it was only in 1980 that the Central Government constituted a Committee for Implementing Legal Aid Schemes (CILAS) and asked it to oversee legal aid schemes and programmes throughout the country. The relevance, the importance of legal aid schemes and the public acceptance of Lok Adalats prompted the Central Government to enact legislation for giving a statutory basis to legal aid schemes and programmes which resulted in the enactment of the Legal Services Authorities Act, 1987.

Originally, the practice of constituting the Ombudsman was initiated as far back as in the year 1809 in Sweeden when Swedish Justice Ombudsman was first appointed and this concept was later adopted by many European countries. In India, the concept of Ombudsman was firstly introduced in banking sector and having found it to be easy, economical and effective, the Government introduced

---

Speech delivered at the seminar on 'The Role of Insurance Ombudsman in Redressal of Insured Public', Hyderabad on 24th August, 2002.

14

this concept in insurance sector also. Ombudsman, as an Attorney or legal representative or an official appointed, would investigate individual complaints against mal-administration, especially, by public authority. The framework for providing the protection to the Policy holders includes the Ombudsman Scheme which is intended to provide a grievance redressal mechanism and thereby increase the confidence of the public in insurance companies. The aim is to 'resolve all complaints relating to settlement of claim on the part of insurance companies in a cost effective, efficient and impartial manner'. The Central Government notified the Redressal of Public Grievance Rules, 1998 in November 1998 and the same were amended on 10th June, 1999. The rules apply to all personal lines business and provide for the appointment of an Ombudsman from a wide pool including but not limited to those with judicial, insurance or administrative experience. The insured's first port of call will be the insurer. If the insurer rejects the complaint or fails to reply to it within one month, then the insured can take his complaint to the Ombudsman provided, that he does so within a year of the Insurer's rejection and he has not brought his complaint before the Courts or the Consumer Forum.

The insurance claims are governed by Civil Law. If policy holders approach the Civil Courts, it will take years. If they approach the Ombudsman, the claim will be decided with consent at the earliest point of time. Here, the Ombudsman can play a dual role. The first is the quasi-judicial role one would expect. The second, upon the agreement of the insurer and insured, is as a mediator in a form of semi-binding mediation.

Dealing with the quasi-judicial role, the Ombudsman can rule on personal lines policies where the subject-matter of the complaint falls within Rule 12 of the Rules namely:

    (a) The premium paid or payable;

    (b) The absence of policy documentation;

    (c) The interpretation of a policy to the extent that this is claim related;

    (d) Delay in settlement;

    (e) An insurer's partial or total repudiation of a claim.

The semi-binding mediation role is a consensual process and in that the Ombudsman needs the consent of insurer and insured to act in the capacity.

Where the Ombudsman is acting in a quasi-judicial capacity, his award is to be issued within three months of the insured's complaint. If the insured accepts the award, the insurer has 15 days to make payment. Where the Ombudsman has mediated, his recommendation is to be issued within one month of the date of receipt of the complaint. In theory, an award acceptable to the insured will be payable by the insurer within 30 days of the Ombudsman having made his recommendation. The Ombudsman's award is binding on the insurer excepting on the points of law but not on the insured, for whom other remedies remain open to pursue.

The Central Government has established the Offices of Insurance Ombudsmen principally to provide a fair, equitable and independent machinery to deal with the insurance disputes and claims. At present, the insured can move the controlling offices for the redressal of any of his grievances. As a consumer of a service provided by the Insurance Companies, he is free to file complaints in the Consumer Forum set up under the Consumer Protection Act, 1986 or in the Civil Courts. He may also seek his remedies through Arbitration under the Arbitration and Conciliation Act, 1996. Establishment of the Ombudsman system is a welcome continuation of the process to strengthen the consumer protection movement against the vagaries of monolithic organizations. Its basic object is to resolve the differences and disputes between the insurer and the insured in a speedy and impartial manner involving the least possible formalities and cost, in the spirit, in which the Ombudsman system is understood the world over, wherever it has been functioning as a quasi-judicial authority and watch dog against any arbitrary or unreasonable action on the part of the public establishments/corporations.

Insurance sector is floating for a rapid growth with the enactment of the Insurance Regulatory and Development Authority Act, 1999.

Recognizing the importance of Andhra Pradesh, insofar as it relates to insurance sector, the Central Government has notified Hyderabad for setting up the Headquarters.

The Government of India, in exercise of the powers conferred by section 114 of the Insurance Act, 1938, promulgated the 'Redressal of Public Grievances Rules in 1998'. Creation of 'Ombudsman Scheme' was envisaged under the aforesaid rules, basically to provide justice to insuring public in a cost-effective, efficient, and impartial manner, particularly in view of time and cost implications involved in approaching Courts of Law. The insurance companies, both in private and public sector, have come forward to fund this institution. Thus, it will be seen that the Ombudsman Scheme is a self-correcting and independent mechanism set up by the Insurance companies themselves to ensure fair, just, equitable and timely settlement of claims to their policy holders. The mistakes committed by their administrative offices in the settlement of claims are expected to be expeditiously corrected by this independent mechanism, through mediation within a month, failing which by passing an Award in three months, after formally hearing the arguments on both the sides.

In order to instill a sense of confidence among the insuring public, officers of eminence, standing and integrity, backed by vast experience in Higher Judicial, Civil, and Insurance Company Services, are appointed to hold this exalted position in the Insurance Sector. The conglomerate of Insurance Companies represented by their apex body - Insurance Council, is vested with the power of appointment of Insurance Ombudsman, out of the panel prepared by a committee comprising of the Chairman of the Insurance Regulatory Authority, Secretary looking after Insurance portfolio in the Department of Economic Affairs, Chairman of the Life Insurance Corporation of India and the General Insurance Corporation of India. The tenure of the post is for a period of three years and the incumbent to the post will draw a pay equivalent to the Highest Civil Servant *viz.*, Secretary to the Government of India (Rs. 26,000 p.m. plus allowances as admissible to such Central Government Officials).

The jurisdiction of the Insurance Ombudsman presently extends to personal lines of Insurance business covering cases, both in Life and General Insurance Sectors, upto a maximum amount of Rs. 20 Lakhs. The decision of the Insurance Ombudsman will be final for the Insurance Companies, who do not appeal against it in a Court of Law. However, the policy holder, if he is dissatisfied, has the right to approach a Court of Law.

This Institution is still nascent and is in its swaddling clothes. Precedents and interpretation of Insurance law is still in making and not yet made. Concerted efforts are required to be made to evolve a common practice in settlement of claims at least in the case of personal lines of Insurance business. This will take time & blessings of the higher judiciary.

If we examine the functions of an Ombudsman, he shall act as a Counsellor and mediator in matters which are within his terms of reference and if requested to do so by mutual agreement, by the complainant and the Insurers. When a complaint is settled by mediation, Ombudsman shall make a recommendation. Such recommendation shall be made not later than one month from the date of receipt of the complaint. Complainant shall communicate acceptance of recommendation within fifteen days of receipt of the same to Ombudsman. In turn, the Insurance Company has to comply with the recommendations within 15 days after receipt of recommendations, together with acceptance letter of complainant from Ombudsman.

The life of the persons in this world-village, say in business life, professional life, personal life is moving with rapid pace and things are changing in split second. However, the other side of this fast moving life is a sense of insecurity and a feeling of lack of confidence. The trust, confidence and security, which the contracting parties, reposed between them, is of paramount importance. As has been stated above, with a trustworthy insurance company around, the people in all walks of life can rest assured and cherish a feeling of security in the event of any untoward contingencies. Therefore, it is necessary for an insurance company, especially in this nerve-cutting competition, to instill confidence and the sense of security in the persons who would like to take insurance. In this direction, the institution of Ombudsman plays a vital and key role. However, this institution of Ombudsman is created under the Redressal of Public Grievance Rules notified by the Central Government inheriting the source of power from a remote provision from Insurance Act, 1938. *Therefore, there is every need for the institution of Ombudsman to be given a exclusive statutory basis. Furthermore, the award of the Ombudsman must be made executable in a court of law just like a decree passed by an Arbitrator*, by which the institution of Ombudsman would be more effective. So also, the *public must be made aware of the institution* of Ombudsman and its role in the redressal of grievances of the insured.

శుభం

WORK CULTURE IN COURTS

Law of Entropy afflicts as much our judicial system as it pervades the universe. All things move from order to disorder. But, the human mind has always imposed order even on Chaos. This is the time for us, to clean up our house and set it back into order.

We are all too familiar with the symptoms and the disease afflicting our judicial system - sky rocketing litigation, the arrears of cases and consequently, the delayed justice. The causes for these *mala fides* are not far to seek: Increase in the population and the increase in literacy rate, has bred litigation. The lack of courts, the vacancies on the Bench, the poor infrastructures of the courts has undermined our ability to cope with the mounting litigation. The consequences are that the poor litigant must go through labyrinthine judicial processes, must wait for years on end to see even a glimmer of justice.

The malice is not curable. But the illness calls for a multipronged cure. The foundation of any system is the knowledge of the people who work the system. Therefore, the first task before us, is to improve the quality of legal education in the country. With bad seeds, one cannot expect a good harvest. Unless our law students are taught properly, they can neither make good lawyers, nor good Judges. Good lawyers and good Judges will dispose of cases at a faster rate and with less cacophony.

In order to reduce the number of cases coming into courts, Alternative Dispute Redressal, such as Arbitration, Lok Adalats, Panchayat Courts should be encouraged amongst the people. Since the Government is the biggest litigant, it needs to evolve a method of solving the disputes within the Government department. This will certainly reduce service-cases, to a large extent. These ADR Fora will also reduce the number of litigation, coming into the Court.

Since the lower judiciary does the bulk of judicial work, it needs to be strengthened. Not only the infrastructure of the lower court needs to be improved, but also the service conditions of the judicial officers need to be revamped. More courts need to be created, so that justice is taken to the door-steps of the people. The recent creation by the Union Government of Fast Track Courts at the district level, to dispose of old cases, is a step in the right direction.

Speech delivered on the 'Administration of Judicial System in Rajasthan', Jaipur.

In our country, the ratio between the population and the Judges, is unrealistic. Therefore, the judiciary is unable to cope up with the flood of litigation. More the Judges, less the arrears of cases. Therefore, the number of Judges needs to be increased in proportion to the population.

Our antediluvian laws either need to be deleted or rejuvenated. The procedural laws should be pruned and streamlined. The right to appeal needs to be restricted both on the civil and criminal side.

New technologies, such as computers, should be introduced in the courts. This will facilitate the dissemination of information, the collection of data and the upkeep of the judicial records.

The work-culture of the courts should be improved. The relationship between the Bar and the Bench should be cordial. Strikes and adjournments only delay the disposal of the cases.

The quality of legislation needs to be improved. Poorly drafted laws encourage litigation. If the law is clear, there is less litigation.

To avoid inordinate delay in furnishing certified copies of Judgments and final orders etc., a copy of the judgment/order should be taken and authenticated immediately after its pronouncement and preserved in the copying-section, for the purposes of issuing certified copies, whenever necessary.

Sufficient number of photo-copying machines should be supplied to the copying-section, for prompt issue of certified copies. Photostat-copies should be authenticated and certified as true-copies.

Judicial reform is not only the concern of the judiciary. It is the responsibility of the Executive, of the Legislature, of the Bar and the Bench and of the people. It is not a one-time remedy, but an on-going process. We must stop blaming each other, for the malice. We must unite, to prevent and control the litigation epidemic. Healthy litigation should be entertained, frivolous one should be discouraged.

The other problem, which usually bags down the courts, is the pendency of large number of cases of under-trial prisoners.

All the Chief Judicial Magistrates in the State were directed to hold court, once or twice in a month, depending upon the work-load in the jails, within their respective jurisdictions, to take up the cases of those under-trial prisoners, involved in petty offences, who are keen to confess their guilt and are unable to furnish bail-bonds, for getting released on bail. All the CJMs were further directed to send quarterly statements, pertaining to the disposal of such cases, to the High Court.

The Legal Services Authority has also agreed to provide the legal aid and assistance of counsel to such prisoners. Faith of the people in system is the touch-stone, to gauge the relevance of a particular system serving the society. This fact equally applies to judicial system, the administration of which is being discussed. Of late, it was observed that senior citizen/old persons in the twilight of their life, are made to wait endlessly for the decision of their cases. Therefore, in order to find solution to this problem, it was also considered and all the Presiding Officers of the subordinate courts were directed to identify all such matters and to take appropriate steps for their disposal, on priority-basis, and they were directed to send necessary statistics, indicating necessary compliance of directions.

Some directions were issued to the Registrar at Jodhpur and Jaipur, and respective Deputy Registrars were directed to prepare the lists of such cases, in which, matters of persons above 65 years of age, are involved, for early disposal. In light of this, large number of cases have already been decided.

Disposal of cases is directly linked with number of functional courts. During this period, 29 new courts of different categories have been created/established.

Dealing with this problem, permanent and continuous Lok Adalats have been constituted at High Court Level and also at District and Tehsil levels.

It is well-known that whatever system a society adopts for itself, is not viable, unless the masses are properly educated, to reap the benefits of such mechanism. Legal remedy can be provided only when one asks for it and lot many people suffer injustice due to sheer ignorance, therefore, it is necessary to have legal awareness and to educate the people about their legal rights. In July, 2000, Legal Awareness Committees, at all levels, *i.e.*, High Court, District and Tehsil, have been constituted. These Legal Awareness Committees hold camps, distribute literature on general laws, deliver speeches and approach the public, through social organisation to serve the cause. The High Court has also introduced and strengthened Para-Legal Clinic, Legal Aid Counsel Scheme.

Before I close, I quote Robert Frost:

"The woods are lovely, dark and deep,

But I have promises to keep,

And miles to go before I sleep,

And miles to go before I sleep."

ಬಬಬ

VIGILANCE AWARENESS

Chanakya (Kautilya) is known as the founding father of economic study in India and he is a great social thinker. He wrote about corruption in the administration of State, by saying that it is difficult to detect the corruption of the Officers of State Administration, just as a fish moving deep under water cannot be possibly found out either as drinking water or not. Chanakya in his *Arthashastra*, further says, just as it is impossible not to taste a drop of honey or poison that is placed at the tip of the tongue, so it is rather impossible for the government servant not to eat up at least a bit of the king's revenue. Though twenty five centuries passed, there is no change in the situation. Not even a single society, completely free from corruption of its officers, is known in the annals of history. It has become a part of human and social life. Even the so-called Socialist or Communist societies, where the means of production are communalised, could not escape from the clutches of this menace. Often it is wondered, whether it is an individual's disease or a social phenomenon.

We can say that, it is the resultant behaviour of a man in his attempt to satisfy his unlimited wants, to the maximum extent possible, out of the limited means for achieving the same. We have to realise that we cannot confine these wants to the basic needs like food, cloth and shelter. After satisfaction of these needs based on basic instincts, next priority needs like satisfaction of psychological needs crop up. *By nature man is not dishonest or corrupt. But it is the society that surrounds him, makes him, corrupt.* The social goals and the approved means to achieve them are important. Goals are set by individuals according to their perception of achieving social respect. Means to achieve the goals are not available to all the persons equally. Basically, the goals and means to achieve the results are the products of the value and normative structure of the society.

If we examine the root of corruption, we will find that it arises perhaps from extreme desire for leaving behind him the unlimited wealth to their families. Nepotism is natural in this situation. Corruption is defined by the World Bank as the use of public office for private profit. A person in office feels that he should earn not only for himself in his lifetime but also for his children, grand children,

---

Speech delivered at the Veledictory Function of the 'Vigilance Awareness Week', Hyderabad on 6th November, 2002.

perhaps for seven generations. This is probably the basic motive behind the enormous accumulation of wealth by the corrupt in our country.

Even the Kautilya's *Arthashastra* has set down highly sophisticated account of anatomy of corruption which has relevance to the conditions obtaining in the modern society. According to Kautilya, there are about 40 ways of embezzlements .... what is realised earlier is entered later on, what is realised later is entered earlier, what ought to be realised is not realised, what is collected is shown as not collected, what is collected is one sort while what is entered is another sort. What is payable is not paid, what is not payable is paid, commodities of greater value are bartered for those of smaller value and misrepresentation of source of income and so on.

Corruption and venality in administration exist in different forms in different countries depending among other things on the stages of economic and political development. New developments, social, political and economic give rise to new ways of corruption. The concept of integrity amongst public servants in the sense that they should not use their official position to obtain any personal advantage is enforced through rule of law.

Till World War II, corruption was generally prevalent only amongst lower grades in certain departments. The immense war efforts during 1939 to 1945 which involved in an expenditure of hundreds of crores created unprecedented opportunities for acquisition of wealth by doubtful means. The war time controls and scarcity provided ample scope for bribery, corruption and favoritism. Sudden extension of economic activities by the Government which was armed with numerous regulations and controls and a pernicious system of license and permits provided new and larger opportunities for those interested in easy money. Complaints against the highly placed officials were not dealt with severally so public confidence was badly shaken. Cynicism peeped into the people who felt that while the government was against corruption, it was not against corrupt individuals if they had the requisite amount of power, influence and protection. With the independence came, rigid economic planning, rapid expansion of government activity involving larger public expenditure which added impetus to the unscrupulous elements in public service and public life. In view of cumbersome and curious procedures and practices in the government departments, the anxiety on the part of the common man to avoid delay had encouraged practising of paying 'speed money'. This has become a fairly common type of corrupt practice, particularly in matters relating to grant of licenses and permits. Besides being a most objectionable corrupt practice, this custom of 'speed money' has become one of the most serious causes of delay and inefficiency. The scope of corruption is greater at such levels in the organization where substantive decisions are taken in matters like assessment, collection of taxes, determination of eligibility for obtaining licenses, grant of license and giving contracts, approval of work and acceptance of supplies etc.

The prime need to check corruption is acceptance of common standard of morality. The corruption thrives where there is conflict of values. The administrative norms require that decisions be made without regard to personal interest or group pressure. But the norms of the society place greater value on loyalty, family or communal group etc. The bureaucracy must wear heavy armour to keep itself from being overwhelmed by the other norms of society. It must adopt measures to strengthen itself internally and to insulate itself from the debilitating influences of life around it.

The quantum of detachment or isolation of bureaucracy from the pressures of the society is important. In every system the officials who wield power must avoid entanglement which would obligate them to any particular group or dilute disinterestedness of their decision.

Some Remedial Measures

Transparency or the diffusion of knowledge about governmental activity is bound to have corrective effect. The scholars, bureaucrats and press must work together responsibly to achieve a just government.

Reports of all aspects of governmental activity should be published freely and discussed critically. The Administration plans and activities must be ground analytically in the mills of scholarly criticism and debated in the public forum.

Mechanical efficiency, speedy in-flow of paper work and decision making are other means to combat corruption. Illicit gratification and bribery thrive on slow and uncertain process.

Careful scientific work flow analysis and ruthless inspection of work flow are some practical means of effectively dealing with the corruption.

Quick investigation and action is yet another pre-requisite to ensure probity. It is noticed that in many cases the existing Anti-corruption Agencies do not launch any prosecution because of procedural difficulties.

The cardinal principle of departmental action is that it should be initiated and completed as promptly as possible. It is for this reason that summary procedure free from the more severe restrictions of Evidence Act has been prescribed for such enquiries. One of the most objectionable features is inordinate delay in the time taken to reach a decision based on the report of the preliminary enquiries. The long delays afford golden opportunities for pressure tactics to be used.

Providing channels for ventilation of grievances is bound to have a sobering effect on the erratic administration.

Public vigilance is the basis of any anti-corruption strategy. Notwithstanding the fact that the Law is tightened or new institutions for investigations are set up, the real remedy lies in the preparedness of the public to put up staff fight against corruption.

For every corrupt official, there are hundreds of members of the public desiring to make use of him and feed him. There is natural human tendency to take advantage of whatever is going without bothering about moral and social aspects. It will be difficult to tackle this growing evil unless we mobilize the best elements in the society to fight it.

If a man is allowed to keep his ill-gotten wealth after paying nominal fine or serving few months in prison, he would gladly do this and enjoy the rest of his life with the society having forgotten or forgiven his crime. The approach should be that the corrupt should not enjoy the fruits of the corruption. Apart from long terms of rigorous imprisonment and heavy fines, confiscation of assets and debarring from holding public offices are also to be resorted to.

The punishment imposed on those involved in corruption should have a deterrent effect on others, so that this pernicious menace is kept under check.

Corruption undermines the rule of law, strangles economic growth and hurts the poor most severally. However, the biggest problems in our country are illiteracy and poverty. The fight against corruption has to be thought of as a cleansing operation which when successful, would encourage effective economic and social activity within and outside the country. This fight obviously cannot be fought only by individual agencies like the Central Vigilance Commission or Central Bureau of Investigation and it can be rooted out only with the help of all forms of society and all levels of citizens of India. An ethical culture and a mindset of honesty and integrity must be encouraged. The observance of vigilance would mark a significant step towards creating a transparent and responsive administrative system and lead us on a path to achieve hundred percent non-corrupt nation and to bring total transparency in our dealings, both official and personal.

ಬಬಬಬ

RESOLUTION OF FAMILY DISPUTES

I am extremely happy and delighted to associate myself with this function when, the International Centre for Alternate Dispute Resolution (ICADR) in collaboration with NALSAR, Universely of Law, Hyderabad has introduced a Post Graduate Diploma Course in Family Dispute Resolution. Both are prestigious institutions, striving hard to promote and propagate the concept of Alternative Dispute Resolution mechanisms with a view to expedite the resolution of disputes in all areas other than criminal offences, so that the disputants get justice in a quicker manner and in the process, the burden on the courts is reduced leaving them free to attend to more important and pressing matters. Litigants cannot afford to wait indefinitely for justice. With a view to expedite the resolution of disputes, it was resolved in a Conference held on 4th December, 1993 by the Chief Ministers, Chief Justices of the States under the Chairmanship of the then Prime Minister of India and presided over by the Chief Justice of India, that "the courts were not in a position to bear the entire burden of justice system and that a number of disputes lent themselves to resolution by alternative modes such as arbitration, mediation and negotiation and emphasised the desirability of disputants taking advantage of alternative dispute resolution which provided procedural flexibility, saved valuable time and money and avoided the stress of a conventional trial".

Subsequent to this resolution, the Arbitration and Conciliation Act of 1996 was enacted by the Parliament which came into force from 22nd August, 1996 repealing the Arbitration Act of 1940. While the Arbitration Act of 1940 was more or less court controlled, the new Arbitration and Conciliation Act of 1996 modelled on the Model Law of United National Commission on Trade Laws (UNCITRAL) laid emphasis on party autonomy with the court intervention reduced to the minimum.

The effort of ICADR and NALSAR to start of P.G. Diploma Course in Family Dispute Resolution to train candidates for the resolution of family disputes of all kinds is a step in the right direction.

One of the oldest of the social institutions, which has survived the ravages of time and social revolutions, is the family. India's contribution to the evolution of

---

Speech delivered at the inauguration of 'Post-Graduate Diploma Course in Family Dispute Resolution', Hyderabad on 27th February, 2002.

social institutions is the joint family system, which has taken deep roots under Hindu Law. Almost all the *Smritis* gave prominence to the family, because it was realised that family is the nucleus and if only that family is happy the society will be happier. The concept of joint family has acquired an Indianness of its own, irrespective of the individual personal laws and has truly acquired secular dimensions for the last so many centuries. Joint family has been associated with agricultural societies and, as Alvin Toffler points out in his famous book "The Third Wave", joint family as an institution has suffered radical changes with the advent of the industrial revolution. The industrial revolution compelled working people to live near factories and away from their homes and this led to break up of joint family system and ushered in nuclear families consisting of husband and wife and their children. Sometimes even husband and wife are forced to live separately because their places of work are located in different cities or towns. This has also led to the so-called single – parent families.

The joint family system broke down slowly by degrees for a variety of reasons. With the break up of the joint family, the domestic front naturally suffered in the process and this meant that children who needed greater attention from the parents didn't get enough of it. Such a scenario contributed to considerable tensions within the family. Husband and wife who are exposed to stress and tension at their respective work places come home to find the home not as a place where they can happily relax but as a domestic extension of tension-ridden atmosphere. Such a situation is an invitation to matrimonial disputes.

Apart from the problems mentioned above, the weakening of familial bonds has also led to disputes relating to custody of children between parents and property distribution between husband and wife after divorce. Then there is the traditional fertile breeding ground of disputes relating to partition, inheritance and succession. Even issues relating to legitimacy and adoption of children also have occupied the attention of courts of law. In fact, according to one estimate, more than 60% of the time of the courts has come to be taken by disputes relating to family disputes. Once the disputes between husband and wife or the siblings or parents and children or brothers are taken to the courts for settlement, there is always the risk of causing greater animosity and rancour between blood relations. We are all aware of the extent of damage that protracted court proceedings can cause to domestic happiness.

Consequently, the legislature thought it necessary to constitute separate family courts for the resolution of domestic disputes and the Family Courts Act of 1984 was passed for this purpose. Naturally, the focus of these courts is to facilitate resolution of family disputes in an amicable fashion so that there is as little bitterness as possible. The families should ideally be in a position to continue with their normal filial bonds even if there is some dispute and it is sought to be settled through third party settlement. However, in practice, it has been found that due to several constraints, the family courts are not in a position to resolve disputes amicably and the delay in deciding these cases has only contributed to further growing of bitterness in the relationship amongst the parties. Legislature has also realized the importance of ADR methods in settling the family disputes, particularly, the tested and tried methods of conciliation. All over the democratic world, conciliation has come to be recognized as the preferred method in the amicable settlement of even international disputes through by bilateral negotiations. The method of conciliation is treated as mandatory in certain family disputes. Counselling by experts is a *sine qua non* in domestic disputes in advanced countries like the U.S.A. etc. The Family Courts Act of 1984 also enables the courts to refer the parties to counselling and to other ADR methods. The recent amendments to Civil Procedure Code in India also enable the courts to refer the parties to ADR methods as a first recourse to amicable settlement of disputes.

It is gratifying to note that the Regional Centre of ICADR at Hyderabad has started a Post Graduate Diploma Course in Alternative Dispute Resolution in collaboration with NALSAR University of Law in the year 2000 and already a few batches of students have completed their courses. It is in the fitness of things that both these institutions are coming together again in starting a diploma course in Family Dispute Resolution from the current year. This is an area with tremendous promise for the peaceful and amicable settlement of disputes that affects a very vital social institution, namely, the family and in the present social scenario, there is a genuine need for professional and well-trained Arbitrators and Conciliators.

This course is not, as its name may suggest, confined to settle only family disputes as mentioned in Family Courts Act of 1984 in the Explanation to Section 7 of the Act. It is enlarged to encompass all disputes in which the family is a nucleus namely, partitions, settlements, adoption, maintenance, care of old aged parents, the object being that such disputes instead of coming to courts for settlement, which will take enormous time for resolution, can by these techniques and skills acquired in these training programmes be resolved much faster, and leave the families free to continue the same old bonds of love and bonhomie as before. This course has thus great potential in the years to come and it is the first of its kind in the country.

ಲಲಲ

FOR WANT OF A NAIL

The Faculty of Law, Jai Narain Vyas University is an institution of excellence in legal academics that has contributed a lot to the growth of legal professionalism in Rajasthan. The Institution has given birth to many a legal luminaries, jurists and members of judicial hierarchy and rendered yeoman service in moulding young students into full-fledged lawyers.

Here, I would life to pay my sincere tributes to late Sh. M.M. Singhvi, an eminent Lawyer and doyen of the Rajasthan Bar, who possessed rarest of the rare quality, of never telling the presiding officer that he is wrong even if the presiding officer was wrong. But, at the same time, he would persuade the presiding officer to accept his contention. Due to his hard work and dedication to the profession, he soon made a mark in the profession and became an eminent lawyer of Rajasthan. He was very actively associated with various social organisations and had rendered social services in the field of education, environment and health.

Legal education in India is a combination of professional training and academic study. Students of law absorb and master the theory of law, its philosophy, its functions and its role in democratic society. Legal profession is the only profession that strives hard to upkeep the democratic policy of the State and maintain social justice. Legal profession demands willingness to work hard, critical understanding in human problems and values. The brightest qualities of head and heart creates among them, honesty and integrity. Success in the profession, which you participants here have chosen can be assumed only through hard working and integrity of character. There is no substitute for hard worker in the profession of law.

I have had no occasion to see the Late Shri M.M. Singhvi, the great soul but I have learnt from others that Shri M.M. Singhvi was exceptionally outstanding as a lawyer and remarkably efficient as a counsel.

Justice Shri G.S. Singhvi, a worthy son of worthy father is now presently functioning as an eminent Judge of Punjab & Haryana High Court.

It is now time for a fresh view on legal curriculum for promoting social change and social justice. Law students have to orient and organise themselves

---

* Speech delivered at 'Fourth All India Moot Court Competition, in Memory of Lt. Sh. M.M. Singhvi', Faculty of Law, Jodhpur.

so as to meet the growing needs of the society. Apart from protecting the constitutionally guaranteed freedoms of the individual, a law student has to prepare himself to assume the role of a saviour, to the socially disabled, the poor, downtrodden, discriminated and the under privileged section of our society.

A law student can develop into a full-fledged professional only by developing his faculties of lawyering. Moot Courts offer immense opportunities to a law student to expand his knowledge and to develop the power of articulation, analysis and legal reasoning.

In the words of Glanville Williams, *"Mooting not only gives practice in Court Procedure but helps to develop the aplomb that every advocate should possess"*.

As a part of the legal curriculum, there should be regular conduct of Moot Court and Moot Trials. The preliminary statement of Committee on Legal Education of the Harvard Law School had delineated the twin purposes of a law school as (1) to train men for the legal profession, and (2) to provide a centre where scholars might contribute to an understanding of law and government and participate creatively in their growth and improvement.

Apart from being equipped with knowledge inputs, a law student has to develop his overall personality to prepare himself to face the challenges of the society. Legal Profession demands willingness to work hard, critical understanding of human problems and capacity to work the legal machinery to suit the complex structure of the Indian Society.

Fresh law graduates lack practical training. Moot Courts and certain other projects like Lok Adalats, have been introduced in law colleges, but still not much interest is shown by the students.

Practical Training Lacking

The main reason for the problem is because of the legal education system which is more or less divorced from the practical aspects of law. The syllabus for the law degree is quite heavy; this should be shortened and practical training programme should be made compulsory with an internal assessment framework. Lack of funds in the universities is also a barrier to the proper flow of teaching as well as learning. Specifically, the lack of grant for law college libraries forces the students to refer to only what is available.

It is a known saying by Franklin: *"For want of a nail, the shoe was lost. For want of shoe, the horse was lost. For want of a horse, the rider was lost. For want of a rider, the battle was lost. For want of the battle, the kingdom was lost. All for the want of horse-shoe nail"*. The king lost his kingdom because he ignored a horse-shoe nail. A student would lose his kingdom of knowledge if he ignores a book. For want of a proper book, the argument is lost, and for want of an argument, the case is lost. For want of a case, the client is lost, and for want of a client, the practice is lost, which is the very life of a lawyer. A law student must be provided with the best of books, journals, magazines, reports etc. for widening his horizons.

ಬಲಬಲಬಲ

FUNDAMENTAL DUTIES

Preamble to the Constitution and Fundamental Duties in the Constitutional Scheme

The Preamble is the blue print for the young republic. It contains not only the aspirations and the vision of our founding fathers, but also reveals the Constitutional Rites of Passage. In *Gopalan* v. *State of Madras*, AIR 1955 SC 88, the majority view of the Hon'ble Apex Court was that the language of law in Article 21 of the Constitution of India cannot be modified with reference to the Preamble. The same view continued upto *Kesvanand Bharti's case*, AIR 1973 SC 1461, where the Preamble was not considered to be part of the Constitution. In the post Keshavanand Bharti period, it is considered as an integral part thereof, since it contains the philosophical bedrock of the Constitution. When we are lost in the sea of ambiguity, it is the Preamble that guides us like a lighthouse. The word "Socialist" read with Art. 39(d) enabled the apex Court to uphold the Constitutionality of laws of nationalization of private property in the case of *Excel Wear* v. *Union of India*, AIR 1979 SC 25: (1978) 1 SCR 1009: (1979) 1 SCJ 299. Similarly, the word "socialist" enabled the apex Court to deduce the fundamental right of "equal pay for equal work" in case of *Randhir Singh* v. *Union of India*, AIR 1982 SC 879: (1982) 1 SCC 618: (1982) 3 SCR 298.

Considering the plight of millions of people who are voiceless and faceless, the Supreme Court used the phrase "Social Justice" to Indianise our Jurisprudence so as to give them a voice, and a social status. The concept of "Social Justice" was interpreted as the recognition of greater good to a larger number without deprivation or accrual of legal rights to anybody. The constitutional concern of Social Justice, as an elastic continuous process, is to accord justice to all sections of the society by providing facilities and opportunities to remove handicaps and disabilities with which the poor are languishing and secure dignity of their person. *Consumer Education and Research Center* v. *Union of India*, AIR 1995 SC 922: (1995) 3 SCC 42. Since one of the functions of Law is social engineering, the doctrine of "Social Justice" is seen as a comprehensive form to remove social imbalance of law, harmonizing the rival claims or the interests of different groups and/or sections in the social structure

---

Speech delivered at The Indian Association of Lawyers, Jodhpur, on 5th May, 2001.

or individuals by means on which alone, it would be possible to build up a welfare state. *Dalmia Cement (Bharat) Ltd.* v. *Union of India,* (1996) 10 SCC 104; *Air India Statutory Corpn.* v. *United Labour Union,* AIR 1997 SC 645: (1997) 9 SCC 377. In the case of *Municipal Corporation of Delhi* v. *Female Workers (Muster Roll),* (2000) 3 SCC 224, the Supreme Court has used the doctrine of Social Justice to extend the benefit of maternity leave to even those women who are casual labourers of Municipal Corporation of Delhi.

The concept of Social Justice is closely related to the dynamic concept of "Economic Justice". Both these concepts have "Distributive Justice" which connotes the removal of economic inequalities and rectifying the injustice resulting from dealings or transactions between unequals in society. The ideal of economic justice is to make equality of opportunity meaningful and of status social, economic and political; *Dalmia Cement (Bharat) Ltd.* v. *Union of India,* (1996) 10 SCC 104.

The concept of Social Justice, when read with Art. 39A of the Constitution of India, leads to the concept of "Legal Justice". Legal Justice requires that the administration of Justice must provide a cheap, expeditious and effective instrument for realisation of their social or economic position or their financial resources; *Babu Ram L* v. *Raghunathji Maharaj,* AIR 1976 SC 1734. The concepts of social, economic and political justice are not pious hopes, but are dynamic philosophies that must permeate our thinking and functioning, both inside and outside the courts. While deciding cases, we cannot afford to be hyper-technical or pedantic in our reasoning. We must be alive and sensitive to the plight of the poor litigant who has approached the portals of justice. Justice, in all her manifestation, must not only be done, but it must appear to be done. By doing Justice we ensure the faith of the people in the institution; we eliminate the anomalies in society and we contribute to the making of a better world.

Rights do not exist without duties. Rights and duties are necessary corollaries of each other. They are two sides of the same coin. A man is a civil animal and hence lives in society. A disciplined society, governed by rule of law, emerges into State. There comes into play the inter-relationship of State and citizens and of citizens and citizens. Rights are incapable of being enjoyed or enforced without a corresponding obligation called duty. What is known as *Dharma, i.e.,* religion, is nothing but a texture woven from the warp and woof of rights and duties, blended by the principles of ethics and morals. The distinctions between the principles of spiritualism and materialism is: while the philosophy of spiritualism proceeds, on defining and dictating the duties, leaving the rights to follow naturally there from, in materialistic world, the rights are emphasized leaving the duties to follow. Such principles are to be found in ancient Indian literature of whatever religion it may be, *Shastras* and *Vedas, Shariat* and *Quran,* Bible and Testaments and so on.

There are more than 35 nations of the world, the Constitutions of which contain specific provisions on fundamental duties.

Nearly a quarter century after the date when the people of India gave unto themselves, the Constitution of India, 42nd amendment was passed by the

Parliament in the year 1976 wherein, Part IVA entitled Fundamental Duties consisting of singular article, namely Article 51A, was introduced into the constitution in accordance with the recommendations of the Swaran Singh Committee. The 42nd amendment extensively curtailed fundamental freedoms guaranteed by the Constitution and made a severe dent on the power of judicial review, a forceful protector of democratic values and human rights, which is a basic feature of the Constitution. Viewed objectively, incorporation of fundamental duties is a remarkable part of our constitution, both in content and expression. In my opinion, the ten fundamental duties enshrined in Article 51A are equivalent to ten commandments of *Bible* and are essential characteristics of a good citizen. They have been beautifully articulated.

The concept of fundamental duties is not unique to the Constitution of India alone.

Chapter III of the Japanese Constitution, 1946, is titled 'Rights and Duties of the People'. Though most of the provisions of the chapter relate to 'Rights', and the Duties that can be discerned are—

(a) Parents have the obligation to send their children to receive the compulsory free education provided by the State (Art. 26).

(b) All people shall have the obligation to work (Art. 27).

The 1997-Constitution of U.S.S.R. (follows earlier Constitutions), had Chapter 7, with the flowing heading: 'The basic rights, freedoms and duties of citizens'. Under the Scheme of U.S.S.R. Constitution, while the rights themselves are non-justifiable, rights and duties are placed on the same footing by Art. 59 which says *"Citizens exercise of their rights and freedoms is separable from the performance of their duties and obligation"*.

Chapter II of the Chinese Constitution of 1982 clubs 'fundamental rights and duties' of citizens together. Article 33(3) makes the performance of the duties, a condition for enjoyment of the rights. Some of the duties enjoyed by Chinese Constitution are—(i) Duty towards motherland—to safeguard the security, honour and interest of the motherland, to defend the motherland and resist aggression, to maintain national unity and integrity, (ii) to abide by the Constitution, (iii) protect public property, (iv) to respect social ethics (v) to pay taxes, (vi) to word etc.

American Constitution does not enumerate fundamental duties of an individual. The United Kingdom does not have any written Constitution and in general Common Law and duties of a citizen are the same in the U.K. and U.S.A. They are, (i) allegiance to the State, (ii) to disclose any treason or felony of which he has the knowledge and (iii) to assist in the detection and suppression of the crime.

Under the constitution of Greece and Cyprus, there is a fundamental duty, cast upon the citizen, to exercise his right of franchise founded on the doctrine of compulsory voting. A failure to exercise the right to vote is an offence, punishable under the Law.

In several cases, the Supreme Court has upheld the validity of laws relating to ecology and environment and has made directions, binding the citizen and the State, finding the source of power to do so in Article 51A. In *Rural Litigation and Entitlement Kendra* v. *State of Uttar Pradesh*, AIR 1987 SC 359: (1986) Supp SCC 517: (1987) 1 SCR 641, Ranganath Misra, J. held.

Preservation of the environment and keeping the ecological balance unaffected is a task which not only governments but also every citizen must undertake. It is a social obligation and let us remind every Indian citizen that it is his fundamental duty, as enshrined is Article 51(A)(g) of the Constitution."

In *M.C. Mehta (II)* v. *Union of India*, AIR 1988 SC 1115: (1988) 1 SCC 471: (1988) 2 SCR 530, Article 51A enacting fundamental duties of citizens was read as casting duties on the government and for issuing certain directions consistently with Article 51A.

Directions were:

(i) The Central Government shall direct the educational institutions throughout India to teach at least for one hour in a week, lessons relating to protection and the improvement of the natural environment including forests, lakes, rivers and wild life in the first ten classes;

(ii) The Central Government shall get text-books written for the said purpose and distribute them to the educational institutions free of costs;

(iii) The Children shall be taught about the need for maintaining cleanliness, commencing with the cleanliness of the house, both inside and outside and in the street in which they live;

(iv) The Central Government shall consider training of teachers who teach this subject by the introduction of short-term courses for such training;

(v) The Central Government, the Governments of the States and all the Union Territories shall consider desirability of organizing "keep the city/town/village clean" week;

(vi) To create a national awareness of the problems faced by the people, by the appalling all-round deterioration of the environment.

Article 51A of the Constitution of India, dealing with Fundamental Duties, has not attracted too much of legal attention. However, in the case of *Mohan K. Singhania* v. *Union of India*, AIR 1992 SC 1: 1992 Supp (1) SCC 594: 1991 Supp (1) SCR 46, it was considered as an external aid for interpretation of statutes. Since the restriction contained in statutory rules were found to be in consonance with Art. 51A(i), the validity of the rule was upheld. Interestingly, a new external aid was discovered in the shape of Fundamental Duties. Supreme Court has revealed other aspects of fundamental Duties, as well. In *M.C. Mehta* v. *Union of India*, AIR 1988 SC 1115: (1988) 1 SCC 471: (1988) 2 SCR 530, the Apex Court directed the Central Government to introduce lessons of Environmental Pollution in the curriculum for the students in the school. After all, protection and promotion of clean environment is a Fundamental Duty of every citizen under Article 51A(g) of the Constitution of India. Similarly, when the issue arose whether bestowing of awards like *Bharat Ratna* is against Art. 18 of the Constitution of India, the

Supreme Court relied on the fundamental duty to excel. "All spheres of individual and collective activity so that the nation constantly rises to higher level of endeavor and achievement" in order to uphold the validity of these awards. The apex Court held "the theory of equality does not mandate that merit should not be recognised. Art. 51A of the Constitution speaks of Fundamental Duty of every citizen of India. In view of Clause (j) of Article 51A, it is necessary that there should be a system of awards and decorations to recognise excellence in the performance of these duties"; *Balaji Raghavan* v. *Union of India*, AIR 1996 SC 770: (1996) 1 SCC 361: (1996) 1 SCJ 457.

The Rajasthan High Court, in a Full Bench decision, has interpreted "the duty to adhere to truth" as part of Fundamental Duty, prescribed by Article 51A(f) of the Constitution of India. *Dharampal* v. *State of Rajasthan,* 2000 (2) WLC 400. In the cases of *Air India Statutory Corp.* v. *United Labour Union,* (1997) 9 SCC 377, and in the case of *Samantha* v. *State of Andhra Pradesh,* AIR 1997 SC 3297: (1997) 8 SCC 191, the Supreme Court has read the Fundamental Rights and the Directive Principles alongwith the Fundamental Duties. Thus, the recent judicial trend is to read the Constitution as a holistic document. Slowly but surely, the Fundamental Duties are emerging on our judicial horizon.

The Fundamental Duties are not just important for judicial interpretations and for case law, they are equally important for us, as individuals. They are the political mantras that define the contributions that the citizens are to make for the republic. As John F. Kennedy rightly said in his inaugural Speech in 1960:

"Ask not what the nation can do for you, ask what you can do for the nation."

The Fundamental Duties remind us of what we should do for the nation. We must protect the sovereignty, unity and integrity of India; we must preserve its rich heritage; we must promote harmony and spirit of common brotherhood amongst all the people transcending religious, linguistic and regional or sectional diversities; we must renounce practices, derogatory to the dignity of women; and we must excel in all spheres of individual and collective activity. In *Balbir Kaur* v. *Steel Authority of India,* (2000) 6 SCC 493. The Supreme Court held:

"The Constitutional Philosophy should be allowed to become a part of every man's life and only then the Constitution can reach everyone."

These are the prescriptions for making the nation strong and invincible.

Conclusion

Article 51A, in the opinion of jurists, suffers from several infirmities. Firstly, it suffers from vagueness. The fundamental duties, set out, are high-sounding morals but mean nothing and lead to nowhere. Secondly, it is a toothless provision. We Indians, today, do not act without compulsions and so would be the fate of fundamental duties. Thirdly, the duties are cast on citizens without casting any duties on the State and hence they are not comprehensive and lack in reciprocity. In spite of such criticism, the significance of the chapter on fundamental duties cannot be belittled. It has set in a new philosophy and line of thinking in the minds of citizens. It has its educative value and character building potential. It is creating awareness. It is full of immense potentialities and, if judicially explored, it would have far reaching implications in shaping the India of this new century. The Chapter on fundamental duties can act as a tab on wild exercise of fundamental rights and on their being stretched beyond permissible limits.

Our Constitution has four pillars to stand on; the Legislature, the Executive, the Judiciary and the Press. A letter written by Shri Ranganath Mishra, the retired Chief Justice of India, has been entertained and registered by the Supreme Court of India as a petition under Article 32 of the constitution to devise ways and means of enforcement of fundamental duties. The matter is being monitored by a Bench, presided over by the Hon'ble Chief Justice of India.

The Government of India in the Ministry of Human Resources Development (Department of Education) has set up a Committee under the Chairmanship of Justice J.S. Verma, former Chief Justice of India to operationalise the suggestion to teach fundamental duties to the citizens of the country. NCERT has devised extensive curriculum and textbooks, incorporating the text of fundamental duties and essays and stories thereon so as to teach and instruct. In my opinion, the future of India lies in acting, implementing and invigorating compliance with fundamental duties. Solution to many a problem of the day, lethargy and incompetence eating into the roots of society and governance, fanatic non-secular regional linguistic forces raising their heads, mounting arrears in law courts—can all be resolved if only we are true to ourselves and do our duty. We have to rededicate ourselves for building a better India, *i.e.*, *Bharat Mata*, if not for ourselves, at least for our children, for our kith and kin, our friends and relations. A serious thinking on fundamental duties and translating them into action would enable us to leave behind a better world to live in for the upcoming generations.

ಬಲಬಲಬಲ

CONSUMER AWARENESS

Consumer Law all over the world has been growing in its volume, content and complexity. Our country is no exception. The consumer awareness has the origin in the United States of America. The first era of consumer activism in USA ended in 1910s, it was an outgrowth of the massive changes brought by the early stages of industrialisation. The period between 1920s and 1930s marks the second era of consumer activism. President John Kennedy's "consumer message" to Congress serves as a convenient starting point for the third era of consumer activism in the United States. The message, the first one by the President of United States of America on the topic of consumer protection, was delivered on 15th March, 1962. In it, President Kennedy enunciated a Consumer Bill of Rights, including the rights to (1) safety, (2) information, (3) choice among a variety of products and services at competitive prices and (4) a fair hearing by government in the formulation of consumer policy.

The statute book at the Centre contains as many as 20 Acts of direct importance to the consumer, not to mention the host of minor Acts and the plethora of subordinate legislation in the shape of statutory Rules and Orders, issued under various Acts. It is not easy – even for lawyers and Judges to acquire mastery of all these laws. But it may be useful if, the ordinary citizen is provided with a bird's eye view of major Central Acts, which are of recurring relevance to the consumer.

The Consumer Protection Act, 1986 enacted by the Parliament is not the only law that deals with the consumer protection and is not the first of its kind. There are number of pre-constitutional laws and also the post-constitutional laws that aim at the protection of the consumer interests. These laws have a direct or indirect bearing on interest of the consumers. They include:

- The Usurious Loans Act, 1918
- The Sale of Goods Act, 1930
- The Agricultural Produce (Grading and Marking) Act, 1937.

Speech delivered at VIth State Convention of Consumer Activists, conducted by Confederation of Andhra Pradesh Consumer's Org. (APCO), Hydrerabad on 27th January, 2002.

- The Drugs and Cosmetics Act, 1940.
- The Drugs and Magic Remedies (Objectionable Advertisements) Act, 1954.
- The Prevention of Food Adulteration Act, 1954.
- The Protection of Civil Rights Act, 1955.
- The Essential Commodities Act, 1955.
- The Standards of Weights and Measures Act, 1956.
- The Trade and Merchandise Marks Act, 1958.
- The Export (Quality Control and Inspection) Act, 1963.
- The Monopolies and Restrictive Trade Practices Act, 1969. [*Repealed*]
- The Water (Prevention and Control of Pollution) Act, 1981.
- The Bureau of Indian Standard Act, 1986.
- The Environment (Protection) Act, 1986.

There are also various provisions in Code of Criminal Procedure like sections 406, 407, 408, 410 and 482 and sections 264, 276, 277, 278 and other laws dealing with the subject.

Further, the Constitution of India, which is the fundamental law of the land, also contains a number of provisions, which go a long way in protecting the rights of the consumers. These provisions include Article 21, which deals with the Right to life and personal liberty, Article 47, which guarantees the Right to health, and Article 48A which aims at a pollution free environment for all citizens etc.

The only difference between these laws and the Consumer Protection Act of 1986 is that in the case of former, each enactment deals with a special class of consumers and that too, with regard to only a particular area of consumer behaviour, whereas latter is a general legislation which lays down a uniform set of laws procedure and fora for protecting the rights of all kinds of consumers. Thus, it bring into existence a separate class of people called consumers and endeavours to protect that rights irrespective of the nature of the transaction that takes place between the consumer and the seller. The advantage of this legislation is that it provides a speedy, informal, inexpensive justice within the reach of all the consumers.

I may now briefly refer to some of the important enactments, which have a direct bearing on the consumers.

Sale of goods constitutes an important topic of consumer law. The statutory law on the subject in India is contained in the Sale of Goods Act, 1930. As regards the question of defective services, most of the legal rules on the subject are non-statutory in character. The obligation to render service of a particular quality may arise either from contract or from principle drawn mainly from the law of torts. Where a specific stipulation exists in the contract, the stipulation must be honoured by the supplier of services. In case of the contract, he would become liable to pay damage for the breach and such damages are governed by two important sections of the Indian Contract Act, 1972, namely, section 73 and section 74. If the contract does not fix the quantum of damages, then section 73 regulates the matter. Where there is no contractual stipulation as to the quality of service, then the matter is governed by uncodified law. In this context, special mention must be made of one principle of the law of torts. The principle is, that a person who undertakes to render professional service to another person is bound to exercise reasonable care and skill, while rendering the service. This principle is to be taken extending to all professions at least to all learned professions, such as accountancy, business consultancy, law management consultancy, medicines and allied professions, nursing, surveying, technical consultancy, valuation etc. A breach of this obligation of care has come to be known as "professional negligence" of which medical negligence is only an illustration.

Sale of Goods Act

The Sale of Goods Act defines *"goods"* as every kind of movable property, excluding actionable claim *e.g.* a claim to debt and money, stock and shares, growing crops, grass and things which are attached to or are part of the land, but have to be separated therefrom before or under the term of a contract, are goods. There can be a valid contract to sell goods, which are yet to be manufactured, produced or acquired by the seller under the terms of the contract. Sale is transfer of ownership in goods in consideration (exchange) of price. A contract of sale is formed by an offer to buy or sell goods for a price and its acceptance.

The Agricultural Produce (Grading and Marking) Act, 1937

The Agricultural Produce (Grading and Marking) Act, 1937 received the assent of the Governor-General on 24th February, 1937. It provides for the grading and marking of agricultural produce and other produce. The Act is generally treated as falling under Constitution Seventh Schedule, Entry 49, which relates to the prescription and protection of merchandise marks. The Act provides for the grading and marking of agricultural and other allied commodities, with the objectives of making available quality agricultural produce including horticulture and livestock produce to the consumers. The insignia used for grading is 'AGMARK'. Under sections 4, 5 and 5A of the Act, penalty is provided for unauthorised marking of an article with grade designation mark, or counterfeiting grade designation mark, or selling misgraded article. Section 58, which has been inserted by Act 76 of 1986, empowers the Central Government to introduce compulsory grading with respect to the commodities where such grading is given in the public interest and for the protection of the consumer. This is to be introduced in respect of notified articles for specific areas.

The Bureau of Indian Standards Act, 1986

The Bureau of Indian Standards (formerly the Indian Standards Institution) is established under the Bureau of Indian Standards Act, 1986, which is an Act of Parliament. It is an expert body whose function is to lay down standards for various kinds of goods. These standards, if complied with, authorise the manufacturer so authorised, to use the ISI mark. Where the goods purport to carry ISI marks but do not actually conform to those standards, the purchaser (on discovering the defect) can claim damages from the seller for breach of contract.

In case of deliberate falsehood, it is permissible to prosecute him also for cheating.

Drugs

The Drugs and Cosmetics Act, 1940 is a Central Act, which is primarily intended to regulate the purity and quality of drugs and cosmetics. The Act is aimed at prevention of substandard drugs, misbranded drugs, adulterated drugs and spurious drugs. These adjectives indicate several varieties of malpractices regarding drugs, which malpractices are distinguishable from one another though occasionally overlapping. The Act also covers cosmetics, which are not of a standard quality or rare misbranded or spurious. Section 18(a)(i) and section 18(a)(ii) of the Act prohibits the manufacture for sale or manufacture for distribution or sale of stocking or offer for sale, or distribution of i) any substandard drug or cosmetic; ii) any misbranded drug or cosmetic; or iii) any spurious drug or cosmetic.

The Drugs and Magic Remedies (Objectionable Advertisements) Act, 1954 was enacted to prohibit advertisements relating to certain types of drugs and "magic remedies". The object of the Act is to prevent unscrupulous persons from misleading prospective customers by including them to waste money on so-called magic cures, which have no potency. This Act principally covers drugs or remedies, which promise to cure sexual impotency, menstrual disorders and so on.

Essential Commodities Act, 1955

The Essential Commodities Act, 1955 is the principal enactment intended to regulate the distribution, sale, marketing and prices of essential commodities Act. The list of essential commodities is given in section 2 of the Essential Commodities Act, 1955. Under section 7 of the Act, any person contravening certain orders made under the Act, shall be punished with imprisonment up to 7 years and with fine. There is also provision for confiscation.

Monopolies and Restrictive Trade Practices Act, 1969

Section 36A of MRTP Act, *inter alia*, says that a person who permits the hoarding or destruction of goods, or refuses to sell the goods or to make these available for sale, or to provide any service, is guilty of unfair trade practice, if such hoarding or destruction or refusal raises or tends to raise the cost of those or other similar goods or services.

The Export (Quality Control and Inspection) Act, 1963

This Act came into force on 1st January, 1964 and is intended to provide for the sound development of the export trade of India through quality control and inspection. The principal object of the Act is to empower the Central Government to create machinery for establishing or recognising agencies for quality control or inspection or both, in respect of goods to be exported. Goods covered by certain notifications are required to be examined by the agency either at the time of export or earlier, in approved testing houses or by approved surveyors or samplers. They must satisfy "standards specification" – an expression which is not defined in the Act, but whose meaning can be ascertained from the context in which certain other expressions, such as "inspection" and "quality control" as defined in the Act, occur. Though this Act has no direct relevance, however, it has an indirect relevance to consumers in India inasmuch as very often one finds advertisements of sale of export-rejected goods. A knowledge of the provisions of the Act would at least put the consumers on guard and make them aware that the goods in question would have been rejected because they were not in accordance with the standard specifications or otherwise were of inferior quality.

Indian Contract Act, 1872

In India, the general law of contracts is contained in the Indian Contract Act, 1872. The Act defines *"contract"* as an agreement enforceable by law. The essentials of a valid contract are (i) intention to create a contract; (ii) offer and acceptance, (iii) consideration, (iv) capacity to enter into contract; (v) free consent of the parties; and (vi) lawful object of the agreement. Writing is not essential for the validity of a contract, except where a specific statutory provision requires writing. An arbitration clause must be in writing. Intention to create legal relations is the most essential requirement.

The principal remedies for beach of contracts are: (i) damages, (ii) specific performance of the contract, and (iii) injunction. When a contract has been broken, the party who suffers by such breach is entitled to receive from the party who has broken the contract, compensation for any loss or damage caused to him thereby, being loss or damages which naturally arose in the usual course of things from such breach or which the parties knew, when they made the contract to be likely to result from the breach of it. In certain special areas, dealt with in the Specific Relief Act, 1963, the court may direct, against the party in default, "specific performance" of the contract, that is to say, the party may be directed to perform the very obligation, which he has undertaken, by the contract.

Prevention of Black-marketing

While the general Parliamentary legislation relating to the control of prices and the prevention of hoarding is to be found in the Essential Commodities Act, 1955, there is a special law providing for the detention of persons indulging in these malpractices, to be found in the Prevention of Black-Marketing and Maintenance of Supplies of Essential Commodities Act, 1980. This Act supplies additional machinery and a further sanction against persons indulging in such activities.

Prevention of Food Adulteration

In India, the principal legislation relating to food adulteration is the Prevention of Food Adulteration Act, 1954. Although provisions on the subject were already contained in certain sections of the Indian Penal Code, it was considered necessary to enact this Act for dealing more effectively with malpractice. The main object of the legislation is to prevent the adulteration and misbranding of foods, and to secure the purity of food and to inform the public about the nature of the substance of the food which they are buying, and to prevent fraud on the consuming public generally. The Act is primarily concerned with investigation, prosecution and punishment of offences under the Act. This does not mean that civil liability is excluded. Such liability is governed, in general, not by any statutory provision (as the position stands at present in India), but by uncodified law. If, through the negligence of the defendant, a consumer is injured, the consumer has the right to claim compensation, the award of which is governed by the general principles of the law of torts. In case of death of the consumer, the specified relatives can claim compensation under the Fatal Accidents Act, 1855.

Standards of Weights and Measures

The Standards of Weights and Measures Act, 1976 establishes standards of weights and measures and regulates inter-state trade or commerce therein. Use of non-standard weights and measures is prohibited. No weight, measure or numeral other than the standard one, can be used. The main object of the Act is to ensure that only the standard weights and measures are resorted to in business transactions.

Unfair Trade Practices

The Monopolies and Restrictive Trade Practices Act, 1969 contains numerous provisions to check monopolies and restrictive trade practices and (as amended) it also provides protection to consumers against unfair trade practices. The definition of unfair practice, as contained in section 36A of the Act, is a very lengthy one. Again, while previously this Act was mainly being administered by the MRTP Commission, it is now permissible for Consumer Fora etc. to entertain complaints of unfair trade practices and by sections 2(r) of the Consumer Protection Act, 1986, the expression *"unfair trade practice"* is defined as having the same meaning as in section 36A of the Monopolies and Restrictive Trade Practices Act 1969. The definition of *"complaint"* in section 2(1)(c) of the Consumer Protection Act, 1986, *inter alia*, covers a written allegation made by a complainant that "as a result of any unfair trade practice adopted by any trader, the complainant has suffered loss or damages".

The Indian Penal Code

The Indian Penal Code constitutes the general criminal law of the country. It contains several sections, which are relevant to consumer transactions. The enactment by the Legislature, of separate Acts devoted to various facets of consumer law does not mean that the Indian Penal Code is no more useful. In fact, the code itself contemplates that there may be special laws for dealing with the special objects (see section 4). Special laws can exist side by side with the Indian Penal Code. There may be overlapping also in certain cases. But that does not destroy the validity of the relevant provisions of Indian Penal Code. Those provisions still survive and can be made use of in appropriate cases.

Insurance

The law of insurance is contained in part in the Insurance Act, 1938 and in part in a few other enactments, but these enactments and their provisions have to be read along with the content of the rules derived from uncodified law, based on case law. The Act is mostly devoted to matters relating to the organisation of insurance business. However, sections 38 to 45 of the Act are some of important provisions of relevance to life insurance. Nationalisation of life insurance business or its intended denationalisation does not have any material effect on the content and operation of insurance policies, so far as the consumer is concerned.

Marine Insurance Act, 1963 is almost an exhaustive code dealing with marine insurance policies. Marine insurance policies usually covers loss of, or damage to the ship which is insured, loss of or damage to the cargo which is insured and loss of freight where freight is insured. Some of the doctrines dealt within the Act, though enacted in the context of marine insurance, are often invoked in regard to other 'insurance transactions also – for example the doctrine of subrogation. The Transfer of Property Act, 1882 relating to actionable claims, contains certain provisions as to the assignment of insurance policies.

Law of Interest

Whenever a judgement is passed by a Court or tribunal or other forum awarding a monetary claim, the question naturally arises about the power of the court etc. to award interest on the principal sum. This question has to be decided with reference to certain statutory provisions, supplemented by rules derived from uncodified law.

The law of interest may become relevant for the period before the commencement of the litigation or other legal proceedings as also for the period thereafter. So far as the period before the commencement of the litigation or other legal proceedings are concerned, the matter belongs to the region, of substantive law. Interest for the period thereafter belongs to the region of, procedural law.

As regards the substantive law of interest, the same may be governed by (a) the contractual provision, if any, (b) the Interest Act, 1978, where applicable and (c) special enactments such as section 80, Negotiable Instruments Act, 1881 and section 51(2) of Sale of Goods Act, 1930.

So far as the period after the institution of litigation or legal proceedings is concerned, the matter is governed by the appropriate statutory provisions (wherever it has been enacted) or by the relevant case law (case law being relevant where there is no statutory provision or the statutory provision is not exhaustive. In the case of Civil Courts, in regard to decrease for the payment of money (other than a decree in a mortgage suit) section 34 of the Code of Civil Procedure, 1908 takes care of the situation. In the case of arbitration, section 29 of the Arbitration Act, 1940 takes care, in part of the situation.

Post Office

Transmission of letters and other articles through post still remains one of the most important modes of communication of information and views, in India. The person sending the message through post desires that it should reach the person for whom the letter is intended within a reasonably quick time and that it should reach the addressee without interception. Cases where it is alleged that the post office has not performed its expected obligations properly can raise legal issues. For dealing with such issues, we need statutory provisions and such provisions form part of the Indian Post Office Act, 1898. As regards insured articles, under section 33, India Post Office Act, 1898 subject to the prescribed conditions, the liability of the Central Government is to pay to the sender of the article (in case of loss) compensation not exceeding the amount for which the postal article was insured.

Banks

The banker-customer relationship is a relationship of debtor-creditor. The banker is a debtor and the customer who has placed money with bank is a creditor. The rights and liabilities depend on the contract between the two. For example, where the question is of withdrawal of money from a bank, the terms of the account govern the matter. If money is placed in fixed deposit for a particular terms, withdrawal before the term cannot be demanded as of right, but only on terms allowed by the contract. Nevertheless, there are certain obligations flowing from statute, particularly the Negotiable Instruments Act. For example, a cheque drawn by a customer must be hounoured by the bank, if there is enough money in the bank, unless special circumstances justify dishonour. Thus, the signature must tally, failing which the cheque may be dishonoured. Banks must exercise reasonable care in dealing with customer's money. For example, if a customer's signature on cheque is forged, the bank, if it pays the cheque, cannot debit the amount to the customer's account. Any breach of contract or departure from statutory duty by the bank is "deficiency" for which the customer can demand compensation through court of consumer forum.

Carriers and Couriers

Liability of carriers of goods and passengers is governed by the statutory provisions (where applicable) and subject to those provisions, by contract. For carriers by road, the Carriers Act, 1885 is the principal Act. For carriage by rail, there is the Act known as the Railways Act and for carriage of goods by ship, the Merchant Shipping Act, 1958 has to be seen. For carriage by air, the Carriage of Goods by Air Act is to be looked into. For multi-model transport, the Act of Parliament on multi-model transport (1993) is to be seen.

The principles of law applicable to a transaction of carriage of goods or passengers basically rest in contract. When a person hands over goods to a road transport carrier, the carrier enters into a contract with the customer to carry the goods to the destination. The goods must be transported within the agreed period, if not specified within a reasonable time. This is because of the general principle of the law of contracts that, in the absence of a specific stipulation, performance of a contract must be delivered to the addressee only, after the conditions, if any, on which they are to be delivered, are satisfied. Where goods are to be delivered only on surrender of certain documents by the consignee to the carrier, the consignor is entitled to compensation for the consequential loss.

The legal liability of couriers *i.e.* persons who undertake to carry letters, packets etc. may now be considered. Usually, they do not themselves undertake to carry the goods, they utilise the service of transporters like rail or air. They may be outside the purview of the Carriers Act, 1985 but they are all the same bound by the contract and must deliver the pack a) in safe condition b) to the named addressee and c) within reasonable time.

The Air (Prevention and Control of Pollution) Act, 1981

Every citizen has a right to pollution free environment. Article 48A of the Constitution of India provides that, it shall be the duty of the State to take steps to protect and improve the environment to safeguard the forests and wildlife of the country. The Supreme Court of India has declared in number of cases that the right to live in pollution free environment is a part of every person's right to life and personal liberty under status of a fundamental right.

Consumer Protection Act, 1986

The Act creates a series of special forums for the adjudication of consumer disputes relating to the sale or supply of goods or services for consideration. The important aspect to be noted is, that the "loss" about which the consumer can complain before the special forum, so created, must be a loss based on some deficiency or defect. Section 2(1)(f) of the Act defines "defect" as any fault, imperfection or shortcoming in the quantity, potency, purity or standard which is required to be maintained, by or under any law for the time being in force or as is "claimed" by the trader in any manner whatsoever, in relation to any goods. Section 2(1)(g) of the Act defines "*deficiency*" as any fault, in the nature and manner of performance which is required to be maintained, by or under any law for the time being in force, or which has been undertaken to be performed by a person in pursuance of a contract or otherwise in relation to any service.

Broadly speaking, under the Consumer Protection Act, 1986, the right to make a complaint to the appropriate Consumer Forum or Commission is given by section 12 of the Act to the following:

(a) the consumer, to whom such goods are sold or delivered or agreed to be delivered or such services provided or agreed to be provided;

(b) Any recognised consumer association, whether the consumer to whom the goods sold or delivered or agreed to be sold or delivered or service provided or agreed to be provided is a member of such association or not;

(c) One or more consumers, where there are numerous consumers having the same interest, with the permission of the District forum, on behalf of, or for the benefit of, all consumers so interested; or

(d) The Central or the State Government.

The definition of "*consumer*" in section 2(1)(d)(i) of the Act requires that the consumer must have bought goods or hired or availed of services for consideration. But, any user of such goods other than the actual buyer is also covered, if the use is with the approval of the actual buyer. Similarly, a beneficiary of services other than the actual hirer etc. is also covered, if the beneficiary avails the services with the approval of the actual hirer. However, a person who obtains goods for re-sale or for commercial purpose is excluded. The expression "*commercial purpose*" as defined by the explanation to section 2(1)(d) does not include use by a consumer of goods bought and used by him exclusively for earning his livelihood by self employment.

Section 24A of the Act, as amended in 1993 provides that the District forum, the State Commission or the National Commission shall not admit a complaint, unless it is filed within two years from the date on which the cause of action has arisen. But the District forum etc., may for reasons to be recorded, entertain a complaint even after two years, if it is satisfied that the complainant has sufficient cause for not filing the complaint within such period.

Under the Consumer Protection Act, the Legislature has taken precaution not only to define complaint", "complainant", "consumer" but even to mention in detail what would amount to unfair trade practice by giving an elaborate definition in clause (r) and even to define 'defect' and 'deficiency' by clauses (f) and (g) for which a consumer can approach the Commission. The Act thus aims at the protection of the economic interest of a consumer as understood in commercial sense as a purchaser of goods and in the larger sense, as a user of services. It is a milestone in history of socio-economic legislation and is directed towards achieving public benefit.

The Act has to be construed in favour of the consumer to achieve the purpose of enactment, as it is a social oriented legislation. The primary duty of the court while construing the provisions of such an Act is to adopt a constructive approach, subject to that it should not do violence to the language of the provisions and should not be contrary to the attempted objective of the enactment.

My endeavour in mentioning the above enactments in some detail is to present some of the important legal aspects of interest to consumers. If the consumers have knowledge of at least the primary aspects of the beneficial provisions of the important enactments and their rights, it would create an awareness among them to demand for supply of quality goods and services at affordable prices. The subject of consumerism has come to stay in India. A large bulk of the consumer awareness, involves familiarity with legal materials regarding various aspects of consumer transactions and my speech is a modest attempt in that direction. The law is a vast field and consumer law itself is growing in dimension as complexity. I hope that my wants will be of some help to all persons interested in the consumer movement, and will facilitate their understanding of the niceties and complexities of this growing branch of the law.

Though the people residing in urban areas are some how enlightened about their rights under the consumer law, due to the various programmes taken by various organizations, much has not been done in rural areas to bring about awareness among the rural masses which constitute a large chunk of the Indian population and majority of whom are illiterate. I hope that the CAPCO and the Consumer Awareness & Research Society will take steps in that direction and enlighten the rural masses also about their rights under the consumer law and should see that the consumers are organised into a powerful movement not only in the urban areas but also in rural areas as well, so that they can get quality goods and services at reasonable prices for better living.

ಐಐಐ

CONSUMER RIGHTS IN THE TELECOM SECTOR

Several years back, I never thought that I would be able to get in touch with my driver, plumber, electrician etc. round the clock. The telecom revolution is here to stay and greater the connectivity and tele-density, better it is for the nation and the consumers.

The present day telecom sector is characterized by simultaneous existence of state and private owned multiple operators, fast changing technologies, convergence of ideas, services and markets, liberalized and customer oriented regulatory regimes. Today, there is more transparency and awareness of the various value added services, offered by various players. The subscribers now demand Value Added Services using IP, wireless and broadband technologies rather than Plain Old Telephony Services (POTS).

However, there has to be harmony between the technology and consumers and this harmony could only be achieved with proper dispute settlement mechanisms in place and the protection of consumer rights.

I would first address the issue of instituting a proper dispute settlement mechanism, and then go on to discuss the issue of consumer rights.

A. DISPUTE SETTLEMENT MECHANISM

Benefits of Proper Dispute Settlement Mechanism

The telecom sector, being highly capital intensive, requires huge capital investments. Having a proper dispute settlement mechanism would assure investors of quick, fair and effective dispute resolution, which in turn would benefit subscribers in getting more add on services at lower tariffs. A prolonged dispute resolution process would be immensely detrimental to the interests of all the stake-holders.

Slower growth of telecom sector would retard general economic and technical development of the country and in order to avoid disruptions and delay in development of telecom markets, disputes need to be resolved expeditiously.

Successful dispute resolution would facilitate investment climate, stimulate growth and is of prime importance to developing countries, targeting greater

Delivered at the seminar on Settlement of Disputes & Protection of Consumer Rights in the Telecom Sector on 20th December, 2004 at Chennai.

teledensities and the even spread of telecom across all the regions. A swift and competent dispute resolution mechanism can play a determinative role in regulating market competition and requires to be as speedy as the networks and technologies they serve.

In my opinion, effective dispute settlement is based on following factors:—

(a) Transparency.

(b) Speed.

(c) Clear and Effective right to recourse.

(d) Consistency.

(e) Certainty.

(f) Expertise.

(g) Focus on Core bottlenecks but technology neutral.

Present Status of Dispute Mechanism

The Indian model of dispute resolution, since 2000, is perhaps the most novel. In India, the regulatory functions are vested with the Telecom Regulatory Authority of India (TRAI), whereas, policy and licensing functions are retained by the Department of Telecommunications (DoT), wing of the Union Government. The adjudication function has been vested with a specialized high-powered tribunal, the Telecom Dispute Settlement & Appellate Tribunal (TDSAT).

The TDSAT was constituted vide an amendment in the Telecom Regulatory Authority of India Act in the year 2000. At this point, it would be relevant for me to explain the reconstitution of the TRAI as was brought about by this amendment.

TRAI is now empowered to provide recommendations on various aspects relating to functioning of the telecom service providers and discharge of certain regulatory functions such as:

(a) laying down the standards of quality of services to be provided by the service providers and ensuring the quality of service;

(b) conducting periodical survey of such services provided by the service providers so as to protect the interest of the consumers of telecommunication services;

(c) fixing tariffs of various services; and

(d) ensuring effective compliance of Universal service obligations.

Adjudicatory

It is interesting to note that the jurisdiction of Civil Courts has been ousted for all telecom related disputes and have been re-routed to TDSAT.

The TDSAT has the following powers:

1. To adjudicate any dispute:

(a) Between a licensor and licensee;

(b) Between two or more service providers; and

(c) Between a service providers and a group of consumers.

2. To hear and dispose of appeal against any directions, decision or order of Telecom Regulatory Authority.

The TDSAT does not hear:

(a) restrictive and monopolistic practices issues; and

(b) individual consumer complaints.

TDSAT has wide original and appellate jurisdiction and as the only Telecom adjudicator, it hears questions of facts and law.

The Tribunal is headed by the Chairperson who may be a serving or retired judge of the Supreme Court or the Chief Justice of the High Court alongwith two members, who are well versed in the areas of technology, communication, industry, commerce or administration or have been Secretary to Union of India for a minimum of 2 years.

The TDSAT has been given the authority to regulate its own procedure and appeal against the TDSAT order lies only before the Supreme Court, thereby reducing the time frame of dispute resolution.

I am happy to know that TDSAT, over the years, has gathered the required expertise and as such very few matters are pending before it. The Tribunal has passed orders on interconnection issues, license agreement, interpretation, pricing, jurisdictional issues, policy interpretation, level playing field.

The very fact that very few decisions of TDSAT were appealed against before the Supreme Court speaks volumes about the effective expertise within the tribunal to deal with very complex matters. It would be appropriate to mention here that except for one case which was remanded back to TDSAT, the Supreme Court did not reverse any order of the TDSAT. I am compelled to repeatedly praise the Tribunal for its efficient dispute resolution. Even complex matters like the challenge to limited mobility services reached finality in less than 3 years despite an appeal to the Supreme Court.

B. CONSUMER'S RIGHTS

The Government has taken various legislative steps in the past to protect the interests of the consumers. The courts have evolved appropriate remedies in common law to cater to the needs of the times. It would not be an exaggeration for me to say that parliamentary legislation and judicial intervention coupled with the role of social reformers and voluntary organizations have in the recent years given consumer protection the shape of a forceful consumer movement.

Individual consumers in India are protected under the Consumer Protection Act, 1986. The Preamble to the Act provides "An Act to provide for better protection of the interests of consumers and for that purpose to make provision for the establishment of consumer councils and other authorities for the settlement of consumers' disputes and for matters connected therewith."

The definition of complainant includes an individual consumer under section 2 of the Act and the procedure for filing the complaint is given under section 12 of the Act and admission of complaint procedure is provided under section 13 of the Act. The Act provides that any person, aggrieved by an order made by the District Forum or State Commission may prefer an appeal against such order to the State or National Commission respectively, within a period of 30 days from the date of the order.

A recent amendment to the Consumer Protection Act also requires payment of certain filing fees.

Section 12 of the Consumer Protection Act, 1986 has been amended as under:—

> "....
>
> (2) Every complaint filed under sub-section (1) shall be accompanied with such amount of fee and payable in such manner as may be prescribed........."

I feel that there is an urgent need to ensure that the interests of the consumers of Telecom Services are specifically safeguarded, considering that the telecom sector is undergoing a continuous technological change and offering a multitude of complex services. Various types of telecommunication services like Voice and Data, Wireline and Wireless, GSM and CDMA, Satellite and VSAT's, GMPCS, Radio Paging and Trunking, Internet Services and Cable and Broadcasting, etc. are being made available to millions of users across the country.

Since there are now several Service Providers providing each of these varied services across the country in each region, it is necessary to regulate and provide uniform and effective guiding principles that would minimize customer grievances and ensure satisfactory provision of Telecom Services by the Service Providers.

The Parliament has provided for certain measures in the TRAI Act, 1997 to address these issues and to protect consumer interest.

1. The TRAI Act, 1997 was enacted to establish the TDSAT to regulate the telecommunication services, adjudicate disputes, dispose of appeals and to protect the interests of service providers and consumers of the telecom sector, to promote and ensure orderly growth of the telecom sector.

2. **Section 11** of the Act provides for the functions of the TRAI in super cession of the Indian Telegraph Act. The section states that the functions of the authority would be to

> (a) make recommendations, either *suo motu* or on a request from the licensor, on the following matters, namely:—
>
> ....
>
> (vii) measures for the development of telecommunication technology and any other matter relatable to telecommunication industry in general;
>
> (b) discharge the following functions, namely:
>
> (v) lay-down the standards of quality of service to be provided by the service providers and ensure the quality of service and conduct the periodical survey of such service provided by the service providers so as to protect interest of the consumers of telecommunication service;
>
> ...."

3. **Section 14** of the Act provides for the establishment of the TDSAT to adjudicate disputes between Service Providers and consumers.

4. Section 14A(1) and (2) and (3) of the Act provides for the entire procedure of dispute redressal as would be applicable qua consumers.

"Application for settlement of disputes and appeals to the Appellate Tribunal

(1) The Central Government or a State Government or a local authority or any person may make an application to the Appellate Tribunal for adjudication of any dispute referred to in clause (a) of section 14.

(2) The Central Government or a State Government or a local authority or any person aggrieved by any direction, decision or order made by the authority may prefer an appeal to the Appellate Tribunal.

(3) Every appeal under sub-section (2) shall be preferred within a period of 30 days from the date on which a copy of the direction or order or decision made by the authority is received by the Central Government or the State Government or the local authority or the aggrieved person and it shall be in such form, verified in such manner and be accompanied by such fee as may be prescribed:

Provided that the Appellate Tribunal may entertain any appeal after the expiry of the said period of 30 days if it is satisfied that there was sufficient cause for not filing it within that period."

5. Section 15 of the Act bars the jurisdiction of any Civil Court.

6. Section 18 of the Act provides for appeal to the Supreme Court directly.

I am happy to state that the TRAI has also notified a list of registered Consumer Associations/NGOs who could interact with it and participate in the various Consultative Processes and other proceedings for evolving appropriate recommendations governing the Telecom Industry. It is to the merit of the TRAI that it has considered consumers to be an important stakeholder in the development and regulation of the Telecom Industry. Each of these consumer organizations/NGOs have participated in the various Consultative Processes and have engaged the TRAI in a dialogue. Their comments and suggestions have also been transparently published on the TRAI Website during each such Consultative Processes.

The TRAI has also issued regulations, requiring the Service Providers to transparently and clearly publish all the Tariffs and alternate packages, and also provide a comparison/financial implications of each of these packages to help the subscriber make a suitable choice. The TRAI is also equally charged with duties and obligations to protect the consumer interest as is evident from its functions, *inter alia*, under section 11(a)(iv) and (v) of the TRAI Act, 1997.

I am pleased to note that the recent landmark decisions of the TDSAT and several recommendations of the TRAI have been aimed at encouraging development and deployment of *New technologies* and encouraging competition and discouraging anti *competition* and predatory prices or arbitrary acts of disconnection so that consumers are benefited and are enabled to access the latest technologies and without suffering arbitrary disconnection and disruptions.

TDSAT REGULATIONS

It is relevant to mention that the TDSAT has also framed certain Regulations governing filing of Original Petition and Appeals before it. These mandate payment of certain minimum fees to meet certain costs of notices and other administrative costs and also to discourage frivolous complaints or appeals being filed.

A Comparison

It would not be out of place to compare the telecom industry and the special needs of this industry with that of the other infrastructure sectors.

The Telecom Industry is a specialized industry. It is governed by several Regulations issued by the TRAI and judgments passed by the TDSAT from time to time. Each of these Regulations is complex and involves several regulatory mechanisms. Each of the Service Providers is bound by such Regulations. The Regulations and decisions of the TRAI may be challenged before the TDSAT, which has been established as a Special Tribunal to oversee the Telecom Regulation in the country. The establishment of such a Special Tribunal with dispute resolution jurisdiction is special to India and is not to be found in most jurisdictions having an evolved Telecom Sector. Those jurisdictions permit a challenge to the decision of a Regulator to the ordinary Civil/Appellate Courts. However, the establishment of the Special Tribunal has its advantage inasmuch as it is well versed with the implications of the complex Telecom Regulations and can ensure faster resolution. Appeals against the decision of the TDSAT lie directly to the Supreme Court, under section 18 of the TRAI Act.

Similar provisions have been introduced in the recent Electricity Act, 2003. I notice that a recommendation of the Supreme Court to this effect is to be found in *West Bengal Electricity Regulatory Commission* v. *CESC Limited*, (2002) 8 SCC 715 (per Justice Santosh Hegde), wherein it was observed that:—

> *"..... Without meaning any disrespect to the Judges of the High Court, we think neither the High Court nor the Supreme Court would in reality be appropriate appellate forums in dealing with this type of factual and technical matters. Therefore, we recommend that the appellate power against an order of the State Commission under the 1998 Act should be conferred either on the Central Electricity Regulatory Commission or on a similar body. We notice that under the Telecom Regulatory Authority of India Act, 1997 in Chapter IV, a similar provision is made for an appeal to a special Appellate Tribunal and thereafter a further appeal to the Supreme Court on questions of law only. We think a similar appellate provision may be considered to make the relief of appeal more effective."*

In a subsequent decision reported as *COAI & Ors.* v. *Union of India & Ors.*, (2003) 3 SCC 186, the Supreme Court observed that:—

> *"...... The contention that until decision of the Tribunal afresh, the fixed service operators may not be permitted to provide WLL with limited mobility to the*

consumers cannot be accepted since that would be grossly detrimental to the consumers' interest and also on account of the fact that several fixed service operators have already provided the facility in question......."

By virtue of section 14(a)(iii), disputes that affect a large body of consumers, generally, can be subject to the jurisdiction of the TDSAT. The exception to this provision is contained in the proviso which retains the jurisdiction of the MRTP Commission etc. But in each of these exceptions, if we note carefully, it is only the individual consumer complaints that can be examined by such bodies/ entities. Whenever there is a dispute that involves a *group of consumers* and is, therefore, a dispute that involves the consumers generally or is otherwise a matter of great importance affecting the Telecom Sector/Telecom Industry and telecom users generally, then these matters ought to be raised before the TDSAT. Matters affecting a large body of Telecom Consumers ought to be referred to the TDSAT by the Consumer Courts in deference to the provisions of section 14(1)(iii) of the TRAI Act. This is because the TDSAT is well equipped to handle such important matters effectively, since it deals with such issues on day to day basis and is also qualified as an expert body under the TRAI Act.

Similar instances are to be found in other countries also where, say a Competition Commission may defer to the jurisdiction of a Specialized Telecom Regulator in matters involving the Telecom Industry.

A dispute came up before the Kerala High Court when I was the Acting Chief Justice of the said Court that whether the Consumer Disputes Redressal Forum, constituted under the Consumer Protection Act, 1986 has jurisdiction to entertain the complaint made by an individual/subscriber with regard to the disconnection of his telephone. The matter came up before me and another learned Judge. The Division Bench held as under:

> *"In our opinion, the learned Single Judge has erred in interpreting section 3 of the Consumer Protection Act without considering section 9 of the CPC and section 7B of the Telegraph Act. The provision order section 3, in our view, is quite specific that the remedy under the Consumer Protection Act is not in derogation of any other law for the time being in force. The learned Single Judge has gone wrong in holding that the remedy under the Consumer Protection Act is more effective and speedy than under section 7B of the Telegraph Act by giving undue credence to the year of enactment. The dispute regarding payment of telephone bill is to be dealt with under the provisions of Arbitration clause contained in the Telegraph Act. The Consumer Protection Act is a general law for all consumers in general and the Telegraph Act is a special law confined to the telephone consumers only. In our view, the principles laid down by the Supreme Court that general law must yield to the special law is applicable in the instant case. The special statute – Telegraph Act – meant for telephone consumers will prevail over the general statute, viz., the Consumer Protection Act, which is available for all who are consumers of various products and services in one way or the other. The stipulation contained under section 3 of the Consumer Protection Act is not in derogation of any other law for the time being in force has been omitted while interpreting the said provision."*

.........the statutory remedy available to a subscriber under section 7B of the Telegraph Act by way of Arbitration has been upheld by the Supreme Court in the decision reported in *Shri M.L. Jaggi* v. *Mahanagar Telephones Nigam Ltd.*, JT 1996 (1) SC 215. In Paragraphs 4 and 8, the Court held as follows:—

It is a statutory remedy provided under the Act and, therefore, in a dispute as regards the amount claimed in the demand raised, the only remedy provided is by way of arbitration under section 7B of the Act. By operation of sub-section (2) thereof, the award of the arbitrator made under sub-section (1) shall be conclusive between the parties to the dispute and shall not be questioned in any court. The statutory remedy under the Arbitration Act, 1940, thus, has been taken away.

It is, thus, settled law that reasons are required to be recorded when it affects the public interest. It is seen that under section 7B, the award is conclusive when the citizen complains that he was not correctly put to bill of the calls he had made and disputed the demand for payment. The statutory remedy open to him is one provided under section 7B of the Act. By necessary implication, when the arbitrator decides the dispute under section 7B, he is enjoined to give reasons in support of his decision since it is final and cannot be questioned in a court of law. The only obvious remedy available to the aggrieved person against the award is judicial review under Article 226 of the Constitution. If the reasons are not given, it would be difficult for the High Court to adjudge as to under what circumstances the arbitrator came to his conclusion that the amount demanded by the Department is correct or the amount disputed by the citizen is unjustified. The reasons would indicate as to how the mind of the arbitrator was applied to the dispute and how he arrived at the decision. The High Court, though does not act in exercising judicial review as a court of appeal but within narrow limits of judicial review, it would consider the correctness and legality of the award.......

...the Forum has no jurisdiction to try the complaint since the dispute raised by the subscriber relates to an instrument, installed at his request by the Telephone Department and that the dispute raised by the complainant relates to the quantum of the bill and, therefore, such disputes come within the purview of section 7B of the Telegraph Act. Consequently, it is submitted that the parties are amenable only to the Arbitration by the authority under section 7B of the Telegraph Act and the jurisdiction of the Forum to entertain a complaint to matters coming within the purview of that section is barred. We have, in the paragraphs above, interpreted the words in section 7B, *viz.* "any dispute concerning any telegraph line, appliance or apparatus, cable chamber tower appliance or apparatus", as found in the said section. In our opinion, the dispute as regards the bill relating to an instrument would come within the purview of section 7B of the Telegraph Act and, consequently, the complaint given to the Forum would be barred. On reading of section 7B of the Telegraph Act, it is clear that the said section has provided a machinery by way of arbitration into claims regarding the instruments and billing.

The correctness of our above judgment was doubted by another Division Bench of the Kerala High Court in Writ Appeal No. 535 of 2002. According to the

Division Bench, our judgment requires reconsideration by a large Bench of the High Court. The matter was, thereafter, placed before the three Judge Bench. The Full Bench was of the opinion that our judgment reported in 2002 KLT 195 does not contain the correct statement of law and does not promote the declared objective of better protection and consequently our decision was over-ruled.

Aggrieved by the decision of the Full Bench of the Kerala High Court, the General Manager, Telecom, BSNL, Kozhikode preferred special leave petition before the Supreme Court of India, questioning the correctness of the order passed by the Full Bench of the Kerala High Court, over ruling our Division Bench Judgment of the High Court reported in *2002 KLT 195.*

I am happy to say that the Supreme Court, by order dated 29-11-2004 granted leave to appeal against the Full Bench decision of the Kerala High Court and have also granted stay of the operation of the Full Bench judgment in Civil Appeal No. 7687 of 2004 (*G.M. Telecom* v. *M. Krishnan & Anr.*). In view of granting of leave and of staying the order of the Full Bench of the Kerala High Court, the parties/subscribers cannot now move to Consumer Disputes Redressal Forum and that the only forum to redress their grievance is the arbitration proceedings provided under section 7B of the Indian Telegraph Act.

The Tribunal's jurisdiction is exclusive as section 15 of the Act, specifically excludes the jurisdiction of any Civil Court in respect of any matter which the Tribunal is empowered, under the Act, to determine. Appeals from the order of the Tribunal lie straight to the Supreme Court and orders passed by the Tribunal are executable as a decree of a Civil Court. In the case of *Cellular Operator Association of India* v. *Union of India*, (2003) 3 SCC 186, the Supreme Court has observed:—

> "...Having regard to the very purpose and object for which the Appellate Tribunal was constituted and having examined the different provisions contained in Chapter IV, more particularly, the provision dealing with ousting the jurisdiction of Civil Court in relation to any matter which the Appellate Tribunal is empowered by or under the Act, as contained in section 15, we have no hesitation in coming to the conclusion that the power of the Appellate Tribunal is quite wide, as has been indicated in the statute itself and the decision of this Court dealing with the power of a Court, exercising appellate or original power, will have no application for limiting the jurisdiction of the Appellate Tribunal under the Act."

With the notifying of Cable and Broadcasting services as telecommunication services within the meaning of the Act, by the Government in 2004, the jurisdiction of the Tribunal has been further widened. Regulating these services and ensuring maintenance of quality standards in Broadcasting and Cable services are important areas of concern for the Tribunal. Protection of the Consumer's right to receive signals has even seized the attention of the Supreme Court in the pending matter of *Ten Sports* v. *Citizens Consumer and Civic Action Group*, SLP (C) Nos. 5204-5205 of 2004.

Thus, the scope and width of the Tribunal's jurisdiction is vast and apart from settlement and adjudication of disputes, the Tribunal has also to be bear in mind the interests of the consumers and ensure a level playing field and orderly growth of the sector. The Tribunal's performance under the Chairmanship of Hon'ble Mr. Justice D.P. Wadhwa in all these aspects has been indeed praiseworthy. It has made decisions and judicial pronouncements on a series of vital issues such as levy and recovery of license fees and penalties and interest, interpretation of license and interconnectivity agreements and regulations. The swift, well reasoned and considered adjudication process employed by the Tribunal has resulted in a determinative, practical and reliable body of law for the Telecom sector. The phenomenal pace of growth of the country's telecom sector itself bears testimony to its confidence in the dispute settlement mechanism system.

To conclude, the telecom sector in India has come a long way and is in fact, in a state of constant flux. So much so that the TRAI and the TDSAT have been established as independent market regulators to provide efficient dispute resolution mechanisms and to safeguard the interests of the consumers. The TDSAT has been doing a commendable job in dispensing with complex technical issues competently and in a short time. Yet, in my opinion, the option of establishing a Telecom Ombudsman for resolution of disputes should seriously be explored especially because it has the potential of resolving telecom related disputes between consumers and the service providers at the initial stages itself without burdening the TDSAT which in any event is a formal procedure.

The task before us is thus heavy and the burden weighty but it is a responsibility that must be shared equally by all the participants in the system— the legislature, the regulatory bodies and the telecom service providers, and one, which bearing in mind the Vibrancy of the sector, will prove equal in performance. The present seminar will thus help in bringing together many minds and contributing new ideas in shaping and strengthening the regulatory dispute settlement mechanisms and in safeguarding the rights of the consumers.

ಬಿಬಿಬಿ

DEVOTION TO JUSTICE

There has been a wide spread talk that of late, the standards of lawyers both in respect of efficiency as well as the ideas have deteriorated. There is also a general belief that the Judges are concerned with Justice whereas, Advocates are concerned only with a successful or unsuccessful attempt in earning money. I am of the view, that the above impression and beliefs are fundamentally unsound.

Advocates are as much devoted to Justice and fair-play, as the Judges. I say this because the Advocate of today is the Judge of tomorrow and if a lawyer is not devoted to Justice and fair-play, it is impossible to make good the same by crossing over from Bar to the Bench. Judges dispense Justice in Courts with the help and assistance of Advocates. If there is decline in the efficiency of the Bar, it will be reflected in the calibre of the Bench. The Bar should be fearless in order to serve the end. While, confidence in the administration of justice is unshaken and is increasing day by day as could be seen from the increasing number of litigants, who approach the portals of Courts seeking Justice.

The difference between law as taught and law as practised is familiar. If I may be excused, I would mention that in law as taught, the facts are clear and the law uncertain; whereas in law as practiced, the law is clear and the facts are uncertain.

Every law student is primarily concerned in acquiring legal knowledge and skill needed for his career and therefore he is selfish. On the other hand, a legal practitioner is essentially selfless, for all his endeavours are bent towards doing the best he can for his client. An advocate shall fearlessly uphold the interest of his client and he must comfort himself in a manner befitting his status, as an officer of the court, a privileged member of the community and gentlemen, bearing in mind that what may be lawful and moral for a person who is not a member of the Bar or for a member of the Bar in his non-professional capacity may still be improper for an Advocate. The standards of professional conduct and etiquette are set out by the Bar Council of India in the rule framed in exercise of its powers under Advocates' Act.

Speech delivered on the occasion of 'Law Fest', 1997 at Tiruchirapalli Law College, Tirruchirapalli, on 9th March, 1997.

An advocate owes a duty to the Court, duty to the client, duty to the opponent and duty to the colleagues. An advocate should conduct himself with dignity and self-respect. The dignity which an advocate commands from his client depends upon the dignity and respect, which he shows to the Court. An Advocate should discourage unjustified litigation.

Many a lawyers have taken a leading part in the Freedom Movement and many have contributed for the development of religion and various Indian languages. Many had undergone incarceration during independent movement and many have played a vital role in Trade Union Movement. An Advocate should be soft spoken and gentle in manners. Advocates have also been the leaders of public opinion as also fighters of freedom. Democracy can have no better champions than Advocates who know precisely what the citizen's rights are in respect of his person, property, faith and freedom of action. An Advocate knows how far a free man may go and how far a free man may achieve the objects of national life by constitutional methods. Some of the lawyers of yester years were makers of modern India - they were statemen, great scholars, philosophers and above all, great humanists.

In England, the bodies concerned with professional conduct are Inns of Courts, General Council of the Bar and the Circuit Mess of each of the several Circuits. It will be interesting to note that in England it is not possible for a Barrister to have a seat in Solicitor's office and a Barrister should not accept a brief for a Company of which he is a Director nor advice or settle documents preferably for the company and a Barrister may not have the words "Barrister at Law" outside the place where he resides or has the Chamber and a Barrister shall not describe himself as a Barrister on his visiting cards. Though the professional conduct and etiquette at the Bar of England and Wales may not strictly apply to the Indian Bar, yet, the standards laid down are worthy of being emulated by at least senior Advocates.

Justice Frank Furter said, *"It is the quality of justice which will establish the Court in the confidence of people and it is the confidence of the people which is the ultimate reliance of the Court".* That the Indian Judiciary is trying to live up to the speech made by Justice Frank Furter.

A good judgement reflects the assistance, which a Judge received from the Bar on either side. A great Bar endowed with ability, integrity and independence is necessary to keep the stream of justice - pure and unsullied. If the High Courts and Supreme Court falter or fail, democracy will be in jeopardy.

Judiciary has a very vital role to play in protecting and preserving human rights and fundamental rights. Law schools and teachers are the backbone of law. I wish for every one, a bright future in the legal profession.

ಬಬಬ

LAWYER AS A CONSCIENCE KEEPER

It gives me great pleasure to participate in the function organized by Coimbatore Bar Association, to felicitate members of the Bar who have completed 80 years of age and those who have completed 50 years of practice in this noble profession.

Completing 50 years of practice in the legal profession is a very great achievement and those who have achieved this feat should be honoured. In this profession, it is the senior lawyers who set the trends and mould junior members. Junior members are trained in logic. It is the senior lawyers who give the profession a true and correct image. The system of establishing and dispersing justice is developed to efficient levels by senior lawyers. The future of our republic depends to a great extent on our maintenance of justice, pure and unsullied. It can be achieved only, by the proper conduct of the members of this legal profession which should receive the approval of all right thinking people.

Irrespective of the incumbents of the judicial office, it is the duty of the members of the Bar to maintain towards the Courts, a respectful attitude. The respect which a Lawyer commands from the litigants would largely depend upon the respect shown by him to Courts. Judges are not free to defend themselves and therefore, the Bar should defend the Judges against unjust criticism and clamour. There should be co-operation between the Bar and the Bench and there should not be confrontation on any account.

What is of utmost importance is to maintain and foster the confidence of litigants, who enter the portals of justice with lot of hope, expectation, trust and confidence. The citadel will fall, the moment the confidence is lost.

It should be the endeavour of everyone who engaged in this profession to belie the words of Lord Brougham, who described a Lawyer as *"Learned gentlemen who rescues your estate from your enemies and keeps it himself"* and that of Jeremy Bentham, an eminent 19th Century British Political Scientist who said that *"Lawyers are the only persons in whom ignorance of the Law is not punished"*.

I remind the words of Justice Oliver Wendel Halmas who spokes of Lawyers as follows:

Speech delivered on the occasion of Honoring the Senior Member of the Bar, Coimbatore on 18th September, 1993.

58

"*The artist sees the line of growth in a tree, the businessman an opportunity in a muddle, the Lawyers, a principle in a lot of dramatic details. The glory of Lawyers like that of men of science is more corporate than individual. Our labour is an endless organic process. The organism whose being is recorded and protected by the law is the undying body of Society.*"

It is the duty of a Lawyer as a conscience keeper of the nation and watch-dog of Society to make his clients respect law and the constitutionally established authority.

ಬಬಬ

SUBORDINATE JUDICIARY – THE ROOT OF OUR JUDICIAL SYSTEM

The Indian Judicial System is constantly exposed to new challenges, new dimensions and new signals and has to survive a world in which perhaps the only real certainty is that the circumstances of tomorrow will not be the same as those of today.

Judiciary today is more deserving of public confidence than ever before.

Our Judiciary, throughout the Union of India have earned a reputation for great integrity and independence. We are proud of it. We, the members of the Judicial hierarchy have inherited the legacy of dedicated collective endeavour by the Bench and the Bar and establishing an unbroken tradition of high efficiency, perfect integrity and fearless independence. The true touch stone for measuring the success of a Judicial institution is the degree of confidence reposed in it by the public and it is a matter of great pride that our country has earned for itself the fullest respect and confidence of the public of the nation. The Judgments of the Courts are treated with respect and its stature in knowledgeable legal circles is equal to be best amongst other Courts in this land.

The Judiciary has a special role to play in the task of achieving socio-economic goals enshrined in the Constitution while maintaining their aloofness and independence, the Judges have to be aware of the social changes in the task of achieving socio-economic justice for the people.

Socrates said that four things improve a great Judge:

    (a) to hear courteously;

    (b) to answer wisely;

    (c) to consider soberly; and

    (d) to decide impartially

The Judges of the subordinate judiciary can be termed as the roots of our judicial system. The society looks forward to have Judicial Officers who may be trusted and who can inspire confidence in the society that it will get justice. It is rightly said that Judicial Officers discharge divine functions though they are

---

Speech delivered at the 'School of Judicial Administration and Rajasthan Judicial Academy', Jodhpur on 9th April, 2005.

not divine themselves. The majority of the Judicial Officers of the State are discharging their judicial functions in a befitting manner but I, being the member of Judiciary in the Supreme Court desire from every Judicial Officer of the Subordinate Judiciary to lead a disciplined life as a Judicial Officer. I expect from Judges of all cadres to strictly observe *punctuality in Court*. Sitting in court late, without reasonable cause, leads to frustration to the litigants attending the Court. Laxity in this behalf is inexcusable. Not adhering to Court timings is a serious aberration. It must be avoided at all cost by all of us. Integrity is an essential quality of a Judicial Officer. A Judicial Officer must follow the standards of integrity, morality and behaviour which he sets for others. If a Judge decides a case wrongly out of motives, it shakes the faith of litigant public and the whole society. Such an officer who does not maintain highest standard of integrity, has no right to continue to occupy the chair as a Judicial Officer. If a Judicial Officer is corrupt, then he cannot be allowed to hold such a divine chair of a Judge.

The members of the judiciary should pronounce the judgments within the stipulated time. Delay in delivering the judgments will cause untold hardship to the litigants since it will deprive them of their chances of preferring appeals/ revisions in time.

The Judicial Officers should not leave headquarters without informing the District Judges or the Controlling Officers, as the case may be. When one is posted to a particular station, one has to meet the superiors either prior to or after taking charge. In the disciplined hierarchy of judiciary, it is imperative that all the officers should maintain cordial relationship with each other so as to maintain the dignity and decorum of the institution.

The Judges must decide cases without fear or favour, affection or illwill, friend or foe. I can assure you that if you are discharging the judicial function as a true Judicial Officer following the norms then you should not be afraid of frivolous complaints made by persons having vested interest.

The officers should apply for permission to leave headquarters with or without pre-fixing or suffixing casual leave and after availing it, extend their period of leave etc. along with the medical certificate. No leave application should be submitted at the time of resuming the duties. Such practice is violative of the clear instructions issued by the High Court. One must give a patient hearing to the litigants/Advocates.

One must work very hard, be very honest, and courteous to the litigants, witnesses and the members of the Bar and discharge the judicial functions with all humility at your command.

When a residential house/flat is allotted which have been constructed by the State Government for the Judicial Officers, you are expected to occupy the same as these houses have been constructed by the State Government in compliance of the directions of the Hon'ble Supreme Court for the welfare of the Judicial Officers.

There are four personalities who have to play vital parts in the conduct of business in Courts. They are: (i) the Judge, (ii) the Members of the Bar, (iii) the officials of the Court, and (iv) the Court staff and the litigant public.

Let us first take the Judge. Many are obsessed with the feeling that a Judge should be of a grandeur personality. This is absolutely wrong. The minimum expected of him is that he should be neat and presentable. He should not be solovently dressed. There is an aversion for the present dress regulations. I am not bold enough to decry it as meaningless. The reason behind this aversion as I could gather, seems to be a prejudice against the English tradition. I do not covet consensus, but I have a conviction that Judges and members of a particular profession should stand apart as distinct from laymen. I have sat in the Bench from 1990 onwards with the present apparel of a Judge hanging on my considerably large – I suppose – physical frame. Personally, when I wore the Judge's dress, then only I felt, I had become ready for the day to dispense justice as a Judge. When the Judge speaks, his accent must be clear. His voice should not be too loud and it should not be too low. It must be clearly audible to those who are present.

Unnecessary and unwarranted utterances are bound to embarrass not only others, but the Judge himself. What should be asked, should be asked, what should not be asked should be avoided by the Judge.

The Judge must learn to hear the Counsel first. What the Counsel says may not be absolutely correct from the point of view of the Judge. The Judge must always remember that his views entertained at the moment, may turn out to be wrong. Hence, with receptivity and with an open mind, the Judge must listen.

Interruption in the middle should not be made by the Judge. A Judge need not exhibit any hastiness in the matter. At a convenient time, the Judge must politely ask the Counsel as to whether he is correct in what he stated before the Court. It would be below the dignity of a Judge to indulge in, argument of the Bar in open Court. If the Judge himself is in doubtful sphere, it is better to listen rather than raising questions, exposing his ignorance. Receive what is given in Court and eschew what is against Law and facts, after thorough analysis and assimilation both in and out of Court, which exercise is part of a Judgeship.

Do not speak out the verdict, unless you propose to pronounce it in open Court then and there. Any shrewd Counsel will certainly discern the mind of the Judge on the verdict. But on no account the Judge shall tell his verdict before he pronounces it.

Courtesy towards the members of the Bar as I already stated is a must for a Judge. In a rarest of rare cases, the language of a member of the Bar may be offensive. Even then the Judge should not loose his temper. Ignoring any such offending behaviour, the Judge must work. But, if offensive behaviour persists, then the Judge has to control it. Otherwise, the decorum of the system will fail. That should not happen. These are all matters of experience of the Judge. There is no hard and fast rule in this regard.

The Judge must give due respect to the staff of the Court. The Court staff is part of the Judge himself. The Court staff may commit mistakes in open court. Be discreet and do not expose the mistakes of the staff to the public eye. The Court staff must be treated by the Judge with due respect and dignity in open court. Not even an attender should feel that he has been slighted and be-littled.

We can now go to the Bar. We cannot think of functioning of Courts without the Members of the Legal Profession. Court etiquette is the topic we are concentrating upon. A member of the Bar must be neatly dressed and must look distinct in his dress. Inconvenience or convenience is not the criterion.

Now, we can talk about the Court staff. Each member of the court staff must be meticulously dressed. The Court despite many odds must look trim. I know, the Courts do not have adequate furniture. Yet the functioning of the Court can be trim, if the people functioning there are trim in person and naturally in mind too. The Court staff must see to the functioning of the Court efficiently and effectively. They must treat the members of the Bar with due respect and courtesy. The Court Officer to a very great extent knows the progress in each case thoroughly and he will also know the facts of each case tried in the Court. He will effectively guide the conduct of the case in Court. He will be of immense help to the Presiding Officer.

The Personal Assistant or Stenographer or Secretary to the Judge must equally be smart and trim. If the judgement has been dictated besides the open Court Hall, the Personal Assistant must keep it an absolute secret. The trend now-a-days noticed is, the members of the Bar and even the public come to know the verdict even before it is pronounced in the open Court. How could this happen! I can only say that it should not happen.

The orderlies of the Court have very significant role to play. They should not forget their importance to the functioning of the Court. The Court staff must have distinct dress regulations. My experience as a Judge has taught that dress regulations for each person functioning for Court business is a necessary paraphernalia. If a member of the Court staff comes to Court casually dressed as if going to a cinema hall, how will he carry respect in the eyes of the public? The present dress regulations, if left alone, will be better which shows the Court staff as a distinct entity.

We will now take up the public entering the Court premises. The very atmosphere must instill a fear into the mind of the public that they are entering a very sanctified place, next to a place of worship. Tea stalls and Pan shops and vending of snacks should not come near the Court functioning. It is not a manner of convenience for the public. Convenience should be provided but not at the sacrifice of the dignity and decorum of the functioning of the Courts.

The public must be asked not to indulge in loud talking in Court Hall. They must remain within the enclosures meant for them.

All said and done the Court must function within the norms of etiquette. I am in favour of strict adherence to Court Etiquette. Now-a-days this is being slowly forgotten. This is a sad state of affairs.

The issue of under-trials detained in various prisons in the country has been a matter of concern. The Hon'ble Prime Minister, while addressing the conference of the Chief Justices, reminded the judiciary of its accountability to ensure the speedy disposal of large number of cases pending before the various Courts. In the same conference, Hon'ble Chief Justice of India, Dr. A.S. Anand identified the "acute shortage of courts", the single largest factor responsible for the accumulation of arrears in subordinate courts. It appears that the Central Government, realizing the plight of under-trials and to ensure justice to common man, made allocation of Rs. 502 crore for creation of 1734 Courts named as "Fast Track Courts" all over the country.

A successful judicial system is a hallmark of any developed civilization. The failure of Criminal Justice System to bring criminal conduct under tight control is viewed as leading to the break down of the public order and to the disappearance of an important condition of human freedom. The Criminal Justice System has failed to achieve its twin primary goals viz; the *Control of the crime* and the *protection of individual rights.* The crime control implies orderly efficient method for arresting, prosecuting, convicting and punishing the guilty and for deterring crime by others. The protection of individual rights is necessary to guard the accused against arbitrary exercise of powers by the State. The rising crime rate clearly indicates that the system is not an effective deterrent. The graph of cases of murder, rape, theft, assault, robbery, disorderly conduct and bride burning is in ascending order. The open violation of laws, bribery in public service, presence of professional criminals and intimidation to victims and witnesses are experienced in day-to-day life.

It is not uncommon for any criminal case to drag on for years. During this time, the accused travels from the zone of "anguish" to one of "sympathy". The witnesses are either won over by muscle or money power or they become sympathetic towards the accused. As a result, the witness turn hostile and prosecution fails. In some cases, the recollection fades, or the witnesses die. Thus, long delay in courts causes great hardship not only to the accused but even to the victim and the State. The accused, who is not out on bail, may sit in jail for number of months or even years, awaiting conclusion of the trial. Thus, effort is required to be made to improve the management of the prosecution in order to increase the certainty of conviction and punishment for most serious offenders. It is experienced that there is increasing laxity in the Court-work by the police personnel, empowered to investigate the case. On the eve of establishment of Fast Track Courts on 11th June, 2001, I asked the State Government to take up the issue of fair and meaningful investigation on high priority. I further add that it is high time the State Government created a Special Wing in the Police Department solely for the purpose of investigation and attending Court work.

The prosecutorial set up consists of "Public Prosecutors including Additional Public Prosecutors, Special Public Prosecutors and Assistant Public Prosecutors". A prosecutor occupies a unique position in Criminal Justice System. In *Hitendra Vishnu Thakur* v. *State of Maharashtra,* AIR 1994 SC 2623: (1994) 4 SCC 602, the Hon'ble Supreme Court observed that a Public Prosecutor is an important office of the State Government and is appointed by the State under the Code of Criminal Procedure. He is not a part of the investigating agency. He is an independent statutory authority. The success of the trial depends mainly on effective prosecution, which is possible only through well qualified, trained, fair and dedicated prosecutors. It goes without saying that integrity and impartiality of the Public Prosecutor is essential in the administration of justice. It is unfortunate that no sincere efforts are being made to improve the quality of the management of prosecution in order to secure the fair, just and expeditious conclusion of the trial.

The role of a Judge in controlling the Court proceedings is very important. A Judge is expected to actively participate in the trial, elicit necessary material from the witnesses at the appropriate context, which he feels necessary for reaching the correct conclusion. In this context, the apex Court, in *Ram Chandra v. State of Haryana*, reported in AIR 1981 SC 1036, has observed that:

> *"The adversary system of trial being what it is, there is an unfortunate tendency for a Judge presiding over a trial to assume the role of a referee or an umpire and to allow the trial to develop into a contest between the prosecution and the defence with inevitable distortions flowing from combative and competitive elements entering the trial procedure. If a Criminal Court is to be an effective instrument in dispensing justice, the presiding Judge must cease to be a spectator and a mere recording machine. He must become a participant in the trial by evincing intelligent active interest by putting questions to witnesses in order to ascertain the truth."*

Thus, a Judge is expected to go through the nature of the evidence, oral and documentary to be adduced in a case, consult the lawyers of both the sides, more particularly, the accused's lawyer to know the probable time within which he expects to complete the cross-examination of a witness. This would enable the Court to formulate the trial schedule for each witness scientifically. A trial Judge must ascertain the whereabouts of each and every witness including the investigating officer so that for want of proper whereabouts of witnesses, trial schedule is not delayed.

Judges have been called the Men of Robes. As Men of Robes, at times, we forget that we belong to the same fraternity as the other Men in Robes, namely the lawyers. The Bar and the Bench are the two wheels of the chariot of Justice. If one wheel is neglected, the other can not gain speed and efficiency. Therefore, be courteous to and polite with the Bar members. But politeness does not mean that one should be like a carpet, letting every one trample over oneself. One should be polite but firm like an ant: willing to walk on earth, but strong enough to annoy an elephant. Therefore, be polite to the lawyers but firm when need arises. While understanding their difficulties, while adjusting their problems, balance the interest of the litigant as well. Accommodate a lawyer in adjournment when the need is genuine. But if the need is frivolous, be firm and refuse the adjournment. As a judge, one must set the discipline of the Court, the decorum of the Court. It is a fine balancing act to be firm and yet generous. But it is a skill all Judges must develop.

Of course, the Judge has to gain the respect of the people and of the Bar with his behavior and knowledge. The Caesar's wife must be above board. The image both inside and outside the Court must be pristine and crystal clear. For this, the dress is the first indication of one's virtues, of one's personality. If a person is shabby, if he is unkept, he reflects a poor self-image, he reflects disorganized thoughts and habits. Beauty soothes the troubled souls; remember, the first impression is the last impression. Therefore, pay attention to the appearance.

Of course, the knowledge of Law must be up-to-date. The knowledge would be tested everyday in every case. Legal issues are first framed and posed in the trial Court. Thus, it is the Judge who would have to tackle the legal issues first. The trial Court lawyer is street smart and knowledgeable. Even in the far-flung areas of this State, one will discover lawyers who know their laws, and case laws. While the Judge should always be willing to learn from their experience and knowledge, one should sharpen one's own knowledge and intellectual capacity. For this, follow the latest amendment, the creation of new laws, and read the latest case law. Be aware of the latest trends emerging in judicial thinking. The Apex Court and the High Court go through different phases. Follow their fluctuations. But it is not sufficient to know the judgment, think about the logic of the judgment, about its facts, its reasoning. See if the judgment covers the case before you or is it distinguishable on the basis of its reasoning, its logic. In order to achieve the legal expertise, burn the mid-night lamp. You will be the winner.

Besides reading, cultivate the art of writing. Judgment writing is a creative process. The language should be plain, precise and pointed. Long sentences lose their punch. Words should be chosen with certain amount of precision. The facts should be stated precisely. The issues should be written clearly. The evidence should be discussed thread bare. The reasoning should be logical and should follow from one point to another. A rambling Judgment is a bundle of confusion. Initially, learn from the Judgments of the superior officers, from the Judgments of the High Courts and the Apex Court. Dissect the Judgments, examine its strength and weaknesses. Learn the craft of writing Judgments.

Be bold in the Judgments. Decide a case without fear or favour. Fear and favour come in many hues and colors. Fear of one's own past, of peer pressure, of public criticism. Favour includes not only monetary favour, but also nepotism, casteism, personal bias and prejudices. If the faith of the people is to be maintained in the Judiciary, then the river of judicial process has to be kept clean. Hence, one must avoid fear or favour at every cost. If people think your Judgment is biased, is colored, is partial, they would doubt the judicial process and the river of justice will stand contaminated. It is our pious duty to keep the river clean. Impartiality is the hallmark of a Judge. Be impartial in your Judgment.

Thus, to provide skill, attitude and professionalism to Judges, presiding over the Fast Track Courts, a short term training programme has been arranged. In the present times, judicial education has become a principal tool to provide accountability to the judiciary. In the words of Paul M. Lee—

"Judicial education is one of the most effective and perhaps an indispensable means for enhancing the fair administration of justice."

"Judicial Education" and "training" are not synonymous, though they aim at the objective of judicial competence and efficiency. "Education" is more concerned with the knowledge and sensitivity, whereas "training" revolves around skills, attitude and professionalism. The two reinforce each other in judicial performance. The Law Commission in its 54th Report recommended a National Judicial Academy for uniform judicial training on all India basis at-least at the initial level. A National Judicial Academy, under the Chairmanship of Chief Justice of India, has since started functioning in Bhopal, though regular training programme has not yet begun. I am informed that few courses on Criminal Justice for trial Judges are sometimes organized by the Indian Institute of Public Administration, New Delhi and the Institute of Criminology and Forensic Science, New Delhi. Outside this occasional programme, there is no organized training for the Judicial Officers at the national level, at present. There are few State level Judicial Academies or Training Directorates established in the recent past under the respective High Courts at Lucknow, Hyderabad, Nagpur, Cochin and perhaps, in few more States.

ಐ ಐ ಐ

JUDICIAL REFORMS FOR A MARKET ECONOMY

The Constitution of India established "Rule of Law" in our country and entrusted the constitutional responsibility of watching and balancing various National interests to the Judiciary. The Judiciary is "absolutely independent" and totally free from executive control while adjudicating cases. The decision of the Supreme Court in *S.P. Gupta Case*, AIR 1982 SC 149: (1981) Supp SCC 87: (1982) 2 SCR 365; *All India Judges Association*, AIR 1993 SC 2493; and *Supreme Court Advocates' on Record Association Case*, AIR 1994 SC 268: (1993) 4 SCC 441, has ensured Judicial Independence in the matter of appointment and transfer of Chief Justices and Judges of High Courts. Fixation of Judges' strength in the High Court is made justiciable and if it is established that the existing strength in any High Court is inadequate to promote speedy justice to the people, Court is empowered to assess the need and fix and increase the strength of Judges to provide speedy justice. Directive Principles contained in Article 39A make it obligatory on the part of the State to so work the system as to secure speedy justice on the basis of equality. The Preamble to the Constitution is to secure Economical and Political Justice. It is true that 'Justice delayed is Justice Denied' and it is equally true that 'Justice hurried is Justice buried'. It is, therefore, imperative to take suitable measures and steps to ensure speedy justice rather than deny justice.

The Bench is *"The Last Bulwark of individual liberty"* and this statement is profoundly true. Every Judge is making some small contribution to the well being of his fellow-men to ensure that the innocent shall go free, that none shall be persecuted or oppressed, that all should be allowed to earn their daily bread and live in peace, free from any unjustifiable interference from whatever quarters it may be threatened.

The present system of Administration of Justice has done its best to give speedy justice to the people. It has fulfilled the aspiration of litigant public. Therefore, there is nothing wrong in the present system of Administration of Justice. Nonetheless, there is scope for making it more efficient. The strength of Judges should correspond to the number of cases. This should be the best method

Speech delivered at the Seminar on 'Judicial Reforms for the Market Economy' conducted by the Madras Chamber of Commerce and Industry, Chennai on 26th March, 1996.

of avoiding delay in disposal of cases. Independence of Judiciary is the basic structure of our Constitution. The doors of Higher Courts should be kept open for all categories of litigants.

In fact, Lok Adalats have been accepted as a mechanism to prevent litigation in Motor Accident Claim Cases, Labour Disputes, Bank Loan Recovery Cases and Summary Criminal Cases. Necessary changes should be introduced in the existing laws to enable the Judges to induce the parties to refer their disputes for Arbitration. In appropriate cases, the Court should introduce the system of submission of written arguments. The Legal Aid Movement and the officials attached to Legal Aid should be required to function as Conciliators to prevent litigation.

The concept of free legal aid has taken good shape and is gathering momentum. This concept of free legal aid is not confined merely to rendering free legal aid to litigants, in the matter of conducting cases and proceedings in the Courts of Law, but, is a wider concept which includes within its ambit, activities in the direction of Free Legal Aid Clinics where efforts would be made to spread legal literacy among the ignorant and advise the poor litigants in the legal problem in the pre-litigation stage. This is one form in which inexpensive justice could be secured to poor litigants. The main reason for the mounting arrears is because the institution of cases far exceed the disposal in a given year. The arrears of cases talked of by those concerned with legal system has not happened over night. On account of mounting arrears of cases, the backlog has assumed serious proportion and is causing great problem to the litigants. The problem of clearing and mounting arrears is primarily connected with various other factors. If competent, quick and efficient Judges are allowed to man the Courts, it may to some extent clear the backlog.

In the last decade, there has been growing awareness amongst the public about their legal rights, resulting in increased approach by them to Courts of Law, particularly to the writ jurisdiction. Not only the number of individual litigants have increased but public interest litigations have also considerably developed. Notwithstanding the establishment of Special Tribunals, the number of cases against the State Government, coming into regular law courts have increased. The discovery of new judicial technique like Lok Adalat has not been able to encompass within its fold all categories of cases. The State Government can encourage the settlement of its cases through LOK ADALAT. Today, the State Government is the biggest litigant in this country and steps should be taken to curb the litigative attitude of the State.

In order to tackle the problem of arrears, Arrears Committee was appointed in 1989, which went into the various causes responsible for the accumulation of arrears of cases and submitted its report in two parts. As a matter of fact, the Committee, after referring to the 126th Report of the Law Commission, has said that the Central Government should issue a binding direction to the Public Sector Undertakings, regarding the reference of disputes *inter se* between them, on one hand and the Government on the other, to Arbitration and also recommended that Arbitration should be made compulsory for the resolution of the disputes of the other parties with the Government and Public Sector Undertakings. The Committee also recommended the re-introduction of the system of appointing Honorary Magistrates, drawn from the rank of retired members of Judiciary and empowering them to do the work of Stipendiary Magistrates. The recommendations of the Arrears Committee cover almost all areas of disputes. If the recommendation of the Arrears Committee is accepted and implemented, it may go a long way in reducing the pendency of arrears.

There is no need to search for an alternative to the existing Judicial System except to rejuvenate the same. Courts are perforce made to intervene and call upon the Executive to perform its duties and that too without fear or favour. It is undoubtedly true that Executive and Legislature have to perform their duties within the areas assigned to them.

Delay in the Administration of Justice is the most widely discussed topic of the day. A good solution for avoiding delay is to reduce the number of cases, accelerate the procedure and discharge the Judge from cumbersome burden. A pre-trial procedure could be introduced for reducing the arrears of cases pending in Courts and, thus, eliminate delays. An *adhoc* pre-trial procedure can take place at the first hearing of the suit or proceeding, as suggested by the Law Department Group, Bombay, which is the branch of the Indian Commission and Jurist and concerns with the maintenance of the Rule of Law. The pre-trial procedure envisages Judicial scrutiny even at the initial stage. A pre-trial conference can be held soon after the parties file their pleadings and if necessary, the Judge can find out before hand whether all the preliminary steps have been completed for holding the pre-trial procedure.

There was a time when it was thought that it would be indecent to suggest that Judges make the Law. They only declare it. Some of the eminent Judges of the pre-Independent era and post-Independent era have played a constructive and creative role in the Judicial history of our country. I quote the speech of Mr. Justice M.N. Venkatachaliah, former Chief Justice of India, on 'Indian Judges as Law Makers: Some Glimpses of the Past' (delivered under the auspices of M.C. Bhandari Memorial Lecture).

"The 20th Century witnessed the phenomenal growth and ramification of Government as a welfare State and the consequent explosion of the legal and administrative expediencies for implementing the new found social and economic aspirations of the State as provider of social security; as regulator of the economy; as adjudicator of industrial disputes. The Myriad social roles of the State created the need for resolving problems in administering this area of State's role. Administrative Law became vital to the proper adjudication and resolution of complex disputes, quite often involving specialized technical matters, between man and man, and man and State. The problem was 'to strike the right balance between efficient Government on the one hand and the protection of the citizen against mis-government on the other'. This balance has been struck by 'some of the more sensational judicial exploits."

Any power is open to abuse whether it be executive, legislative and judicial. Judges do make law. The Judge cannot make law merely because he is a Judge.

It does not mean that the Judiciary is usurping the power of law making. The Judiciary is doing its best to make the basic human right more meaningful and assure social and economic justice. The Supreme Court of India by implementing the cases of public interest litigation has shown a revolutionary movement in the realm of judicial functioning to ameliorate the miseries of the masses. There has been increasing use of law as a device of organised social action for bringing about socio economic changes.

Transnational Commercial Transactions, with the internalization of market have grown in number and thereby, involve greater potential for International Trade Dispute. Resolution mechanism can provide for negotiation, conciliation, arbitration and litigation. Direct negotiation and conciliation may end in resolving of disputes and conflicts. When parties try to solve their differences and disputes through negotiations, they have choice of either litigation or arbitration. With the view to find relatively efficacious and cheap remedy, party to an international contract can resort to International Commercial Arbitration. Such arbitration proceedings, unlike litigation, enable the parties to exercise a high degree of control over the arbitral proceedings, the terms of arbitral relief and composition of Arbitral Tribunal. Such forum offers more informal, cheap and quick remedy to resolve International Trade Disputes.

It has been the long felt need to replace the present Arbitration Act, 1940 by a new enactment. The Parliament has not yet passed the Arbitration and Conciliation Bill, 1995. The Government of India and several representative bodies of Trade and Industry have suggested amendments to Arbitration Act, 1940, to meet the requirements of the day. The Economic Reforms may not become fully effective if the law dealing with the Court of both Civil and Criminal disputes remains out of tune with such reforms. Therefore, the Arbitration the Conciliation Ordinance, 1996, has been promulgated by the President of India and the same was published in Gazette of India, Extraordinary dated 16th January, 1996 and it has come into force with effect from 25th January, 1996. The Ordinance consolidates and amends the law relating to Domestic Arbitration, International Commercial Arbitration, Enforcement of Foreign Arbitral Award and defines the law relating to conciliation taking into account the United Nations Commission of International Trade Law and the Model Law and the Rules.

The Ordinance providing for an arbitral procedure and Arbitral Tribunal is obliged to give reason for its Award. The supervisory role of Courts in the Arbitral proceedings has been minimized. The Arbitral Tribunal has been permitted to use mediation, conciliation or other procedures during the Arbitral Procedure to encourage the settlement of disputes. Such Arbitral Award is made enforceable as if it were a decree of Court. The settlement reached between the parties, as a result of conciliation proceedings, is placed on the same pedestal as an Arbitration Award.

The Narasimhan Committee followed by Tiwari Committee and the Committee on Legal Aspects, headed by Shri V.S. Hegde, recommended the setting up of Special Tribunals with special powers of adjudication for speedy recovery of dues of Bank and Financial Institutions. Accordingly, Recovery of Debts due to Banks and Financial Institutions Act, 1993, has been enacted to provide for the establishment of Tribunals for expeditious adjudication and recovery of debts due to Banks and Financial Institutions where the debt due is not less than Rs. 10 lakhs. The said Act also provides for constitution of Appellate Tribunals. Company Law Board has been constituted under section 10(E) of the Companies Act, 1956 read with Article 245 of the Constitution of India. Land Reform Tribunals have been constituted under Article 247 of the Constitution of India, Administrative Tribunals have been constituted to deal with service matters of civil servants. Parliament is enabled to make law, providing for the establishment of any Additional Courts for the better administration of law, made by Parliament or of any existing laws, with respect to a matter enumerated in the Union List.

Lok Adalat is a new system of dispensation of justice which came into existence to grapple with a problem of giving cheap and speedy justice to people. Certainly, Lok Adalat is not a substitute for the present judicial system but it only plays a supplementary role in that. It provides for resolution of certain type of disputes by discussion, counselling, persuasion and conciliation.

It is undoubtedly true that the three organs of the State, namely Legislature, Judiciary and Executive are supreme in their respective sphere of activity. No organ can usurp the function assigned to the other. Judiciary has power to ensure that the Legislature and the Executive function within their constitutional limits. Judiciary is conjoined to attend to the task of ensuring that the Legislature and the Executive do not cross their limits. When Executive remains inactive and fails to perform on serious issues of public importance, the Courts can come to the rescue of aggrieved persons because the Courts are "Sentinel of Democracy". Judicial review is a powerful weapon to restrain unconstitutional exercise of power by the Legislature and the Executive. Delivering Dr. Zakir Hussain Lecture, the Chief Justice of India, Hon'ble Sri A.M. Ahmadi, has said that the Supreme Court was compelled, by a force of circumstances, to expand its jurisdiction by, at times issuing normal direction to the Executive, something it would have never resorted to, had the other democratic institution functioned in an effective manner. It has been rightly said that Supreme is the Sentinel on qui-vive. If other organs of the Government are unwilling to discharge their duties, Judiciary has to step in. It is the Court which enthusiastically took up cudgels on behalf of the Civil Society, so that bonded labourers were freed, human rights activists were given protection and public interest litigation was encouraged. Courts do concede the supremacy of the other organs.

Hard decisions have to be taken by Courts when Executive exhibits lack of courage and supine indifference. In fact, polluting industries are directed to be closed to preserve and protect the beauty of Taj Mahal.

Various reforms have been introduced in the Administration of Justice and; Court Management and Technology, by reduction of adjournments through a constant monitoring and tracking process by the officials of the Courts by notifying the lawyers in advance to be ready with the cases to be listed. Lawyer-based delay should be avoided as much as possible. Time frame must be set to move through different judicial process and hierarchy Courts. Extensive use of computer and appropriate software programmes can be made available to avoid delay in disposal of cases. Time parameters should be set with regard to various categories of cases. The Planning Commission of India with the National Information Centre (NIC), has created a Special Courts Informatics Division and it has four broad programmes under implementation *viz.*, Computer Aided Query Servicing Programmes on matters related to Constitution of India, developed for the Legislative Department of Ministry of Law; a Computer based case law information retrievals system for the Supreme Court to enable Judges to have access to information on decided cases of Supreme Court as well as Computer based system for preparation of the cause list of the Supreme Court. The Supreme Court has introduced the compilation of entire listing process which enables the Court to list fresh cases for preliminary hearing within ten days at the most. The computer classifies the cases, allocates it to appropriate courts and the Bench generates both as advance and final Court list. Certainly, our legal system has made a beginning in the right direction and it is bound to succeed.

ಐ ಐ ಐ

MADRAS HIGH COURT – A TEMPLE OF JUSTICE – A TEMPLE OF GOD

I am delighted to participate in this morning's function, since I have been very closely associated with the Madras Bar Association. I am proud to say that it was during my tenure as Secretary of the Madras Bar Association that the Post Centenary celebrations took place. It was a memorable occasion and I recall the words of the then President of India, Mr. R. Venkataraman in his message to the Association. I quote "The Bench and the Bar are two pillars on which the edifice of justice stands. It is essential for success of our democracy. I feel that a strong Bar is an essential input for successful implementation of law and free flow of justice without favours or fear".

The Madras Bar Association has produced many giants, both in the legal profession and in the movement for freedom struggle. Late Prakasam, Dr. Subbarayan, Mr. Mohan Kumaramangalam were all members of the Association and also in the forefront of the struggle for independence. There were many others who were part of this Association. Mr. T. Chengalvarayan, a freedom fighter is still an active member of this Association. The list of legal luminaries who were members of the Association is an endless one. I shall confine myself only to the office bearers of this Association, Mr. V.L. Ethiraj, Sir Nugent Grant, M.O. Parthasarathy Iyengar M.K. Nambiar, have all held the high office of the President of the Bar Association. Incidentally. Mr. Parthasarathy Iyengar was the first Indian President of this Association. In the year 1984, when the first non-barrister was elected as President, I had the honour of serving the committee. I am mentioning all this only to show what a great institution the Madras Bar Association is and it is in the fitness of things that they should celebrate the centenary of this Grand High Court Building. Even today, this building holds good after 100 years of wear and tear.

One historical fact which might have escaped our attention is that an old temple of Chenna Kesava and Chennai Malleswarar Temples were erected at this site, and, therefore, this building has been blessed by Gods. I remember the

---

Speech delivered at the function organised by Madras Bar Association, Chennai on 8th August, 1992.

words of Chief Justice S. Ramachandra Iyar, who remarked as follows, on the occasion of High Court Centenary:

"On the site that the temple of God was located that the temple of Justice came to be built."

I would like to mention few words about this great building. All the materials used in the construction of this building, except the steel girders and some ornamental tiling, were manufactured locally. The style of the building was of Hindu Sarracenia architecture and it took nearly four years for completion. The novelty of this was the light house tower. It has cross ventilation and there has been an optimum use of space without in any way spoiling the architecture. The cost of the building was well near Rs. 13 lakhs. The High Court moved to this place on 12th July, 1892. A building of this age and character is a constant source of inspiration for both the Bench and the Bar and to the litigant public.

Barrister President Mr. Kumar Rajarathnam quoted the words of the then Chief Justice Sir Arthur Collins, when the key of this building was handed over to him by the then Governor, Lord Whenlock. While handing over the key, the Governor concluded with the words, *'and now, my Lord Chief Justice, I have pleasure in handing you the key, as a token that the building has been entrusted to your hands by the Government, in full confidence that the administration of justice will be carried on with the ability and integrity that has always marked the Madras High Court. To you, my Lord, and to the other gentlemen who hold with you the high position of Judges of the High Court, and to those gentlemen who occupy themselves in the Honourable and learned profession of law, in all your hands the administration of justice may be safely left, and we may look forward, for many years to come, with the full knowledge and full satisfaction that the best years of your lives will be devoted to carrying on one of the noblest of works, the uninterrupted administration of justice"*

It is our singular good fortune that those Honourable Judges who have hailed from other States have been extremely kind, good and courteous to the Members of the Bar. I have been personally associated as a Member of the Bar, both in my capacity as Government Pleader and as Secretary of this Association, and I can tell you without fear of contradiction that we will always remember Judges like Govinda Nair, K.B.N. Singh, Chandrakuar, Dr. A.S. Anand and last but not the least Justice Mishra and My Lord the Chief Justice. Barrister President, Mr. Kumar Rajarathinam made a very reasonable request as I know that there is dearth of chambers and that the number of members have increased. Many Senior Advocates are prepared to contribute books to complete the library. But unfortunately due to paucity of space, the Association could not accept their munificent donations. But a time has now come when my Lord, the Chief Justice, will be happy to seriously consider the request of the President and with the inspiring personality like Justice Mishra, who is in-charge of the buildings.

ಐ಄ಐ಄ಐ಄

LAW DAY

The Constituent Assembly, though constituted in terms of a statement (May 16th, 1946) by the British Government, represented the cream of our national leadership and had among its membership, some of the best talents available in the country at that time. It was a unique body in many respects. Its independent and sovereign character was beyond question, and no outside authority could sit in judgment over the Constitution framed by it. Among the members of the Assembly were the Presidents of the Indian National Congress (including five ex-Presidents), the Depressed Classes League, the Muslim League, the All India Scheduled Castes Federation, the All India Women's Conference, the All India Landholders Association, the Hindu Maha Sabha, the Servants of India Society and the Anglo-Indian Association. There were also some Vice Chancellors, businessmen, working class representatives, journalists and authors.

Out of the 296 members of the Assembly originally allotted to what were then known as the Governors' Provinces and Chief Commissioners' Provinces, 208 were elected on the Congress vote. The then Indian States, whose representatives joined the Assembly later, had been allotted 93 seats. Out of its strength of 208, as many as 30 were from outside the party. From the minorities, the Scheduled Castes accounted for 29; the Scheduled Tribes 4, the Indian Christians 6, the Anglo-Indians 3 and the Parsis 3, thereby ensuring liberal representation to all minorities. Out of the 4 seats allotted to the Sikhs, the Congress had 3.

The desire of the Constituent Assembly to secure the largest measure of agreement for the Constitution could also be seen from the composition of the Drafting Committee. Dr. B.R. Ambedkar, its Chairman, was not only a Congressman but was a vigorous critic of the Congress and its policies for many years. Of the remaining members of the Committee, only two, namely, K.M. Munshi and later T.T. Krishnamachari were members of the Party. One member, Muhammad Saddulla of Assam, was a member of the Muslim League and the others, Alladi Krishnaswami Ayyar, N. Gopalaswami Ayyangar, N.Madhava Rao and D.P. Khaitan were independent members.

Speech delivered on occasion of 'The Celebration of Passing of the Constitution of India by the Constituent Assembly', Tamil Nadu on 26th November, 1992.

In framing the Constitution, the paramount consideration, present in the minds of our founding fathers was to make it a living instrument, truly reflecting the sovereign Will of the people. Our great leader, Jawaharlal Nehru, explained in the Constituent Assembly, the philosophy behind the Constitution:

> "A Constitution, if it is out of touch with the people's life, aims and aspirations it becomes rather empty; if it falls behind those aims, it drags the people down. It should be something ahead to keep people's eyes and minds upto a certain high mark (C.A. Deb. 8-11-1948, P.318)".

Till the year 1991, our Constitution had undergone corrective surgery 68 times, by way of amendments. The first amendment was in the year 1951 (AIR 1951 SC 458), within about one year of the passing of the Constitution and even before the Parliament, under the Constitution, could be constituted.

What is a Constitution? It is a collective declaration of the determination of the people of a nation, to live in an orderly fashion for the common good and well-being of the whole nation. The Constitution should be a live and responding document to meet the needs, necessities and exigencies of changing socio, economic and political environment of not only of the nation but of the entire globe. If the Constitution does not admit the changing concepts of human economical conditions, it shall not only retard the march of the nation towards its logical goal but also generate socio-economic-political tension which shall eventually pave way for the undoing of the Constitution.

The higher judiciary of our land which is entrusted with the onerous task of protecting, preserving and enforcing the Constitution cannot and should not be unaware and unmindful of marching trends of human aspirations and the fall outs of conflicting rights and equalities. The success of the Constitution also rests with the Bar and the Judiciary in a very large measure. Wooden interpretation and technical enforcement of the Constitution, just by its words and not by its spirit, shall prove to be destructive of the Constitution. The Law should march in parallel line with the aspirations of the people of the nation. The march of law is largely controlled by the Judiciary. The law is unable to keep pace with the march of the nation, resort to amendment of law, be it Constitutional law or ordinary law, becomes inescapable. It is true that the Courts interpret the law as it is and the Legislature amends the law as it ought to be.

It is often misunderstood that the Courts act against the progressive acts of the States. Can you imagine, an automobile without brakes? Would you venture to travel on such automobile without brakes? Is it difficult to visualise as to what would be the fate of the automobile and its occupants when it moves, that too, fast without brakes? No sane person shall recommend an automobile without the brakes or hamper the efficient operation of the brakes. It is common knowledge that the brakes are used only when necessary, that too, proportionately to regulate the speed and direction of the automobile to ensure that no tragedy occurs either to the automobile or to the third party, so that the automobile and its occupants reach the destination safely and definitely. It is needless to say that the Judiciary is only a regulating machinery and not an unwanted appendage in our Constitutional frame work. It is because of that, that our Constitution has given due and important place to the Judiciary in the State mechanism of our nation.

As Indians, we are justly entitled to be proud of our nation and its endearing and enduring democratic institutions. Needless for me to state that almost all nations which had attained independence from the colonial rule of British, French and Portugal, in Asia, Africa, Middle and Far East, have lost their independence to dictators and usurpers of powers of all sorts. In the dark sky of anti-democratic forces, India, our India, shines like a bright star emitting rays of light of Freedom, Democracy and Rule of Law. But for our Constitution, this unique place to us, in the comity of nations, would not have been possible. One cannot help pointing out the inescapable reality that a Democratic State with all its faults, based on comparatively flexible and responding Constitution is the best of all the governing institutions.

The fall of the monolithic giant, *viz.*, the Soviet Union, like a pack of cards, after three quarters of a centuries of Dictatorship of the Proletariat is an eye opener. The revelations of brutal suppressions, rampant corruptions, total lack of productions and the unmindful apathy of the unquestionable, ruling class to the needs and sufferings of the people has greatly disillusioned the world as to the efficacy of the alternative form of Socialistic State.

Therefore, it is the duty of every citizen to address himself as to how and what he could contribute to the efficient and improved working of our Constitution and the Institutions created under the sacred document. I am reminded of a story which runs as follows:

A king arranged for the marriage of his daughter with the Prince of a neighbouring Kingdom. He required large quantities of milk for the marriage. Hence he appealed to his people to contribute their day's production of milk into a huge vessel with a narrow opening for pouring the milk. After some time, the vessel was brought to the kitchen and the contents poured in another vessel to cook the necessary edibles to feed the royal wedding guests of the prince. To the shock of the King, it was found that there was only water and no milk. Each of the people had poured water thinking the other would pour milk. Consequently, the Royal Wedding guests, who could not be treated with proper food, got insulted and infuriated, which resulted in the disruption of the Royal Wedding. A war broke out, in which the Kingdom of the princes and its people were defeated and destroyed. Like-wise, if we; the citizens think individual misdeeds may not affect the nation, it shall in the long run prove to be fatal.

Therefore, as the guardians of law, let us resolve to rededicate ourselves to preserve and protect the Constitution and its institutions from the onslaught of individual and group misdemeanours so that we ourselves and our posterity may live in a civilised state of democracy.

ಬಬಬ

BE YOU EVER SO HIGH, THE LAW
IS ABOVE YOU

The phrase **"Rule of Law"** reminds one of the famous words of Bracton **"The King is under no man but under God and the Law"**. No one can claim to be above law. Denning's dictum **"be you ever so high, the law is above you"** is applicable to one and all, irrespective of his position, sex, creed, caste or birth.

The Constitution being a supreme law, every institution be it Legislature, Executive or Judiciary, created under the Constitution is expected to respect its command and no organ or instrumentality of the Government, be it Parliament, Police or even Judiciary can ignore it. To affirm the faith of the people in the 'Rule of Law', to preserve democracy and confirm the belief in the Latin Maxim *"ibi jus ibi remedium"* that there is remedy under the law for every legal injury, the Judiciary under the Constitution is invested with vast powers to remedy the maladies that emnate from the failure of other branches of the Government to fulfil their constitutional obligations. Courts cannot shut their doors when executive excesses or legislative aberrations infringe upon valuable rights of the citizens or else people will take to the streets which will sound the death- knell of Rule of Law.

Very often the weak, the deprived and the under-privileged groups in the society flood the prisons where as the rich and the powerful manage to escape the hands of law through money and muscle power.

A careful study of cases in which the power of withdrawal of cases has been exercised would reveal that the power has been abused by the executive for political consideration and personal gains. In a society governed by the Rule of Law, moral turpitude cannot be condoned. Under such circumstances, Courts have a solemn duty to protect and preserve the administration of Criminal Justice against possible misuse and abuse of authority by the executive by resorting to withdrawal of cases against those in power and influential.

Human mind has creativity. When Citizens and bureaucrats go hand in hand to assist Administration, most of the problems get solved. There is reluctance on

---

Delivered at the All India Conference of Intellectuals in Chennai on 28th December, 2003.

the part of Citizens to report cases to the police. The facts that deter people are many. They are: (1) ignorance or indifference; (2) fear of annoyance or publicity; (3) ineffectiveness of police or their callous attitude; (4) the fear of reprisal and harassment; (5) inconvenience and expense of getting involved in police cases and (6) non-registration of Crimes due to influence of politicians and influential.

There is need for spread of legal literacy among the masses especially the under-privileged lots. Legal literacy is not just about learning what the law says but also learning how to go about accessing it. The duty of the public to uphold the Rule of Law rests on reciprocity. Since Citizens have a duty to aid in law enforcement, the Government owes them a duty of protection when such aid places them in jeopardy.

POLICE:

It is noteworthy that police in our country have to perform a difficult and delicate task, particularly, in view of the deteriorating law and order situation, communal riots, political turmoil, student unrest, terrorist activities and among other, the increasing number of underworld and organized gangs and criminals. Many hardcore criminals like extremists, terrorists, drug peddlers, smugglers have taken strong roots in the society. Therefore, the police has to act very diligently and if they do not act diligently and carefully, the culprits go unpunished and that is also danger for the rule of law. To deal with such a situation, a balanced approach is needed to meet the ends of justice. The police should deal with the criminals in an efficient and effective manner and bring to book those who are involved in the crime. It is pertinent to note that the action of the State must be right, just and fair. Using any form of torture or extracting information is neither right nor just and fair and so it is impermissible and offensive of liberty guaranteed under the Constitution. The police should change their attitude and become friendly towards the society by gaining faith of the people that they are there to control the crime and maintain the rule of law for the progress of the welfare State. The human rights, which are paramount for protection of the life, liberty and dignity of the person are supreme in constitutionally governed democracy. The mere existence of human rights is not sufficient unless they are well protected. Therefore, protection of human rights at all costs is necessary for proper functioning of the welfare State and maintenance of the rule of law.

The police, at the helm of affairs, should be trained in the course containing human rights and fundamental constitutional rights of the citizens so as to sensitize them about these rights so that there is change in attitude and approach and that they conduct investigation in a scientific manner leaving aside the obsolete method of investigation by torture. This can be achieved by providing adequate training to the police officers by the Government. Thirdly, the judiciary has already started taking action by giving guidelines and seeking their enforcement and whenever occasion requires, by taking severe action for violation of human rights. Human Rights Commissions and Committees should also take appropriate action to protect the human rights. Thus, if three organs of the State *i.e.* Legislature, Executive and the Judiciary, take appropriate steps as stated supra, definitely human rights will be upheld and the goal enshrined in the Constitution will be achieved.

I am perfectly frank in saying that since after independence, in many areas, political reasons have been allowed to govern in the direction and management of the force, especially in matters of appointments, promotions, punishments, transfers, and assignments, and the evil has injured the efficiency of the force.

Frequent complaints are received from citizens that policemen use vulgar, indecent and profane language; they are maltreated, insulted or driven away when they go to police stations with a just complaint or for reasonable information. In the interest of discipline, the officers on the top must be earnest and they themselves must set the example. Lack of courtesy is among the most frequent charges by citizens against the police, and contrasts to their disadvantage in this respect with similar bodies in foreign countries is often made.

JUDICIARY:

The Indian Judicial System is constantly exposed to new challenges, new dimensions and new signals and has to survive in a world in which perhaps the only real certainty is that the circumstances of tomorrow will not be the same as those of today.

Judiciary today is more deserving of public confidence than ever before.

Our Judiciary, throughout the Union of India has earned a reputation for great integrity and independence. We are proud of it. We, the members of the Judicial hierarchy have inherited the legacy of dedicated collective endeavour by the Bench and the Bar and established an unbroken tradition of high efficiency, perfect integrity and fearless independence. The true touch stone for measuring the success of a Judicial institution is the degree of confidence reposed in it by the public and it is a matter of great pride that our country has earned for itself the fullest respect and confidence of the public of the nation. The Judgments of the Courts are treated with respect and its stature, in knowledgeable legal circles, is equal to be best amongst other Courts in this land.

The Judiciary has a special role to play in the task of achieving socio-economic goals, enshrined in the Constitution and while maintaining their aloofness and independence, the Judges have to be aware of the social changes in the task of achieving socio-economic justice for the people.

Socrates said that four things improve a great Judge:

    (a) to hear courteously;

    (b) to answer wisely;

    (c) to consider soberly; and

    (d) to decide impartially.

I expect Judges of all cadres to strictly observe punctuality in Court. Integrity is an essential polity of a judicial officer. A Judicial Officer must follow the standards of integrity, morality and behaviour which he sets for others. The Judges must decide cases without fear or favour, affection or illwill, friend or foe.

The Judges, I conclude with strong belief and immense faith, as judicial officers will conform to established time-tested Court etiquette and uphold the dignity and enhance the decorum of Temples of Justice.

The speedy trial of offences is a desirable goal and essence of an organized society. Due to liberal interpretations of Article 21 of the Constitution, the right to speedy trial has received the status of a fundamental right. The right cannot be denied on the ground of financial and administrative inability of the State.

ಜಜಜ

JURISDICTION – (TERRITORIAL, PECUNIARY AND INHERENT)

Dispensation of Justice is a Divine Work. It is, therefore, said that justice should be administered without fear or favour, affection or ill-will. In the discharge of your judicial duties, the one and the only consideration should be to render justice to the litigants within the legal frame work.

The concept of imparting training to directly recruited District Munsifs is the wonderful brain child of Hon'ble Mr. Justice K.A. Swami, the Chief Justice of our Chartered High Court. He has been bestowing his attention more and more in improving the judicial system. The training to Judicial Officers is a novel concept, conceived by him. Nobody had ever thought of this kind of training programme, before.

This type of training is bound to tone up the administration of justice and improve the equipment of judicial officers.

The subject assigned to me is "Jurisdiction, Territorial, Pecuniary and Inherent".

Pecuniary Jurisdiction

1. The pecuniary limit of jurisdiction of a District Munsif's Court on the original side is Rs. 15,000.

2. That of Sub Court on the original side is one exceeding Rs. 15,000.

3. That the pecuniary limit of jurisdiction of a District Munsif Court on the Small Cause side is Rs. 500.

4. That of the Sub Court where Small Cause jurisdiction is conferred on it is Rs. 2,000.

One will thus find that according to the pecuniary value of the causes, the jurisdiction of Courts vary. This goes by the name of pecuniary jurisdiction in legal parlance. How this arises and under what provisions, I shall come to it later, to deal in detail. It is sufficient at this stage that this arises by virtue of two enactments known as Tamil Nadu Civil Courts Act of 1873 and Provincial Small

---

Lecture delivered in Training Programme for newly recruited Civil Judges (Junior Division) Judicial Magistrates, 17th November, 1995.

Causes Courts Act. As already stated, the above relates to the jurisdiction of Courts subordinate to High Court and functioning in several places in our State.

Let us turn to Madras city and the Civil Courts functioning here.

Just as the pecuniary limits of jurisdiction of Moffussil Courts are governed by two enactments, I have already referred, the Civil Courts in Madras City are also governed by two enactments. They are,

1. Madras City Civil Court Act, 1892.
2. Presidency Towns Small Causes Courts Act.

The Civil Courts functioning in Chennai City are,

1. The City Civil Courts.
2. The Courts of Small Causes.

Originally, all cases even upto the value of Rs. 2,000 were filed in the High Court. It was found that it entailed a good wastage of time of the High Court and that it was also expensive for the poorer sections of society. Hence, it was proposed to confer jurisdiction on the regular side of the Small Causes Court upto the pecuniary limit of Rs. 2,000. Later, the Bill was modified, constituting a separate Court as a City Civil Court, conferring on it jurisdiction to receive, try and dispose of all suits and other proceedings of a civil nature, not exceeding Rs. 2,500 arising within the City of Madras.

The said Court had no jurisdiction,

(a) In respect of proceedings relating to admirality, as the High Court alone was exclusively given jurisdiction as a Court of Admirality or a Colonial Court of Admirality having testamentary intestate and matrimonial jurisdiction.

(b) The City Civil Court had also no jurisdiction to deal with insolvency matter.

(c) The City Civil Court had also no jurisdiction in respect of matters exclusively within the jurisdiction of Small Causes Court.

With the advance of time, the number of City Civil Courts have increased, all of them, however, still having no jurisdiction in respect of matters enumerated as above.

But, with the advance of time, the pecuniary jurisdiction of City Civil Court was enhanced from time to time, the same reaching a limit of Rs. 50,000 till 1980. By a further Amending Act, the same was enhanced to Rupees One lakh. Now, by a recent enactment in the current year, the same has come to be enhanced to Rs. 10 lakhs.

The above pecuniary limits of jurisdiction of the Courts in the City of Madras, entertaining suits of a civil nature, has been dealt with by the above two enactments. This disposes of the pecuniary jurisdiction of the Civil Courts in Madras City. It will thus be seen that by virtue of two enactments, the Courts in the Moffussil have been dealt with relating to their pecuniary jurisdiction. Likewise, by virtue of two other enactments, the pecuniary jurisdiction of the Civil Courts of the Madras City have been dealt with. Thus, the pecuniary jurisdiction of all Civil Courts functioning in the Moffussil and in the Madras City have been dealt with in the above four enactments. For the matter dealt with, relating to pecuniary jurisdiction of Courts, reference to be given to section 12 of the Tamil Nadu Civil Courts Act, 1873, and sections 3 and 3A of the Madras city Civil Courts Act, 1892.

It may be relevant, at this stage, to deal with the pecuniary limits of appellate jurisdiction of Courts in the Moffussil as well as Courts in the Madras City. So far as the Courts in the Moffussil are concerned, there is a three tier hierarchy. At the top is the District Court. At the base is the District Munsif's Court. In between is the Subordinate Judge's Court. The District Court as well as the Subordinate Judges Courts have appellate jurisdiction over the District Munsif's Court. The pecuniary limit of appellate jurisdiction of the District Court is Rs. 30,000. Hence, all appeals from the District Munsif's Court and the subordinate Judge's Court lie to the District Court if the pecuniary limit does not exceed Rs. 30,000. If it exceeds the said limit, the appeal lies only to the High Court where the matters appealed against are from the Subordinate Judge's Court or the District Court. This is dealt with in section 13 of the Tamil Nadu Civil Courts Act, 1873. Correspondingly, in regard to the pecuniary limits of appellate jurisdiction regarding City Civil Courts, established under the Madras City Civil Courts Act, 1892, the relevant provisions for reference are sections 3A and 15 of the said Act. This topic of pecuniary jurisdiction dealt with above may be concluded with a reference to section 6 of the Code of Civil Procedure which says that,

> "Save in so far as is otherwise expressly provided, nothing herein contained shall operate to give any Court jurisdiction over suits amounts or value of the subject-matter of which exceeds the pecuniary limits of its ordinary jurisdiction."

It now remains to deal with the High Court of Judicature at Madras. The Madras High Court is a Chartered High Court. The other Chartered High Courts are the Bombay and Calcutta High Courts. These High Courts are governed by Letters Patent in regard to their jurisdiction in Civil, Criminal, Admirality and Vice Admirality, Testamentary, Intestate and Matrimonial jurisdiction and also Original and Appellate jurisdiction. It covers a very wide field and cannot be dealt with, even in a sketchy or a cursory manner, the implications of such jurisdictions as conferred on the High Court by the Letters Patent. Those interested in the same may read the extract of the amended Letters Patent – High Court, Madras, incorporated in the Original Side Rules published by the M.L.J. office.

Territorial Jurisdiction

Black's Law Dictionary, 5th Edn., defines Territorial Jurisdiction as follows:

> "Territory over which a government or a sub-division thereof has jurisdiction—jurisdiction considered as limited to cases arising or person residing within a defined territory. The authority of the Court is limited by the boundaries fixed. As obvious, territorial jurisdiction means the territory within which the power of a Court is to be exercised. Section 10 of the Tamil Nadu Civil Courts Act, 1873, provides that the State Government shall fix and may, from time to time, vary the local limits of the jurisdiction of any District Court or Subordinate Judges Court. Likewise, the High Court shall fix and may, from time to time, modify the local limits of District Munsifs' Courts."

By virtue of the aforesaid section, the territorial jurisdiction of the District Court, Sub-Court and of the District Munsif's Courts have been fixed, which means that the extent of jurisdiction of the said Courts is limited to the limits of the territory within which they have to function, dealing with cases arising therefrom and trying and disposing of the same.

So far as the courts in the Madras City are concerned, the territorial jurisdiction of the City Civil Court and the Small Causes Court is co-terminus with the territorial jurisdiction of the High Court. The territorial jurisdiction of the High Court is dealt with, under Article 11 of the Letters Patent, which states that the said High Court of Judicature at Madras shall have and exercise Ordinary Original Civil Jurisdiction within such local limits as may, from time to time, be declared, by the law made by the Governor-in-Council and until some local limits shall be so declared and prescribed within the local limits of the local jurisdiction at the said High Court of Madras at the date of the publication of these presents, and the Ordinary Original Civil Jurisdiction of the said High Court shall not extend beyond the limits for the time being declared and prescribed as the local limits of such jurisdiction.

Inherent Jurisdiction

As most of you, by this time must be aware or ought to be aware, the one section of the Code of Civil Procedure dealing with the same is section 151, C.P.C. It is to be noted how the section is worded to comprehend its import.

Section 151, C.P.C. reads as follows:

"Nothing in this section shall be deemed to limit or otherwise affect inherent power of the Court to make such orders as may be necessary for the ends of justice or to prevent abuse of the process of the Court."

It is to be noted from the wording of the said section that inherent jurisdiction of a Court is that in hearing in a Court established in accordance with law, the said jurisdiction is available to a Court not by reason of any conferment or by any extraneous authority. In other words, Courts whenever they get established, get so established together with jurisdiction in hearing by the sheer force of its establishment. An approximate analogy to the concept of inherent jurisdiction is, referable to the concept of right by birth under Hindu Law. Under Hindu Law, where a son is born to a co-parcener, his very birth confers on him a right in the property of his father. It is not an acquisition, not an inheritance but one sprouting from his very birth. In other words, it is an infrastructure as it were to a body born to a co-parcener. This analogy, in my opinion, highlights the significance of the concept of inherent jurisdiction as enshrined in section 151, C.P.C.

Now, the amplitude of legal literature on this legal concept is too vast to be summarized within any reasonable limits. This section has come in for interpretation from ancient times, down to date, at the hands of the Privy Council, the Supreme Court and almost all the High Courts in India, giving it a shape and a permanent habitat to discern the force and significance of its application in varied pastures and circumstances. As expatiated by the Supreme Court, section 151, C.P.C., does not confer a new power in the Court but makes a statutory regulation of the inherent power of the Court to do things "exdebito Justitial".

In AIR 1970, Supreme Court, page 998, in paragraph 4, the learned Judge deals with the confines of the said section as follows:

> "*Under the inherent power of Courts, as recognised by section 151, C.P.C., a Court has no power to do that which is prohibited by the law. Inherent jurisdiction of the Court must be exercised, subject to the rule that if the code does contain certain provisions which would meet the necessities of the case, such provision should be followed and inherent jurisdiction should not be invoked.*"

In other words, the said jurisdiction is not an appellate power. The subject of this jurisdiction contains a mass of literature dealt with, by all the High Courts and the Supreme Court and therefore, a correct comprehension and appraisal of its real import can be had in the course of the practice as and when engaged in a research into the doctrine under various circumstances. To quote *Black-*in this context, the word 'jurisdiction' is a term of large comprehensive import and embraces of judicial action. It is the authority by which Courts and Judicial Officers take cognizance and decide cases." *Black* concludes to say that the jurisdiction is "the legal right" by which the Judges exercise their authority."

Tomlin's Law Dictionary states the 'jurisdiction' as—

> "*An authority or power which a man hath to do justice in causes of complaint brought before him.*"

One will thus find that the focus of the word 'jurisdiction' is targeted in exercise of authority. In this sense, jurisdiction is in some instances;

Taken away and in other instances, specifically conferred.

Let me, in the first instance, deal with matters where jurisdiction is taken away:

Under Order 50 of the First Schedule to the Code of Civil Procedure, a Small Causes Court, functioning in the Moffussil has no jurisdiction to exercise authority in the matters dealt with in the said order. Hence, those of you to function as such in the Moffussil have to acquaint yourselves with order 50 of Schedule I of the Code of Civil Procedure to know that you have no jurisdiction in the matters dealt with therein.

Under Order 51 of the First Schedule to C.P.C., the Small Causes Court, functioning in the Madras City under the Presidency Towns Small Causes Court Act has no jurisdiction to exercise powers dealt with therein. Hence, those of you who may come to man the said Court should acquaint yourselves to know on what matters you have no authority. Thus, the said two Orders of the First Schedule to the Code of Civil Procedure have to be studied to ascertain the extent of jurisdiction taken away.

One more significant section of the Code of Civil Procedure whose parameters of exercise of power your may have to acquaint yourselves to know to what extent your exercise of power, functioning as Judges, is restricted or taken away is section 9, C.P.C. You will find from a reading of the said section that you are invested with jurisdiction to try all cases of a civil nature excepting suits of which their cognizance is either expressly or impliedly barred. This is a very important section, required to be studied deeply. This is a section on which a mass of legal literature has already piled up as not to be dealt with within a narrow compass of time. Let me tell you that the emphasis in this regard is to know what suits of a civil nature are. The section starts with a presumption of exercise of jurisdiction, barring such exercise where there is implied and express prohibition. In this regard, the land mark judgment delivered by the Supreme Court and reported in Judgment Today (1995), Part 5, page 1, dated 13th July, 1995. The Supreme Court has to say on the scope of the section and its magnitude, as follows:—

> "One of the basic principles of law is that every right has a remedy. "Ubi Jus Ibi Remedium" is the well known maxim. Every civil suit of a civil nature and unless the suit is barred by statute, one may at one's peril, bring a suit of one's choice. It is no answer to a suit howsoever frivolous the claim that the law confers, no such right to sue. The expansive nature of the section is demonstrated by use of phraseology both positive and negative. The earlier part opens the door widely and the latter debars entry to only those which are expressly and impliedly barred. The two explanations, one existing from the inception and the latter added in 1976, bring out clearly the legislative intention extending operation of the section."

We are now in a very complex society. The pattern of litigation coming up before Courts has undergone a transformation. One will find in the nature of time, several statutes, coming into force, taking away the jurisdiction of Courts. Statutes regarding farms and lands and factories and industries are intended to take away the jurisdiction of Civil Court. Service sector, Banking sector, Taxation sector and several other sectors of the kind have come about in the establishment of Special Tribunals to deal with rights and obligations arising, taking away the jurisdiction of Courts. This process of denudation of the powers of the Civil Courts is on the increase. But, nevertheless, it must be borne in mind that ultimately you may be drafted into those Tribunals, as an inevitable phenomenon, to deal with matters arising therein. Thus, there is no need for getting disheartened at such denudation of powers of Civil Court. In essence, it only results in taking power of one sector and to confer the same on the other. But, ultimately, the one or the other has to be manned by the one having judicial training.

Ancillary.—Power of Court to adjudicate and determine matters incidental to the exercise of primary jurisdiction, *i.e.*, acquiring jurisdiction of a case as an entirety and incidental to disposition of the matters, possess jurisdiction, to decide the other matters raised by the case.

Appellate Jurisdiction.—Power vested in an Appellate Court to review and revise the judicial action of an inferior Court.

Continuing.—A doctrine invoked commonly in child custody or support cases by which a Court which has once acquired jurisdiction continues to possess it for purposes of amending or modifying orders therein.

Co-ordinate.—That which is possessed by Courts of equal rank, degree or authority, equally competent to deal with the matter in question.

Criminal.—Power to hear and dispose of criminal cases.

Equity.—Jurisdiction belonging to a Court of Equity by Chancery Courts in England. In India, there are no such District Courts, but the Courts deal with the principles therein laid.

Exclusive.—The power which a Court or other Tribunal exercises over an action or over a person to the exclusion of all other Courts.

Foreign.—Any jurisdiction foreign to that of the forum, *e.g.*, of a sister State.

General.—Such as extends to all controversies that may be brought before a Court within the legal bounds of rights and remedies as opposed to limited or special jurisdiction which covers only a particular class of cases.

International.—Power of Court or other organization to hear and determine matters between different countries or persons of different countries or foreign States.

International Court of Justice is a judicial arm of the United Nations. It has jurisdiction to give advisory opinion on matters of law and treaty – Construction when requested by the General Assembly, Security Council or any other International Agency, authorised by the General Assembly to petition for such opinion. It has jurisdiction also to settle legal disputes between Nations when voluntarily submitted to it. Its judgment may be enforced by the Security Council. Its jurisdiction and powers are determined by statutes to which all Member-States of the United Nations are parties. Judges of such Courts are elected by the General Assembly and Security Council.

Legislative.—The sphere of authority of a legislative body to enact laws and to conduct all business, incidental to its law making function.

Plenary.—Full and complete jurisdiction or powers of a Court over the subject matter as well as to parties to controversy.

Probate.—Jurisdiction relating to Wills.

Summary.—Jurisdiction of a Court to give a judgment or make an order itself forthwith, *e.g.*, to commit to prison for contempt.

Territorial.—Already dealt with.

Extra-territorial.—Judicial power which extends beyond the limits of a particular State or country – Long arm statutes.

Original Jurisdiction.—Jurisdiction in the first instance, *i.e.*, jurisdiction to take cognizance of a cause at its inception, try it and pass judgment upon the law and facts – distinguished from Appellate Jurisdiction. Original Jurisdiction does not mean exclusive jurisdiction and two or more Courts may have Original Jurisdiction and it may be of the same actions.

The above are different kinds of jurisdictions whose scope, content and target differ. There are many more such as Military, Admirality, Matrimonial, etc. Further, more jurisdictions are in the offing to deal with Ecology, Environment, Space, etc.

ಋಋಋ

BEAR THE AGONY TO ENJOY THE ECSTASY

While inaugurating the Bar Association of India in 1960, India's first President had said:

"The Courts are helped and assisted by the members of the Bar in carrying on their functions. They only make submissions; they do not advise the Courts, and when the Bar is strong it also provides the Government with the field for the recruitment of good judges. The tendency now is to confine all appointments to the higher posts in the Judiciary to the members of the Bar. If the Bar is weak the Judiciary will be weak. There can be no question about that, and if we want to have a strong judiciary, we must start with a strong Bar, so that it can furnish the right type and the right caliber of judges."

These words of wisdom hold true even more today.

At the inauguration of the Bar Association of India, the Chief Justice of India observed that it is *"a red letter day in the history of the legal profession of India when we are, for the first time, laying the foundations of an all-India Bar which, let us hope, will develop on the right lines and will lay down healthy traditions and sound conventions for the legal profession to follow."*

Since the time of its inception, the Bar Association of India has laid down healthy traditions and sound conventions for the legal profession to follow. The Bar Association of India has about 2000 individual members and more than 100 corporate members consisting of the High Court Bar Association and District Court Bar Association. This Association unites all the members of the Bar, practicing throughout the country. It fulfils the need of the country wide organisation of lawyers. The objects of the Association are broad based and aim at the furtherance of interest of the profession to set about different task of public and national welfare in many directions. The Association has fulfilled the interest of a strong and united Bar. The Judiciary, with high ideals and a strong and a united Bar, is very much necessary for the administration of justice to succeed. It is not possible to have a strong Bar unless Bar Association takes the lead of ensuring that the profession runs on the right lines.

Speech delivered at the Bar Association of India (Tamil Nadu & Pondicherry) on 15th March, 2003.

It is in the fitness of things that the Bar Association of India has set up a chapter in yet another State, which will help in spreading the message of unity and high ideals to the State and the Districts of Tamil Nadu.

The first thing, we in the legal fraternity shall have to take care of, is to see that the arrears of cases which have mounted up get eradicated at the earliest. This will not be possible without the full and unstinted cooperation of Members of the bar.

Again, there is the question of unequal fight between the party, with ample resources, and the litigant without adequate legal aid. The cost of fighting a case, whatever might be the justice of the matter, is too exorbitant which most citizens can ill-afford to bear.

Today, by and large, the Indian legal system enjoys immense public confidence. The common man considers the judiciary as "the ultimate guardian of his rights and liberties" This institution has stood the test of time and we owe it to the great institution to which we belong that we maintain the confidence of the common man in the judiciary by giving even-handed justice in all cases.

If our legal system is to prove effective and retain the faith and confidence of the average man, it must find an answer to the abovementioned problems.

It is the duty of the Bar Associations to ensure that, the younger deserving members of the Bar are helped by the senior members in the profession. They must be given the opportunity to work and show their skills and they must be provided reasonable remuneration to survive in the profession. Newer areas are emerging everyday which include biodiversity, biotechnology, information technology, environmental sciences, air and space technologies, ocean and marine sciences, forensic sciences, public health, petroleum and minerals related subjects etc. and specialized knowledge and skills hitherto not contemplated by legal profession will be required. Lawyers will be naturally called upon to specialize in assorted branches of legal practice as it is impossible to be a practitioner in all new emerging areas of legal practice.

ಌಌಌ

ADVISE TO NEWLY ENROLLED ADVOCATES

I have been a part of the legal system for more than 36 years now and an well aware of the zeal which the newly enrolled Advocates experience on the day of their enrolment. The day of enrolment as an Advocate is a day of pleasant fulfillment of an ambition for all those aspiring to be a member of the legal fraternity. It is also a day of strong resolve to make a mark in the new field you are going to enter shortly.

The legal profession is one of the most ancient, the most noble and honourable profession. There is unprecedented erosion of human values taking place in almost all fields of activities of mankind. All human activities and institutions are affected very badly by those catastrophic phenomenon. As well informed youths expected to be equipped to practice law in the 21st century, one must be knowing that legal profession and for that matter judiciary is also not totally an exception to it. However, I must hasten to add that it is heartening to note that the condition of the judiciary, meaning thereby, the Bench and the Bar is not that bad when compared to the other institutions. If one wants to hear a shocking description of the degrading standard in the legal profession one may hear the following observations of the Supreme Court in *Bar Council, Maharashtra v. M.V. Dabholkar*, AIR 1976 SC 242: (1976) 2 SCC 291: (1976) 2 SCR 48:

> "*Briefly expressed, these practitioners, according to testimony recorded by the State Disciplinary Tribunal, positioned themselves at the entrance to the Magistrates' Courts, watchful of the arrival of potential litigants. At sight, they rushed towards the clients in an ugly scrcniurage to snatch the briefs, to lay claim to the engagements even by physical fight, to undercut fees and by this unedifying exhibition, sometimes carried even into the Bar Library, solicited and secured work for themselves. If these charges were true, any member of the Bar with elementary ethics in his bosom would be outraged at his brethren's conduct.*"

If, you do not want to be unduly perturbed, you may take it that Dabholkar's case was only an occasional aberration and not a general condition. But, nobody can even for a moment, doubt the severity of the moral crisis. No individual and no society can ignore except at its own peril, the challenge posed by moral crisis

---

Speech delivered to the Newly Enrolled Advocates at the Rajasthan State Bar Council, Jaipur.

taking place all over the world. The crisis has got a very serious impact on the legal profession and the system of administration of law also. Therefore, as new entrants in the legal profession, who are bound to take the role of the leaders of the contemporary society, one must have to act as leaders of a renaissance movement with the object of averting the moral crisis and restoring the moral standards of the community and thereby, restore the past glory honour and nobility of the profession which has at least to some extent, suffered degradation in the near past. This is the foremost thought for consideration, because I feel that it may be difficult for the present generation to redeem itself from the present plight easily. The new entrants in this field are the hopes of tomorrow. It may be easy for them to be men of character and conduct of a high standard since they are not already affected substantially by the global phenomenon of moral crisis. Prevention is always better than cure. The present generation is thus pinning their hopes on who, the new entrants, must take a vow that come what may, they will not allow themselves to be affected by the moral crisis which has affected the present generation very badly. They must be able to put up a strong fight against the social evils that has spread among the community, as wild fire, as a consequence of erosion of values in life. They must grow as a new generation, of men, of law or leaders of the society who care for values in life and lead a value based life as example to the members of the community at large. The sure way to improve the moral standard of the society is to improve the sense of morality of each individual, who ultimately constitutes the society or community and the humanity. Only when all the members of the community decide to live a value based life, the moral standards of the community and humanity can be improved. It may a truly difficult task to perform, but before it is too late, a determined effort in that direction is a must.

In a democratic country like India, Rule of Law is of fundamental importance. Rule of law requires justice to be administered among the citizens. Administration of justice is possible as per the existing system only through Civil and Criminal Courts, other Tribunals and other established forums for adjudication of disputes. Thus, so long as the present system of administration of justice continues, an efficient Bar is the *sine qua non* for due administration of justice and for preservation of Rule of law. Therefore, Bar has a very responsible constitutional function to play and nobody who becomes an advocate need have any fear about his future if only one realises one's own responsibilities in the proper perspective and discharges them duly and creditably. Justice V.R. Krishna Iyer, the living legend of Indian Judiciary, has said about the role of advocates in a democracy and their responsibilities to the society and the nation:

> *"The rule of law cannot be built on the ruins of democracy, for where law ends, tyranny begins. If such be the keynote thought for the very survival of our Republic, the integral bond between the lawyer and the public is unbreakable. And the vital role of the lawyer depends upon his probity and professional life-style. Be it remembered that the central function of the legal profession is to promote the administration of justice. If the practice of law is thus a public utility of great implications and a monopoly is statutorily granted by the nation, it obligates the*

lawyer to observe scrupulously those norms which make him worthy of the confidence of the community in him as a vehicle of justice – social justice. The Bar cannot behave with doubtful scruples or strive to thrive on litigation".

It will be advantageous for you to remember the above words of Justice Krishna Iyer.

Yet another point which I want to stress is that the law is a learned profession par excellence and an advocate is not learned if his learning is confined to law reports and statutes. As Lord Me Mill, no other profession touches human life at so many points. Like the legal maxim *"once a mortgage always a mortgage'*; an advocate must always be a student. He can never put an end to the process of learning, acquiring wisdom is an endless process and the success of an advocate will depend upon the extent of the wisdom possessed by him. The legal profession, though a source of living, is mainly a career of service to the community. Besides administration of justice, the services of lawmen are in great demand in other fields like legislation and politics. It is the high function of advocates in modern society to be the guardian and vindicators of the two most precious things in life - justice and liberty. As men of law and as such leaders of the society, one cannot leave politics to a group of persons who have treated politics as a mere source of their living. As learned men and leaders of the society, you must involve in almost all activities of the society especially in politics, is my view. You must try to form public opinion to the effect that the service of law-men should be utilized more and more in the administration of the country, since the same is to be carried on in accordance with law. In all departments of administration, more and more number of persons trained in law should be appointed for the purpose of betterment of administration, is my firm belief, of course, persons trained in law must equip themselves to act as learned men and must render the service realizing and recognizing the high position, the society has accorded to them with a view to justify the recognition granted to them by the society. Then and there alone they will be able to keep up the status, the society has granted to them and the nobility of the profession. The varied social activities in which an advocate can usefully participate will definitely help him to be a successful advocate also. If proper care is taken, such social activities can never go against the professional success of an advocate. It can only brighten the chance of success in the profession.

Life at the Bar is never a Bed of Roses. This is very much true at least in the initial stages of the career. It requires a constant and deliberate attempt on the part of its members to keep abreast with the latest developments taking place in the field of law and the society and to equip themselves in all respects. To start with, you may not get much work you may feel that you are being neglected by all concerned. However, this is the time when you should patiently work hard and study with devotion all branches of law from books and from courts where they are applied to resolve the human problems. Understanding law is quite different from applying it to the different factual situations. The application part of the law is the most difficult part of the profession. Success of any practicing advocate depends much upon the skill with which he is able to apply his knowledge of law to the facts of particular case he is called upon to handle. To equip oneself with sufficient knowledge of law and the skill to apply the same to the factual situations, it takes a reasonably long time. Such training cannot be had within a specified time. Even though at the initial stages, the struggle for existence is bound to be seen in the upper tiers, there is sufficient and more room to accommodate any number of talented ones. In fact, there is an actual dearth of the really talented ones. So, my firm belief is that nobody, who is ready to work hard and take real interest in the profession with a firm resolution that he will reach the top, need not have any fear about his/her future.

About professional ethics and the skills to be developed for a successful career, I think I need not mention anything. Because professional ethics, I suppose is a subject expected to be learnt by the new advocates themselves by you. As such I will conclude my words once again quoting V.R. Krishna Iyer J., from Dabholkar's case where the learned judge has delineated the moral standard expected from a practitioner of law. He is of the view that the professional conduct of advocates must be complete in tune with

> *"The setting of a calling to which Lincoln, Gandhi, Lenin and a galaxy of great men belonged. The high moral tone and the considerable public service the Bar is associated with and its key role in the developmental and dispute-processing activities and, above all, in the building up of a just society and constitutional order has earned for it a monopoly to practice law and an autonomy to regulate its own internal discipline. This heavy public trust should not be forfeited by legalizing or licensing fights for briefs, affrays in the rush towards clients, under-cutting and wrangling among members"*

ಐ ಐ ಐ

PART III

HUMAN RIGHTS

HUMAN RIGHTS

The year 1948 is memorable for any serious advocate of the Protection of Human Rights. It was in that year that the world witnessed the culmination of a long and arduous task - the task of drafting and adopting the Universal Declaration of Human Rights (UDHR). It was in that year that the world saw the realization of some of its long - standing aspirations; the aspirations of seeing itself as a single international community. To be exact, it was on the 10th of December, that year, that the United Nations adopted the Universal Declaration of Human Rights, the *"Magna Carta for all humanity"*. That was a great beginning; a big step forward. Behind it, was the sad spectacle of the ruins of two disastrous world wars which acted as an impetus for the various people to sit together, to set aside their petty differences and to seek a solution for the problem of human rights violation.

It is the 50th anniversary year. Having come a long way through these fifty years, we unite once more to strengthen our resolutions and to march forward with the motto *"All Human Rights for All"*. That, indeed, is a comprehensive one, covering a wide area of civil, cultural, economic, political and social rights.

The United Nations Commission on Human Rights, while drafting the outline of the Declaration, had a tough time in identifying all the pockets of our complex societies where the issue was relevant. "Where to begin" was the question that perturbed the concerned member-states. *Jananeethi* has already made it clear that the above motto comes into effect only when the lowest stratum of our society is benefitted by its work. Gandhiji's concept - that "the fight for human rights begins from the village, the lowest cadre, the down-trodden, and the highly unorganized sectors" has been a guideline for *Jananeethi*. In going ahead with its designs. *Jananeethi* has found that this Gandhian concept fits into the slot at least as far as the Indian subcontinent is concerned. That's why all attempts were made to incorporate this into its plan and prospects, as part of the Percolation of Justice. In fact, that's not far from what the UN itself had visualised: Universal Human Rights begin, it said, *"in small places where every man, woman, and child seeks equal Justice"*.

Speech delivered on Human Right's at Cochin on 4th December, 1998.

Thus, the 1948 Declaration, had in it a clear vision, as to how the world should be in future. It recognized that *"the inherent dignity of all members of the human family is the foundation of freedom, justice and peace in the world"*. It aims at the fulfilment of our right to a life with dignity, which includes a whole lot of related rights. And what's more, these rights are rights indeed, not mere "gifts" granted or taken back at some individuals whim and fancy.

The 50th anniversary is an apt occasion for the entire world to mobilise more effort and to reinforce its struggle against the anti-human right forces. We must see to it that an awareness is created as to what really are our rights, and when, where and how they are violated. As for that, the Declaration has already been translated into not less than 200 languages. *Jananeethi* has translated into Malayalam, the 1948 Declaration along with all the major covenants that have come by in the year that followed. It is a significant contribution to a noble cause from Kerala, this comparatively obscure side of the world. Nations all over the universe have taken consideration of the various aspects of the Declaration while exercising acts of legislation. It has come to such a level that one can't be blind to the existence, relevance and importance of the Declaration.

As can be expected, the future of any planned or non-planned action in this area is not without challenge. They were there ever since its inception. "In human" rights are still on the rise and the world is far from being non-discriminatory. Millions of people in the various corners of the globe are denied the right to live with dignity. They are looking up towards the upholders of human rights with expectant eyes. The task we have taken up is not a silly one; the path is not without hazards. We have on our shoulders a huge piece of rock. We have better learn to walk with it than being crippled by it.

శుశుశు

FREEDOM & DIGNITY – BIRTHRIGHT OF ALL HUMAN BEINGS

Individual freedom and dignity are the birth right of all human beings. Rights and duties are the two faces of the same coin *viz.*, the individual human being and they are inter-related in all activities – socio-economic and political, – of that individual. Fulfilment of duties becomes the prerequisite to enjoy rights. While rights exalt individual liberty, duties express the dignity of that liberty.

Human being like all other forms of life is part of the nature. Every form of life, in its most-minutest form 'cell', gets synthesized and adopted to sustain itself and perishes in a natural way. Necessarily, therefore, human beings follow the same pattern from the beginning to end of life. During the period from birth to death, a human being as a social animal acquires claims and liberties. These claims, liberties, powers and immunities are described under the homonym 'rights'.

These rights do not owe their existence to any law. They are gifts of nature. Thomas Jefferson declared that *"all men are created equally and they are endowed with certain inalienable rights to life, liberty and pursuit of happiness."* These rights of man and woman compendiously came to be accepted as 'Human Rights'. These are 'irreducible minima' which belong to every member of human race when pitted against the State or other public authorities or groups, gangs and other oppressive communities. They are inviolable and cannot be legitimately denied or abrogated by any power of the State.

The movement for 'Human Rights' is part of human history and it is never a lone sojourner. Everytime, there is a disquieting tendency in the history leading colossal catastrophe, the aftermath necessarily instigated eruption and escalation of thoughts, directed towards 'Human Rights'. In 1188 AD, the Federal Assembly of kingdom of Leon received from King Alfonsa* IX of Hungary guaranteed rights against arbitrary arrest and most famous and influential beginning in the saga of 'Human Rights' – *Magnacarta* was accepted by King John in 1215 AD,

---

Inaugural speech delivered at the conference on 'Human Rights, Duties and Safeguards Contemporary Indian Context', at Hyderabad on 14th June, 2002.

* The confirmation of series of rights. King Adnew II.

after a struggle. The French Declaration of the 'Human Rights' of Man and Citizen, 1789 which is an invaluable contribution in the Global Struggle for 'Human Rights', Covenant of League of Nations, 1919, Universal Declaration of Human Rights (UDHR), 1948 and its related charters were added to Human Rights jurisprudence only after tremendous struggle. The history of 'Human Rights' movement is also the history of the challenges faced by it. It also scripted with prognosis for the ailment which we suffer *i.e.* "Human Rights" violations.

Constitution of India and Human Rights

It is not possible to define "Human Rights" in an objective manner. The Universal Declaration of Human Rights, 1948 enumerated at least 27 such broad rights, which are necessary for the establishment of social and International order in which the rights and freedoms can be realised.

Protection of Human Rights Act, 1993 defines "Human Rights' as to mean the rights relating to life, liberty, equality and dignity of the individual guaranteed by the Constitution or embodied in International Covenants on Civil and Political Rights (ICCPR) and International Covenant on Economic, Social and Cultural Rights (ICESCR) which were adopted by the General Assembly of United Nations on 16th December, 1966. This Act was made by the Parliament 'having regard to the changing social realities and growing concern in India and brought about issues relating to 'Human Rights' with a view to bring about greater accountability and transparency in enforcement of laws of the nation'. In India, the movement of Human Rights is a part of social justice which is a conceived and perceived Constitutional goal, intended to be practiced with all sincerity by the three wings of the State: Legislature, Executive and Judiciary.

Child & Human Rights

The child is a person within the legal meaning. All the rights, claim, liberties, which inhere a human being, also belong to the child. Greed, helplessness, poverty and exploitation, however, are inimically dispossessed of to the child. Ignorance and tenderness make a child gullible to adults' evil design. In times of war and peace, it is the child who suffers more than the elder. Despite Universal Declaration of Human Rights and other such international efforts, billions of children were denied human rights. Ultimately in 1989, the General Assembly of U.N.O., in the Convension on Rights of the Child (CRC), adopted the rights drafted by UN Commission on human rights. It is a set of international standards and measures intended to protect and promote the well being of the children in the society. The Charter is guided by the principle 'first call for children' - a principle that the essential needs of the children should be given highest priority in allocation of resources at all times. It obligates signatory States to respect and ensure that children get a fair and equitable deal in society. The Charter contains 41 Articles and recognises the right of the child to live with dignity, right to health, nutritious food and right to beauty of childhood.

The society and other groups have, thus far, denied the right of the child to education and decent life. The child was economically exploited by forcibly engaging him as commercial, farm, domestic and industrial servant and was treated as a slave with or without connivance of the parents. A large body of

Legislations like Apprentices Act, 1961; The Children (Pledging of Labour) Act, 1933; The Child Labour (Prevention and Regulation) Act, 1986; The Bonded Labour System (Abolition) Act, 1976; Motor Transport Workers Act, 1961; Factories Act, 1948; The Minimum Wages Act, 1948; The Plantations Labour Act, 1951; The Trade Unions Act, 1926; The Workmen's Compensation Act, 1923; The Mines Act, 1952; Beedi and Cigar Workers (Conditions of Employment) Act, 1966 and Merchant Shipping Act, 1958 either abolish or regulate child labour.

The Supreme Court of India, in a large number of cases, has strenuously come down against the executive and against those who exploit children, and issued appropriate directions. In *Unni Krishnan v. State of A.P.,* AIR 1993 SC 2178: (1993) 1 SCC 645: (1993) 1 SCR 594, the Supreme Court held that it is the fundamental right of every child to have education upto the age of fourteen years. The decision in Unnikrishnan's case lead to far-reaching directions given by the Supreme Court in *M.C. Mehta v. State of Tamil Nadu,* AIR 1997 SC 699: (1996) 6 SCC 756: (1997) 1 LLN 12, where the Supreme Court in its activist role directed every state Government to deposit an amount of Rs. 25,000 as detrained expenses of the child if he is to be compulsorily weaned from economic activity and given education. *Anganwadi* and *Balwadi* Schemes and Integrated Child Development Programmes aim at good health and nutrition to the children.

Notwithstanding the State efforts, legislatively as well as executively, social evil of child abuse continues. This is the perennial challenge to the human rights movement. Whether the legislation is insufficient or whether implementation is inadequate are the two questions to which all of us have to address ourselves. In majority of African Nations, South American Nations as well as Indian sub-continent, still billions of children suffer from poverty, ill-health and exploitation. A concerted unified effort on the part of everyone is more than desired.

In so far as the judiciary is concerned, we have accepted the principle that our fundamental rights chapter is required to be interpreted compatibly in accordance with international law.

Women & Human Rights

As per the U.N. Report, 1980, women constitute fifty percent of world's population. They perform two-third of work hours, but receive one-tenth of world's income and own one-hundredth percent of world's property. They constitute more than half of Indian population. They are denied life, liberty and dignity. The right to equality before law is available only to a fortunate few. They suffer discrimination and their self-sacrifice or self-denial further add to the problem. Vienna Declaration on Elimination of All Forms of Discrimination against Woman (CEDAW), 1979 ratified by UNO on 18th December, 1979 takes note of the discrimination against women and mandates all member states to take all appropriate measures including legislation to modify or abolish gender based discrimination in the existing laws, regulations, customs and practice. All forms of discrimination on ground of gender is violative of fundamental freedoms and human rights. The General Assembly of U.N.O. on 4th December, 1986, adopted resolution on Right to development recognising the right of every woman to develop. The escalating emergence of women's rights is not an accidental or sporadic occurrence. The Constitution of India prohibits discrimination only on the basis of sex. Further, it empowers the state to take all necessary steps for the upliftment of women. In *Government of A.P.* v. *P.B. Vijay Kumar*, AIR 1995 SC 1648: (1995) 4 SCC 520: (1995) Lab IC 2236, for the first time, the Supreme Court laid down that Article 15(3) can be read into Article 16 to sustain any special provision favouring women.

The employment statistics show that in agricultural sector which I call 'earth collar' jobs, seventy per cent of the labour is women. The dominant classes in the rural areas seldom treat these agricultural labour as human beings and at slightest opportunity they exploit them sexually. In payment of wages and supply of food etc., the women are discriminated. In blue collar and white collar employment sectors, there is an increasing presence of women as employees at all levels. The insult, verbally or by sign language, is tolerated by women in silence for the fear of losing respect in the society. All the cases of harassment are not reported. But still women continue to suffer insult at the work place which is again a perennial challenge to the human rights activists.

Prisoners & Human Rights

The old exploiting the young; the man exploiting the woman; the rich exploiting the poor; and the anti-social exploiting the citizen are all aspects of open society. There is another society behind the prison walls where large number of human beings are denied human rights. Legal justice requires that offenders of law should be brought to book and punished. Within this, they should be constitutionally accepted as human beings, at the stage of investigation, as suspects; at the stage of trial, as under-trials; and at the stage of punishment, as incarcerated human beings citizens are denied the rights. Though human approach to reformation of the prisoners is very much part of the social science of criminology, there is much to be done in this field. In the precincts of jail, what happens is known to the jail administrator. For fear of facing torture, the principle of silence is rule and does not allow the violators to come to the fore. Under-trial prisoners are denied the right to speedy trial which is a human right. The prisoners are denied the rights of human beings. The Supreme Court of India in a catena of decisions has recognised this.

HIV-AIDS & Human Rights

Caught in the coils of HIV-AIDS, human kind is struggling to extricate itself from the recent scourge of the 20th century. The recent State-wide statistics of a number of such patients shows that the situation is alarming. The problem throws up lot of challenges to the Human Rights Law. The Indian Legal system is not fully geared up to face the challenges. There is lot of legislative vacuum in the field. Whether HIV-AIDS disease can be treated as a problem of public health bringing under the Epidemic Diseases Act, 1897 and Public Health Act? Whether sex workers who are imprisoned under Immoral Traffic (Prevention) Act, 1956 can be denied right to life by denying the release after their period of sentence, on the ground that they require treatment for HIV-AIDS? Whether the Doctor treating the patient is under obligation to reveal to the society about the disease without violating hippocratic oath? Whether the State and society can deny fundamental rights and human rights to HIV-AIDS patients. These are some of the challenges we should be prepared to face.

In *P.N. Swamy* v. *Station House Officer*, 1998 (1) ALD 755, a Division Bench of Andhra Pradesh High Court directed that women rescued from brothel houses who were found to be infected with HIV, be taken to welfare houses to make them learn vocational courses. It was also directed to separate the children of these women to be sent to welfare hostel having regard to the rights of the children. The court recognised the fundamental right to life and liberty of even those who suffer from HIV-AIDS.

Refugees & Human Rights

Universal Declaration of Human Rights specifically recognises the right to seek and enjoy asylum in an alien country. The cross-border exodus of exploited human beings everywhere has created new problem area of "stateless citizens". The disturbing trends of religious bigotry and ethnicism has created social tensions, sometimes resulting in genocide and large scale migration. In East Asia, Europe, Central Africa, the history during the past decade has thrown challenges to the Human Rights in this area of Human Rights.

International Refugee law seems to revolve around two main pillars - the norm making process at the international level with a strong focus on the evolution of a right regime to protect and provide for refugees and the practical aspects of international and domestic State policies, which are reflected in the actual observance of or modified compliance with these international norms, or simply put, in the practice of States. The implications of providing asylum have several ramifications on the individual state in its social, political and economical structure. Any such decision must remain the prerogative of the individual state and therefore immigration laws have been under the exclusive jurisdiction of the individual State, with minimal international interference. Thus, we have two seemingly irreconcilable perspectives. One provides for the protection and the prevention of violation of human rights, both at the domestic and international level, and the other provides for the importance of state interests and the sovereign power of the state to determine its policies with regard to immigration and asylum rights. The main hurdle in incorporating a strong human rights regime in refugee protection is the failure to point out a clear addressee of the obligations of human rights protection. Treaty and customary human rights obligations usually rest clearly on one state, and the relation can be clearly established between individuals or groups of the Government or the State in question. This domestic framework is open to international concern and coercion, in the form of sanctions by the international community. This framework, however, is lacking, in the context of refugee protection, as no obligations are spelt out *vis-a-vis* the refugee with respect to the receiving state or any other state of the international community.

Other Challenges

Activities of followers of political ideology with faith in extremist violence and radicalism have resulted in conditions which are appalling. The people are denied the right to choice as to the residence and avocation. The people who lost limbs due to land mine blasts and those who lost the limbs due to terrorists' amputation heckle at human rights activists who bring the cases of law breakers before courts, complaining human rights violations. The complaint of violation of human rights by the State in the case of those who themselves violate human rights of others is a big challenge in a democratic system. Apart from this, the state sponsored terrorism, either in enforcing the municipal law or for enforcing the foreign policy, for various reasons, assumes a subject of perennial debate. Thus, larger issues are a cause for the convenient gloss over the human rights of those unfortunate people who are physically challenged (handicapped) and mentally challenged (handicapped) for no fault of theirs. Needless to reiterate, human rights of those challenged persons are not recognised at all.

Conclusion

The world is caught up in economic liberalisation and global market syndrome. Increasing awareness in the affluent countries for better comforts for their citizens would necessarily result in depriving the human rights in other countries. As we discuss, human rights in this hall, elsewhere the children are denied the right to dignified life and women are subjected to deprivation and insult. The more emphasis on the practice of human rights results in equally forceful opposite reaction and there are more and more violation of human rights. But there need not be scope for pessimism, for an honest appraisal of human rights practices would go a long way for giving effect to international treaty or convention rights as well as Human Rights in the Constitution.

The idea of human rights as fundamental universal standards which have been codified in documents with a special status and to be reviewed by an independent judiciary, is a notion which has (with reference to the English constitution) "not been made but grown". Where contract thinkers founded human rights in natural law and, subsequently, during the French and American revolutions, a phase began codifying human rights in Declarations and Constitutions, the evolution of human rights eventually resulted in justiciable norms. The process of realising human rights as higher law to be invoked before the judiciary thus took shape in the course of centuries.

ಬಬಬ

CONSTITUTIONAL RIGHTS OF
WEAKER SECTIONS

The objective of equality, which implies social and economic justice in the wider sense, permeates the provisions of Part IV of the Constitution of India.

The Constitution opened a new horizon of hope for women in our developing nation, with the engrafting of non-discrimination and special clauses, intended to protect and promote the rights and legitimate aspirations of women as equal citizens of India. These special clauses are found in Articles 15, 39, 42 and 51A of our Constitution. These provisions hold out the promise of a new social order in what women would prefer to call a "male dominated society".

In the Indian Constitution, the rights of women are traceable to the non-discrimination law contained in Article 15 and 15(3), besides Articles 39 and 42. Special attention to the legitimate interests of women has been paid by incorporating articles of far reaching benefits. The women are guaranteed equal political and civil rights such as suffrage, employment, access to places of public resort, etc. They are also afforded extra special protection on account of their general health, responsibilities of mother hood, etc.

Under the Civil Procedure Code, there is provision for the arrest of man who is a judgement-debtor for non-payment of decretal amount. There is no such provision against a woman judgement-debtor. Perhaps, this is due to certain relevant factors like the natural health of women, and duties arising out of mother hood and home or house hold duties, etc.

Various Co-operative Societies Acts and Panchayats Acts envisage co-option of women to the management of panchayats and co-operative societies if no women was elected. It is interesting to notice that the Apex Court, in the case reported in *Bombay Labour Union* v. *Franchises (P) Ltd.*, AIR 1966 SC 942, struck down a draconian rule under which women employees were prohibited from continuing in employment on getting married. It is interesting to notice the reasoning of the learned judges:

Speech delivered on the occasion of 'Third Conference of Bar Federation of Tamil Nadu and Pondicheery', Madras on 10th April, 1993.

"It is the married working women's intermittent pre-occupation with the House that is at the root of the belief that employment and marriage are mutually exclusive. It is a pity that this is being made out to be a conflict between basic human rights, the right of the child to the mother and the right of the woman to work. In reality, it is a question of reconciling certain basic facts. The married woman who works because of necessity or because she has a strong sense of social purpose or a desire to participate in the economic activity of the nation must be considered as making two kinds of contribution to the society and to the nation. One directly in the sense of productive work done in an office or factory or laboratory or school room and the other indirectly and without payment to society as a mother. The latter must, of course, remain the first charge upon a woman, if withheld it would make society extinct. But, just because mother hood is taken or granted as the natural functions of women and because from it she often deriver the deepest psychological satisfaction, it does not make any less, labour, and I am not speaking biologically it is labour even in terms of man-hours of work. Women themselves have accepted both these rules gladly. They have only to be helped to harmonise the two through the creation of certain facilities like nurseries, part-time employment opportunities, maternity leave benefits and re-orientation course in certain careers".

A division bench of the Bombay High Court in *Charan Singh v. Union of India,* dealing with Articles 14, 15 and 16 of the Constitution in relation to women, upheld reservation for women for appointment to clerical posts in the enquiry and reservation offices of the railways in the metropolitan cities of India on the following grounds:

1. Under-representation of women in the railway services, particularly because they were excluded from field jobs.
2. They are specially suitable for the job of reservation clerks because their nature is gentle and courteous.
3. They were not as easy to contact by the racketeers in black-marketing of railway tickets as men.
4. Because they could be regarded as socially and educationally backward class.

The committee appointed, on the status of women, by the Government of India in 1974, bears testimony to the fact that inequality exists between men and women, and the report says that women are economically backward, particularly in relation to employment, and they are also educationally backward.

Article 39(d) of the Constitution enjoins on the State to direct its policy towards securing equal pay for equal work for both men and women. This Article is based on Article 41 of the Constitution of the International Labour Organisation, 1919 and Article 23(2) of the Universal Declaration of Human Rights, 1948, which is couched in almost identical language.

Article 46 of the Constitution provides for special care of the educational and economic interest of the weaker sections of the people, particularly scheduled castes and scheduled tribes and for their protection from social injustice and all forms of social exploitation. Obviously, this Article intends to promote the welfare of those who are socially handicapped in the peculiar Indian context. This article again is replica of Article 45(4)(1) of the Irish Constitution.

Education and economic advancement go together. Without education, economic assistance may not be really fruitful or effective. Untouchability, bonded labour, discriminatory wages, usurious loans in rural areas, dowry, child marriage, discriminatory laws against women relating to marriage, divorce, inheritance are but a few examples of social injustice against, and exploitation of weaker sections in the highly stratified society.

Article 46 of the Constitution was invoked by the then State of Madras in the case of *State of Madras* v. *Chempagam Dorairajan*, AIR 1951 SC 226 where reservation of seats in favour of Backward classes in Engineering colleges was made according to certain formula. The state, unsuccessfully, pleaded the communal G.O. to be upheld having regard to the provisions of Article 46 of the Constitution even if it violated the fundamental rights under Article 29(2). The Supreme Court rejected this argument and held that the Directive Principles of State Policy have to conform to and run as subsidiary to the chapter of Fundamental Rights. However, this judgment was over ruled by the Constitution (First Amendment Act, 1951), which added clause (4) to Articles 15.

The subsequent trends of judgements of the Supreme Court has also gone to the extent of saying that the directive principles should be read into the fundamental rights.

Article 39(f) of the Constitution imposes the obligation on the State "That childhood and youth are protected against exploitation and against moral and material abandonment". This article is based on Articles 45 of the Cuban Republican Constitution of 1940, and also derives support from Article 41 of the Constitution of the International Labour Organisation, 1919.

By the 42nd Amendment, 1976, the following phrase was added to the original clause in Article 39(f) of the Constitution, *viz.*,

> "*That children are given opportunities and facilities to develop in a healthy manner and in conditions of freedom and dignity*".

Article 39(e) follows the phraseology of Article 45(4)(2) of the Irish Constitution. It enshrines, on the one hand, that men, women and children are put in employments suited to their health and strength, and on the other hand, to see that economic necessity does not force them into a vocation, unsuited to their age or strength. These articles aim at securing just and humane conditions of work and the need to provide for maternity relief.

Social security component, which is necessary concomitant of the welfare state, has been provided by Article 41. Article 43 has been invoked, particularly in the case of 'living wage'.

Women form the most vulnerable section of the Indian society by tradition and social attitudes. They constitute almost half of the population of the country. There has been change in the social attitudes and necessary provisions are made for participation of women in the management of Panchayat and Co-operative societies besides their active participation in Legislature and Parliament.

The Apex Court, in the case of *Air India* v. *Nargosh Meerza*, AIR 1981 SC 1829: (1981) 4 SCC 335: (1982) 1 SCR 438: (1981) Lab IC 1313: (1981) 2 LLJ 314, held unconstitutional a clause in the service rules providing for retirement of air-hostesses in the event of first pregnancy.

The weakest sections of the society are scheduled castes and tribes. Economic planning alone cannot tackle the aim of establishing a social democracy in the absence of direct action to fight social attitudes and tendencies. Constitutional safeguards and guarantees provide solace to the weaker sections. States have been promulgating various social welfare legislations, opening new vistas of progress and opportunity to the weaker sections so that they could attain excellence in the chosen field.

Before the Constitution was adopted by the Sovereign people of India, Dr. Bhim Rao Sahib Ambedkar remarked,

> "On January 26, 1950, we will have equality in politics and inequality in social and economic life. We must remove the contradictions at the earliest moment or else those who suffer from inequality will blow up the structure of political democracy.

The term "Scheduled" is a British legacy. When the alleged lowest ranking caste in the dehumanizing social stratification were listed in the schedule appended to the Govt. of India Act, 1935, for special safeguards and benefits, Mahatma Gandhi chose to Christine them as "Harijans" meaning thereby children of God. The scheduled castes and tribes consist of 165 million in our country.

The country has aimed at the upliftment of weaker sections who have suffered at the hands of stronger sections for centuries through constitutional provisions and parliamentary and legislative enactments, evolving preference programmes which consist of the following:

1. Reservation in the legislature, in Government service and in public sector.

2. Programmes entailing expenditure or provisions of service like scholarship, grants, loans, etc.

3. Special protection accompanying distributive schemes to protect the backward classes in general from being victimised or exploited like forced labour, reliefs from debt, bondage, regulating money lending, restricting and transfer, etc.

These measures are re-calculated to safeguard against exploitation of socially degraded classes by the socially upgraded and more sophisticated predatory neighbours.

The problem of weaker sections is a human problem and not just a sociological problem. It is a peculiar problem of our country which needs a healing touch and human understanding.

If Articles 14, 15, 16 and 17, read with the directive principles of state policy are to be meaningful and effective, there should be a radical change in the mental attitude and thinking process of the people who matter. The Constitution cannot work by itself. The dream of Mahatma Gandhi was:

> "An India in which the poorest shall feel that it is their country in whose making they have an effective voice: an India in which all communities shall live in perfect harmony. There can be no room in such an India for the curse of untouchability or the curse of intoxicating drinks and drugs..."

> The relevance of political fundamental rights may not be so much appreciated by the less fortunate unless there is a reasonable standard of material existence and a fair degree of homogeneity if quality of life is the ultimate criterion."

As rightly observed, Prof. Earnest Barket:

> "If the problems of national homogeneity are still insistent and there is no common feeling of fellowship if some sections of the community are regarded by others as essentially alien and heterogeneous, either on the ground of their inferior education or on the ground of their inferior stock or decent or on any other ground, the ideal of common life of freedom will seem equally illusory."

The convention concerning equal remuneration for men and women workers for work of equal value was adopted by the General Conference of the International Labour Organisation on 29-6-1951. In order to implement Article 39(d) of the Constitution of India and Equal Remuneral Convention, 1951, the Equal remuneration ordinance was promulgated, which was subsequently replaced by the Equal Remuneration Act, 1976. This Act imposes a duty on the employer to pay equal remuneration to men and women workers for same work or work of a similar nature and prohibits discrimination being made while recruiting men and women workers.

No exemption from Equal Remuneration Act was held to be available on the ground of financial incapacity – *Mackinon Mackenzie* v. *Andrey D'Costa*, AIR 1987 SC 1281: (1987) 2 SCC 469: (1987) 2 SCR 659: (1987) 2 SCJ 562: (1987) Lab IC 961.

The Supreme Court, in the case of *Peoples Union for Democratic Rights* v. *Union of India*, AIR 1982 SC 1473: (1982) 3 SCC 235: (1983) 1 SCR 456: (1982) Lab IC 1646 has held that execution of labour and services against payment of less than the minimum wage amounts to "forced labour" and violates Article 23 of the Constitution. "Begar" has been described as labour or service which a person is forced to give without receiving any remuneration and thus it is a form of forced labour.

In another case, bonded labourers working in a brick kiln were freed from the clutches of owners, despite the fact that some large amounts were due from the labourers to the kiln owners. Employment of children below 14 years in construction work was deprecated in *Shiv Dayal Srivatsava* v. *Union of India*, (1982) 3 SCC 181.

Bonded labourers families have been granted financial assistance as a rehabilitation measure and such bonded labourers have been repatriated to their State of origin, in the case of *P. Sivasami* v. *State of Andhra Pradesh*, AIR 1988 SC 1863: (1988) 4 SCC 466: 1988 Supp (2) SCR 346: (1988) Lab IC 1680.

ೲೲೲ

RIGHT TO LIVE

R ight to live is a fundamental right guaranteed under the Constitution.

When the term Life is used here, something more is meant than mere existence. Supreme Court held in *Sunil Batra* v. *Delhi Administration*, AIR 1980 SC 1579: (1980) 3 SCC 488: (1980) 2 SCR 557. that the right to live includes right to live consistent with human dignity and decency.

In *Frances Caraliemullin* v. *Union Territory of Delhi*, AIR 1981 SC 746: (1981) 1 SCC 608: (1981) 2 SCR 516: (1981) 2 SCJ 18, Justice Bhagwati elaborated by observing:

> The right of life includes right to live with human dignity and all that goes along with it namely, the very necessaries of life such as adequate nutrition, clothing and shelter over head and facilities for reading, writing and expressing oneself in diverse forms, freely moving about and mixing and mingling with fellow human beings. The right includes right to basic necessities of life and also right to carry on such activities that constitute the bear minimum expression of human self.

In *Umed Ram's* case, the Court held:

> The right to life in Art 21 embraces not only physical existence of life but also the quality of life. It observed, "in case of residents of hilly area, access to roads is access to life itself.

Article 47 contains directive principles of state policy to raise the level of nutrition and standard of living of its people and the improvement of public health. The medical profession has an important role to play in improving health of the individuals.

The Supreme Court, in *Pashchim Banga Khet Mazdoor Samity* v. *State of West Bengal*, AIR 1996 SC 2426: (1996) 4 SCC 37: (1996) 3 SCJ 25: (1996) Lab IC 2054, ruled that providing adequate medical facilities for the people is an essential part of the obligations, undertaken by the government in a welfare state.

Speech delivered at the Seminar on 'Consumer Awareness on Quality, Cost and Prevailing Practices is Medical Services', Hyderabad on 23rd December, 2001.

Now the facilities provided by the state are supplemented by private hospitals, particularlys corporate hospitals, in a big way.

With the advancement of science and therapeutic methods, the medical profession is playing a commendable role in improving health and the longevity of human being. Treatment is available to several diseases, which were hitherto treated as incurable.

The Indian traditional approach of treating the medical professional as God is no more present. With modernization and increased values of material wealth, the medical profession has become commercial, leading to large scale mushrooming of hospitals and nursing homes which has changed the attitude of the patients in general towards doctors. The high cost paid by the patient makes him question whether he is getting his money's worth.

The profession differs from other occupations for the reason that the profession operates in spheres where success cannot be achieved in every case and very often success or failure depends upon the factors beyond the professional man's control. Yet, the law prescribes a liability on the professional, it, an advocate or the like.

With the emergence of the Consumer Protection Act, no doubt, there is a spate of litigation since no court fee is payable. There has been a growing awareness in the public mind to bring the negligence of such professional doctors to light.

The Indian Medical Association, as a matter of fact, contended before the Supreme Court that the relationship between the patient and the doctor was based on contract of personal service which was, in fact, excluded from the definition of service under the Act. The contract of personal service is distinct from contract for personal service. In the absence of relationship of master and servant between patient and the medical practitioner, the service rendered by the medical practitioner to the patient cannot be regarded as service rendered under a contract of personal service. As such service rendered by medical profession is under a contract for personal service to which exclusionary clause of the definition of 'service' does not apply. The example of contract of personal service is employment of domestic servants or service rendered by the medical officer to his employer.

The service rendered by a doctor or hospital, free of charge, is not covered under the Act but where hospital charges the fee from some patients and renders free treatment to others, the service rendered by such hospital is covered under the Act, as the law stands now (in *Indian Medical Association* v. *V.P. Shanta*, AIR 1996 SC 550: (1995) 6 SCC 651).

Incidentally, Government hospitals, health centers and dispensaries also fall under the purview of the Act if for any category of patients, charges are collected. They are exempt only if they offer free service to all patients. Collection of nominal registration fee, of course, does not attract the Act.

The liability of a medical professional is—(i) statutory, or (ii) contractual or (iii) based on tort. The Indian Medical Council Act, 1956 empowers the Medical

Council to prescribe standards of professional conduct and etiquette and code of ethics for medical professionals (section 20A). As in the case of Bar Council Act in relation to advocates, while the Bar council punishes misconduct of advocates, many a time no instances of a doctor being punished for any misconduct by the medical council are reported.

In general, a professional man owes to his client a duty in tort as well as in contract to exercise reasonable care in giving advice or performance of services (Jackson and Power) as Lord Denning puts it:

> *The professional man gives advice under a contract for reward; or without a contract in pursuance of voluntary assumption of responsibility gratuitously. In either case, he is under one and the same duty to use reasonable care..... In one case, it is by reason of a term implied by law, in the other, it is by reason of duty imposed by law. For a breach of that duty is liable in damages and those damages should be and are the same whether he is sued in contract or tort.*

A mistake in diagnosis, of course, is not necessarily a negligent diagnosis (*Hatcher* v. *Black*). No human being is infallible. In the present state of science, even the most eminent specialists may be at fault in detecting a diseased condition. A practitioner is liable, in respect of his diagnosis, only when it is palpably wrong *i.e.*, its mistake is of such a nature as to imply absence of reasonable skill and care on his part, regard being had to the ordinary level of skill in the practitioner.

Justice Mc Nair, J observed:

> *A doctor is not guilty of negligence if he acted in accordance with a practice adopted and treated as proper by a responsible body of medical men skilled in that particular part.*

The Supreme Court in *Dr. Laxman Balakrishna Joshi* held as follows:

> *The duties, which a doctor owes to his patient, are clear. A person who holds himself out, ready to give medical advice and treatment, impliedly undertakes that he is possessed of skill and knowledge for the purpose. Such a person, when consulted by a patient, owes him certain duties, viz., a duty of care in deciding whether to undertake the case, a duty of care in deciding what treatment to give or a duty of care in the administration of that treatment. A breach of any of these duties gives a right of action for negligence to the patient. The practitioner must bring to his task a reasonable degree of skill and knowledge and must exercise a reasonable degree of care. Neither the very highest nor a very low degree of care and competence, judged in the light of the particular circumstances of each case is what the law requires.*

The Supreme Court held that a homeopath prescribing Allopathic drugs is negligence *per se* in *Poonam Verma* v. *Dr. Aswini Patel*, AIR 1996 SC 2111: (1996) 4 SCC 332.

Use of wrong drugs or wrong gases, excessive use of anesthesia, excessive dosage of injection, operating on the wrong organ, transfusion of mismatching blood, leaving surgical sponge or forceps, prescription of drugs without examining the patient are considered as negligence.

A criticism that the medical practitioners tend to over-prescribe and refer for unnecessary tests does not appear to be totally unfounded. It is for the medical profession to absolve themselves of this criticism by their own conduct.

Liabilities of Hospitals

At one time, it was argued that the hospital employs doctors and specialists who do their job on their own and are hence not liable for their negligence. In *Cassidy v. Ministry of Health*, a leading authority on the subject, Lord Denning observed:

> If a man goes to a doctor because he is ill, no one doubts that the doctor must exercise reasonable care and skill in his treatment of him: and that is so whether the doctor is paid for his services or not. But, if the doctor is unable to treat the man himself and sends him to hospital, are not the hospital authorities then under a duty of care in their treatment of him? I think they are.

> In my opinion, authorities who run a hospital, be they local authorities, government boards, or any other corporation, are in law under the selfsame duty as the humblest doctor; whenever they accept a patient for treatment, they must use reasonable care and skill to cure him of his ailment. The hospital authorities cannot, of course, do it by themselves: they have no ears to listen through the stethoscope, and no hands to hold the surgeon's knife. They must do it by the staff which they employ: and if their staff are negligent in giving the treatment, they are just as liable for their negligence as is anyone else who employs others to do his duties for him. What possible difference in law, I ask, can there be between hospital authorities who accept a patient for treatment, and railway or shipping authorities who accept a passenger for carriage? None whatever. Once they undertake the task, they come under a duty to use care in the doing of it, and that is so whether they do it for reward or not.

> It is no answer for them to say that their staff is of professional men and women who do not tolerate any interference by their lay masters in the way they do their work. The doctor who treats a patient in the Walton Hospital can say equally with the ship's captain who sails his ship from Liverpool, and with the crane driver, who works his crane in the docks, "I take no orders from anybody". That "sturdy answer", as Lord Simonds described it, only means in each case that he is a skilled man who knows his work and will carry it out in his own way; but it does not mean that the authorities who employ him are not liable for his negligence. .... The reason why the employers are liable in such cases is not because they can control the way in which the work is done - they often have not sufficient knowledge to do so - but because they employ the staff and have chosen them for the task and have in their hands the ultimate sanction for good conduct, the power of dismissal". (1951 2 KB 3453).

On the question of evidence, this is what Lord Denning said in his characteristic style:

> If the plaintiff had to prove that some particular doctor or nurse was negligent, he would not be able to do it. But if he was put to that impossible task: he says, "I went into the hospital to be cured of two stiff fingers. I have come out with four stiff fingers, and my hand is useless. That should not have happened if due care

had been used. Explain it, if you can". I am quite clearly of opinion that that raises a prima facie *case against the hospital authorities.... They have nowhere explained how it could happen without negligence. They have busied themselves in saying that this or that member of their staff was not negligent. But they have called not a single person to say that the injuries were consistent with due care on the part of all the members of their staff. They called some of the people who actually treated the man, each of whom protested that he was careful in his part; but they did not call any expert at all, to say that this might happen despite all care. They have not therefore displaced the prima facie case against them and are liable to damages to the plaintiff.*

The only difference under consumer jurisprudence is that the doctors and the hospitals which tender totally free service to all the patients are exempt from the jurisdiction of Consumer Fora. But it does not mean that the party cannot approach the Civil Court or the High Court.

Costs

Coming to the aspect of costs, it is commented that the treatment in corporate hospitals is very high. Of course, we cannot overlook the high price of modern equipment and the use of other infrastructure in these hospitals. But at the same time, the feeling of a common patient is that he is fleeced. They attribute unnecessary reference to clinical tests for the sake of commission and over drugging for encouraging their favorite pharmaceutical concern. It is for the medical profession to strip itself of this criticism by evolving suitable code of conduct or norm by arranging vigilance and appropriate methods to identify such bad elements in the profession to get them de-registered. The consumer has got right to have the goods or services at competitive price and has a right to choice. Associations of medical practitioners or hospitals should strive to bring down the cost to the lowest. Even if the doctors maintain high standards and norms, the result of the patient depends on other factors also such as quality of service provided by nursing staff and the clinical labs attached to the hospital. It is commented that several hospitals are run with unqualified nurses or student nurses and clinical jobs are carried out without full time pathologists or well-qualified technicians. If the state does not effectively check and implement the standards for these two wings of medical care, the associations of doctors, nurses and technicians should evolve a code of ethics.

Another important factor in medical care is the environment in the hospital *i.e.,* infection level. It is reported that the mortality rate and inflectional level for various hospital is regularly monitored and published in the U.S. We do not seem to have any such practice inspite of the fact that the cases of hospital infection in India are much more than in U.S. Right to informed choice of a patient will be effectively exercised only if such practice is adopted in India also.

The exorbitant costs are another disturbing feature. It is for the medical profession to evolve the methods and bring down the costs of medical treatments.

The consumer/patient has a right to be informed about the progress of treatment and the full details of treatment given to him at the time of discharge.

He should be able to exercise his choice during the course of treatment itself whether to continue the treatment with the same doctor/hospital or to go to another, depending upon the progress of the treatment. It is necessary that the hospitals should maintain full, accurate case records, provide access of the same and copy of the full report at the time of discharge on payment of charges.

As in U.S., it is desirable that the Government and the managements of private hospitals formulate standards in support of patient's safety, medical/health care and error reduction.

Finally, it is not only desirable to restore to mutual trust between the doctor and the patient but also to provide the best possible treatment at lowest possible cost.

ಐ೮೮ಐ೮೮ಐ

LIFE AND LIBERTY OF A CITIZEN

The expression 'Human Rights' means the right relating to life, liberty, equality and dignity of the individual, guaranteed by the Constitution or embodied in International Covenants, enforceable by the Courts in India.

The concept of human right is involved almost in every aspect of the life. The framers of our Constitution have made in-depth study before framing the Constitution and incorporated Articles 21 and 22, guaranteeing life and liberty to every individual and prohibiting arbitrary arrest. If any person is arrested, he has to be produced before the Court within twenty-four hours of his arrest. The methodology and the ways and means of the investigation introduced by the Colonial Rulers is being continued by the police. The custodial torture and the custodial deaths are increasing day by day in the country. Therefore, the protection of Human Rights Act, 1993 was enacted to provide for the constitution of a National Human Rights Commission, State Human Rights Commissions in States and Human Rights Court for better protection of human rights and for matters connected therewith or incidental thereto.

As the increased instances of custodial torture and death have assumed alarming proportions, the credibility of Rule of Law and the administration of criminal justice system are being affected. The Apex Court, therefore, has been reminding every time that the custodial torture is a naked violation of human dignity and degradation which destroys the individual personality to a very large extent. It has also observed that it is a calculated assault on human dignity and whenever human dignity is wounded, the civilization takes a step backward - flag of humanity must on each such occasion fly half-mast. Custodial torture not only involves infliction of bodily pain but also the mental agony, which a person undergoes within the four walls of police station or lock-up. The extent of trauma, which a person experiences is beyond the purview of law in case of either physical assault or rape in police custody.

It is also noteworthy that the police in this country have to perform a difficult and delicate task, particularly in view of the deteriorating law and order

---

Speech delivered at 'Inauguration of Human Rights Committee', Hyderabad a 14th October, 2002.

situation, communal riots, political turmoil, student unrest, terrorist activities and the increasing underworld and armed gangs of criminals. The terrorists, drug peddlers and smugglers, who have organized gangs, have taken strong roots in the society. Therefore, the police have to be tough in controlling crime by preventing commission of crime and bringing the culprits before the courts for prosecuting them. In doing so, they have to adopt a balanced approach to deal with the situation, which is essential to meet the ends of justice and in view of the expectation of the society that the police must deal with the criminals in an efficient and effective manner for the purpose of controlling crime. Therefore, the police have to maintain balance between fundamental rights, guaranteed to the citizens and the societal requirements of the crime control.

The Universal Declaration of Human Rights in 1948 which marked the emergence of a worldwide trend of protection and guarantee of certain basic human rights, stipulates in Article 5 that no one shall be subjected to torture or to cruel, inhuman or degrading treatment or punishment. Despite the said declaration, the crime continues unabated, though every civilized nation shows its concern and takes steps for its eradication. This declaration is the starting point to remind the society, all over the globe, that liberty and dignity of the individual as a person, is supreme, subject to the reasonable restrictions imposed by the respective Constitutions or laws of the countries. There is obligation on the State machinery, which looks after crime control, to act effectively in consonance with the constitutional scheme and societal requirements by democratizing its process of investigation in scientific manner, leaving aside the obsolete methods of torture under colonial rule. Considering the importance of the issue regarding deaths in police lock-ups and custody, the Supreme Court in *D.K. Basu* v. *State of W.B.*, AIR 1997 SC 610 laid down eleven requirements to be followed by the law enforcing agencies in all cases of arrest or detention till legal provisions are made in that behalf as preventive measures. When it was brought to the notice of the Supreme Court, the Supreme Court gave directions to appoint sub-committees by the Human Rights Commissions of the State where there are Human Rights Commissions and where there are no Human Rights commissions, the Chief Justices were asked to appoint the Committees.

In pursuance of the said direction, I recommended for the appointment of the Committee consisting of Hon'ble Sri Justice Y. Bhaskar Rao, as Chairman, Hon'ble Sri Justice A.Hanumanthu, and Sri. N. Subba Raju, as Members. Justice Bhaskar Rao, former Chief Justice, is known for his intelligence, administrative ability and human approach. Likewise, Hon'ble Sri Justice A. Hanumanthu and Shri. N. Subba Raju have been known for their competence and have proved themselves to be the best Judges of their days.

I would also like to thank also Hon'ble Chief Minister N. Chandra Babu Naidu for his ready response for constituting this Human Rights Committee in the State of Andhra Pradesh.

With my experience during my stay in the State, I could say that the police is doing good work and I hope that they will continue their good work for the welfare of the State. But, at the same time, they should see that the rights of the citizens, guaranteed by the Constitution are not violated by their actions or inactions. While dealing with the criminals or people approaching them for redressal of their grievances, they should be very cautious that their fundamental rights are not violated in any form by their actions and they should always keep in mind the various instructions and observations made by the Apex Court in cases arising out of violation of human rights. Now that a Human Rights Committee has been constituted in the State, the Committee will monitor the situation in the State and examine cases where violations of human rights are complained and aid protection of human rights by the police.

The Supreme Court has evolved eleven requirements to be followed by the law enforcing agencies in all the cases of arrest or detention. I have no manner of doubt whatsoever that the Committee will do its best to see that the eleven guidelines are followed in letter and spirit and guide the police administration in the State so that life and liberty of the citizen is protected as echoed by the Supreme Court.

ಬ೦ಬ೦ಬ೦

HUMAN RIGHTS AND POVERTY

The United Nations Committee on Economic, Social and Cultural Rights defines poverty as a human condition, characterized by sustained or chronic deprivation of the resources, capabilities, choices, security and power, necessary for the enjoyment of an adequate standard of living and other civil, cultural, economic, political and social rights. Poverty has been and remains a constructed social and economic reality. The poor are not poor simply because they are less human or because they are physiologically or mentally inferior to others whose conditions are better off. On the contrary, their poverty is often a direct or indirect consequence of society's failure to establish equity and fairness as the basis of its social and economic relations.

Every man and woman has the human right to a standard of living, adequate health and well-being, to food, clothing, housing, medical care and social services. These fundamental human rights are defined in our Constitution. In the Universal Declaration of Human Rights, 1948, the General Assembly proclaimed the Universal Declaration of Human Rights as a common standard of achievement for all people and all nations. Article 1 of the General Assembly proclaims thus:—

> "All human beings are born free and equal in dignity and rights. They are endowed with reason and conscience and should act towards one another in spirit of brotherhood."

The human right to live in dignity, free from want, is itself a fundamental right, and is also essential to the realization of all other human rights — rights that are universal, indivisible, interconnected and interdependent. The right to be free from poverty includes the human right to an adequate standard of living. Poverty is a human rights violation. The right to be free from poverty includes:

The human right to an adequate standard of living.

The human right to work and receive wages that contribute to an adequate standard of living.

The human right to a healthy and safe environment.

The human right to live in adequate housing.

An Article on Human Rights and Poverty.

The human right to be free from hunger.

The human right to safe drinking water.

The human right to primary health care and medical attention in case of illness.

The human right to have access to basic social services.

The human right to education.

The human right to be free of gender or racial discrimination.

The human right to participate in shaping decisions that affect oneself and one's community.

The human right for children to develop in an environment appropriate for their physical, mental, spiritual, moral and social development.

The Supreme Court of India has considered these aspects in many judgments, rendered in recognition of the human right on poverty.

The landmark judgment of the Supreme Court [*Jolly George Varghese* v. *Bank of Cochin*, AIR 1980 SC 470: (1980) 2 SCC 360: (1980) 2 SCR 913] on the subject was rendered by his lordship Justice Sri. V.R. Krishna Iyer. The question of putting a person in prison in execution of a money decree, who does not have the necessary means to pay the debt, has been considered by the Court. The court while dealing with the issue has adopted that Sec. 51 of the CPC has the flavor of Art. 11 of the Human Rights Covenants. The court has held that a simple default to discharge is not enough to detain a person in prison. "*There must be some element of bad faith beyond mere indifference to pay, some deliberate of recusant disposition in the past or alternatively, current means to pay the decree or a substantial part of it.*" The court stressed the need to help the debtors who are in distress because of the blanket restraint of their properties.

In *People's Union for Democratic Rights* v. *Union of India*, (1982) 2 SCC 494, public interest litigation, which is a strategic arm of the legal aid movement and which is intended to bring justice within the reach of the poor masses who constitute the low visibility area of humanity, is a totally different kind of litigation from the ordinary traditional litigation which is essentially of an adversary character where there is a dispute between two litigating parties, one making claim or seeking relief against the other and the other opposing such claim or resisting such relief. Public interest litigation is brought before the court not for the purpose of enforcing the right of one individual against another as happens in the case of ordinary litigation, but it is intended to promote and vindicate public interest which demands that violations of constitutional or legal rights of large numbers of people who are poor, ignorant or in a socially or economically disadvantageous position should not go unnoticed and unredressed. The poor too have civil and political rights and the rule of law is meant for them also, though today it exists only on paper and not in reality.

The poor working in quarries were put to distress due to the inhuman conditions. Taking cognizance of the issue, Supreme Court directed the State Government to exercise proper control and to act as a welfare state and to see that workers whether the continued to work with improved conditions. In

Bandhua Mukti Morcha v. *Union of India*, AIR 1984 SC 802: (1984) 3 SCC 161: (1984) 2 SCR 67, Hon'ble Justice Sri P.N. Bhagwati, speaking for the bench has widened the scope of public interest litigation. According to the court, public interest litigation is not in the nature of adversary litigation but it is a challenge and an opportunity to the Government and its officers to make basic human rights meaningful to the deprived and vulnerable sections of the community and to assure them social and economic justice.

Though the Constitution of India, through Art. 24, prohibits the employment of the children below the age of 14 years in any factory, or mine or in any hazardous employment, it is a hard reality that, due to poverty, a child is driven to such employment. Court has found that several enactments intended to prohibit the employment of children have failed in implementation. While considering these aspects, the Hon'ble Supreme Court in *Bandhua Mukti Morcha* v. *Union of India*, AIR 1997 SC 2218: (1997) 10 SCC 549: (1997) Lab IC 1209 reiterated the implementation of its speedy implementation.

Conceptually, the *parens patriae* is the theory of obligation of the State to protect and take into custody the rights and privileges of its citizens for discharging its obligations. The Constitution makes it imperative for the State to secure to its citizens rights guaranteed by Constitution and where the citizens are not in a position to assert and claim their rights, the State can be activated and approached to effectively come upon the scene and protect the human rights of victims of a disaster.

A newspaper carried a report about the non-payment of wages to a large number of people in a factory. The report also indicated that several employees died due to starvation or committed suicide owing to financial crisis. A writ petition was filed by the lawyer on the basis of the said news. In *Kapila Hingorani* v. *State of Bihar*, (2003) 6 SCC 1, the Supreme Court interfered with the matter in public interest and held that there is failure to perform the constitutional duties by the State in controlling the functions of the public sector companies. In such circumstances, the court would not hesitate to lift the corporate veil when corporate personality is found to be opposed to justice, convenience and interest of revenue or workman or against public interest.

To help the poor litigants, the Supreme Court has evolved the concept of Free Legal Aid. Even Senior Counsel should volunteer to defend the indigent accused. Accepting Art. 39A of the Constitution and the Universal declaration of Human rights, Supreme Court had held that it is the duty of the State to provide *amicus curiae* to defend the indigent accused. Otherwise, he would be meted out with unequal defense. If as a common knowledge, the youngster from the Bar who has either a little experience or no experience is assigned to defend him, it is high time that senior counsels practicing in the Court concerned, volunteered to defend such indigent accused as a part of their professional duty, Supreme Court added [In *Kishore Chand* v. *State of Himachal Pradesh*, AIR 1990 SC 2140: (1991) 1 SCC 286: 1990 Supp (1) SCR 518].

The Supreme Court has again reiterated the constitutional right to life guaranteed to ensure the equality of the "weaker segments of society", and found that meeting basic needs is indispensable to the development of individuals. The court declared that the basic needs of man have traditionally been accepted to be three—food, clothing and shelter. The right to life is guaranteed in any civilized society. That would take within its sweep the right to food, right to clothing, the right to a decent environment and a reasonable accommodation to live in. The difference between the need of an animal and the human being for shelter has to be kept in view. For the animal, it is the bare protection of body; for the human being, it has to be a suitable accommodation that would allow him to grow in every aspect physical, mental and intellectual. The Constitution aims at ensuring fuller development of every child.

There are numerous judgments of the Supreme Court where the court has helped the poor. The very recent case is the famous Best Bakery case, when a lot of poor people who have been denied justice, Supreme Court came to their rescue helped them and removed all technical objections.

Poverty is indisputably the most potent violation of all human rights, and constitutes a threat to the survival of the greatest numbers of the human population. As poverty has intensified in both rich and poor nations alike, the view of poverty as a human rights and social justice issue has gained increased recognition. The United Nations General Assembly (UNGA) has resolved that extreme poverty and exclusion from society constituted a violation of human dignity.

The speech made by His Excellency The President of India, Dr. A.P.J. Abdul Kalam at the Human Rights Day function held at Vigyan Bhavan, New Delhi, on 10th December, 2002 stresses the need for the removal of Poverty through vision for the nation. His Excellency has stated that:

> *"People, who are economically or socially in the lower strata, are vulnerable to human rights exploitation by those who are in the higher strata. One way to reduce this exploitation is to narrow this divide. In our country, about 300 million people are below the poverty line. After five decades of progress, the aspirations of people are rightly mounting that India should become a developed country. This is the second vision for the nation."*

In safeguarding, human rights Judiciary is the guardian of our Constitution. Wherever life exists in our planet, no life can be allowed to be devalued by anybody. The system cannot be a mute witness to this inhuman act.

In the Human Rights Day Message, this year, the UN Secretary General, Mr. Kofi Annan has re-emphasized the commitment to the rule of law. He said:

> *"... we must be guided by one clear principle beyond any other: respect for the international rule of law."*

> *which*

> *"... is the most effective tool to fight criminality and terrorism, and the best guarantee of safety, security and freedom for us all."*

The President, Mr. Zail Singh, had suggested that no person in the country should be allowed to have more than one house, as a measure of reducing economic disparities and ensuring proper distribution of prosperity.

Inaugurating a rural housing colony at Ragannaguda village, in the Hayatnagar Mandal of Ranga Reddi district, 25 km. from Hyderabad, he pointed out that some people had a number of houses at different places—in their city, district headquarters, in Delhi, as also at summer and winter resorts. This was unfair. Permitting one house per person, the extra houses could be given to the needy who should be facilitated to pay for them in instalments.

The President, Mr. Zail Singh regretted that nearly four decades after independence, the rich-poor disparities still existed in the country, with about 36 per cent of the population living below the poverty line. The rich had been getting richer and the poor poorer.

The Centre and the State Governments, he said, should ensure that the fruits of their planned development reached the poor. They should strive to reduce the disparities between the rich and the poor. If the disparities continued, he warned, they could lead to 'unrest'. (THE HINDU, Dated 4-1-1987)

"The abolishing of slums is perfectly feasible and the accommodation of everyone is reasonably possible provided we have a political and economic zest. The human resources of these millions in search of accommodation may be fully utilized in the very construction of homesteads. So also the Land Reform Laws and the Urban Ceiling Legislations, if implemented *bona fide*, may yield enough surpluses for housing to every Indian. China has done it. The Soviets have done it. Cuba has done it. Even Kampuchea and Vietnam are doing it. The moneyocracy of India may not permit it and the elite economists and the high-tech strategists and their political comparators will undermine the Constitution from within. This perspective drives us to a re-examination of its mandates."

"Equal protection of the laws is not a formal declaration but a dynamic actualization. So, to create conditions of life where social and economic disabilities do not deny equal justice in the enjoyment of basic facilities is the task of the legal system. Articles 14, 15 and 39A, read together, mean nothing less, nothing else. The right to life, preserved in Article 21, has the same broad élan, viewed in the benign light of the Preamble which assures to all citizens liberty, equal opportunity, fraternity and the dignity of the individual. There is need to brain-scan Article 21 because judicial illusion raises false expectation and the Court, viewed as a whole, being stuffed with artists of the Establishment, may give a jolt when the right to life is pressed, seriously, disturbing the status quo conscience of the robed brethren. Article 21 which has incarnated as the last hope of the least and the lost of our countrymen, is a proud heritage of the judicial revolution, mid wifed by the Supreme Court in all innocence. The provision may first be read here:

"Article 21 – Protection of life and personal liberty – No person shall be deprived of his life or personal liberty except according to procedure established by law."

"Its anatomy is in two parts. First, a basic assumption that everyone has a right to life and personal liberty, too fundamental to be negotiable if our democratic order is not but a legal bubble. Second, this basic postulate of liberty may be truncated or annihilated if the power to do so is duly legislated. Two inevitable issues then arise. What is life and liberty? Next, can a cannibal legislation do away with life or personal liberty regardless of humanism and realism?"

"What is guaranteed by this fundamental right is not mere animal existence nor vegetable survival but rightful opportunity to unfold the human potential and share in the joy of creative living." [Law and the Urban Poor in India – Justice V.R. Krishna Iyer, 1988]

In fact, what is said in the Universal Declaration of Human Rights is derived from the Rig Veda "It is the duty of every man not to inflict suffering and misery on a fellow being and it is the right of every human being to be happy.

ಐ಑ಐ಑ಐ಑

NO COUNTRY IS AN ISLAND IN THE VAST OCEAN OF HUMANITY

The decade in which India gained its independence was marred with the bloodiest war, the world had seen since the advent of civilization. It was a period of complete mistrust and disharmony. Alliances were being formed between the erstwhile allies of the Second World War. But they were alliances, which were polarizing the World and creating a chasm, which was never seen before. Having gained independence, one of the greatest challenges faced by our country was to preserve our sovereignty at any cost. Yet, at the same time, it was the need of the hour to embrace the new world order which was sought to be based on social and economic progress by fostering co-operation and recognizing the mutual rights and liabilities of each country.

No country can survive as an island in this vast ocean of humanity. A web of unseen bridges joins all the nations into a global village. Just like the traffic on any road, there are certain rules and regulations, which have to be followed on these bridges to avoid any mishap. International law and International Conventions lay down these rules and regulations for a smooth flow of traffic. International law and International Conventions are themselves a quintessence of the desire of the people of the world to live in peace and harmony.

The founding fathers, incorporated into the Constitution, the aspirations of the people of the country to consolidate peace and security in the world and for paving the way for the establishment of a just social order. In 1949, Pandit Jawaharlal Nehru addressed the U.S. Congress and said that the objectives of the foreign policies of the new nation would be preservation of the world peace and enlargement of human freedom. Thereafter, he evolved the principle of Panchsheel, the five principles of harmonious co-existence of nations for establishing lasting peace on earth.

Before India became independent, the Indian Courts, under British rule administered the English Common law. They accepted the basic principles governing the relationship between international law and municipal law under the common law doctrine. Under the English Common law doctrine, rules of

---

Delivered at Lucknow to the Chief Justices of and other eminent Jurists of the World on 11th February, 2003.

international law, in general, were not accepted as part of municipal law. If, however, there was no conflict between these rules and the rules of municipal law, international law was accepted in municipal law without any incorporation.

Keeping in view the aspirations of the people of the country to consolidate peace and security in the world, the founding fathers incorporated into the Constitution, Article 51 of the Indian Constitution, which directs the State to:—

(a) promote international peace and security;

(b) maintain just and honourable relations between nations;

(c) foster respect for international law and treaty obligations in the dealings of organized people with one another; and

(d) encourage settlement of international disputes by arbitration for paving the way for the establishment of a just social order.

Leaving a little confusion, this provision differentiates between international law and treaty obligations. It is however, interpreted and understood that "international law" represents international customary law and "treaty obligations" represent international conventional law.

Article 51 as well as other Articles of the Directive Principles are considered, by well-known Jurists, to be of no potency and that they were only mere platitudes. They did not reckon with the pro-activism of the Indian Judiciary.

Prof. Weir, in his thesis "India's new Constitution Analysed", said:

"As these principles cannot be enforced in any Court, they amount to a little more than a manifesto of aims and aspirations."

Sir Ivor Jennings, in an article in the Hindu, a daily newspaper, about the Directive Principles, said:

"They can be used for the purpose of political and private criticism but they confer no legal rights and create no legal remedy......it all reads like, and is, a political manifesto."

It is a general criticism that since Article 51(c) is placed under the Directive Principles of State Policy in Part IV of the Indian Constitution; it means it is not an enforceable provision. Since the principle laid down in Article 51 is not enforceable and India has merely to endeavor to foster respect for international law, this Article would mean *prima facie* that international law is not incorporated into the Indian Municipal Law, which is binding and enforceable. However, when Article 51(c) is read in the light of judicial opinion and foreign policy statements, it suggests otherwise.

One such landmark judgment is of the Supreme Court of India which has dealt with the applicability of international conventions to the country; the Apex Court in the case of *Vishaka* v. *State of Rajasthan*, AIR 1997 SC 3011: (1997) 6 SCC 241 held:

"In the absence of domestic law occupying the field, to formulate effective measures to check the evil of sexual harassment of working women at all workplaces, the contents of international conventions and norms are significant for the purpose of interpretation of the guarantee of gender equality, right to work

with human dignity in Articles 14, 15, 19(1)(g) and 21 of the Constitution and the safeguards against sexual harassment implicit therein."

"...Any international convention not inconsistent with the fundamental rights and in harmony with its spirit must be read into these provisions to enlarge the meaning and content thereof, to promote the object of the constitutional guarantee......regard must be had to international conventions and norms for construing domestic law when there is no inconsistency between them and there is a void in the domestic law".

Similarly in a string of landmark judgments, the Supreme Court has read the provisions of various International Conventions into Article 21 and the other Articles relating to Fundamental Rights. It would, therefore, appear that using Article 51 as a tool in its hands, the Supreme Court has been able to inject into Part III of the Constitution, the vast number of rights flowing from the United Nations Charter, from the various conventions ratified by India and, in particular, the International Conventions on Civil and Political Rights, 1966 and the Convention on the Elimination of All Forms of Discrimination Against Women, 1979.

It is often said that, judicial activism in this field cuts into the prerogative of the Parliament to make laws and to the extent to which Article 51 should be implemented, by enacting laws for achieving objects of an international convention, is within the realm of Parliament's legislative competence, under the Constitution. But the Courts, utilizing international conventions for interpreting the different provisions of the Constitution and implementing them *de hors*, such provisions could be criticized as encroaching upon the power given to the Parliament under Article 253 of the Constitution.

In *S.R. Bommai v. Union of India*, AIR 1994 SC 1918: (1994) 3 SCC 1, the Supreme Court of India rejected any such approach and said that for the present, it would suffice it to state that the provisions of the covenant, which elucidate and go to effectuate the fundamental rights guaranteed by our Constitution, can certainly be relied upon by Courts as facets of those fundamental rights and hence, enforceable as such. The Supreme Court of India has a self imposed restraint when it is faced with a situation where it has to balance between the interpretation of the Constitution in such a way that the lacunae in the municipal laws can be filled without overstepping its limit, in its zeal of judicial activism.

Article 51(c) embodies the dream of the founding fathers of our Constitution, who wanted peace and harmony in the world. They were keen to incorporate whatever was the best in the interest of our nation. At the same time, they also had to safeguard against the over enthusiasm of the legislature, lest in their zeal they compromise on the basic integrity of our country and incorporate or ratify conventions which we neither need nor can afford due to the complex and intricate character of our nation. Therefore, the Constitution envisages a goal for the legislature in the form of Directive Principles. Article 51(c) is one such goal and the tool to fulfil this goal is in the form of enabling power of the Parliament, under Article 253 read with Entry 14 of the Union List in Seventh Schedule of the Constitution.

People's Union for Civil Liberties v. *Union of India*, AIR 1997 SC 568: (1997) 1 SCC 301, referred to Article 17 of the International Covenant on Civil and Political Rights, 1966 and Article 12 of the Universal Declaration of Human Rights, 1948, so as to derive from Article 21, a right to privacy in India. The Court observed in this connection:

> "*International law today is not confined to regulating the relations between the States. Scope continues to extend. Today matters of social concern, such as health education and economics apart from human rights fall within the ambit of International Regulations. International law is more than ever aimed at individuals. It is almost an accepted proposition of law that the Rules of customary international law which are not contrary to the municipal law shall be deemed to be incorporated in the domestic law.*"

All these would indicate the pre-eminent position that Article 51 of the Constitution enjoys in this country, fostering respect for international laws and treaty obligations with one another. This has resulted in international law being injected into the domestic law with the Constitution being classified as municipal law for this purpose. As a result, through a very pro-active judiciary which has utilized interpretative skill by utilizing the provisions of Article 51 for extending vast rights and expanding the existing rights, by giving effect to International Conventions which it has ratified, though no municipal law has been enacted to implement these treaties.

The demand for a world Parliament has often been raised, at different forums for achieving peace and harmony in the world. This, however, is not the solution to the existing problems in the world. We have sufficient provisions in our respective Constitutions to achieve the peace and harmony which has been deluding us since time immemorial. What is actually needed is the spirit of harmony and mutual respect for each others rights and duties. If we are ever to achieve that state of complete harmony as in the fables, we have to rise above the petty issues, which have been dividing us. In conclusion, I would like to quote the words of former President of India – Dr. Radhakrishnan *"The World has got together as a body: it is groping for a soul."*

ಐಐಐಐ

Part IV

Gender Justice

STATUS OF WOMEN IN INDIA

The year 1999, marked the Golden Jubilee of Indian Council of Social Welfare which was founded by Mrs. Mary Clubwala Jadhav in 1949. It was the Indian Council of Social Welfare that founded the Madras School of Social work in 1952 through the good offices of Mrs. Mary Clubwala Jadhav, who was also the founder of Madras School of Social work.

During national struggle for independence, Mrs. Jadhav progressively indianised the guild of service. It was her vision that led to the setting up of surrogate home for orphaned, destitute, children coming from economically weaker sections of society. It was through her tireless efforts that she founded the Indian conference of social work in Madras now known as Indian Council of Social Welfare. She was the founder Hon. Secretary of Madras School of Social Work which has now grown into a premier institute of social work in the country. Her death in 1975 left a vacuum in the field of voluntary social work in Tamil Nadu and in India.

Considering the fierceful and vibrant battle, let loose by the fairer sex against men to fight gender inequality, male dominance and discrimination.

In ancient India, women had enjoyed equal status and equal rights with men. But they lost all their freedom during the Mughal period. Now with the advent of the modern era, women have proved that both in efficiency and intellect they are at par with men. Many avenues and opportunities are available to women with the advent of the Industrial Revolution. In every field, women are competing with men. But due to casteism, illiteracy, outdated customs and tradition, the full potential of Indian women could not be gauged and recognised.

Due to their vulnerability and lack of opportunities, women of our country still are considered as belonging to the group of 'backward classes'. Constitution of India, though ensured gender equality through Article 14, a special provision by way of Article 15 had to be enacted to treat women as a 'special category' so as to create variety of opportunities and avenues for women to utilise their abilities.

Apart from the Constitutional guarantees, various statutes were enacted to protect the rights of women. Statutory Commissions like the – National and State

---

Speech delivered on the occasion of Mary Clubwala Jadhav Fourth Memorial Endowment Lecture on 'Status of Women in India' at Chennai on 6th February, 1999.

Women's Commissions – are constituted under the National Women's Commission Act, 1990. But inspite of the various protective laws, we keep on hearing instances of sexual harassment, exploitation and oppression of women.

In this context, it is heartening to note that judiciary had always taken a strong stand whenever it came to cases of sexual exploitation and harassment of women.

In *Vishaka* v. *Rajasthan*, AIR 1997 SC 3011: (1997) 6 SCC 241 our Supreme court had held strongly against sexual harassment in working places. Recently, the Supreme court, in a case headed by the Hon'ble Chief Justice of India, Dr. A.S. Anand, had raised the right against sexual harassment to the level of Fundamental Right. But the stark reality is that inspite of statutory provisions and strong judicial reprimand, the sexual harassment and exploitation continue unabated. It is a pity that women who constitute 50% of our population have to lead a life of insecurity and oppression.

The only panacea to liberate women from the clutches of harassment and exploitation is empowering them so as to create a congenial atmosphere to develop and progress. In this connection, we have to adhere to the suggestion put forth by no less a man than Nobel Laureate, Amartya Sen, that unless women are empowered, issues like health, illiteracy, population will remain problems for ever in countries like India.

Women of India are the most unrepresented sections in the present political system. Their representation has never exceeded 8% in Parliament and 10% in State Assemblies. On the Executive side, only 5.8% of senior management and administration posts are occupied by women.

In Judiciary, only 3% of the Judges are women. In the 12th Lok Sabha, there were only 43 women MPs and 19 in Rajya Sabha. These figures are quite disheartening. Though Women's Reservation Bill, providing for 33% reservation for women in legislatures was introduced after much difficulty, the Bill could not be passed. Unless women are educated and made to shed off their inhibitions, this state-of-affairs will continue.

State Governments and the Department of Public Grievances in the Government of India should set up special cells for the enforcement of laws to ensure women's right and protection. A special division under a Commissioner for Women's rights may be created in the nodal department to liaise with such special cells.

Women's guidance centres in every district should be organised by voluntary organisations with qualified social workers, lawyers, doctors and family counsellors. Free legal aid services should be initiated wherever possible.

Larger number of women Judges must be appointed to judiciary and more so in the family courts.

I conclude with a hope that the women in our country will realise their true potential and assume positions of high authority.

ಏಲಾಲ

WOMENS' EDUCATION

It gives me great pleasure to inaugurate the "College Students' Union" in the august presence of my Reveared Brother Judge. Hon'ble Mr. Justice S. Natarajan. There is no denying the fact that the students of your college are wonderful and unique. Your college union is ably piloted by your President assisted by Vice President, working in Unison with General Secretary and Treasurers. I am told that the students have contributed richly to the College and to you all my dear students, my sincere congratulations, appreciation and Good Wishes from the judiciary.

This august institution was started under the dynamic guard and patronage of late Shri V.L. Ethiraj. He has rendered yeoman service for the cause of education in general and women's education in particular. The college is a standing monument for the dynamic leadership qualities of Shri V.L. Ethiraj.

Despite the fact that women constitute almost half of human population, their importance as individuals has never been recognised in the social and economic scenario. Traditional women had been confined to four walls of the house, children, household and family rituals and thus remain 'invisible'.

The International Labour Organisation in its report submitted in 1982 had reported that women, who constitute 50% of the world population, contribute 23rd of world's work hour and receive 10% of world's income and own less than 1% of the world's property, all because of sheer accident of birth. But, there has been rapid change in the modern times and national leaders have been advocating and concentrating on women's education.

The Father of our nation has said that 'If a man is educated, an individual is educated, but, if a woman is educated, the entire family is educated'. Our great poet, Subramania Bharathi, has said that of all charitable activities, imparting knowledge to the poor is glorious. These are his words in his inimitable style.

"It is for better and noble to educate a poor man than building thousand temples and choultries of more numbers".

This institution has grown from strength to strength and has established high academic achievements and eminence in co-curricular activities, thanks to the

---

Speech delivered on the "Inauguration of the College Students' of Ethiraj College Union", Chennai.

efforts of teaching staff and the committee of management headed by Hon'ble Mr. Justice Natarajan. Twenty-first century is going to usher in a new era in which women are going to take great part in the economic activities.

The union of students has got useful and constructive role to play in improving the educational levels and standards of students.

The students' union, can play a dominant role in ensuring that the students get the best all-round education so as to shape and mould them as better and useful citizens of our nation.

The students are requested not to drift from the rich heritage and traditional and moral values. One must develop humility, patience, intelligence, initiative and modesty.

Institutions grow like Banyan trees, but their success depends on the way the objectives of the institutions are realised and sustained. It is a matter of great mental satisfaction that the institution, started under the dynamic name of late Sri V.L. Ethiraj, is now administered by a team headed by Hon'ble Mr. Justice S. Natarajan. Justice S. Natarajan has been rendering service for the cause of education in general and women's education in particular.

Let's hope and aspire that this banyan tree spreads far and deep and extends charity to the deserving, in the coming years.

The exemplary way in which Mr. Justice – S. Natarajan and his team is running the institution would really attract anybody towards this institution. His deep sense of involvement in women's education has no parallel. The Ethiraj College, which is occupying a unique place in the cause of women's education, is a standing example in the city of Madras. It is my earnest desire and appeal to Hon'ble Mr. Justice S. Natarajan to start many more educational institutions and in particular a private Law College, which would cater exclusively to the needs of women students.

I am reminded of the words of Mahakavi Bharathiyar, who said:

When he was appealing for fund raising:

"Those flushed with funds pour forth gold to as those with lesser wealth gives as coins those who do not possess both, give us, at least words of support."

Since I belong to the last of the above categories, I can only give my words of encouragement and good wishes which I give them heartily in abundance.

To conclude let us recall, with reverence and gratitude, the vision of the far sighted and selfless founder Sri. V.L. Ethiraj. I request the students (the beneficiaries) of the priceless legacy to pledge themselves today to take this citadel of learning to glorious heights into 21st Century, striving for excellence, seeking true knowledge and finding a new consciousness without yielding to the vile and low.

ಐಐಐಐ

THE HEALING POWER

Paediatric Science has in recent times made extraordinary advances in responding to the desire of men and women to have children. Great unbelievable strides have been made particularly in the area of reproduction which has witnessed phenomenal revolution. Recent development in the area of development of reproductive technologies that allows reproduction without the usual traditional intercourse between partners is noteworthy. Couples who are unable to have children on their own are availing of the technique called "Assisted Reproductive Technologies" (ART). These techniques began in the Western countries as far back as 1960. Controversial technologies like the "Invitro Fertilization" (IVF) and "Cryopreservation ECG and Sperm Donation", "Surrogacy" and more recent "Cloning" are now being adopted in various countries. These developments are, no doubt, a great victory for modern medicine and huge relief for the couples who are not only childless but face the increasing difficulties and societal hostilities towards "Adoption". No doubt, these advances in Medicine have not been free from moral and legal difficulties, which has given rise to a plethora of medical and controversial legal questions.

Practice of the Art of Medicine necessitates one to acquire many qualities like Gentleness, Humility, Understanding, Compassion, Empathy, Foresight, Altruism and, of course, a Human Touch. It is needless to say that the most powerful drugs ever produced are "TWO KIND WORDS OF THE DOCTOR". It is the duty of the Doctor to instill courage into the minds of the suffering people. A survey done in Thailand showed that all kinds of Doctors, ranging from Quacks to the best trained Modern Medicine Practitioners, have been equally effective in society, since they have human qualities of "Head and Heart", required to encourage the patient's own "Healing power".

A Surgeon should play the role of a compassionate and kind-hearted human being behind the knife. Even in an emergency case, human compassion can do a lot to assist the protean machines which are frightening for the critically ill patient. Unfortunately, Medical Education of today does not lay much emphasis on the Art of Medicine and role of human aspect in the treatment of patients. It

Delivered at the 12th Dr. M.S. Ramakrishnan Memorial Endowment Oration on 4th May, 2003.

would be pertinent to mention here that the University of Brisbane in Australia, has made a beginning in recruiting students into Medical Schools after they have graduated in Arts, Music, Philosophy etc., and they have made a beginning in realizing the needs in the field of Medical Education. Best results can be achieved by patiently "Listening" to the patient and then making a complete physical examination. The art of Clinical Medicine is gradually dying in the present teaching set up with hi-tech gadgets.

In one of the meetings of the American Heart Association, the key note address was on "How to Auscultate the Heart". Many Cardiologists do not know the art of using a Stethoscope, which has both diagnostic and therapeutic roles to play. If one has to become a good Surgeon, one needs to be a good human being. The knife only cuts. The healing is done by the body's Immune System which can be better stimulated by a humane Surgeon. Prof. M.S. Ramakrishnan had human qualities in abundance which was the real secret of his success as a Paediatric Surgeon, besides being an excellent academician. He was a great visionist.

ಬಎಬಎಬಎ

PART V

LAW AND SCIENCE

PLASTIC SURGERY

It is great to know that the M.B.R. Medical Trust is doing yeoman and dedicated service to the ailing and suffering people and has made tremendous strides in the field of micro vascular surgery and plastic surgery. Success in any field of activity can be achieved only through hardwork, dedication and commitment. It is heartening to know that M.B.R. Trust is doing charitable activities by providing free treatment to the needy and the poor. Advanced medical treatment involves expenditure which is burdensome on the purse of the common man. I laud the services rendered by the M.B.R. Trust in repairing deformities and disfigurements and treatment of kidney diseases and orthopaedics to the poor patients and hope this will continue in the years to come.

The Trust was formed by a group of people who were interested in rendering services to ailing people. The Chief of Plastic Surgery unit is Dr. K.R. Rajappan, a qualified Plastic Surgeon with 32 years of experience in plastic surgery. After a vast experience in medical college service and as Chief Plastic surgeon in Kottayam Medical College, he organised the unit at Ernakulam with the help of other trustees and with a team of devoted specialists.

This Specialists' Hospital is doing free service to the tune of about Rs.20 to 25 lakhs, for the poor, every year. Other special service organisations like Lion's Club and other Charitable Organisations help co-ordinate the work of free service. Main work is confined to repair of deformities and disfigurements and replantations and treatment of kidney diseases and orthopaedics.

M.B.R. Medical trust used to send plastic surgeons to various centres in Kerala, from Payyanoor to Trivandrum to organise and do plastic re-constructive surgeries free of charges. During 1980, they performed 189 major operations of plastic re-constructive surgeries in different Hospitals, all over Kerala, and won the Lion's International Award for medical service.

I was invited to inaugurate the workshop on cosmetic Raino Plastery. The real interpretation of this term, Plastic Surgery, is reconstructive and reparative surgery to reconstruct and repair the defect of human body, whether it is from

---

Inaugural speech delivered on the seminar and workshop on 'Cosmetic Raino Plastry' conducted by M.B.R. Medical Trust, Cochin.

141

birth or acquired after birth as a result of injuries, accidents, diseases or operations. There were days when the efforts of the surgeons, to change the shape of body created by God was accused. A French Surgeon, Thangliacozzi, who was supposed to be a famous plastic reconstructive surgeon of those days, when died, was first buried in crematorium meant for gentlemen and later his body was exhumed from the burial ground and cremated in burial grounds kept for criminals and accused.

Now those days are gone and it is such a common branch of surgery in a developed country that some of the surgeons confine their work to one field alone for example repair of nose or lip or ear or breast.

I have been told that cosmetic branch of plastic surgery is supposed to be dear in developed countries. But the necessities of the developing countries is different from the developed countries. The cost of a cosmetic surgery in developed countries is not compatible with the cost of treatment in developing countries because of the low per capita income of the people.

The service of a doctor within our country, is a sacrifice. It is impossible for a doctor to charge heavily for the treatment of a patient inspite of all the adverse factors he faces in the society, as our culture and belief is different from that of the developed countries.

Plastic surgery, even after 32 years of its onset in Kerala, is in the infancy. This narrow speciality has created confusion and chaos among the public. The surmise that plastic surgery is a beautification treatment, still lingers in the mind of lay public. They come to you as if they are attending a beauty clinic but will be disappointed if beauty touch is not provided according to their imagination. Your touch with knife is sharper than they think and leaves a scar for them to remember throughout their life.

I am of the opinion that it is the mandatory duty on the part of a doctor to explain facts to the patients before treatment. A detailed counseling may make them aware of the possibilities and bring them out of the blind belief of imagination and ignorance.

Still there may be people whose minds are not cleared. Precipitated ideas stay back in the subconscious mind. These groups require psycho analysis before treatment especially when you plan cosmetic surgery.

We belong to a developing country where the cost of living is high and the per capita income is law and – common men live with difficulties. Do not forget these facts. Give due consideration to the have nots. When they need medical help, give them consideration, treat them on compassionate grounds behave gently and render them kindness. They will be happy – you will have peace and peace of mind and immense satisfaction.

I was told that the concept that plastic surgery is costly is not correct. It is as costly as any other surgery but there is one factor which influences this belief. Most of our countrymen find it difficult to spend time and money for a cause that deals with figure and not functional involvement of the body.

Today's global outlook for the coming century lists the growing gap in living standards between rich and the poor. Futurists cite the advent of faster and different communication system, new sources of energies and genetically based productions are already in progression and they will improve life in the coming century. We are moving towards a future that will be characterised at once by desperate needs and vast potential. To keep pace with the fast developing technological scenario is a real challenge, faced by professionals, especially by those in the medical filed. But the real challenge faced by the medical professionals in their pursuit for excellence is the erosion of values in the profession. The canker that eats upon the growth of the medical profession is the spirit of commercialism.

If medical profession is looked upon as a profession of dedicated service to the ailing and the suffering, the future of the profession will be well secured. Our country needs the services of the dedicated professionals, who have imbibed values in their practice. A medical professional has to update and equip himself with the necessary knowledge regarding medical advancements to serve efficiently. We have to stop the outflow of the rich and the affluent into developed countries for advanced treatment when the necessary infrastructure, technical know-how and the required potential are available in our country. Continuing professional development programmes, Seminars and workshops help, in a way, to augment one's knowledge and information.

I exhort the members of the medical profession to strive hard to maintain the public confidence in the medical system of our country. For this, one has to maintain a strong sense of identity, solidarity and commitment and build up a better public image through hard work and sense of values.

I hope that the members of the medical profession will rise to the occasion and meet the various challenges with vigour and a sense of commitment.

The challenge of the new millennium is the changing technological scenario. This will envelop the professionals of plastic surgeons also. They will have to keep pace with the fast developing technological arena.

ಋ ಋ ಋ

ORGAN DONATION

I deem it a privilege to be a part of this Symposium that deals with a subject, the importance of which cannot be gauged. I congratulate the organisers for their efforts to bring about awareness regarding organ donation among the masses— both rural and urban areas.

I am glad to note that K.G. Hospital has been rendering yeoman and dedicated service to the ailing and suffering and has made tremendous strides in the field of medicine and health. The growth of this hospital into a reputed health care centre, catering to every conceivable health problem has been phenomenal. Success in any field of activity can be achieved only through hard work, dedication and commitment. The contribution of Dr. Bakthavathsalam, the man behind the success of this institution, will remain as a mark in the annals of this hospital.

I am delighted to note that community service, with special stress on health care, has been rendered meaningful and effective by the Rotarians of Coimbatore. An oranisation can achieve its objectives in letter and spirit only through able leadership, vision and selfless service. Dr. Muruganathan has fitted himself into the post of Governor, Rotary District 3200, possessing all these qualities in abundance. I have had the opportunity of inaugurating the Mega Project of Rotary District 3200 in Cochin where 40 Ambulances were donated.

I feel privileged to be in the presence of Dr. B. Ramamurthy who is a colossus in the field of neurosurgery. His presence here, today, in Coimbatore, is a loss to those people in Chennai who are waiting in a long queue to get an appointment.

Today's subject of deliberation is of global importance, especially in this age of advanced medical treatment and technology. It is a pity that people of our country have to look to the western countries for effective and advanced medical treatment when the necessary infrastructure, technical know-how and the required potential are available in our country. This is mainly due to lack of encouragement and awareness.

Speech delivered at the function of 'Organ Donation' Awareness Programme and Trauma Care Symposium organised by K.G. Hospital and Post-Graduate Medical Institute, Coimbatore on 17th February, 2000.

Western countries have made vast strides in the field of organ transplantation through research and experimentation. Superstitions, myths, illiteracy and poverty are the major factors that mar the growth of organ transplantation in our country. Creating awareness through continued educational programmes is the only panacea for this malady.

When countries like Belgium, Austria and Singapore have adopted procedures that facilitates easy organ transplantations from the 'Brain-stem-dead' persons, we are still embroiled in legal entanglements in this area.

Organ donation is the greatest legacy a man can leave behind after death. One can live after death not through re-birth but through organ donation. Organ donation not only keeps a dead man alive through his organs, but helps another man escape from the clutches of death. Organ transplantation is yet to develop and gain momentum in our country. This can be achieved only through active participation and support from the people.

I conclude with a sanguine hope that deliberations today will set forth a revolution in the field of organ transplantation, making more and more people come forward to donate the greatest gift a man can give to another man.

ಬಿಬಿಬಿ

FORENSIC SCIENCE

Forensic Science is defined as application of science to law. It owes its origins first to those individuals who developed the principles and techniques needed to identify or compare the physical evidence and secondly, to those who recognized the necessity of merging these principles into a comprehensive discipline. Today, many believe that Sir Arthur Conan Doyle had a considerable influence on popularizing scientific crime detection methods in his several fictions through his character Sherlock Holmes.

Nevertheless, the existence of law-medicine problems can be dated back to the days of Manu. The central theme of the great Tamil Epic—the Story of Anklet "Silapadhikaram" is to stress the supremacy of physical evidence over oral evidence. Evidence of tracking footprints has been recorded in a Tamil poem written several hundred years ago, to unravel the mystery of a missing girl.

This poem is written as if the Sevili (governess of the heroine) addresses the heroine's mother. Observing the footsteps on the sands of the thorny path, the Sevili says thus: 'After all, your daughter has chosen the right person. Her man will certainly look after her well, a tactful lad, indeed! First he made his steps, carefully avoiding the thorns and then asked his girl to follow him, stepping on his own foot prints so that thorns won't prick her delicate feet. That's why there is only one set of big foot prints. The insets are those of your deer-eyed daughter'.

It is very difficult to translate the true essence expressed in the original Tamil Verses.

The poem describes the intricacies of elopement, which is one of the accepted norms of love marriages of the ancient Tamils. The word "adi" in Tamil, means 'a foot step'. It also means a 'line of verse'. Naladiar is a famous composition of poems, each poem comprising of four lines, while Thirukkural comprising of two lines. The Sevili says humorously that this young man who is eloping with the girl he loved, had converted Naladiar (fourlined verse, into Valluvar's (two lined verse), meaning that the walking of two persons, one following the foot steps of another had resulted in one set of bigger footprints.

Speech delivered in National Seminar of Forensic Science and Application in Investigation and Prosecution, Hyderabad on 28th July, 2002.

146

Similar evidence may be available in the literature of other Indian languages. But, Forensic Science as an organized discipline came into existence n India after Independence. Prior to Independence, scientific service to the criminal administration system was rendered by institutions known as Chemical Examiners Laboratories, established in the middle of the 9th century. The first Chemical Examiners Laboratory was established in Chennai and then in Calcutta n 1853, in Agra in 1864 and then in Bombay in 1870.

Today in India, there are more than twenty well established Forensic Science Laboratories, four of them being administered by the Central Government, while he rest are run by State Governments. In addition, a separate DNA laboratory, a Serologist's Laboratory and Chemical Examiner's Laboratories and Document Examiners Laboratories continue to exist separately. Thus in total there are more han 30 forensic science and allied institutions in India.

However, the forensic science education is available only in five or six universities in this vast country of ours as compared to ninety odd universities n USA, conducting several need based forensic educational programs.

Thus, I appeal to the universities in India to offer comprehensive courses on forensic science and training programmes, if necessary, in collaboration with well reputed forensic science laboratories, in order to augment the shortage of trained manpower.

The revolutionary growth of various disciplines of science & technology, especially in the field of molecular biology has made a tremendous impact on the growth of forensic science.

The small magnifying lens of Sherlock Holmes has been replaced by the giant Scanning Electron Microscope. Calculators have given way to computers. Laser beams have already taken the place of brushes and powders to uncover the latent fingerprints. Forensic molecular biologists can tell now, with certainty, that this is the blood of Mr. X. The police investigator need not struggle any more to obtain semen sample from the rapists since even a few strands of hair forcefully removed from his scalp is sufficient to fix him up, thanks to the DNA technology.

Even the very concept of Forensic Science has considerably changed. Forensic Science does not confine any more to matters relating to crime alone. It has become the ever expanding branch of applied science used to unravel the mysteries in civil, criminal, regulatory and even non-litigious matters. In America, for example, forensic scientists are found deployed in State and Federal Food and Drug Administrations, Insurance Companies, independent testing laboratories such as Underwriters Laboratory, U.S. Post Office, Customs Service Agency, Internal Revenue Service, State Gambling Commissions, and City Fire Departments etc. Even the New York State Racing Commission employs a forensic chemist to investigate unfair competition by the detection of doping of racing horses.

I do not know whether you have considered the fact that in India, Forensic Science has been the monopoly of Government experts. The majority of Forensic Science Laboratories in India is administratively controlled by the Police. There are no independent laboratories in India as is the practice in developed countries.

However, in America the Governmental experts constitute only less than 25% of experts while the rest are independent experts or experts attached to universities and other academic bodies.

In England, the Forensic Science service is corporatised and in such system, even the investigating agencies have to pay for the services just like defence. Even a common man can approach the Forensic Science Laboratories there to get an expert opinion. The courts in some countries have their own role of neutral experts to be consulted when there is difference of opinion between the experts, appearing for different parties. In some of the forgery cases in Singapore courts, four different document experts have tendered expert opinion on four different tones.

I am sure that the deliberations made in this seminar will make fruitful recommendations to be taken up for consideration by the Committee on the Reforms of Criminal Justice System. However, my suggestion is that the Committee may kindly examine the prevailing forensic science practice in India *vis-a-vis* the practice in other parts of the world and suitably make their recommendations.

ಜಿಜಿಜಿ

MEDICAL JURISPRUDENCE IN THE LEGAL EDUCATION

Law is one of the means to regulate human conduct. It permits legal activities and provides punishments for unwanted or illegal actions in our society. Legal education has a number of purposes, both academic and practical ones, but not all of those could be achieved within the three years or five years time frame. It is also not possible to acquire mastery over all the subjects included in the law syllabus, simultaneously. All the students of law must become acquainted with the judicial process - which includes, the making of laws their application – and the techniques necessary to effect conciliation between disputing parties and also acquire competency to assist the Law Courts in arriving at truth and just conclusions. However, this is not the sole purpose of law for which we impart legal education in our Law Colleges and Universities. The law student cannot be a master of the whole body of substantive law. But he can reasonably be expected to be acquainted with the general principles of the main branches of law, like the Constitution of India, Law of Contracts, C.P.C., Cr. P.C., Torts, Penal law, and laws relating to the institutions of family and property.

In our experience, we have realized that there is a deficiency in the syllabus followed in our colleges, for two fundamental reasons. First one is that the cases before the Courts of law, with which these students have to deal at a future point of time, emanate from real lives and in the social context which has a tendency to change continuously and perennially. They are of variations and combinations of infinite variety of social facts including the family and property relations, and involving crimes having origin in socio, economic and political background. The other one is that a student of law need not always opt to practise before Civil Courts. He may pursue a profession which requires expert knowledge in a particular branch of law or a profession outside the practising of law, but still have some nexus with law and legal institutions like legal advisers to financial institutions or to the investigating agencies or in the field of forensic medicine and science.

Speech delivered at the Seminar on 'Need for Inclusion of Medical Jurisprudence in Legal Education', Hyderabad on 7th September, 2002.

Lawbreakers are always engaged in searching new scientific devices of committing offences. They are clever enough and hardly leave direct evidence on the place of occurrence.

The increasing trend of using scientific devices in committing offences has led to the origin and development of forensic science. There is substantial progress in the field of forensic science and the forensic experts are of great help to the courts in the administration of justice. This may include applying medical knowledge in deciding cases of injuries, hanging, sexual offence, infant death, poisonery, dowry death, bride burning etc. Administration of justice is an indispensable task of every modern welfare State but it is much arduous to accomplish it. The person, while sitting in the chair of a Judge, is always surrounded by the clouds of facts.

Education in our law colleges today is mainly aimed at imparting the law student knowledge necessary to ascertain the law from the books but not exposing the students to different other disciplines like Forensic Science and medicine, which are, strictly speaking, outside the practice of law, but with definite relationship with law. He is driven to depend upon the expertise of the medical man or books, without any basic exposure at the law colleges. Irresistible consequence is that a poor performance is shown in Courts while dealing with medico legal cases. Naturally, this leaves the Courts without much help from the legal practitioner. For example, in most of the Criminal Cases involving injury to the human body, medical men are called as witnesses. When a medical man appears in Court, he speaks on two aspects. One is, those facts which he observed physically. We have no problem so far as this aspect is concerned. But when the medical practitioner starts interpreting those facts and expresses an opinion, such opinion is considered as an expert opinion under section 45 of Indian Evidence Act. The persons expressing these opinions are generally persons, having no interest in litigation or its subject matter; as such they are expected to present their opinions fairly and without bias towards the litigant by whom they have been called. But our experience tells us that often the matter is not so smooth and simple, and it may also appear that medicine and law do not go hand in hand because conflicts of opinions, more particularly of medical opinions, in our courts are quite common. An injury through a blunt force like stick on any hard substance like a bone or skull would look like an incised wound caused by a sharpened weapon like a knife on skin, but an expert can decipher and understand the transaction. But a lawyer without this knowledge would argue that the medical evidence runs contrary to the visual evidence, and a Judge without this knowledge may find contradiction between the expert's and visual evidence. Unless the lawyer and the Judge are competent enough to resolve these conflicting opinions in their common pursuit of arriving at truth, the process would result in miscarriage of justice, and the accused, deriving benefit of doubt in quite undeserving cases.

When we understand the purpose of legal education as being that of preparing the Law student to be able to reconcile the academic law with the problems that arise in his practice before law courts or in their new occupation having nexus with law, we are bound to realize that the present day syllabus prescribed for law students is quite deficient. That is why generally it is criticized that our law courses are not practical enough to be useful in resolving the practical problems that arise in discharge of our day to day functions in Courts. Further students' requirements and tastes differ. That is the reason why there has been a choice for the students to elect certain subjects like Taxation, Labour Laws, Legal remedies in some Universities, as their optional subjects, besides the basic subjects like Constitution of India, Law of Contracts, C.P.C., Cr. P.C., Torts, Crimes etc., being compulsory. I do earnestly believe that, if Medico-Legal Jurisprudence and Forensic Science are included, at least, as optional subjects, it would be of immense help to the students who have an inclination to practice on Criminal side. We all know that Medico Legal Jurisprudence is the science that deals with the application of medical knowledge to legal questions. The extent to which this branch would be taught in our college may vary depending upon the necessities. The fruits of science and technology are being utilized for both constructive and destructive works. Criminals are making use of latest techniques to remain unidentified. Generally, criminals commit crimes with due care and caution, taking all the precautions to omit witnesses to the incident. This is so particular in cases of offences against women. By their very nature, offences against women are prone to be committed in clandestine. Even in cases of domestic violence, we cannot expect any witnesses to such crimes. We know well that for variety of reasons witnesses hesitate to speak truth before the Court. Even when the witnesses speak the truth, their evidence suffers from many variations like perceptional variations, memory variations, and expression variations. Besides these, there is likelihood of it being tainted with bias on socio, political, economic, religious, caste, creed, status, sex etc. lines. Further, we cannot rule out the mental attitude of the witness who may, by their nature, be prone to exaggerate or belittle the events, based on their understanding of men and matters. Even though the experts are expected to be unbiased, still they are no exception in respect of these inherent deficiencies. Physical and material objects and circumstances are free from these shortcomings, subject to the condition that these are not contaminated or manipulated by human agency at any stage.

The definition of an expert, as envisaged under the Indian Evidence Act, is somewhat restrictive and narrow. The section 45 of the Act provides that when the court has to form an opinion upon a point of foreign law or science or art or as to identification of handwriting or finger impressions, the opinion of persons specially skilled upon the point of foreign law or science or art or handwriting or finger impression are relevant. Thus a person skilled in a field not covered under section 45 is not treated as an expert for the purpose of giving expert opinion. As a matter of fact, the use of the term "Expert" is not confined to a professional man. The court has to critically examine and to decide about the competency of an expert. Usually academic qualification is taken into consideration but in number of cases testimony of an expert has been rejected for want of experience.

The expert opinion is admissible in evidence where subject matter of the case is technical and where more positive and direct evidence is not available. When

it appears that expert opinion will not affect the substantial rights of the partie
such opinion may not be called for. Again, expert opinion is not admissible up
the question of law. Such questions are to be decided by court itself.

The opinion of an expert, however eminent in his field he may be, must n
be taken as conclusive. An ambiguous and contradictory opinion carries litt
weight. Confused opinion is held to be wholly unsafe to uphold the convictio.
Expert opinion is fallible, therefore, it is always unsafe to base conviction sole.
upon expert evidence without there being substantial corroboration. The Judg
holds the final authority in deciding a matter put before it and all witnesse
including experts, have the function only to render their assistance and help i
reaching a decision. Therefore, the court is not bound to rely upon the opinio
of an expert and can apply its own mind to reach a conclusion. After all, Judg
is not an expert, but is directly accountable for the delivery of justice.

If it is true that an expert cannot be a substitute of court, then it is equall
true that the court can also not become a good substitute of experts. If a Judg
not possessing the specialized knowledge, tries to draw any conclusion i
technical matters without the aid and assistance of an expert, such a recours
may be most unsatisfactory and may amount to travesty of justice. We shoul
take a rational and harmonious view by keeping in mind that expert opinion i
not binding upon the court, nevertheless, it has great significance in th
administration of justice. The court should try to reap the fruits of advancemen
of science.

Therefore, there has been increasing necessity to rely upon the physica
evidence, which is the domain of forensic science and medico-lega
jurisprudence. In fact, law and medicine go hand in hand in forensic medicine
a medical speciality that assists in the detection of crime. Knowledge in forensi
medicine is of great assistance to the Court while dealing with the Criminal cases
Besides, in Criminal Courts, forensic medicine has got its relevancy while dealing
with the matters concerning the determination of age, depending upon severa
parameters like dentition, development of organs etc. Ignorance of basic medico
legal knowledge leads to undesirable consequences. Lawyer or Judge with good
working knowledge in science and forensic medicine is an asset to the Court.

Justice Brandies said that, a lawyer who has not studied economics and
sociology is very apt to become a public enemy. It occurs to my mind that i
applies with equal force to the lawyer not possessing any knowledge in forensic
medicine, but practising in Criminal side. The curricula of the Law Colleges must
include diversified subjects like medico-legal jurisprudence at least as optional
subject, to see that the students are exposed to the basic concepts of law and
medicine equally, so that the student is well prepared to apply his knowledge to
practise while dealing with medico-legal cases.

ಐಐಐ

PHILOSOPHY & SCIENCE IN HUMAN DEVELOPMENT

His Holiness Vethathiri Maharishi, the founder of the World Community Center, in his pursuit of spiritual truth, had found that certain techniques of physical exercise and meditation were useful, even necessary, tools – in that these serve exercises serve to keep the body sufficiently healthy so that one could pursue one's spiritual search without the worry and suffering of disease; and meditation served to quiet the mind to enhance insight, sharpen awareness and enable deeper, subtler states of introspection and analysis of nature.

This Conference has selected a very important/current topic for discussion and deliberation, namely, Philosophy, Science and Human Development. This topic is a very close to my heart. Few words about each subject:—

Philosophy: Philosophy is the endeavour to understand the imperceptible; Science is the pursuit of an empirical understanding of perceivable phenomena.

Science: Science has grown to a marvellous level and has made a tremendous impact on the masses. It has helped us to meet the ever-growing demands of humanity through fresh inventions and technological prowess.

Human Development: For a virtuous way of living, Maharishi has synthesized a package of five core principles which, when followed in letter and spirit, will usher the individual and the world to peace and prosperity. These five principles are:

1. Every person should live by his own earnings;
2. One should not harm anyone, either in body or mind.
3. One may not kill any living being, except as dictated by law.
4. To safeguard the possessions and the freedom of others.
5. One should try to help relieve the pains and difficulties of other living beings.

Delivered at the Inauguration of the National Conference on "Philosophy, Science and Human Development" at Aliyar, Anamalai Hills on 7th August, 2004.

Meditation and introspection have become a part of Maharishi's teachings s
as to realize and practice the above principles in our day-to-day life.

The Vethathirian Philosophy comprises of fourteen points:

1. World without War.
2. Economic Justice.
3. A Fair Judiciary.
4. One World Federal Government.
5. Reformation of Culture.
6. Living under the Guidance of Intellectuals.
7. Respecting Womanhood and Giving them Full Equal Rights.
8. Living in Tune with the Law of Nature.
9. Avoiding Unnecessary Rituals and Festivals.
10. Sports to be made non-commercial and only for children.
11. The Educational Curriculum to include Teaching of the Law of Cause and Effect.
12. Expounding the Philosophy of Magnetism.
13. Food and Water to be available for Each Person of the World.
14. Universal Agreement on One Truth (God) to bring about true realization of God and self.

In the month of June, 2004, I visited this Holy Ashram and came to know that Maharishi has dedicated his entire lifetime to realize and bring out this universal system. This system is a result of his application of scientific enquiry into everyone of his experiences and his courage and conviction to live by his wisdom rather than by unexamined habits. His courage and conviction, his ability to tune his mind to the depth of Nature, his concern for the masses to see what he has seen, and his ability to declare the noblest truths without any fear and favour have made him one of the greatest seers that this century has produced.

To Philosophy, Science and Human Development, I, as a Judge of the Highest Court of India, desire to address you all on spiritual empowerment of the Jurists, which is the need of the hour to rejuvenate them to fulfil the expectations of the society and repose faith and confidence in the justice delivery system.

Law enforcement or sustenance of law and order is becoming a prime issue day by day. The quantum of piling of the cases in the Courts and the cumulative growth in its rate is giving us an indication that there is a need of deep concern in this matter worldwide. Merely increasing the number of courts and the number of Judicial authorities may not be the solution for this. There is a need for an attitudinal change and overall structural change in the society, which should be brought about in all walks of life of the community. The increase in the number of people approaching the Judiciary for proper justice shows their confidence of getting proper justice from the Judiciary but the matter of concern is that this increase is proving us that there is a constant increase of injustice outside in the society.

The basic spirit of our Constitution is to provide each and every person of the nation, equal opportunity irrespective of race, religion, caste, community and social status and the structure of the Constitution is built with the bricks of moral and ethical values, which have really made the whole nation stand inspite of facing so many adverse situations.

A fair Judiciary is the Vethathirian philosophy. Though the Judiciary is only one of the three organs of the State, it plays very responsible role in building up the confidence and integrity of the nation. It is like the foundation of the nation. This is the reason, which make the jurists of the country to think about the future of the nation. Is it not the time to think about some permanent solutions for these problems? Is it not the time to bring about a change in the attitudes of the people? Is it not the time to make them realize more about their responsibilities along with their rights? It is said that 'Prevention is Better than Cure'. Doctors deal with the problems of physical and mental health of the patients. It is said that the social health is also an important factor. I feel the jurists are those doctors who take care of the overall social health of the society at large. Only when there is a problem in the social health, a person approaches jurist – doctor of social health. The punishment and sentence we give is in principle to bring about a change in the behaviour of a person or criminal. The very spirit is to make him realize the mistake and change his behaviour. Any effort in bringing about this realization before breaking the law is highly appreciable and is in fact strengthening the law and order of the nation. The value system of the culture of our nation is in fact protecting the structure of justice. There is a need to strengthen this value system. Values like; truthfulness, non-violence, self-less services, honesty, tolerance, sincerity etc., when inculcated with dedication will solve so many present day problems. It will promote a natural law abiding culture. It is wonderful to note that the basic spirit of spiritual education of any religion is primarily based on inculcating such values as universal brotherhood. It means to see every human being as a child of God and as his own brother. Then he shares his resources with his brothers who are in need of it. Spirituality teaches selfless service and having a feeling of global family. When spirituality is inculcated in practical life, a person becomes a natural embodiment of moral and ethical values.

The nation should now give birth to a new generation with tremendous strength of moral values and with an uncompromising will towards the spirit of truth, justice and non-violence. This is possible only when the elder generation sets an example before them.

The spirit of our profession is not calculative … arguments for winning over the case, but is for the protection of justice.

Legal profession has vital role to play in the administration of justice, not merely as representing one of the parties to the litigation but as officers of the court. The profession is a commitment to the people to protect their legal and fundamental rights, but unfortunately over the years, the legal profession appears to have put the true purpose of the profession on a back burner an allowed aggressive materialism to overtake it. Moral values and professiona ethics have suffered in the bargain. The bar and the bench have to act collectivel to retrieve the image of the profession by taking stringent steps agains malpractices and their practitioners.

For discharging the judicial obligations, many challenges have to be met i order to provide inexpensive, speedy and unpolluted justice to the people. W should respond to the hope and aspirations of the citizens.

Unless the justice delivery system functions smoothly, cordially, effectivel and maintains balance between love and law, it will lose its vibrancy i delivering the justice. Function of judiciary is to administer justice according t law and in doing so, the system must respond to the hopes and aspirations of th people who have reposed confidence in the judiciary to secure Justice. Th progress of the society depends upon proper application of law to the needy i achieving the constitutional goal *i.e.*, justice, liberty, equality, peace, purity an happiness. We believe that once upon a time, Satyuga – (Paradise – the age c Truth) existed on this earth. But presently we are living in a World of fea insecurity, distrust, intolerance, hatred, violence and injustice. We are living in world where human, moral and spiritual values stand at a distanc Consequently, happiness which is the birth right of every human being ha become an elusive dream. The man is suffering from hopelessness, carelessnes and depression. Material progress is like a squeezed sugarcane devoid of its juic and sweetness. The evils like eve-teasing, rape, abduction, prostitution, use c filthy and abusive language, obscenity in art and literature as well as on scree and stage, exhibition of some human nude pictures in commerci advertisements, instances of divorce and the suicide and diseases of variou kinds are all attributable to sex and lust. Renunciation of this vice of sex will lea to establishment of a healthy society. Similarly, if the vice of anger, hate an malice are eschewed for establishment of peace in the globe, we should establis peace within us. Self-transformation leads to the Universal transformation.

The present day society requires only those quintessential, fundament principles whether within history, philosophy, ethics, culture, jurisprudence c other disciplines which ennoble attitudes and behaviours and which improv human understanding and the quality of life. It is the need of the day t introduce value-based education in legal system and in law colleges and thereb create men and women of character based on the values and integrity.

My message to the jurists is that the jurists is must be fair, righteous, uprigl in their work or profession and in all other walks of life. Jurists shall wor together in achieving the objectives of the jurisprudence and spiritual prudenc in promoting the culture of peace, justice and harmony. We must devote som time daily on introspection, meditation, silence and study for our spiritual an moral development. We shall endeavour in affirming the brotherhood of a human beings for achieving the spiritual values and divine qualities. 'Be goo and do good'. *Sarvey Jana Sukhino Bhawantu* (Universal Love and Benediction) a is being imparted by this spiritual organization. We shall endeavour at all stag of life in rendering positive and substantial justice to all, more specially to th poorer and under privileged section of the society with affordable cost and quicker pace for achieving purified and holistic world.

Every Judge in India bears faith in, and allegiance to the Constitution of India. This faith and allegiance have a meaning only if he truly shares the social, economic and political philosophy that forms the vital parts and the background of the Constitution and determines its thrust and its strategy of action. This philosophy and strategy are reflected, besides other parts of the Constitution, in its Preamble, Directive Principles of State Policy, Fundamental Rights, Fundamental Duties, etc.

The Directive Principles of State Policy depict the ambitions and aspirations of the Fathers of the Constitution. These Directive Principles indicate the objects and goals of the Republic and also lay the strategy of action to achieve these. So, Judiciary which constitutes one of the four pillars of the State and is an important agency, empowered to work for realization of these goals, must interpret, apply and enforce the law in accordance with the guidelines provided by these Directive Principles.

The very attitude of a judge towards a criminal ought to be spiritual and a reformist's attitude instead of merely judicative or punitive, for before a person committed a crime, he was a normal being and he can be reformed to become a normal person again. Therefore, goes the saying:

"Every saint has a past; every sinner has a future;" It would, therefore, be wrong to think that a criminal was always a criminal and would always remain a criminal. Let the judiciary and the law enforcing agencies, therefore, not snatch away from him his sense of individual dignity, his feeling of respect and let not his divine spark be attacked so hard as to give smoke instead of a shine. At the same time, your scales say that you have to strike a balance, there should not be a compromise in delivering the Justice. Steps towards transformation and realization are highly appreciable.

ಖಿಖಿಖಿ

NEW ADVANCES IN FORENSIC SCIENCE

The Practice of Forensic Science and Forensic Medicine

Definition

Forensic Science is defined as the application of the laws of nature to th laws of man. In the broader sense, forensic science is the application c various physical and social sciences to problems of law. Professc Chandra Sekharan, India's most renowned forensic scientist has come ou recently with a comprehensive definition. Forensic Scientists examine an interpret evidence and facts in legal cases and offer their expert opinior regarding their findings in Courts of law on the majority of occasions, while the also offer their expert opinions to private individuals in non-litigious matters.

Pathologists, criminalists, documents examiners, finger print examiner, forensic chemists, serologists and other specialists most often apply the expertise to cases. Judges, attorneys, police and other Investigating Officers hav come to rely upon forensic experts to help resolve issues of fact and in makin decisions of guilt and innocence.

Etymology

Etymologically, the word 'forensic' is derived from the Latin word *'forensi* that means public. This Latin term is related to the English word "Forum" whic means a market place where Roman Courts originally used to conduct the sessions. The term forensic can best be defined as "related to Court procedures The term forensic science covers all those medical, biological, chemical ar physical techniques employed in the investigation of crime, in the evaluation civil disputes and also in non-litigious matters such as the investigation sudden natural death. The term in a broader sense will include forensic medicin chemistry, biology, physics, odontology, anthropology, psychiatry, psycholog toxicology, geology and examination of questioned documents, fire arm, to mark and finger prints. Forensic engineering, forensic neuropathology ar forensic account and fraud auditing are some of the recent additions. Forens science would thus appear to-day as a very complex conglomerate of bits human knowledge and endeavour.

Speech delivered at the National Seminar on 'New Advances in the field of Forens Science and Medical Jurisprudence', Pune on 8th January, 2005.

Criminalistics

The term forensic science is sometimes used as synonym for criminalistics. Criminalistics is concerned with the recognition, identification, individualization and evaluation of physical evidence, using the methods of the natural sciences in matters of legal significance. It includes all the areas of tracing evidence of forensic chemistry. It also includes the reconstruction of events based on physical evidence analysis. People who are engaged in criminalistics as profession are called criminalist while those who are engaged in forensic science are called 'forensic scientists".

Special areas of forensic sciences

Forensic Medicine is the application of medicine and medical science to legal problems. Practitioners of forensic medicine are doctors of medicine with speciality certification in pathology and forensic pathology. Most of them are medical examiners. They are concerned with determining the cause and circumstances in cases of questioned death. They also become involved in matters having to do with insurance claims and sometimes in cases of medical malpractice.

Forensic medicine is also known as *legal medicine* or *medical jurisprudence.* This discipline is considered to be one of the most fascinating of all the many branches of medicine. All branches of medicine, including anatomy, pathology, dentistry, physiology, biochemistry, pharmacology, obstetrics, pediatrics and many others play their vital role in medico-legal problems. The medical examination of the body of the dead or alive, the observations made thereon, the accurate scientific assembly of the evidence gathered, and the reconstruction of reasonable inferences, based on these findings would indeed create a lot of interest and satisfaction among those who choose to practice this branch of medicine.

Cheiloscopy refers to the utilization of lip prints as means of personal identification in much the same manner as fingerprints. Lip print identification is analogous in several respects to bite mark analysis and employs many of the same general methods. Lip prints on drinking glasses, facial tissues, undergarments and pornographic magazines have been used as evidence in actual court cases.

Rugoscopy: The morphology of the palatal rugae may be sufficiently characteristic of the individual for identification purposes. Generally more prominent in males, these apparently persist unchanged over many years and presumably will reappear even if surgically removed. Men have slightly better developed rugae than women. The palatal rugae can be used to confirm the ownership of upper dentures (often a problem in nursing homes) or even denture fragments since the reverse image of the rugae are reproduced on the palatal surface. Comparison is usually accomplished using ante mortem impressions made for study of models or prosthodontics consideration.

Forensic geology is the application of earth sciences in crime investigation. Comparison and analysis of soil and related earth materials, encountered in criminal cases are the thrust areas of forensic geology. This speciality also includes forensic identification of gems and precious stones and the various types of mines and mineral frauds.

Forensic psychology is the application of psychology on matters of litigation and jurisprudence. The interface between psychology and the law covers expert opinions, concerning questions of child custody, competence, criminal responsibility, personal injury or handicap suitability to work in law enforcement and candidacy for probation or parole. It also includes expert opinions on such matters as the reliability of eyewitness testimony and lie detection. The lie detector test is not relied as forensic evidence.

Lie detection is a scientific topic about which everyone has strong feelings. It is appraised by some as the court of last resort – a way to establish guilt or innocence in cases that cannot be resolved by other means. Some feel that lie detection is an applied technology that has gone out of control and a threat to basic civil liberties. Harvard psychologist, William Marston, first introduced the technique in 1917. In India a few Forensic Science Laboratories have a separate lie detection section. Polygraph is the instrument used in lie detection technique. Polygraph monitors the bodily activity that accompanies responses to test questions. Expandable pneumatic belts, positioned around the upper thorax and abdomen, provide two separate recordings of the chest movements associated with inspiration and expiration. Changes in skin resistance (the galvanic skin response or GSR) are detected by electrodes attached to the fingertips. A partly inflated blood pressure cuff, attached to the cardio channel reflects relative changes in blood pressure and provides an index of pulse.

The polygraph itself is not capable of detecting lies, and there is no pattern of physiological response that is unique to lying. All one can infer by examining polygraph charts is that the subject showed a greater physiological arousal to one question than to another. Although lying may account for this differential arousal, other factors may also cause one question to be more disturbing than another; for example, a question could elicit a large response because it provoked feelings of anger or grief or because it was threatening or embarrassing. The extent to which such factors affect the outcome of polygraph tests is unknown. The age-old Polygraph tests, narco-analysis tests and the most recent brain fingerprinting tests have raised lot of controversies regarding their reliability.

Forensic psychiatry is the application of this speciality of medicine in theory and practice to a variety of legal issues. A forensic psychiatrist's work starts with the preparation of psychiatric reports for the Court on the mental state of offenders, suspected of having a mental abnormality.

Forensic radiology is the application of radiological techniques to forensic problems. It also includes the situation where the practice of radiology itself gives rise to some medico legal consequences. Forensic radiological techniques are employed in the identification of skeletal and dental material, the location of missiles and foreign bodies and the detection of bone injuries. A much wider and more diffuse field, where radiology has an interface with jurisprudence and medical ethics, occurs, when the professional activities and conduct of the radiologist becomes the subject of legal notice.

Forensic anthropology has to do with personal identification based on bodily (particularly skeletal) remains. Practitioners are physical anthropologists who are interested in forensic problems. Other areas of forensic anthropology include establishing databases on bodily structures as functions of sex, age, race, stature and so forth. Interpretations of footprint or shoe-print evidence are also included.

Forensic toxicology has to do with the determination of toxic substances in human tissues and organs. Much of the work concerns the role played by the toxic agents in causing or contributing to the death of a person.

Questioned documents examination includes comparisons and interpretation of handwriting, mechanically produced material (typing, printing) and photocopied material. Analysis of papers, inks and other materials used to produce documents are also included.

Firearms examination has to do with firearm identification, comparison of markings on bullets and other projectiles, cartridge cases, and shell cases, especially for the purpose of determining whether a bullet or cartridge case has been fired from a particular weapon or not.

Tool Mark examinations are concerned with the association of particular impressions with particular tools such as screw driver, cutting pliers, scissors, shears etc.

Fingerprint examination is concerned with the classification of fingerprints and the organization of sets of prints into usable files. Development of latent prints on crime scene objects and comparisons of known and unknown fingerprints are a part of the work as well.

Voice analysis in this era of telephone, radio, and tape recorder communications may often prove to be valuable evidence for associating an individual with a criminal act. The telephoned bomb threat, the obscene phone call, or tape recorded kidnap ransom messages have all become frequent enough occurrences to warrant the interest of law enforcement officials in scientific techniques capable of transforming the voice into a form suitable for personal identification.

The sound spectrograph is an instrument that converts speech into a visual graphic display. Voice spectrograms, or "voiceprints", could provide a valuable means of personal identification. The sound spectrograph was first developed at Bell Telephone Laboratories in 1941.

Each voice has its own unique quality and character, arising out of individual variations in the vocal mechanism. The probability that any two individuals will have the same size vocal cavities (throat, nasal, and two oral cavities formed by positioning the tongue) and will coordinate their articulators (lips, teeth, tongue, soft palate, and jaw muscles) in a like manner is so small as to make the human voice a unique personal trait. The voiceprint is simply a graphic display of the unique characteristics of the voice.

The Practice of Forensic Science in India

Prior to independence, institutions known as Chemical Examiner's Laboratories established in India in the middle of the 19th Century rendered scientific service to the criminal justice administration system. The first chemical Examiner's Laboratory came into existence in Madras in the year 1849 and the first case tackled by the laboratory is concerned with the examination of wood in a case of cheating. Similar laboratories were established later in Calcutta (1853), Agra (1864), Bombay (1870) and other places. These age-old reputed institutions formed the nuclei of the Forensic Science Laboratories that were formed in the 1950s after Independence.

In all these institutions, about 2,000 scientists are tackling, every day, evidence materials to bring out truth and to serve the cause of justice. Thus scientific methods are being adopted in crime investigation in India in an organized way from 1849 onwards. This, however, does not mean that scientific principles were not used in this country in crime investigation earlier. The existence of law medicine problems can be dated back to the days of Manu (start of Christian era). The central theme of Ilangovadigal's great Tamil epic "Silapathikaram" (story of Anklet) which dates back to second century A.D. is to stress the supremacy of physical evidence over oral evidence. Evidence of tracking footprints to unravel the mystery of a missing girl has been recorded in a Tamil poem, written possibly a few hundred years before Christian era.

Pioneer forensic scientist

Sir Arthur Coman Dyle through his several celebrated works has left a deep impression in the minds of his readers world over that Sherlock Holmes was the pioneer forensic scientist. Some went on to say that Archimedis is the real pioneer forensic scientist, quoting the legendary example. Nevertheless, the following are the pioneers in the field of forensic science.

- Alphonese Bertillon devised the first scientific system of personal identification.
- Calvin Gaddard determined first whether or not a particular gun has fired a bullet by comparing the suspected bullet with the one that has been test fired from the suspect's weapon.
- Albert S. Osborn developed the fundamental principles of document examination and made acceptance of documents as scientific evidence by courts.
- Edmond Locard founded the Institute of Criminalistics, the first of its kind at the University of Lyons, France.

Locard's Principle of Exchange

Prof Locard propounded the famous "Locard's Principle of Exchange" which states that every criminal can be connected to his crime by contact traces carried from the scene of crime or left by him at the scene of crime. Whenever two objects come into contact, they always leave a trace on the other. Wherever the criminal steps, whatever he touches, whatever he leaves, will serve as physical evidence against him. His finger prints caused by his touch, his shoe prints, his hair, the fibres from his clothes, the glass he breaks, the tool mark he leaves, the paint he scratches, the blood or semen that he deposits or collects – all these will bear witness against him.

The functions of forensic scientists are:

1. Analysis of physical evidence.
2. Provision of expert testimony.
3. Furnishing training in the proper recognition, collection, preservation and transportation of physical evidence.

Common types of physical evidence

The common types of physical evidence include: blood, semen and saliva documents, drugs, explosives, fibres, finger prints, fire arms and ammunition, glass, hair, impressions, organs and physiological fluids (Viscera), paint, petroleum products, powder residues, serial numbers – restoration of erased identification numbers, soils and minerals, tool marks, wood and other vegetative matter. Thus, physical evidence can by anything from massive objects to microscopic traces. The examination of physical evidence by a forensic scientist is undertaken for (1) Identification or (2) comparison.

(a) **Identification** has as its purpose, the determination of the physical or chemical identification of a substance with a near absolute certainty, as analytical procedure will permit. Example – Identification of illicit drugs, like heroin, cocaine, barbiturates or identification of poison or identification of arson residues or identification of explosive residues. Each of these requires the analysis and ultimate identification of a specific chemical substance to the exclusion of all other possible chemicals.

(b) **Comparison:** A comparative analysis subjects a suspect and control specimen to the same tests and examination for the ultimate purpose of determining whether or not they have a common origin. Examples: Similarities of hair found at the scene of crime to hair removed from a suspects head – comparison of paint chips found on the garments of a victim in a 'Hit and Run' case with the paint removed from the suspect's car.

Comparison is made by selection of a set of properties of the crime sample and control specimen. If one or two properties selected disagree, then we can say that the specimen does not originate from the same source. If all properties do agree and the specimens are indistinguishable, can we say that they come from the same source? Yes, with certain limitation – not necessarily in all cases. Evidence that can be associated with a common source with an extremely high degree of probability is said to possess **individual characteristics.** Example: matching ridge characteristics of two finger prints; striation of bullets; comparison of wear and tear marks in foot wear impressions and handwriting characteristics. Evidences that can be associated with a common group and never with a single source possess class characteristics. Example: blood grouping, type pattern.

In forensic science, when opinion regarding common source of origin is given, it will mean that the presence of a certain number of individual characteristics establishes the common source of origin since there is only the remotest chance (Probability) of the occurrence of a similar set of characteristics from some other source.

This reasoning depends on the law of compound probability which states that two or more independent events that will happen is equal to the products of their separate probabilities. Thus when the probability of finding two identical finger prints or paint flakes is quite small, the presence of the finger prints of a culprit in the scene of crime or the presence of a chip of paint from the culprit's car in the garments of the victims in a 'hit and run' case will themselves be sufficient to support a conviction.

Physical evidences are the most valuable mute witnesses. It is not confused by the excitement of the moment. Neither is it absent as human witnesses; nor it can be wrong. It is actual evidence. It cannot perjure itself. It cannot be wholly absent. Forensic scientists are, therefore, considered to be the watchdogs of society and their services are very essential to the crime-prone society.

Forensic Science is defined as application of science to law. It owes its origins first to those individuals who developed the principles and techniques needed to identify or compare the physical evidence and secondly to those who recognized the necessity of merging these principles into a comprehensive discipline. Today, many believe that Sir Arthur Conan Doyle had a considerable influence on popularizing scientific crime detection methods in his several fictions through his character Sherlock Holmes.

Nevertheless, the existence of law-medicine problems can be dated back to the days of Manu. The central theme of the great Tamil Epic—the Story of Anklet "Silapadhikaram" is to stress the supremacy of physical evidence over oral evidence. Evidence of tracking foot prints has been recorded in a Tamil poem, written several hundred years ago, to unravel the mystery of a missing girl.

Today in India, there are about twenty and odd well established Forensic Science Laboratories, four of them being administered by the Central Government, while the rest are run by the State Governments. In addition, a separate DNA laboratory, a Serologist's Laboratory and Chemical Examiner's Laboratories and Document examiners Laboratories continue to exist separately. Thus in total there are more than 30 forensic science and allied institutions in India.

It is gratifying to note that some of the above laboratories have excellent scientific facilities but that "a number of State laboratories have chronic problems even to survive specifically for severe shortage of trained manpower."

I am also distressed to note that forensic science education is available only in five or six universities in this vast country of ours as compared to ninety and odd universities in USA, conducting several need based forensic educational programs.

I appeal to the universities in India to offer comprehensive courses on forensic science, technology and law and training programmes, if necessary, in collaboration with well reputed forensic science laboratories, in order to augment the shortage of trained manpower. Though, some effort, has been made as former founder Chancellor of the National Law University, Jodhpur, by establishing the School of Science and Forensic Sciences as one of the twelve Schools, under the stewardship of one of our internationally reputed forensic scientist,

Padmabhushan Dr. P. Chandra Sekharan.

Even the modern forensic science of yesteryears is no more modern. The revolutionary growth of various disciplines of Science and Technology, especially in the field of molecular biology has made a tremendous impact on the growth of Forensic Science.

The small magnifying lens of Sherlock Holmes has been replaced by the giant Scanning Electron Microscope. Calculators have given way to computers. Laser beams have already taken the place of brushes and powders to uncover the latent fingerprints. Forensic molecular biologists can tell now with certainty that this is the blood of Mr. X. The police investigator need not struggle any more to obtain semen sample from the rapists since even a few strands of hair, forcefully removed from his scalp is sufficient to fix him up, thanks to the DNA technology.

It is a matter on record that it is only the meticulous use of forensic science by Professor P. Chandra Sekharan, the World-renowned forensic scientist, gave the world the news within 24 hours that Rajiv Gandhi was killed by a human bomb and that the human bomb is a woman, wearing the explosive-loaded belt bomb around her waist. At this juncture, I want to make an earnest appeal to the Central and State Governments to establish a full-fledged University for Forensic Science studies. I have read in the newspaper, as early as in 1993, that the Government of Karnataka was prepared to offer land and need money to establish a National School of Forensic Sciences following the pattern of the first Law University in Bangalore. But that proposal has not fructified. Now, there are five or six Law Universities at national level. But forensic science studies are offered only in piece-meal in a few universities. The Madras University has discontinued the M.Sc. forensic science course. Therefore, there is immediate necessity to establish an exclusive University for Forensic Science studies and research. I hope and trust the Governments at the Centre and States would give their serious consideration to my plea.

Education in our law colleges today is mainly aimed at imparting the law student knowledge, necessary to ascertain the law from the books but not exposing the students to different other disciplines like forensic Science and medicine, which are, strictly speaking, outside the practice of law, but with definite relationship with law. He is driven to depend upon the expertise of the medical man or books, without any basic exposure at the law colleges.

The task before us is thus heavy, the burden weighty but it is a responsibility that must be shared equally by all, namely, the participants, the students, teachers, colleges and the Universities. The present seminar will thus help in bringing together many minds and contributing new ideas in shaping and strengthening the forensic science.

In my opinion, law and medicine go hand in hand in forensic medicine, a medical speciality that assists in the detection of crime. Knowledge in forensic medicine is of great assistance to the Court while dealing with the Criminal cases. Besides in Criminal Courts, forensic medicine has got its relevancy while dealing with the matters concerning the determination of age depending upon several parameters like detention, development of organs etc. Ignorance of basic medico-legal knowledge leads to undesirable consequences. A lawyer or a Judge with good working knowledge in science and forensic medicine is an asset to the Court. I, therefore, suggest that the curricula of the law colleges must include diversified subjects like medico-legal jurisprudence to see that the students are exposed to the basic concepts of law and medicine equally, so that the student is well prepared to apply his knowledge to practice, while dealing with medico legal cases.

ෙ෯ෙ෯ෙ෯

SCIENTIFIC MANAGEMENT

The Conference was organised to study in depth, how best to use and employ techniques of Scientific Management for the development of our nation. Such a study could be useful and meaningful, if we realise that we have to look at our development plans in such a way that the principles enshrined in our Constitution are scrupulously followed and implemented. These principles are broadly summarised in the Preamble to our Constitution. We have to secure for all our citizens.

JUSTICE, *social, economic and political;*

LIBERTY *of thought, expression, belief, faith and worship;*

EQUALITY *of status and of opportunity;*

FRATERNITY *assuring the dignity of the individual and the unity and integrity of Nation.*

The development of our nation has to be planned, keeping in view these goals and objectives. As you are all aware, 'management' identifies a particular set of people whose job is to direct the efforts and activities of other people towards achieving common objectives. It is generally said, that a manager is one who gets things done rather than doing them himself. Management is a process by which certain objectives are realised. No doubt, in this process one has to employ scientific techniques and bring in an analytical approach towards solving problems that might develop during the process. The functions of management include-decision making, organising, staffing, planning, controlling, communicating and above all, directing. These functions are related to each other and cannot be looked at in isolation.

Planning, more so, strategic planning or deciding on broad courses of action is termed policy making or decision making. Policy making for the development of our nation is the function of the Executive and the Legislature, which create laws, rules and regulations and administer them, which in turn determine the direction the country should take its march towards development and progress.

Inaugural speech delivered on Annual Conference on 'Scientific Management for National Development' at Loyola Instt. of Business Admn., Madras on 21st March, 1993.

167

The judiciary also makes policy through Court decisions which strike down legislation, require modification of legislation or even imply the need for new legislation. Certain decisions of the United States Supreme Court rendering unconstitutional racial segregation in public schools, eventually gave birth to civil rights legislation at both the national and state levels there. In India too, Courts make policies. The recent Supreme Court Judgement in what is popularly known as *Mandal Commission Report case* quotes with approval, the observations of Sir Anthony Mason, Chief Justice of Australia. The learned Chief Justice observed that "Society exhibits more signs of conflict and disagreement to-day than it did before.... Governments have always had the option of leaving questions to be determined by the Courts according to law .... There are other reasons, of course, that cause Governments to leave decisions to be made by Courts. They are of expedient political character. The community may be so divided on a particular issue that a Government feels that the safe course for it to pursue is to leave the issue to be resolved by the Courts, thereby diminishing the risk, it will alienate significant sections of the community."

The learned Chief Justice further said, ".....My own feeling is, that the people accept the courts as the appropriate means of resolving disputes when Governments decide not to attempt to solve the disputes by the political process".

The law is not an abstract concept removed from the society it serves. The Courts constantly strive to narrow the gap between the ideal of equal justice and the reality of social inequality. The youth of today have a vital responsibility to discharge. The country is on the threshold of 21st Century. We are at a crucial stage in the march towards development. We are a developing nation and our people have great ambitions and aspirations. The object of development is to improve the standard and quality of the life of the people. In the recent past, tremendous changes which we have not witnessed in the first forty years after independence, have happened. A thorough review of the development policies that were in operation in the first four decades has resulted in a total change in the direction of our economy. In this changed context, the management of change or management of challenges caused by the changes appears to me as the major issue this Conference should address itself.

Problems facing the country in its development are numerous and complicated and they will have to be managed and solved with a single minded determination, keeping in mind, the unity and integrity of our nation. Development plans should not be lopsided and should take into account the progress of all the States and the Union Territories.

Service institutions – Government agencies, armed services, Schools and Colleges, Universities, research laboratories, hospitals and other health care institutions, labour unions, professionals, firms, trade associations and many others are in need of management. Management more often than not is attributed to industry only. But non-industry institutions, are in dire need of efficient management. As inefficient management is not management, I would say that management is nothing, but efficiency and effectiveness in approach and action and in achieving the goals set. Perfection and excellence are ideals to which managers should strive for constantly in their endeavours. Professionalism is part of management. Therefore, one could see that the management boils down to professionalism, perfection, efficiency, effectiveness and above all, excellence in any activity that one is engaged in. A manager should manage the resources, environment and more importantly, human beings. In getting the job done through other people, management of such people plays a vital part.

Public Service Institutions are the real growth sector of any society. In the coming century, service institutions will be more powerful and larger. Scientific Management should, therefore, go much beyond business administration. Business needs the service institutions to serve them without which it cannot grow. Business management, therefore, should include service sector management also. Business has a social responsibility and must be accountable to the public. When business derives benefits from society, it has a duty to contribute to the society as well. In the modern context, it is the duty of business to protect environment and the pollution laws should sufficiently take care of that so that we do not have another Bhopal Gas tragedy. Management of environment is a duty owed by the present generation to the posterity and this duty is to be discharged properly.

Schools, hospitals, universities, etc., are all bigger and more in number today in our country compared to the past, but they are in no way adequate to meet the requirements of the millions of our population. Our greatest strength is our greatest weakness. The human resources are our strength and the population is our weakness. Infrastructure facilities have not grown to the extent the demand for them has increased. Managers should endeavour to see what plans are necessary to increase the existing infrastructure facilities and to create modern infrastructure necessary for growth.

We should not lag behind in development compared to other countries and we should do everything to achieve faster growth with the help of the 'state of the art' technology. The educated youth and especially the engineers, administrators, accountants, businessmen and the like in our country are in no way inferior to those of the advanced countries and in fact, our professionals in the field of engineering, science, medicine, technology, software, etc., are contributing to the development of countries abroad and this so called brain-drain should stop. This can only be done if opportunities are created in our country and given to our men and woman to exhibit and use their talents and skills to the advantage of our own nation. This is yet another challenge facing the country today, *viz.*, to create here more opportunities as are available in western countries.

Coming to industry trade and business, there is now unfettered freedom to the industry to do whatever they want. Industrial licensing, import licensing, monopoly restrictions, foreign exchange regulations, capital issues control, and all related restrictions have been virtually scrapped. What is now required from the industry is to deliver the goods, increase the export earnings for the country, and provide goods and services at competitive cost and in good quality. With the full convertibility of the rupee on trade account, there can be no complaints hereafter from the industry. What is disturbing is that while they want freedom, liberalisation and removal of controls, which have all been given to them, they are still not ready or equipped enough to face international competition and very often the lack of infrastructure facilities like power are being blamed for the industry not growing. This situation has to change and it is upto the young and promising managers of tomorrow, to find solutions to the problems faced by industry, as industrial growth is vital for the economic growth which is again vital for national development.

ॐॐॐ

NATUROPATHY

A recent study by the Consumer's Forum, Delhi, has found out that the most expensive item in a family budget is medical care. Suppose, an average family has about five members, the medical expenditure easily goes beyond Rs. 150 per month. Given the conditions of sanitation in this country, the people, especially the poorer people, are easy prey to epidemics.

We often read the headlines in papers that gutter water has entered the pipe lines or dead bodies have been recovered from water main storages. This condition spells disaster for the populace. Every home gets into the 'infection net', and all this means heavy strain on the purse of the common man.

In private companies, they bear the medical expenditure of their employees and in Government, some reimbursement measures are available. But, if one makes an analysis of the causes of various indispositions, one can trace it to the food they eat and the water they intake.

To get over this state, we have a boon in Naturopathy. Nature cure can be availed by every one and the cost is very little and more than anything, it is easily available.

Once, I had the opportunity, or shall I say misfortune, to see a village primary health centre. The crowd of patients was huge, including old people. There was only one doctor available and how could he attend to hundreds of patients daily from over 60 villages, to whom he is supposed to cater? The stock of medicines also is not adequate. However, he has to administer some medicine and he goes on doing his job with or without effect. There are not enough beds in the hospitals. But crowds are still pouring in. How to solve this problem. I can surely say, the answer, is naturopathy.

There was an old saying, "What you eat you become". So, you have to choose what you eat.

Naturopathy alone can cover our poor homes. Instead of the patient going to the over-crowded, heavily under-equipped clinics, Naturopathy actually goes to every home.

Advice on regular habits, care of what to eat, when to eat are given to families and we can have hundreds of Naturopathy clinics in and around the rural areas.

Inaugural speech delivered in the seminar on 'National Nature Care for Doctors', Madras on 9th October, 1993.

The key to solve our health problems, which are growing day by day, is held by naturopathy. I am glad, the institute of integral health studies is doing real service.

India found the Ayurvedic system of medicine and the *Siddha* system of medicine and I think, this is again our turn to spread the naturopathy. Naturopathy should be given equal recognition like other systems of medicine.

ಬಬಬ

PART VI

LAW AND ENVIRONMENT

ENVIRONMENTAL PUBLIC HEARING

The Constitution of India is amongst the few in the world that contains specific provisions for the protection of the environment of our country. The national commitment to protect and improve the environment is explicitly enunciated in the Constitution of India. Judiciary has strengthened this mandate. Government of India, recognising the principle embodied in the Constitution to protect the environment of our country, has introduced the system of obtaining clearance for certain categories of industries and development projects for installation/expansion/modernisation. They have issued a notification [1]under the Environment (Protection) Act, that any person who desires to undertake any new project or expansion or modernisation of any existing industry or project, he/she/it is required to seek environmental clearance for a proposed expansion/modernisation activity, if the resultant Pollution load is to exceed the existing levels. The "Pollution Load" in the above context covers emissions, liquid effluents, and solid and semi-solid wastes generated. The project controller will have to approach the State Pollution Control Board for certifying whether the proposed modernization or expansion activity is likely to exceed the existing pollution load or not. The project proponent will have to submit an executive summary, incorporating in brief, the essence of project details and findings of environmental impact assessment study which could be made available to concerned parties or environmental groups on request. The concerned parties or environmental groups will be the *bona fide* residents located at or around the project site of alleged adverse environmental impact. Public hearing is contemplated in case of projects involving large displacement or having severe environmental ramifications.

This system of public hearing was introduced from 1994 onwards based on the broad principle that bodies, like Pollution Control Board, entrusted with legal power for the enforcement of Pollution Control laws will not arbitrarily exercise such power, without first hearing the person who will likely to be affected by the said establishment. With the conduct of the public hearing, the public, especially those affected are getting a chance to have the right information. In most of the cases, the industry seeking sanction will normally say that their project is

---

Inaugural address..... at the seminar organised by The Kerala State Pollution Control Board, 22nd February, 2000.

1. Environment Impact Assessment Notification, 1994.

environmentally sound and there is no chance of pollution. The Pollution Control Board, sometimes, may not be able to know the other side of the pollution aspects. Based on such fundamental rule of fair procedure *"audi alteram partem "*, *i.e.*, "hear the other side"; that the scheme for public hearing was formulated. It is based on the fundamental principle of natural justice that "hear the other side before taking a decision".

The project proponent will have to submit an executive summary, incorporating, in brief, the essence of project details and findings on environmental impact assessment study which could be made available to concerned parties or environmental groups on request. The purpose of conducting public hearing is to gather opinion of the public including the affected people, nearby residents, environmental groups, etc. By conducting the public hearing, the public gets a chance to have prior information about the project and to express their views on the subject. The Summary of the project is made available to the public for their information and for eliciting their views on the project while conducting the public hearing. It may be noted that the people have a fundamental right to information.

A proper hearing must always include a *"fair opportunity to those who are parties in the controversy for correcting or contradicting anything prejudicial to their view"* according to Lord Denning. If the right to be heard is to be a real right, which is worth anything, it must carry with it a right in the public to know the project, which is proposed by the proponent. The public must know all the materials produced by the project holders to substantiate their claim and then only the public must be able to say that they have been given a fair opportunity of hearing to correct or contradict them.

A public hearing will normally be an oral hearing. However, in some matters it may suffice to give an opportunity to make representations in writing, if any adverse material is disclosed and provided so that the demands of fairness are substantially met. The public, attending such public hearing should see that their objections are put in writing so that there shall not be any scope for any missing important points by the authorities. They should also produce evidences like reports, photographs, newspaper reports, etc. in support of their claim.

The authorities also will have to consider all the objections raised by the public. They should not come for hearing the public with a prejudged view. They must consider all the relevant evidence, which the public submits. Arrangements for hearings must be fair and justice may not be sacrificed to speed or haste.

The authorities are doing a quasi-judicial duty while performing their function under the Act. If it is certified that no increase is likely to occur in the existing pollution load due to proposed expansion or modernization and the project proponent will not be required to seek environmental clearance, but copy of such certificate, issued by the SPCB will have to be submitted to the Impact Assessment Agency (IAA), normally the Ministry of Environment and Forest, for further action. The Board should also keep in mind that they are hearing the persons who are going to suffer. The constitutional duty, enshrined on all the citizens to protect the environment of our country shall be remembered while taking a decision. Although there is no general rule of law, requiring of giving reasons, a Board may be unable to show that it has acted lawfully and fairly unless it explains itself. Thus where the Act empowers the Board to refuse sanction, it may be unable to show that it has acted lawfully unless it explains itself. In a series of cases, it has been held that statutory tribunals must give satisfactory reasons so that the losing party may know whether he should exercise his right of appeal on a point of law.

The public has a right to know about the state of pollution, which they are going to suffer. They should utilize this facility in the right manner. The purpose of conducting the public hearing is to minimize the negative impacts of the projects, right from the planning stage to the implementation stage. The benefits and impacts should be weighed in the right spirit to support or object to the project proposal or to suggest or demand changes in the project proposals. The health of our planet earth is ultimately about the health of its people.

The traditional concept that development and ecology are opposed to each other is no longer a good principle. "Sustainable Development" is the solution. Sustainable development meets the needs of the present without compromising the ability of the future generations to meet their own need. It is a balancing concept between ecology and development and has been accepted as a part of the Customary International Law though its salient features have yet to be finalized by the International Law Jurists. Environmental measures by the Pollution Control Board must anticipate, prevent and attack the causes of environmental degradation. Where there is threat of serious and irreversible damages, lack of scientific certainty should not be used as a reason, for postponing measures to prevent environmental degradation. Human beings are at the center of concerns for sustainable development. They are entitled to a healthy and productive life in harmony with nature. The right to development must be fulfilled to equitably meet developmental and environmental needs of present and future generations. In order to achieve sustainable development, environmental protection should constitute an integral part of the development process and cannot be considered in isolation from it. States and people should co-operate in good faith and in a spirit of partnership in the fulfilment of sustainable development of our country. We should not forget our constitutional obligation to protect and improve the natural environment embodied in Art. 51A(g) of the Constitution of India. The system of the Public Hearing, as embodied in the notification, is the acceptance of the right of the people to have fresh air, water and natural resources.

ಬಬಬ

ENVIRONMENT PROTECTION

During 1995, the award instituted by the Earth Care Group in association with the Rotary Club of Madras East was presented to Pallavaram Tanners Industrial Effluents Treatment Company Limited for their successful commissioning of a Common Effluent Treatment Plant with their own private initiative and capital, thereby ensuring safety to the ground water.

Mr. N. Ram's contribution to the promotion of harmony, peace and community amity, all of which do have a positive impact to our living environment, made the Panel of Advisers to select him for the award.

Mr. N. Ram needs no introduction. He is a dynamic person and a very successful Editor of a renowned magazine, Frontline. Because of his kindness, good qualities and uprightness, Mr. N. Ram is considered to be a person of absolute integrity and straight forwardness, which would always enable him to be always in the Front Line. No doubt that he will reach a grand land mark because of his complete dedication and service for humanity through journalism. He deserves my heartiest congratulations and sincerest good wishes.

The Rotary Club of Madras East, chartered in the year 1985, has carved a name in the district by organising programmes beneficial to the community and by holding exhibitions on themes like energy, environment and pollution under the Chairmanship of their honorary member and eminent Agricultural Scientist Dr. M.S. Swaminathan. I have participated in many meetings with Dr. M.S. Swaminathan. It is befitting that the award is instituted in his name for environment protection.

Protecting the world from air pollution, water pollution and environmental hazards has become a major issue before all the countries now. When science and technology advance, naturally, the consequences will also follow. When industrial growth is applauded, it also becomes a source of new problems like affecting the environment from its discharges and effluents. But, science, technology and industrial activities cannot be curtailed for the reason that they will pollute. The only answer to maintain environmental equilibrium of the

---

Speech delivered on the occasion of the presentation of Dr. M.S. Swaminathan Award for Environment Protection, Chennai on 7th August, 1997.

nature is to see that the industrial activities evolve such methods that will not pollute the environment.

The State is also saddled with heavy responsibilities to eradicate such problems. Article 48A of the Constitution casts a duty on the State to endeavour to protect and improve the environment and to safeguard the forests and wild life of the country. Article 51(g) of the Constitution casts a fundamental duty on every citizen to protect and improve the natural environment.

In recent times, the Judiciary is also playing a pivotal role in eradicating pollution problems. The Courts have acted smoothly and sternly in many cases filed as Public Interest Litigations and other environmental related cases.

The first one involving issues relating to environment and ecological balance was reported in AIR 1985 SC 852. In this case, the Supreme Court ordered the closure of stone quarries for causing air pollution. Subsequently, the Supreme Court has delivered various judgements which have created much awareness among the public, of environmental hazards.

In the famous *Tannery* case *Vellore Citizen Welfare Forum* v. *Union of India*, AIR 1996 SC 2715: (1996) 5 SCC 647: JT 1996 (7) SC 375, the Supreme Court while passing orders on Tannery Pollution in Tamil Nadu, requested the Chief Justice of the Madras High Court to constitute a Special Bench 'GREEN BENCH' to deal with environment matters.

In the *Tannery* case referred to above, the Supreme Court monitored about 960 tanneries in Tamil Nadu from the year 1991-92 and directed closure of tanneries which did not have adequate effluent treatment systems. Some of the closed tanneries became sincere, constructed effluent treatment systems and approached the Supreme Court and the Supreme Court after verifying the reports of Tamil Nadu Pollution Board, permitted them to operate. Other tanneries are doing the effluent treatment systems so that they could be re-opened. Hence, it is a successful attempt on the part of the Supreme Court, since it has made the tanneries realise their duties.

In a decision reported in AIR 1992 SC 382, the Apex Court observed that All India Radio and Television should broadcast/telecast information and message on environment in national and regional language, and make environment a compulsory subject in school and college, so that there would be a general growth of awareness.

In another important judgment reported in *S. Jagannath* v. *Union of India*, AIR 1997 SC 811: (1997) 2 SCC 87: JT 1997 (1) SC 160, the Apex Court had gone into the environmental degradation caused by shrimp culture and acqua-culture industries, operating within the coastal regulation zone as defined under the Coastal Regulation Zone Notification and directed them to be demolished and removed from the said area before 31st March, 1997. The various reports and analysis, dealt with in the judgement are a clear indication as to how the judiciary is concerned with the prevention of pollution.

In another case, a Division Bench of the Madras High Court has ruled that no stone quarrying or crushing operation should be allowed within five hundred meters of the residential area.

Let us now come to the Green Bench of the Madras High Court the task before it and its achievements.

The Green Bench directed the Tamil Nadu Pollution Control Board to issue individual notices to all the tanneries in Tamil Nadu, numbering about 960. The Board also filed status report about all tanneries and effluents treatment systems provided by them. It is a clear indication of the Green Bench to monitor the tanneries. The effluents discharged from a tannery is ten times noxious when compared to the domestic sewage. Now the tanneries are seriously and sincerely erecting effluent treatment systems and approaching the Green Bench for direction to operate. Now the tannery industry in Tamil Nadu is under the strict vigilance of the Green Bench. There is a possibility that environment problems caused by the tanneries will be averted in the coming days which are not far away.

Dyeing and Bleaching Industries: On a public interest litigation, filed against water pollution caused to Noyyal River, by various dyeing and bleaching units in Tirupur, the Green Bench directed the Tamil Nadu Pollution Control Board to file status report of all such units in and around Tirupur. The Green Bench by an order dated 6th March, 1997, directed closure of 168 units for not providing or not taking any steps to construct Effluent Treatment Systems.

Foundaries: Foundaries are also one of the highly air polluting industries. The Green Bench, on a Writ Petition filed by a foundary in Coimbatore against closure order issued by the Pollution Control Board, took the entire matter under its control and directed the Pollution Control Board to file a report about all foundaries in Coimbatore. The Board filed a report about 565 foundaries in Coimbatore and the Green Bench, by an order dated 8th March, 1997, directed the closure of foundaries located in primary residential areas or to shift from the area by 15th April, 1997.

City Waterways: Another important and interesting case before the Green Bench is about the water and air pollution caused to city waterways like Cooum, Buckingham canal, Adyar river, etc. The Tamil Nadu Pollution Control Board filed an report before the Green Bench about the causes, sources and the measures to be taken to make the city waterways clean. The Green Bench directed the Pollution Control Board to issue notices to all establishments/ industries who discharge the effluents/sewage directly without any treatment into the Cooum, Buckingham Canal, Adyar river. As expected, this evoked much response from those establishments/industries and without any further notice, they are now taking steps to treat the effluents/sewages.

It is a fact that Cooum can be cleaned only by a joint action of Government of Tamil Nadu, Chennai Corporation, Madras Metropolitan Water Supply and Sewage Board, MMDA, Slum Clearance Board Pollution Control Board and other Government agencies. But, the Green Bench has now initiated a move in the right direction. The Government has also now announced, in the Floor of the Assembly, on 2nd May, 1997 that a Global Tender would be called soon to clean the Cooum river and about Rs. 722 crores have been earmarked for the said project.

Cleaning Garbages in City: In two separate cases filed against the pollution caused by dumping of garbages in Otteri and Bloyds colony, the Green Bench directed the Chennai Corporation to prepare a time bound scheme for cleaning and disposal of garbages in the entire city of Madras. The Madras Corporation is now seriously considering the matter and doing its best with the help of the State Government and other agencies.

Motor Vehicle Emission: The smoke emitted by the motor vehicles is a serious cause of air pollution since it contains harmful air pollutants like carbon monoxide. The suspended particulate matters mix with the atmosphere and spoil the environment. On a public interest litigation filed against such air pollution in Madras city, the Pollution Control Board had filed a comprehensive report about the methods to contain air pollution caused by motor vehicles, to the Green Bench of the Madras High Court. On a direction from the Green Bench, the said report has been forwarded to the Government for approval, since it involves co-ordination of other Government agencies also.

There are cases against air or water pollution caused by saw mill units, poultry farming, automobile work shops, tyre retreating, decadicating units, rice mills, bricks kilns, oil mills, etc., filed by neighbours who have to suffer by the activities of the said units. The Green Bench has interfered in such cases and has directed the said units to adopt adequate measures or to shift from that place so that the neighbours could live in peace and in a pollution free atmosphere.

The Green Bench has also come alive to stop the ecological problem due to deforestation and mining activities.

The Green Bench, while making the industries instal pollution control measures, not only acts as a saviour of environment but also tends to improve the economy of the country. The Green Bench has the duty and responsibility to go into these matters in great details and find out the genuineness of such litigations and to find out a solution to the environmental problems. The Green Bench is marching ahead with soft and at the same time tough stand towards polluting industries.

The formation of Green Bench in Madras High Court can be considered as a major forward step taken by the State Judiciary for the cause of pollution free environment. The Green Bench has been tougher on some occasions, but that was only with the good intention to force the concerned units to do their bit to eradicate pollution hazards, which will line an impact in the long run, on the entire society. The Green Bench has made its impact throughout the State and has definitely created an awareness among the public.

In the coming days, we will be able to hear much more about the Green Bench. But, it is to be noted that the intention of the Green Bench is not to close down the industries, but to regulate them and force them to instal appropriate air, water pollution control devices. The extreme step of closure is taken only in case of unavoidable circumstances. Such industries will be permitted to operate only after they take appropriate measures.

But, it should not be taken as if only the Green Bench should make the environment clean. Each and every individual has the duty in this aspect.

Keeping one's own house neat and tidy, keeping our surroundings clean and green, putting the garbages and other wastes in the specified places is also a primary step which each one of us should follow. We should also keep our car, scooter and other vehicles in good condition and educate our neighbours who are ignorant of environmental awareness.

Environment shall not be considered something confined only to industry or business but a total system as such. It shall also include the attitude and quality of life. Any contribution made towards better environmental quality through peace and harmony shall definitely deserve recognition.

಄಄಄

RIGHT TO BREATHE GOOD AIR

The problems of Environmental Pollution have assumed recognition all over the world and necessary legislations have been enacted by various countries to control environmental pollution. So far as our nation is concerned, control and prevention of environmental pollution has been made a constitutional obligation by virtue of Article 48A of the Constitution of India, which was added by 42nd Amendment Act, 1976. This Article provides that the State shall endeavour to protect and improve the environment and to safeguard the forest and the wild life of the country. Similarly, by virtue of Article 58(1)(A), it is laid down, that every citizen of India has a duty to protect and improve the natural environment including forest, rivers and wild life and to have compassion for living creatures.

Environmental Pollution may be caused by water, air and even noise. State of Orissa was the first to enact in 1953 Orissa River Pollution Prevention Act which was followed by the State of Maharashtra which enacted in 1969 the Maharashtra Prevention of Water Pollution Act, 1969. World Health Organisation is of the opinion that noise pollution is detrimental to the psychology, physiology and behavioural pattern of the people. It is said by the medical experts that noise disturbs biological organisms and causes pupil delation, paling of the skin, dryness of mucous membranes, intestinal spasms and adrenal secretion. The State, in fulfilment of its constitutional obligation, has enacted legislation to control environmental pollution – like the Forest Act, 1927; The Water (Prevention and Control of Pollution) Act, 1974; The Water (Prevention and Control of Pollution) Rules, 1975; The Water (Prevention and Control of Pollution) Cess Act, 1977; The Water Prevention and Control of Pollution (Amendment) Act, 1978; The Water (Prevention and Control of Pollution) Cess Rules, 1978; Thee Air (Prevention and Control of Pollution) Act, 1981; The Air (Prevention and Control of Pollution) Rules, 1982; and The Environment (Protection) Act, 1986.

The above enactments aim to control water, air and environmental pollution. In a landmark judgement, our Supreme Court in Municipal Council, *Ratlam Municipality* v. *Vardichand*, AIR 1980 SC 1622: 1980 4 SCC 162, has upheld the

Speech delivered in the symposium organised by Rotary Club of Madras, Madras on 25th August, 1995.

183

directions of a Sub-Divisional Magistrate to the Ratlam Municipal Council to provide amenities to abate nuisance by constructing drain pipes and flushing them with water to wash the filth and to provide sanitary facilities for the slum dwellers who are using road for that purpose. The Supreme Court further directed the Municipal Council for exercising its statutory powers to stop the discharge of effluent from the alcohol plant into the street even though the Sub Divisional Magistrate did not issue that direction.

The Environment Pollution is also an off-shoot of the industrial development. It is, therefore, imperative that suitable measures should be found out to harmonise the growth of industries without polluting the eco-system.

Similarly, the Supreme Court issued certain directions to maintain ecology and environment in respect of quarrying of lime stone in Dehra Dun District (AIR 1985 SC 652). The Supreme Court observed that preservation of environment and keeping the ecological balance unaffected is a social obligation and a constitutional duty.

In *Sri Ram Foods and Fertilizers* case, AIR 1987 SC 965, the Apex Court impressed upon the Government of India to evolve a national policy for location of chemical and other hazardous industries in areas where population is scarce and there is little hazard to the community. Yet another case, touching environmental issue is reported in AIR 1987 SC 1109. In that case, a plot of four acres out of the land of Zoological Garden of Calcutta was allotted to TAJ Group of Hotels on lease by the Government of India for construction of a Five Star Hotel. The Supreme Court, considering the point of development and ecological disturbance has observed thus:

> "Today, Society's inter-action with nature is so extensive that the environmental question has assumed proportions affecting all humanity. Industrialisation, urbanisation, explosion of population, over exploitation of resources, depletion of traditional sources of energy and raw material, the description of the natural ecological balances, the species for economic reason and some times, for no good reason at all, are all factors which have contributed to environmental deterioration. While the scientific and technological progress of men has invested him with immense power over nature, it has also resulted in the unthinking use of the power, encroaching endlessly on nature. If man is able to transform deserts into Oasis, he is also leaving behind deserts in the place of Oasis."

In a recent pronouncement with regard to pollution in the River Ganga, the Supreme Court issued the following directions.

Coming nearer home, the Supreme Court has issued directions to owners of tanneries in Ambur, North Arcot District, not to discharge the trade effluent without scientific treatment.

Notwithstanding the legislations and judicial verdict, the participation of people is of utmost importance to protect the environment from pollution and maintain ecological balance. Social consciousness is the most vital factor for the effective prevention of environmental pollution and abatement of nuisance. In the interest of the future generation, environmental awareness should be spread amongst the people. It is, indeed, indisputable that industrial development is a must to the growth of the nation and it is equally indisputable that environmental ecology should be maintained by controlling the pollution of air, water and noise. The survival of the future generations is also dependent on a harmonious growth of industries with full control of pollution of environment and maintenance of ecological balance. Economic prosperity will be meaningless and useless unless steps are taken to control pollution of water and air. It is the duty of every citizen to maintain hygienic environment. The Supreme Court has held that act which causes environmental ecological, air, water pollution amounts to violation of Article 21 of the Constitution [(1995) 2 SCC 577]. Local authorities are vested with power to take suitable steps to promote, protect and improve both the man-made and natural environment. Recently, in the decision reported in (1995) 3 SCC 266, the Apex Court has noticed the suffocation of Nainital on account of pollution and has issued directions to take preventive as well as remedial measures to regain Nainital of its consoled beauty.

Right to breathe good air is part of the constitutional "right to life". On account of air pollution, certain respiratory diseases like silicosis and Tuberculosis occur. Inhaling toxic dusts or fumes is much more dangerous. Bhopal Gas Tragedy is an example of air pollution which was as a result of leak of poisonous fumes. Inhalation of polluted air results in the rapid and effective distribution of poisonous substance to all the body tissues, resulting either in death or some other major permanent disablement. Such escape of poisonous fumes or gas affects the people living in the nearby locality. It is, hence, necessary that suitable legislation should be brought about to regulate the growth of industries and at the same time, ensure that people breathe fresh and unpolluted air. It is heartening to find that necessary legislation has been introduced by some states to control the emission of smoke from automobiles to keep the air free from fume and clean.

೮೨೮೨೮೨

STRUGGLE TO SAVE ENVIRONMENT

The subject chosen for the public law lectures is about a matter of grave concern for one and all, especially when we think of the future generations of this world. I am reminded of a joke about a curious child of the third standard millennium asking questions to his father

Child	:	Dad, What is a bird?
Father	:	Child, it is a two winged animal who builds a nest.
Child	:	What is a nest, Dad?
Father	:	It is a home made of branches of a tree.
Then the child asks	:	Dad, What is a tree?
Father	:	Let us enquire and find out from the Archaeological Department.

Going by the lack of awareness among the public as regards environment, such an event can be foreseen in future. What we can give to our children and grand-children are only airconditioned flats, Channel TVs and Computers as our legacies whereas we have inherited from our forefathers, acres of agricultural lands and estates, abounding in natural resources, flora and fauna.

The World Commission on Environment and Development of U.N. General Assembly (1983) in its report entitled *"Our Common Future"* has reflected the concern for future generation.

I Quote:

> *"Our children will inherit the losses. We borrow environmental capital for future generation with no intention or prospect of repaying. They may damn us for our spend thrift ways but they can never collect our debt to them. We act as we do because we can get away with it. Future generations do not vote. They have no political or financial power, they cannot challenge our decision".*

In *Minors Opasa et al* v. *Factron et al,* (1994) 33 ILM 173 and 224 Philippino), the Philippine Supreme Court entertained a Civil Suit filed by 40 Philipino children representing themselves and generations yet unborn against the Philippines Government to stop deforestation. The Philippine Supreme Court granted reliefs based on the concept of 'inter-generational responsibility'.

Inaugural speech on the occasion of 'Public law lectures' of the Cochin University of Science and Technology, School of Legal Studies, Cochin on 19th February, 1999.

We cannot allow our future generation to live in concrete jungles under the garb of development. The Report of the World Commission on Environment and Development had focussed on population, food, security, the loss of species and genetic resources, energy, industry and human settlements, pointing out that they cannot be treated in isolation from one another. The report had called for support from World Bank for environmentally sound projects and policies. The role of multinational companies in sustainable development of developing countries was also stressed.

The United Nations Environment Programme (UNEP) had adopted certain guidelines for environmentally sound development into the 21st Century. The guidelines named *"An Environmental Perspective until the year 2000 and Beyond"* (19th June 1987 at Nairobi) concentrate on the fundamental principle that though growth is akin to development, it shall not deplete the world's natural resources. The Report highlights how long term economic growth is made possible without jeopardizing global environment.

"Law is the last result of human wisdom acting upon human experience for the benefit of the public" (Dr. Samuel Johnson). The Indian Judiciary while entertaining environmental disputes has always been pro-environmental and never shied away from evolving new concepts and applying new principles for protecting environments.

In *Vellore Citizen Welfare Forum* v. *Union of India*, AIR 1996 SC 2715: (1996) 5 SCC 647: JT 1996 7 SC 175, a three-Judge Bench of the Supreme Court had held that the concepts of *'no fault'* liability and *'onus of proof'* in environmental cases are implied under our law. In this case, the Apex Court took note of Articles 47, 48A and 51A(g) of the Constitution and based on International Conferences, held that the precautionary principle and the new concept of 'burden of proof' in environmental matters shall be applied by the authority appointed under Section 3(3) of the Environment Protection Act, 1986. The learned Judges implied that the 'burden of proof' in environmental cases is on the developer or industrialist who is proposing to alter the status quo, as part of the Environmental Law. Similarly, in *A.P. Pollution Control Board* v. *Prof. M.V. Nayadu*, AIR 1999 SC 812: (1999) 2 SCC 718: JT 1999 (1) SC 162, His Lordship Justice Jagannadha Rao has very succinctly delineated the above principles and evolved the principle of Inter-generation equity-rights of the future against the present. The Court had held that to ensure safety to environment and maintain eco balance but at the same time to ensure sustainable development, the Court can seek scientific investigations and expert opinion from bodies such as Appellate Authority under the National Environmental Appellate Authorities Act, 1997.

"Man damaged the Environment : he can rescue it" (Justice V.R. Krishna Iyer). We have to collectively struggle to save the environment for the future progeny through governments and popular movements.

To conclude, I quote Dr. Albert Schweitzer (Out of My Life & Thought 1933):

> *"Anyone who proposes to do good must not expect people to roll any stones out of his way and must calmly accept his lot even it they roll a few more stones into it. Force that grows in the face of obstacles alone can win".*

ಬಂಬಂಬಂ

PART VII

CYBER LAW & IPR

DIGITAL DIVIDE

Information and knowledge have always been great resources. Those who have access to them and those who can use them have gained immense power, power of the intellect and through that, power over men, societies and nations. The acquisition of information and knowledge and their cultivation have led to spectacular scientific and technological inventions and discoveries. These in turn have extended man's physical power immensely. Science and technology have gifted us machines and devices using which, with less and less physical labour, more and more could be produced and created, leaving more time for people to exercise their mind and brain and explore the universe further. Distance, time and place are no barriers for human endeavour and achievement. The exploration of earth's resources, and using them for making life less-dependent on the vagaries of nature, more comfortable, more productive and leisurely have been the pursuits of mankind.

In earlier days, information and knowledge could be stored only in men's memory, transmitted and shared just by physical communion by word of mouth. However, inventions like writing, paper and printing have enabled the storage of information and knowledge in libraries. But profiting from them is possible only by people, physically moving to the libraries or to classrooms, Schools, Colleges and Universities.

Those who are not literate or educated enough, cannot profit from the information and knowledge that the philosophers, scientists and technologists have been creating. The difference between those who have access to information and knowledge and can use them, on the one hand and those who cannot, on the other hand, has been resulting in an economic and cultural divide. Until recently, bridging this gap and narrowing this divide has been extremely difficult.

Since the later half of the 19th century, spectacular discoveries and inventions have been made. The telegraph (1848) enabled people to send written messages over countries and continents in a trice. The telephone (invented 1876) enabled people to speak to one another. The invention of the radio (1896) enabled telephone conversations and voice message to be sent round the globe. The

Speech delivered on 'Bridging the Digital Divide', at Jubilee Hall Andhra Pradesh High Court, Hyderabad on 17th May, 2002.

invention of communications satellites and their deployment from the mid 1960s are enabling transmission and exchange of information from anywhere on the surface of the earth to anywhere else, at any time, instantaneously. Television (late 1920s) has enriched the electrical communication by telephone and radio. Computers (invented in late 1940s) have become so powerful and so small that their incorporation, in every device and system and use for every purpose is transforming our concept of time, distance and computation. While inventions like the steam engine, automobile, aircraft, nuclear power, etc. have extended man's physical power, electronics, telecommunications, satellites, computers and solid state memories are extending man's mind and brain power.

Information is contained in voice as in telephony, images as in video, text as in fax and data as in computers. Voice, images and text are electronified, digitized and are stored on solid-state memories. These solid-state memories are just like our brain cells which also store huge quantities of information and are interconnected. Advances in electronics and computers have made the process of electronified, storing and transmitting information, inexpensive and the costs are falling, spectacularly. The transmission or dissemination and exchange of electronified information is taking place on the globegirdling telecommunications systems. If people are equipped with appropriate devices like the telephone, TV, PC or the mobile handset and many more new devices that are being invented, then they can connect to the telecommunication network anywhere in the world and through it, to the tens of millions of websites in which information about every human activity is being stored for exchange and for retri-review. In other words for the first time, in the history of man-kind, and information generated anywhere in the world, in any form *i.e.* voice, image and text can be made instantaneously available, to any person, by telecommunications network through various devices. Obviously, those who have the appropriate devices and access to the telecom and Internet can get information that they seek, from anywhere in the world. If one is able to organize the information into knowledge that is necessary for his trade or business of vocation, then he can be one of the most endowed persons. Telecommunications, computers and Internet technologies are thus opening up the possibility of equal opportunity for every human being to gain access to every type of information, everywhere in the world.

The question of public policy makers is that can every human being, in the country benefit from this most wonderful gift of technology *i.e.* electronified information, potentially within the reach of every person. We have education but not everyone is availing of it. That is the basis of the divide between the education-haves and education-havenots. We have other divides like those who are born into rich and educated families and therefore, have the initial advantage of great inheritance and those who are born into poor and illiterate families with the terrible disadvantage of not having such education that can enable them to quit poverty. Now, telecommunications and Internet are technologies that will help anybody to gain information and knowledge and therefore, intellectual and economic power. A number of conditions are essential for this technology to benefit all and not only a few, thus accentuating the already existing divisions and disparities. Let me mention but a few of them.

- It is a true to say that without literacy and education, no citizen can benefit from any technology or even from democracy. The devices, through which a person gains access to information and knowledge, should be operable by every one who wants to benefit by the technology. Access to telecommunication and Internet should be affordable and inexpensive. The public policy must see that, if the digital divide is not to further disadvantage the already little educated and poor, there must be an immediate massive programme of eradicating illiteracy and providing education for all.

- People should not be expected to go to towns and cities, where the telecommunication Internet systems are, but these must be extended to all the population centers, to all the 600,000 villages in India. Therefore, it is imperative that a reliable, secure and adequate telecommunications network be extended to cover all the population centers in the entire territory of the country, in the least of time.

- Technologies are bringing down costs, both of telecoms and of computer systems and devices. Competition is bringing down these costs further. The benefit of these cost reductions must be extended to lower prices for accessing and using the telecommunications network and Internet. No costs which are not intrinsically part of a telecommunications and Internet system should be imposed. In this light, I think the entrance fees, license fees, spectrum charges and revenue shares and such things which are imposed upon the companies licensed to provide telecom and Internet systems and services are inappropriate from the point of view of making the Internet and telecom affordable to the masses. These license fees and revenue shares etc. are all costs to the companies and therefore they will be realized through prices charge to users. One can understand that these constitute 30% to 40% of the costs. If these are removed, obviously the prices would be reduced by 30-40%. If communications and Internet are seen as a technology that develops human resource, just like education, I see no reason why the telecoms and Internet usage should be taxed while education is not taxed. It is better that human beings are educated and enabled to be self-employed rather than Governments gathering revenues by sale of licences and using them for unidentifiable purposes, not at all related to the development of human resources.

The telephone-divide *i.e.* the relative advantages that people with a telephone can have over those who cannot, is being solved in India in a very elegant way. The STD/ISD public telephones (PTs) in every street corner in towns and cities and, one at least, in every village is one of the most wonderful solutions to narrow the telephone divide. That 30% of revenues of telephone companies comes from public telephones shows how millions of those who cannot afford a private telephone subscription are, nevertheless, making use of public telephones for their needs and benefits. It is, therefore, wise to upgrade all the STD/ISD public telephones into public Internet kiosks. They may be fitted with a PC and given an Internet connection, through great global communications platform and a mammoth store of information can be made easily available through least costly technical means. Then this eighth wonder of the world, the Internet, can be accessed by all sections of the public even if they cannot purchase a PC or have a telephone subscription. The Internet policy of the Government envisages this transformation but it is not coming through quickly. Private companies are installing the Internet, only in cities and towns, where there is good business proposition. In the villages and small towns, the provision of Internet will, like the telephone, have to be subsidized. Of all subsidies, subsidizing the access to and use of information is the most beneficial subsidy and is essential for bridging the digital divide.

- For quite some time to come, people who have telephones will be the first ones to use the Internet. There are two types of payment involved. One is, for gaining access through the telephone network and the other for using the Internet. Competition, in the provision of Internet service, has drastically brought down the price of Internet usage from Rs. 40 to Rs. 10 per hour. This is wonderful so that the people who are not affluent also can use Internet. But access, by a telephone call, to Internet, for an hour is costing Rs. 25.20. In no other country, the telephone cost is so much more than the cost of Internet use. This must be corrected. In many countries, there are great global communications platform and mammoth store of information is available, as flat rates are charged for the use of telephone to gain access to and use of the Internet. In India also, public policy must bring about this result.

Even as people have access to the telephone, long distance calls, both within the country and abroad, are still costly. Luckily, competition has already halved these rates but they could be further halved or even be 1/4th of what they are, if Internet protocol (IP) telephony is allowed to every telephone subscriber. The policy of permitting only the Internet subscribers and kiosks to avail of Internet telephony must be revised so that the subscribers also have the benefit of the inexpensive I.P telephony. We should not hesitate to allow the deployment of any technology that is coming up for the general benefit of all the sections of people. The interest of people must be more cared for than the interest of a few entrenched incumbent companies.

- Computer education should be imported in all schools, in classes VIII, IX & X. While most of the costly private schools are already giving computer education, charging extra fees from students, the studens of the Government Schools, especially in the rural areas are likely to be deprived. Public policy should be to see that knowledge to use computers, is imparted as part of the literacy and education programmes. I do not mean that students should be taught to become Programmers or Software Engineers. But they should be able to use PCs, to gain access and surf the Internet; to create their own websites and send and receive e-mails and search for and download information that they want. All public libraries should be connected to Internet and users of libraries should be allowed to use the Internet at a nominal fee. Government must, initially start this facility in rural area, so that the digital divide is addressed where it is most necessary.

Governments are migrating to electronic Governance. In our country, the citizen has to seek many services from, and has to exchange so much information with the Government. Government of Andhra Pradesh, for example, is delivering 22 services/transactions from its *e-seva kendras*. This is a great convenience to citizens who are then not required to go to Government offices, which is of great expense and inconvenience. Government has to deliver services to people, through several outlets, electronically and most importantly through the STD/ISD booths, upgraded to Internet kiosks. If the Government itself wants to establish an *e-sava kendra*, it may cost not less than a lakh of rupees per *Kendra* whereas, with a few thousands of rupees, given as an incentive to the STD/ISD booth operators, all of them would deliver the e-services to the people. This is the least costly way of delivering e-services to citizens.

Most importantly, for general mass of the people to benefit, information that is stored and available on the Internet must be in the local languages also. It is good to know English, in which 95% of the content, today, is written. But to expect that everyone would know English is too much. Therefore, Governments and public limited companies should come forward to create content in local languages. It should refer to the daily needs of people like for example, that pertaining to agriculture, seeds, market rates and so on.

It is noteworthy that all over the world telecommunications and information technology-based services are being provided, competitively by private sector companies and that Government Departments and companies are also disinvested or privatized. Even then, Government's policies and regulations should be such as to make telecom and information services more and more affordable to people. Government will always have a role to see that the telecommunication reaches every nook and corner of the country and then every variety of information service that is available in cities, is also available in country side. I.T. Enabled Services have a potential of providing job for millions of people. It is unwise to require the job seekers to come to cities. These opportunities must be available in the rural areas and this will be possible only if broadband telecommunications connectivity is extended to all the small towns. We have about 5,000 of them in the country. If the broadband is available, the I.T. Enabled Services could be provided from small towns also. That is the way we can narrow the gap between the urban and the rural educated people with regard to job opportunities.

Information enables citizens to participate in public debate in governance. Every Government must, therefore, open a portal so that any citizen, by accessing the same can communicate with any Government office and with any Legislator on any issue that he wants. It is for Engineers and Software professionals to see that not much skill and engineering and proficiency in English is needed to navigate to the Government departments and offices, through the portal. Our I.T. professionals should be able to develop such applications and such procedures that require the least skill, on the part of users, for getting all the benefits that can be had from electronic governance and Internet.

Government has realized the importance of convergence and, therefore, the need for a comprehensive new law and regulation. For this purpose, Government utilized the Convergence Bill to create the Communications Commission of India (CCI) to license and regulate telecommunications, Internet and broadcasting. Legislators and legal professionals must study the provisions of this Bills to see that they conduce to narrow the gap between rural and urban areas and that no area of the country is disadvantaged due to lack of broadband telecommunications and the Internet.

ॐ ॐ ॐ

CYBER LAWS

Cyber Space – a term coined by Novelist William Gibson – denotes a place without physical walls or even physical dimensions, which has connected the globe, in the shortest span of time, to the extent no technology has done before in human history. Today, the Internet connects almost 200 million people – people from 195 countries – approximately 3% of the world population and back home the connectivity is estimated to grow around 125%, annually, over the next three years.

The moot point is what does it mean to people? Can Internet provide water or food or will it eradicate AIDS? Will it stop crime or wars? Do we need legislation to promote the phenomenon or to control and regulate it? The answers are much complex than the cyber revolution itself. For optimists, the cyber revolution holds a new path to prosperity, connectivity, exchange of information, trade and business and for those who are sceptical, it will create a digital divide with the division between knows and know-nots, slicing through the haves and have-nots.

If these are extreme viewpoints, there is a huge shade of grey area in which cyber space operates and in such a polarization of views, emerges the cyber jurisprudence, which is chasing the speeding technology on the information highway to formulate the traffic regulations. As the traffic systems are varied and chaotic, depending on the country you drive, the same is true for the cyber laws of the respective environment one operates in.

For a democratic country, participative governance and right to information have been issues of some importance, especially, in the last decade or so, as people loosing faith in their governance have wanted a greater say in the governing process. The time and effort it takes to make for participative decision-making have been the major stumbling blocks. Elections, we are told, is the only method by which the populace of the country can voice its opinion or provide its approval/disapproval of the governors of the country. Hence, whilst notions of public hearing have been built into environmental law, delegated legislation is published in draft form to seek opinion of concerned people. These processes of opinion seeking have, in the main, been symbolic and marginal. Communication

---

Speech delivered at the seminar on 'Emergence of Cyber laws', Hyderabad on 22nd December, 2001.

technology opens up possibilities of people participative law making and administration which could be of Greek vintage. Of course, the Greek did not allow either slaves or women to participate in decision making and we, today, want a greater say to be given to members of the vulnerable groups.

In the field of cyber crimes, there are of course the offences which have been introduced under the Information Technology Act of 2000. Penalties have been provided under the Act for causing damage to any computer or computer system. Monetary penalties, not exceeding Rs. 1,50,000, have also been provided for failure to furnish any document, return or report to the Controller or the certifying authority. For failure to furnish other information, returns and maintenance of books of accounts, penalties of Rs. 5,000 and Rs. 10,000, respectively have been specified under the statute. A residuary penalty provision makes the contravention of any other rule and regulation made under the Act punishable with compensation upto Rs. 25,000. Whilst deciding on the quantum of compensation, the adjudicating officers are required to have due record of the amount of gain of unfair advantage, made by the defaulter, the amount of loss caused by the default and the repetitive nature of the default. Other than the above said compensatory penalties, the statute also introduces criminal sanctions of imprisonment and fine for tampering with computer source documents; hacking computer systems, publishing obscene materials, publishing false digital signature certificates or creating such certificates for fraudulent or unlawful purposes. Along with imprisonment and fines which range from one to two lakh of rupees, the statute also provides for confiscation of computer, computer systems and accessories.

Other than these penalties and offences which are already introduced by the Information Technology Act, the attention is to be drawn to the possibilities of the perfect crime or the impression of such a possibility which computer technology has opened up. The technology renders the perpetrator, relatively, visible and consequently, creates the impression of being able to do wrong and yet not be punished for it. I am thinking the new generation is more comfortable with computer technology than their parents and mentors. And this technology, like all others, will be used for both good and bad.

Another soft spoken possibility of Information Technology is commerce. E-commerce, will revolutionise buying and selling and international trade is never going to be the same again. The question for us as law persons, however, is how do we regulate these buyer-seller transactions. Do concepts such as buyers beware which require a reasonable degree of investigation from buyers be given up in preference to absolute obligation on sellers. Would such obligations torpedo the possibilities of electronic commerce? Further, absolute standards may be appropriate in situations of misrepresentation, cheating or fraud. How do we deal with problems of *bona fide* mistake, possibilities of which are much greater when persons are interacting on a transnational basis in a space which is mentally but not physically real. In these *bona fide* mistakes/disputes, where should the burden fall – on the buyer? Or on the seller? Or will society pick up the costs in the shape of some new kind of cyber insurance?

The question raised should bring home the fact that the new technology will give rise to its own set of disputes. And these disputes would need to be resolved whether by adjudication or through ADR methods. Under the Information Technology Act, for the adjudication of disputes, under the statute, as well as for imposition of penalties, the Central Government has been empowered to appoint officers, not below the rank of Director to the Government, as adjudicating officers. No person can be appointed as adjudication officer without possessing experience in the field of information technology and law. An appeal can be made from the decisions of the controller and adjudicating officer to the Cyber Appellate Tribunal. This Tribunal is a single member body, consisting of an individual who is or has been or is qualified to be a Judge of the High Court or is or has been a member of the Indian Legal Service with at least 3 years experience in Grade-I of that service. The matters within the Jurisdiction of the Tribunal shall not be taken cognizance of by any other court. An appeal from the decisions of the Tribunal can be made to High Court. The above adjudication set up is necessary but at the same time it needs to be recognised that adjudication is a more useful method of deciding disputes when the position of law is definite and certain. Cyber laws are in a stage of development. In this state of flux, where each person is operating on his own perception of what is the law, it may be wiser to conciliate and mediate rather than adjudicate the disputes which occur on clash of perceptions. ADR methods seem appropriate as they do not allow either of the parties to totally lose or totally gain.

Before taking up the legal education possibilities of these developments, the attention is to be drawn to the socio-cultural revolution which information technology is causing to happen. The umpteen chat shops, cyber dating and marriages are causing social interactions, even of the intimate variety, to happen without 'in person' communications. These communications, due to their instantaneous nature, are dramatically different from the pen friends phenomenon which the postal communication network had started. This change in private relations is bound to have its ramifications on family law. For us, in India, we would need to consider whether the contracting of marriage should become more and more a private affair with public intervention only happening to regulate the consequences of a marriage. If such a choice is not taken, there may be a fair number of disputes of misrepresentation and suppression of material facts which courts would have to deal with.

Now how should these various developments be represented in the legal curriculum and what should one teach? I would think that it should be taught from a comparative perspective. Thus, even if we teach the Indian Information Technology Act, we also look at how the matters regulated by the Act have been regulated, elsewhere and what disputes, if any, have occurred in non-Indian jurisdictions and how have courts resolved those disputes. The Cyber Law Courts should also contend with some of the conceptual quandaries. Also the Information Technology revolution would require very many new kinds of contracts on software development, web hostings, hyper linking to be drafted. Hence the negotiating and drafting techniques for such contracts could be an objective study.

Co-ordination-intensive structures can help to develop effective new arrangements. There is a growing recognition that governance is possible without formal government. Social institutions and informal organizations can be created to deal collectively with specific issues, developing rules for the game and settling conflicts. There are physical and biological systems that lie outside the jurisdiction of any one national government, such as Antarctica, the oceans, the electromagnetic spectrum, and the global climate system. Regional or global forms of governance may manage such "International commons". The characteristics of this restructuring is maximum flexibility and coordination and aim is UNITY IN DIVERSITY. An overhaul and streamlining of governance is an essential task in adapting the society to the fluid information intensive environment of the 21st century. Technology, now, offers us, individually and collectively, a remarkably powerful prosthesis of human brain. It makes 'UNITY IN DIVERSITY' and well-being in the global village realizable objectives, but their achievement demands innovative leadership and unprecedented institutional flexibility".

The above excerpt will give one interesting perspective on the interface of technology and e-governance and the link to laws which are instruments of regulating and directing to such desired goals. The subject of 'technology' has been audited from various perspectives-appropriate technology Vs technology for the chosen few, dangerous technologies Vs useful ones, technology as a trading tool in the division of haves and have-nots Vs people oriented and people owned technologies-the debate goes on. Information Technology has added a new dimension of a new matrix of haves and have-nots, combined with know and know-nots, often termed as the digital divide.

To conclude, from the beginning of time, the law has to engage with the developments in science and technology. Some of these engagements may be no more than evidentiary. Thus, just as we have to decide whether a tape recordings or DNA finger printing could be produced in evidence, decisions on video conferencing, digital signature and web contracting may need to be undertaken. In Andhra Pradesh, we have already recongnised that an under-trial can be produced before the court by video link and physical production is not required.

Technology reconstructs societies, alters its concern and law is an instrument through which these altered concerns need to be regulated, managed and facilitated. Technology opens up for us cross-cultural and cross-border diversity. How these diversities are to be dealt with is the challenge of emerging cyber laws.

৪০৪০৪০

INTELLECTUAL PROPERTY

For optimists the cyber revolution holds a new path of prosperity, connectivity, exchange of information, trade and business and for those who are sceptical it will create digital divide with the division of knows and know-nots, slicing through the haves and have-nots.

If these are extreme viewpoints there is a huge shade of Grey area in which cyber space operates and in such a polarization a views, emerges the cyber jurisprudence, which is chasing the speeding technology' on the information highway to formulate the traffic regulations. As the traffic systems are varied and chaotic, depending on the country where you drive, the same is true for the cyber laws of the respective environment one operates in.

New Inventions, discoveries and technologies not only widen scientific horizon but also pose new challenges for the legal world. Information Technology – brought about by Computers, Internet and Cyberspace has also posed new problems in jurisprudence. It has shown inadequacy of law while dealing with the—

    (i) information technology itself;

    (ii) changes induced by the information technology in the way we live, perceive and do business.

The Courts, throughout the world, have been dealing with these problems and coming up with 'inconsistent answers'. Sometimes these problems have arisen in separate tight compartments mentioned above; sometimes in combination with each other. These problems have arisen in almost all areas of law. The law (statutory or otherwise) providing answers to these problems or dealing with the Information Technology is often loosely referred to as the "Computer Laws" or "Information Technology Laws" or "Cyber Laws".

INTELLECTUAL PROPERTY:

'What is worth copying is prima facie worth protecting' is the genesis for the Intellectual Property Rights. They refer to the property that is creation of the mind: inventions, literary and artistic works, symbols, names, images, and designs used in commerce. It is broadly divided into two categories.

Inaugural speech at the workshop on 'Intellectual Property in the Cyber World and Information Technology', Hyderabad on 23rd February, 2002.

1. Copyright, which includes literary and artistic works such as novels, poems and plays, films, musical works, drawings, paintings, photographs, sculptures and architectural designs.

2. Industrial property, which includes inventions (patents), trademarks, industrial designs, and geographic indication of source.

In India, Intellectual Property is protected under five different Acts, namely: The Copyright Act, 1957; The Patents Act, 1970; The Trade Marks Act, 1999; The Design Act, 1911; and The Geographical Indications of Goods (Registration and Protection) Act, 1999. There is another area of intellectual property known as 'trade secret' but as the name suggests it is a secret formula or process known to certain individuals that is not registered under any intellectual property law. It does not prohibit any one else to find it out or develop it. Nevertheless, an employee who has gained knowledge may be prohibited from using it on the ground of breach of confidence or trust. This is still part of common law and is so protected under section 16 of the Copyright Act. Among different areas of intellectual property three, namely, Copyright, Patent and Trademarks, are affected by the Information Technology.

By Act No. 38 of 1994 and Act No. 49 of 1999, the Copyright Act has been amended by introducing sub-section (O) to Section 2, namely, the interpretation clause to change the definition of the word *'literary work'* and it now includes computer programme as well as computer database. The result is that not only the computer programmes are protected but computer database is also protected as a copyright. In India, infringement of a copyright is a penal offence and civil remedies (Injunction, damages etc.) are also available. By the two amending Acts, consequential amendments were also made in other sections to make enforcement more realistic.

A computer that is more-or-less permanently attached to the Internet is sometimes referred to as a 'host'. To facilitate communication between hosts, each host has as unique address, a complicated string of numbers. The question whether one can use trade name of other as domain name has arisen in India and the Delhi High Court (*Yahoo. Inc.* v. *Akash Arora,* 1999 Delhi Law Times 285) and Bombay High Court [*Rediff Communication Ltd.* v. *Cyberbooth,* AIR 2000 Bom 27: (2000) 20 PTC 209 (Bom)] have taken the view that the domain name serves same function as the trademark and is not a mere addressor like finding number on the internet and, therefore, it is entitled to equal protection as trademark. Injunctions were, therefore, granted, restraining the defendants from using names similar to plaintiff's trade names as their domain names. Section 2(zb) of the Trade Marks Act, 1999 specifically incorporates *'services'* in the definition clause and sections 29 and 30 define what constitutes infringement. Under the Act, for infringement of trademark (like that of copyright) is a penal offence and civil remedies of injunction and damages are also available.

MORALITY: FREEDOM OF EXPRESSION

It is often said that if your child is spending too much time alone on a computer then one should be careful. The reason is that the content in the cyberspace is as diverse as human thought. It also contains information and material, which is obscene. As impressionable one can be misled or lured by others. The US in order to curtail it enacted the Communications Decency Act of 1996 (CDA). Section 223(a)(1)(B)(ii) of the CDA criminalized the 'knowing' transmission of 'obscene or indecent' messages to any recipient less than 18 years of age. Section 223(d) prohibited knowingly sending or displaying to a person less than 18 years of age, any message that is patently offensive (sexual or excretory activities or organs) as measured by contemporary community standards. Under the CDA, it was valid defence for those who—

Took in good faith.... effective .... actions' to restrict access by minors to the prohibited communications (Section 223(e)(5) of the CDA and restricted such access, by requiring certain designated forms of age proof, such as a verified credit card or an adult identification number [Section 223(e)(5)(B) of the CDA].

RIGHT OF PRIVACY:

The right of privacy is part of Article 21 but it is not absolute. Disclosure of private information is justified under certain circumstances. Nevertheless, right of privacy, in the light of Information Technology, may have to be dealt by the Courts or suitable legislation may have to be enacted. The right of privacy may be infringed by:

(i) utilising private data already collected for a purpose other than for which it was collected;

(ii) sending of unsolicited e-mails or spamming;

(iii) unauthorised reading of e-mails of others.

For a democratic country, participative governance and right to information have been issues of some importance, especially in the last decade or so as people, loosing faith with their governance have wanted a greater say in the governing process. The time and effort it takes to make for participative decision-making have been the major stumbling blocks. Elections we are told is the only method by which the populace of the country can voice its opinion or provide its approval/disapproval of the governors of the country. Hence, whilst notions of public hearing have been built into environment law or delegated legislation is published in draft form to seek opinion of concerned people. These processes of opinion seeking have in the main been symbolic and marginal. Communication technology opens up possibilities of people participative law making and administration, which could be of Greek vintage. Of course, the Greeks did not allow either slaves or women to participate in decision – making and we today want a greater say to be given to members of vulnerable groups.

In 1996, the United Nations Commission on International Trade Law (UNICITRAL) has a adopted a Model Law on Electronic Commerce and the General Assembly by its Resolution No. 51/162 dated 30th January, 1997 recommended that all States should give favourable considerations to the said Model Law when they enact or revise their laws. In response to the said UNICITRAL resolution and to give effect to the same, the Government of India enacted the Information Technology Act, 2000 on 9th June, 2000. The

UNICITRAL Model Law provides for equal legal treatment of users of electronic communication and paper based communication. The IT Act tried to sort out many problems of cyberspace by suitably making amendments in the Indian Penal Code, 1860; the Indian Evidence Act, 1872; the Bankers' Books Evidence Act, 1891; and the Reserve Bank of India Act, 1934. These provisions give legal sanction to digital signature, electronic records; sort out questions of jurisdiction, evidential issues, security measure and sanction against obscenity. Penalties have been provided under the Act for causing damage to any computer or computer system.

The IT Act has been enacted to provide legal recognition for transactions carried out by means of electronic, data interchange and other means of electronic communication, commonly referred to as "electronic commerce" which involve the use of alternatives to paper-based methods of communication and storage of information, to facilitate electronic filing of documents with the Government agencies etc. and also to give effect to the said resolution and to promote efficient delivery of Government services by means of reliable electronic records.

Section 2 of the Act, namely, the interpretation clause, has exhaustively defined the various electronic terms, legal terms etc. Chapter II deals with digital signatures authentic electronic records. Chapter III brings about an era of electronic governance. In short, it says that all records where the requirements is to be in writing or in the typewritten or printed form can now be satisfied if it is made in the electronic form and it also permits publications of the rules and the regulations in the electronic form. The applications and forms may be accepted electronically. Chapter IV of the Act deals with attribution, acknowledgement and despatch of electronic Records and it will also assist the courts in sorting out problems of jurisdiction in case of breach of contract, lest a dispute goes to court of law. Chapter VI of the Act deals with appointment of controller and grant of licence to certifying authority who, in turn, is authorised to issue digital signature certificate. Chapter VII deals modalities of issuing Digital Signature Certificate.

Chapter IX deals with penalties and adjudication and Chapter XI deals with offences. The IT Act prescribes penalty against a person who, without permission of the owner, accesses, or downloads or introduces virus or causes any damage, or disrupts or denies access to an authorised person to any computer, computer system or computer network or charges, services to the account of any other person. The penalty is to be paid to person affected and it can extend to one crore rupees (Section 43). The quantification of damages is not left to the Civil Courts but has been entrusted to an adjudicating officer having experience in the field of Information Technology (Section 46). The guiding factors for quantification of damage amount is, amount of gain or unfair advantage; amount of loss; and the repetitive nature of the default.

Monetary penalities, not exceeding Rs. 1,50,000 have also been provided for failure to furnish any document, return or report to the Controller or the Certifying authority. For failure to furnish other information, returns and maintenance of books of accounts, penalties of Rs. 5,000 and Rs. 10,000 respectively have been specified under the statute. A residuary penalty provision makes the contravention of any other rule and regulation made under the Act, punishable with compensation upto Rs. 25,000. Whilst deciding on the quantum of compensation, the adjudicating officers are required to have due record to the amount of gain or unfair advantage made by the defaulter, the amount of loss caused by the default and the repetitive nature of the default.

The statute in Chapter XI (Section 65) also introduces criminal sanctions of imprisonment and fine for tampering with computer source documents; hacking computer systems, publishing obscene materials, publishing false digital signature certificates or creating such certificates for fraudulent or unlawful purposes which may extend to three years or fine which may extend upto two lakh rupees or both. Securing access to a protected system is punishable with imprisonment, which may extend to ten years (Section 70). The Act also provides penalty for breach of confidentiality and privacy of the information, received by a person in pursuance of any of the powers conferred under the Act. Apart from providing for other penalties, the Act also provides for confiscation of computer, computer systems and accessories. Publishing or transmitting obscene information in electronic forms is punishable with imprisonment upto five years or fine, which may extend to one lakh rupees and this could be enhanced to ten years or rupees two lakhs in case of second or subsequent conviction. Though the US Courts have invalidated some of the similar provisions, the Indian Courts have not so far dealt with the reasonableness of such provisions.

Other than these penalties and offences, which are already introduced by the Information Technology Act, I wish to draw your attention to the possibilities of the perfect crime or the impression of such a possibility which computer technology has opened up. The technology renders the perpetrator, relatively, visible and consequently, creates the impression of being able to do wrong and yet not be punished for it. I am thinking here of Acts such as hoax bomb calls or the recent case of young teenager setting up a pornographic site. The new generation is more comfortable with computer technology than their parents and mentors. And this technology, like all others, will be used for good and bad. Further, in view of the amendment brought to the Indian Penal Code, the word document now includes an electronic record. The result is that anyone using the forged electronic record is punishable under the Indian Penal Code as he would be using a forged document. It may also be noticed that amendments have been made to the Indian Evidence Act and the Bankers' Books Evidence Act, 1891 in order that electronic record, digital signature and the computer print out may be proved and admitted in Courts of law, subject, of course to the conditions mentioned in the amended sections.

Another oft spoken possibility of Information Technology is commerce. E-commerce, will revolutionise buying and selling and international trade is never going to be the same again. The question for us as law persons, however, is how do we regulate these buyer-seller transactions. Do concepts such as buyers beware which require a reasonable degree of investigation from buyers be given up in preference to absolute obligation on sellers. Would such obligations torpedo the possibilities of electronic commerce? Further, absolute standards may be appropriate in situations of misrepresentation, cheating or fraud. How do we deal with problems of bona fide mistake, possibilities of which are much greater when persons are interacting on a transnational basis in a space, which is mentally but not physically real. In these bonafide mistakes/disputes, where should the burden fall – on the buyer? Or on the seller? Or will society pick up the costs in the shape of some new kind of cyber insurance?

The question raised should bring home the fact that the new technology will give rise to its own set of disputes. And these disputes would need to be resolved whether by adjudication or through ADR methods. Under the Information Technology Act, for the adjudication of disputes, under the statute as well as for imposition of penalties, the Central Government has been empowered to appoint officers, not below the rank of Director to the government, as adjudicating officers. No person can be appointed as adjudication officer without possessing experience in the field of information technology and law. An appeal can be made from the decisions of the controller and adjudicating officer to the Cyber Appellate Tribunal. This Tribunal is a single member body, consisting of an individual who is or has been or is qualified to be a Judge of the High Court or is or has been a member of the Indian Legal Service with at least 3 years experience in Grade-I of that service. The matters within the jurisdiction of the Tribunal shall not be taken cognizance of by any other court. An appeal from the decisions of the Tribunal can be made to High Court. The above adjudication set up is necessary but at the same time it needs to be recognised that adjudication is a more useful method of deciding disputes when the position of law is definite and certain. Cyber laws are in a stage of development. In this state of flux, where each person is operating on his own perception of what is the law, it may be wiser to conciliate and mediate rather than adjudicate the disputes, which occur on clash of perceptions. ADR methods seem appropriate, as they do not allow either of the parties to totally lose or totally gain.

I wish to draw the attention to the socio-cultural revolution which information technology is causing to happen. The umpteen chat shops, cyber dating and marriages are causing social interactions, even of the intimate variety, to happen without 'in person' communications. These communications, due to their instantaneous nature, are dramatically different from the pen friends phenomenon which the postal communication network had started. This change in private relations is bound to have its ramifications on family law. For us, in India, we would need to consider whether the contracting of marriage should become more and more a private affair with public intervention only happening to regulate the consequences of marriage. If such a choice is not taken, there may be a fair number of disputes of misrepresentation and suppression of material facts, which courts would have to deal with.

Now how should these various developments be represented in the legal curriculum? I would think that the Cyber Law Court should be taught from a comparative perspective. While dealing with the matters arising out of the provisions of Information Technology Act, the Court should see how the matters regulated by the Act have been regulated, elsewhere. What disputes, if any, have occurred in non-Indian jurisdiction and how those Courts have resolved those disputes may be relevant. The Cyber Law Courts should also contend with some of the conceptual quandaries. Also the Information Technology revolution would require very many new kinds of contracts on software development, web hosting, and hyper linking to be drafted. Hence the negotiating and drafting techniques for such contracts could be an objective study.

History provides fascinating clues on centralization and decentralization. The vast Roman Empire could only operate with considerable decentralizaton, even though it had outstanding communications for its time. It was physically impossible to exercise centralized day-to-day control. It worked as follows. Great care was taken at the Centre to appoint a provincial governor or military commander. He was highly trained in the way the Roman System operated and Roman policies were deeply ingrained in him. He had to hold high office in Rome before being appointed to a distant post. Thus coordination between the provinces and Rome was assured. The fall of Rome led to decentralization and an attempt by the Catholic Church to effect a new centralized form of governance. The Holy Roman Empire was a temporary compromise. The power struggle, between religious centralized and secular decentralized control, bled Europe for centuries, in the Middle Ages, until the latter won out. The information technology revolution triggered by the printing press played a crucial role. A challenge for the third century is to create, in Madison's words, a new "happy combination", balancing global/regional, national and local governance levels in a way, appropriate to the shrunken global village and the coordination – intensive structure, made possible by today's information technology based revolution.

Coordination – intensive structures can help to develop effective new arrangements. There is a growing recognition that governance is possible without formal government. Social institutions and informal organizations can be created to deal collectively with specific issues, developing rules of the game and settling conflicts. There are physical and biological systems that lie outside the jurisdiction of any one national government, such as Antarctica, the oceans, the electromagnetics spectrum, and the global climate system. Regional or global forms of governance may manage such "International commons". The characteristics of this restructuring is maximum flexibility and coordination and an aim is UNITY IN DIVERSITY. An overhaul and streamlining of governance is an essential task in adapting the society to the fluid information-intensive environment of the 21st century. Technology, now, offers us, individually and collectively a remarkably powerful prosthesis of human brain. It makes "unity in diversity" and well-being in the global village realizable objectives, but their achievement demands innovative leadership and unprecedented institutional flexibility".

The above excerpt will give one interesting perspective on the interface of technology and governance and the link to laws which are instruments of regulating and directing to such desired goals. The subject of 'technology' has been audited from various perspectives - appropriate technology *Vs* technology for the chosen few, dangerous technologies *Vs* useful ones, technology as a trading tool in the division of haves and have-nots *Vs* people oriented and people owned technologies – the debate goes on. Information Technology has added a new dimension of a new matrix of haves and have-nots, combined with know and know-nots, often termed as the digital divide.

To conclude, from the beginning of time, the law has to engage with the developments in science and technology. Some of these engagements may be no more than evidentiary. Thus just as we have to decide whether tape recordings or DNA finger printing could be produced in evidence, decisions on video conferencing, digital signature and web contracting may need to be undertaken. In Andhra Pradesh we have already recognised that an under-trail can be produced before the court by video link and physical production is not required.

Technology reconstructs societies, alters its concern and law is an instrument through which these altered concerns need to be regulated, managed and facilitated. This regulation has been vitally influenced by the kind of people who have had to be regulated and though in India, have always had to battle with difficulties of diversity, communication. Technology opens up for us cross-cultural and cross-border diversity. How etc. these diversities are to be dealt with is the challenge of emerging cyber laws.

ಖುಖುಖು

COPYRIGHT ACT

Copyright Act was originally enacted to help the indigent author. In fact, Copyright Act is an exception to section 20 of CPC. In that, a suit for infringement of copyright can be filed in the place where the plaintiff resides and carries on business (Sec. 62(2) of the Copyright Act).

The Copyright Act, 1957 is an Act to amend and consolidate the law relating to Copyright. The different provisions of the Act as amended upto date are self explanatory. In *Indian Performing Right Society Ltd.* v. *Eastern Indian Motion Picture Association*, AIR 1977 SC 1432, Justice Krishna Iyer says:

> World opinion in defence of human right to intellectual property led to International Covenants and Municipal laws, Commissions, Codes and Organizations, calculated to protect works of art, India responded to the Universal need by enacting Copyright Act, 1957.

In *Pandurgan* v. *Govinda*, 1971 Crl LJ 1399 it was held that reproduction of matter in Official Gazette will not amount to infringement (*See* also 1955 (1) MLJ 01).

In *Entertaining Enterprises* v. *State of Tamilnadu*, AIR 1984 Mad 278, it was held that video tape falls within the definition of Cinematography film. In *Blackwood and Sons Ltd.* v. *Paruraman*, AIR 1959 Mad 410, it was held that even in the case of translation work, there can be copyright. In *Nag Book House* v. *State of West Bengal*, AIR 1982 Cal 245, while dealing with syllabi in circular, containing guidelines of authors and publishers of text books, it was held that they cannot be taken as original work. Performance of a cine artist in a Cinematography film does not fall within the definition of "Cinematography film" (*Fortune Films* v. *Dev Anand*, AIR 1979 Bom 17). In *Thanakappan* v. *Vidyarambhan Press and Book Depot (P) Ltd.*, 1968 Ker LJ 440, it was held that mere acceptance of remuneration or delivering manuscript by itself will not amount to assignment of copyright. Piracy can be detected by making careful examination (*Lallubhai* v. *Laxmi Shanker*, AIR 1945 Bom 51: 45 Bom LR 679). For infringement, there need not be exact reproduction of original – Resemblance with original may be sufficient. (*Anand* v. *Delux Film*, AIR 1978 SC 163).

Speech delivered at the seminar on 'Copyright Law-Emerging Trends', at S.K. University, Anantpur on 17th February, 2002.

Copyright Act gives protection in respect of:

(a) Original literary, dramatic, musical and artistic work.

(b) Cinematography films.

(c) Sound recording. (Section 13(1) of the Act).

The definition of literary work includes computer programs, tables land compilations including computer (databases) (section 2(O) of the Act.)

In the modern world, the law of Copyright provides the legal frame work not only for the protection of the traditional beneficiaries of the copyright, the individual author, composer or artist but also for the investment required for the creation of works by major cultural industries, the publishing, film, broadcasting, satellite television, recording industries and computer software industry. Copyright protects a vast array of items including computer software, television serials, graphics, advertisements, and brochures.

India having become a member of WTO and in compliance with TRIPS, the Parliament has introduced several amendments by the Copyright (Amendment) Act, 1999 especially to protect Computer software. The amendment act has included databases in the definition of literary work.

Section 14(b)(ii) has been introduced to include the definition of exclusive right in Copyright, the right to sell or give on commercial rental or offer for sale or for commercial rental any copy of the computer program.

Section 52(1)(ab), (ac) and (ad) have been introduced to enable computer programs to be used by a lawful possessor to observe study or test functioning of computer program, to make copies for non-commercial personal use etc. These amendments would enable software companies to enforce their rights and protect them in an effective manner.

Copyright has universal application. India is a member of Berne Convention 1886 and Universal Copyright Convention 1952. International Copyright Order has been passed by the Government of India to protect any work, first made or published in a member country in a like manner as if it was first published in India.

Section 40(a) has been introduced by the Copyright Amendment Act, 1999 to protect broadcasting organisations and performers rights of a foreign country, which may not be a member of either the International Conventions mentioned above or a country with which India has entered into a treaty.

With computers, Internet and web, information is accessible through out the world at a click. There have been apprehensions that in the digital age, the rights of copyright owners would be adversely affected especially as copying is easy and accessible. Even if a person does not have a computer, he can walk into a internet cafe and access a computer. Internet cafes are spread far and wide in India in small towns.

To cope with the problems that have arisen by extensive use of computers, Internet surfing courts have set precedents. The Madras High Court held in *Raj Video Vision* v. *Sun TV*, that broadcasting rights do not include the right to exploit or telecast through satellite television. When the agreements in question were entered into in 1985, satellite television was not even contemplated. The Court observed that the plaintiff who was not assigned with satellite broadcasting rights specifically cannot complain infringement of that right. Satellite TV broadcasting right is a separate, independent and specific right. Satellite Television is different from ordinary territorial television as satellite broadcasting can reach a very much larger audience than any ordinary territorial television.

NAPSTER CASE

Napster has designed and operates the systems which permits the transmission and retention of sound recordings, employing digital technology. Napster facilitates the transmission of MP3 files between and among its user. Napster allows its user to: (1) make MP3 music files stores on individual computer hard drives, available for copying by other Napster users; (2) search for MP3 music files stored on other users' computers; and (3) transfer exact copies of the contents of other user' MP3 files from one computer to another via the Internet. These functions are made possible by Napster's Music Share software, available free of charge from Napster's Internet site, and Napster's network servers and server-side software. The plaintiffs claimed that Napster users are engaged in wholesale reproduction and distribution of copyrighted works, all constituting direct infringement. Napster contended that its users did not directly infringe plaintiff's copyright because the users are engaged in fair use of the material. Napster identifies three specific alleged fair uses: sampling, where users make temporary copies of a work before purchasing, space-shifting, where users access a sound recording through the Napster system that they already own in audio CD format; and permissive distribution of recordings by both new and established artists. The District Court determined that Napster users engage in commercial use of the copyrighted materials largely because (1) "a host user sending a file cannot be said to engage in a personal use when distributing that file to an anonymous requester" and (2) Napster users get for free something they would ordinarily have to buy. The Circuit Court affirmed this finding. Direct economic benefit is not required to demonstrate a commercial use. Rather, repeated and exploitative copying of copyrighted works, even if the copies are not offered for sale, may constitute a commercial use. The Court concluded that Napster's activities reduces audio CD sales among college students and it raises barriers to the plaintiff's entry into the market for digital downloading of music. Napster system makes the song available to millions of individuals and not just the original CD owners. The Court held that if a computer operator learns of specific infringing material, available on his system and fails to purge such materials from the system, the operator knows of and contributes to direct infringement.

New York Times Co. v. *Tasini*, a Judgment delivered by the US Supreme Court on 25th June, 2001 held that inclusion of articles in electronic database is not a revision. The litigation was initiated by six freelance authors and relates to articles they contributed to three print periodicals. The freelance authors complained that their copyrights, have been infringed by inclusion of their articles in the databases. The publishers in response relied on the privilege of production and distribution, accorded to them. The Court held that the databases reproduction and distribution of individual articles simply as individual articles would invade the core of the authors' exclusive rights. The Court held that the print publishers and the electronic publishers have infringed the copyrights of the freelance authors.

   Randowm House Inc. v. *Rosetta Books Lic*, (SDNY 07/11/2001) decided on 11th July, 2001, relates to a suit filed by authors against the publishing Company, Random House Inc. The publishing company had entered into an agreement with each author to "print, publish and sell the work in book form". The issue here was whether the publisher was the beneficial owner of the right to publish the works as e-books. Random claimed that it was, by virtue of its licensing agreements with authors. The Court disagreed; explaining that the most reasonable interpretation of the phrase, set out above, did not include the right to publish e-book. The Court held that the grant of right by the agreements convey the rights to publish the books, club editions, reprints, abridged versions, and editions in Braille. Random argued that the authors could not permit the publication of any material that would be injurious to Random sales of their works and, therefore, the authors must have granted it the right to publish e-books. The Court found this reasoning convoluted.

   In the digital age, the Courts have to protect the rights of the authors although the status may not contain all required provisions, especially, as problems totally unforeseen arise everyday. For example, the issue of jurisdiction when Internet is used as a platform for advertisements. Internet is accessible to every computer user having Internet connection and there is no territorial boundary. Courts would have to exercise trans-border jurisdiction against infringements which may not be located within the jurisdiction of the Court.

৪০৪০৪০

INTELLECTUAL PROPERTY RIGHTS

Intellectual Property (IP) refers to property created with the use of intellect. In other words, it is the creation of the mind. Such intellectual creation is equated with the status of property because of the commercial value of the intellectual creation. There are several Intellectual Properties that are commercially very valuable and they are protected by different IP rights. The law governing these rights is the Intellectual Property Laws. These laws relate to various creations including inventions, literary and artistic works, symbols, names, images and designs used in commerce. In the present day world of Cyber Technology, safeguarding of intellectual property rights has more relevance.

What is worth copying is *prima facie* worth protecting is the genesis for the intellectual property rights.

Intellectual Property rights can broadly be divided into two categories, namely, (i) industrial property rights and (ii) copyright. The industrial property rights refer to the vesting of rights over matter that will be useful for industries and in commerce, which include patents, trademarks, industrial designs and geographic indications of source. Copyright, on the other hand, refers to merely, literary and artistic works. This does not mean that it cannot be used in industries. Copyrights are generally vested in novels, poems, plays, films, musical works, artistic works such as drawings, paintings, photographs and sculptures and architectural designs.

The most important international organization, essential, for the understanding and development of intellectual property rights is the World Trade Organization (WTO), which replaced GATT (General Agreement on Tariffs and Trade). The agreement of the WTO system encompasses trade in goods and services. Other areas include agreements relating to protection of IP and dispute settlement.

The existing framework of intellectual property laws, recognized internationally, are those identified by the Trade Related Intellectual Property Rights Agreement (TRIPS) governed by the WTO. They are (a) Patents, (b) Copyrights, (c) Trademarks, (d) Geographical indicators, (e) Protection of

Speech Delivered at the Indian Officer's Association, Chennai on 14th March, 2003.

undisclosed information, (f) Layout Designs of Integrated Circuits and (g) Industrial Designs.

New inventions, discoveries and technologies not only widen scientific horizon but also pose new challenges for the legal world. Information Technology – brought about by Computers, Internet and Cyberspace has also posed new problems in jurisprudence.

I may now briefly refer to some areas of Intellectual Property Rights.

A patent is a document issued upon application by a Government Office and it describes an invention and creates a legal situation in which the patented invention can normally be exploited with the authorization of the owner of the patent. The right created by a patent is a monopoly right. The significance of the right that it is a statutory right is to prevent others from exploiting his invention.

Copyright law deals with the rights of intellectual creation. This area of intellectual property is particularly concerned about protecting creativity and ingenuity. It is an important area of Intellectual Property because it is one of the means of promoting, enriching and disseminating the national cultural heritage. A country's development depends, to a very great extent, on the creativity of its people and encouragement of individual creativity and its dissemination is a *sine qua non* for progress. The protection is afforded to all forms of public communication and is not limited to merely printed publications and protects even software. The rights include right of Reproduction, Performing rights, Motion Picture rights, Broadcasting rights, Translation and Adaptation rights etc.

There is another area in intellectual property known as 'trade secret' but as the name suggests it is a secret formula or process known to certain individuals that is not registered under any Intellectual Property Law. It does not prohibit any one else to find it out or develop it who did not know the secret. Nevertheless, an employee who has gained knowledge may be prohibited in using it on the ground of breach of confidence, or trust. This is still part of common law and is so protected under Section 16 of the Copyright Act. Among different areas of intellectual property three, namely, Copyright, Patent and Trademarks are affected by the Information Technology.

Another important intellectual property is "Trademarks". Like how a name identifies an individual the trademarks provide the identity and origin of a product. The evolution of trademarks, as a right, arose with the evolution of the consumer protection laws. Trademarks started to play an important role with industrialization and they have since become a key factor in the modern world of international trade and market-oriented economies. Trademarks include, words, letters and numerals, devices, signs, etc. Trade Secrets are a relatively newer form of intellectual property. All intellectual properties have protection on disclosure to enable public to use the same after several years. Trade secrets, on the other hand, protect material that has not been disclosed.

Recently, Geographical indicators have also occupied important place in IPRs. Like trademarks, these indicators also help identify the source of the goods. These have been given the status of intellectual property because the product gets more commercial value by its mere association with a particular geographical place. It helps a consumer to identify where the goods originate. This identification is associated with quality of the goods. Therefore, in effect, the indicators help in promoting the product of the geographical area. Just as trademarks are valuable, these indicators are also very valuable to the manufacturer.

The first Indian law on IPR was the Indian Trade and Merchandise Marks Act, 1884. The First Indian Patent Law was enacted in 1856 as a result of recommendations of the Law Commission. The Indian Patents and Designs Act was passed in 1911. The India Patents and Designs Act, 1911 prevailed till it was recently re-enacted in the year 2000.

The Indian Copyright Act introduced the first legislation on copyright in 1847 and the same was replaced by the Indian Copyright Act, 1914. Later, the Indian Trade and Merchandise Marks Act and the Indian Copyrights Act were fully repealed and have been replaced by the Trade and Merchandise Marks Act, 1958 and the Copyright Act, 1957 respectively. There is also an enactment called the Geographical Indications of Goods (Registration and Protection) Act, 1999.

After TRIPS there were several areas where the old legislation needed amendments. Hence the Trade Marks Act, 1999 was passed.

The New 1999 Act included the registration of service marks. The definition of 'trademark' has been amended to include, within its purview, the concept of service marks as well. The Act defines a "mark" to include a device, brand, heading, label, ticket, name, signature, word, letter, numeral, or any combination thereof.

After the emergence of TRIPS, especially for India, the importance of looking at geographical indicators as a separate area, requiring intellectual property protection has become more pronounced. With this in mind, the Indian Parliament has enacted the Geographical Indications of Goods (Registration and Protection) Act, 1999. The Act is restricted in its application to goods only. As per the Act, a geographical indication need not necessarily be the name of a country or territory or locality. The definition of 'goods' states that the term refers to agricultural, natural or manufactured goods or any goods of handicrafts or of industry and includes foodstuff. An indicator serves three main purposes under the Act. They are: 1. Identifies the nature of goods, 2. Identifies the origin of the goods and 3. Connects some quality or characteristic of the goods to the origin of the goods.

The Law governing copyright in India is the Copyright Act, 1957 and the Copyright Order of 1991. This Act has been amended in the years 1984, 1994 and 1999. The Act provides for exclusive rights to authors and other owners of original works. The object is to ensure protection from, unlawful exploitation of their works. There is no mandatory requirement of registration under the Indian Copyright Act to either get copyright protection or to sue against infringement. The only advantage of registration is that it saves the copyright owner the hassle of proving ownership at a later stage.

Copyright is vested in India by virtue of section 13 of the Act on matters such as (a) Original literary, dramatic, musical and artistic works, (b) Cinematograph works and (c) Sound recording. The Act defines each of these works. Section 2(o) of the Information Technology Act, 2000 specifically mentions that literary work includes computer programs, tables and compilations including computer databases. Networking and eventually the Internet in itself has widened the horizon of accessability of all the databases. The result is that the volume of data, processed every day as well as the number of people connected has increased. Therefore, adequate protection of databases has become very important. In India, infringement of a copyright is a penal offence and civil remedies (Injunction, damages etc.) are also available.

Patents policy, pursued by India, enabled it to become a big international player in the generic drug market. In India, the Indian Patent Act, 1970, as modified in 1999, is the governing patent legislation. The patent policy of 1970 has catered to the needs of Indian poor.

The right of privacy is part of Article 21 but it is not absolute. Disclosure of private information is justified under certain circumstances (*X v. Hospital Z*, (1998) 8 SCC 296). Nevertheless, right of privacy in the light of Information Technology may have to be dealt with by the Courts or suitable legislation may have to be enacted. In the field of cyber crimes, there are of course the offences, which have been introduced under the Information Technology Act, 2000. In response to the United Nations Commission on International Trade Law (UNICITRAL), the Government of India enacted the Information Technology Act, 2000 on 9th June, 2000. The UNICITRAL Model Law provides for equal legal treatment of users of electronic communication and paper based communication. The IT Act tried to sort out many problems of cyberspace by suitably making amendments in the Indian Penal Code, 1860, the Indian Evidence Act, 1872, the Bankers' Books Evidence Act, 1891 and the Reserve Bank of India Act, 1934. These provisions give legal sanction to digital signature, electronic records, sort out questions of jurisdiction, evidential issues, security measure and sanction against obscenity. Penalties have been provided under the Act for causing damage to any computer or computer system.

The IT Act has been enacted to provide legal recognition for transactions, carried out by means of electronic, data interchange and other means of electronic communication, commonly referred to as "electronic commerce" which involve the use of alternatives to paper based methods of communication and storage of information, to facilitate electronic filing of documents with the Government agencies etc. and also to give effect to the said resolution and to promote efficient delivery of Government services by means of reliable electronic records.

ॐॐॐ

Part VIII

Criminal Law

A CONVICT ALSO IS A HUMAN BEING

I was very much fascinated by looking at the premises of the Central Prison, more particularly, on the auspicious occasion of the birth anniversary of Mahatma Gandhi, the Father of Nation. We do not celebrate this occasion as an empty formality or rather a ritual, but with full understanding of relevancy of Mahatma Gandhi and his teachings and preaching to the present day world. Gandhiji always believed that light alone can dispel darkness and darkness cannot dispel darkness.

The Civilized Nations have begun to understand that even a convict is a human being and merely because of conviction, he does not cease to be so. He continues to hold all such rights which are fundamental in nature. In India, our Courts expressed their concern and anxiety over the rights of prisoners on many occasions. The indiscriminate handcuffing of prisoners irrespective of the propensity of the Prisoner to escape is violative of their fundamental rights. Any unreasonable restriction on a detenu's right to consult a legal practitioner and to meet family members and relatives is violative of Arts. 14 and 21. The next primary right is speedy trial. The speedy trial is guaranteed under Article 21 of the Constitution of India. Any delay in expeditious disposal of criminal trial, infringes on the right to life and liberty of the prisoners. The police administration shall ensure safety and security of the inmates in police lock-ups and must be conscious of the fact that the right against custodial violence is recognised as an integral part of prisoners' liberty.

In *Charles Sobhraj*, AIR 1978 SC 1514: (1978) 4 SCC 104: (1979) 1 SCR 512: 1979 SCJ 264, it was stated that the Supreme Court would intervene even in prison administration when constitutional rights or statutory prescriptions are contravened to the injury of a prisoner. In this case, the complaint was against custodial torture.

In *Rama Murthy* v. *State of Karnataka*, AIR 1997 SC 1739: (1997) 2 SCC 642, directions were given to improve conditions in jails and for appropriate actions to be taken on the 78th Law Commission Report on 'Congestion of Under Trial Prisoners in Jail', as well as preparation of new Prisons Act. In this case, the

---

Speech delivered at the inauguration of Legal Services Center and observance of 'Prisoners Welfare Day' at Central Prison, Hyderabad on 2nd October, 2002.

Supreme Court pointed out nine major problems which afflict the system and need immediate attention. These are:

- Overcrowding;
- Delay in Trial;
- Torture and ill-treatment;
- Neglect of Health and Hygiene;
- Insubstantial Food and Inadequate Clothing;
- Prison Vices;
- Deficiency in Communication;
- Streamlining of Jail Visits; and
- Management of open-air Prisons.

The courts, which are expected to intervene in exceptional cases; are having to do so on an almost daily basis. The Indian judiciary has been very sensitive and is trying to ensure the protection of human rights of the people behind the four walls of the prisons. Judiciary is serving as an institution for providing effective remedy against the violation of human rights.

In Andhra Pradesh, I was informed that the prisoners' strength is more than thirteen thousands, out of which more than eight thousand and four hundred are undertrials. The major problem of our jails is the increasing number of undertrials resulting in overcrowding in the prisons. On the other hand, presence of undertrials is coming in the way of offering correctional treatment to offenders.

The debate on judicial arrears in criminal cases has thrown up number of ideas on how the judiciary can set its own house in order. Alarmed by the backlog of inordinate delay in disposal of such cases, it has been decided to introduce Fast Track Courts. Thus, Fast Track Courts are to tackle the cases of under trial first, as the graph of such persons in jail has gone high. It is high time to restore the confidence of people in judiciary by providing speedy justice particularly to the under trials.

The pendency of criminal cases in the State of Andhra Pradesh as on 30th June, 2002 is three lakhs ninety-seven thousand and three hundred twenty five. Now that the Fast Track Courts are established in each district, and I have no doubt that the pendency will be reduced considerably.

In regard to the police investigation, the criminal trial as well as prison systems, the criminal laws to some extent have been amended under the State Act No. 31 of 2001. For example, section 167(2)(b) of the Code of Criminal Procedure has been amended in the State of Andhra Pradesh to make the production of the accused for the purpose of remand through video linkage as valid. But for such law, the physical production of the accused for the purpose of remand was mandatory. In Hyderabad, Rangareddy and Nellore districts, this video linkage system has been introduced and I was informed that this system is effectively functioning. Good results are being yielded in saving the State from spending huge exchequer. This is one of steps taken by the High Court of Andhra

Pradesh for ensuring speedy disposal of criminal cases. The State should seriously think over for its expansion to all the districts.

Pursuant to the directions issued by the Supreme Court in *D.K. Basu v. State of West Bengal*, AIR 1997 SC 610: (1997) 1 SCR 416 on 19th October, 2001, a committee was constituted headed by a retired Chief Justice and two members in January, 2002 itself to oversee whether eleven requirements laid down therein by the Apex Court in all cases of arrest or detention are being implemented or not in the State of Andhra Pradesh. The Committee is to send a report to the Apex Court as regards the matters relating to custodial violence. The Government has approved the appointments to the Committee made by me through G.O.Ms No. 282, Home Department dated 17th September, 2002. The Committee headed by Hon'ble Sri Justice Y. Bhaskar Rao assumed charge of the Committee on 18th September, 2002 and it is in the formative stage now.

The Prison administration in the Andhra Pradesh State aims at ensuring the return of the offender to society as a well adjusted individual. The department recognises the fact that protection of society cannot be achieved merely by detention unless the offender is corrected and reformed while in prison. I was happy to learn that towards this objective, the Prisons Department is undertaking a number of measures in its institutions like taking measures to improve accommodation, medical care, sanitation, dietary, recreational facilities, religious activities, educational facilities. The prisoners are also being given vocational training.

I would like to emphasise the fact that open air prisons play an important role in the scheme of reformation of Prisoners. Release of offenders keeping in view their behaviour on probation, home leave to prisoners, introduction of wage system, release on parole, educational, moral and vocational training of prisoners are some of the features of the open air prison (camp) system. The whole thrust is to see that after release the prisoners may not relapse into crimes, for which purpose they are given incentives to live normal life, as they are trained in the fields of agriculture, horticulture etc. Games, sports and other recreational facilities, which form part of the routine life at the open air camps, inculcate in the prisoners a sense of discipline and social responsibility. The prayers made regularly by the prisoners provide a spiritual strength to them.

Whatever may be the facilities or arrangements that are provided at jail, basically a jail is a jail and it can never be a substitute for liberty. Whether of iron or golden, a cage is a cage. Human beings do not live with food alone. True liberation should be from our greed and lust. When we achieve it, the walls of jail stand nowhere. As Justice Krishna Iyer said, prisons are constructed with stones of law, and law is out here at the doorsteps of poor and needy with human touch. The enactment of the Legal Services Authorities Act which aims at providing a protective umbrella to the weaker and poorer sections of the society against all injustices is a major step towards the fulfilment of the constitutional goals of socio-economic justice. Hence, the Legal Services Centre inaugurated will be a great help to the prisoners in providing free legal aid and in filing and pursuing appeals and in matters where legal assistance is required.

In the end, I would like to mention that the concern of the authorities whether they are of judicial administration or of prison administration, is in the well being and in the usefulness to this society and to bring all the convicts back the prosperity and peace and to see that they do not continue to be a burden or liability to the society, and on the other hand, convicts are reformed into a law abiding citizens to contribute to the social well being.

ಜಿಜಿಜಿ

SPEEDY TRIAL IN CRIMINAL COURTS

It is said that justice hurried is justice buried and at the same time justice delayed is justice denied. We have to read these two sayings with another important factor *i.e.*, justice should not only be done, but should also manifestly appear to have been done. A perfect blend of these sayings strikes a nice balance between the quantitative and qualitative aspects of the justice delivery system. Rendering speedy and substantive justice is the need of the day. It is observed by the Hon'ble Apex Court also that in some instances justice was rendered only after the person entitled thereto left this World. Law is the product of operation of social forces in a given society at a particular point of time. In a dynamic and progressive society, when the social life is much complicated by technological innovations, exposure to the new regions of hitherto unknown value systems and ever changing normative structures in our society, strong undercurrents of litigative tendencies are causing enormous arrears of work in Courts.

The consequences of judicial delays for ordinary litigants are immense, and in some cases, even tragic. Recently, a senior citizen who had invested his life's savings in a non-banking financial company attempted self-immolation after a Delhi Court granted yet another postponement of the proceedings for recovery of his savings from the defaulting company. Judicial delays, whether in cases involving high-profile persons or those relating to ordinary litigants, are not justifiable, and so there is a dire need to alleviate their consequences. The speedy trial is guaranteed under Article 21 of the Constitution of India. Any delay in expeditious disposal of criminal trial infringes the right to life and liberty guaranteed under Article 21 of the Constitution of India. Therefore, a lawyer being an Officer of the Court shall not seek adjournments for silly reasons and he owes a duty to assist the Court in speedy disposal of cases. Accordingly, the Officers also shall not grant adjournments on mere asking. They must think judiciously for granting even a single adjournment. Otherwise, it will create mental agony for the parties. Especially in matrimonial cases, during the prime and blissful part of their age, the parties are going round the corridors of the Courts keeping immense faith in the administration of justice that their cases will be disposed of at the earliest point of time and that they can also live happily in

Speech delivered at the 'Decennial Celebration of Criminal Courts Bar Association', Hyderabad on 7th October, 2002.

the later part of their lives. We, all connected with the administration of justice pledge ourselves that we will put in all efforts for early disposal of such cases

If we look at the statistics, the pendency of the Criminal Courts, in the year 1993 was nearly twenty thousand seven hundred only, but now as on 30th June, 2002, the pendency stands at the figure of nearly fifty thousand cases. Thus there is a steep increase by two and half times in the total number of cases in the twin cities of Hyderabad and Secunderabad within a span of ten years. Society at large, is subjected to deceitful and dishonest activities by unscrupulous elements in all walks of life. *White collar and economic offences are on the rise when compared to traditional crimes and human rights violations, posing a great threat to the civilized society.* The major chunk of the cases in the Criminal Courts relate to the cases arising out of section 138 of Negotiable Instruments Act. Majority of the cases are pending for want of service of summons or execution of NBWs. As on 30th June, 2002, a very alarming figure of 9,610 NBWs were pending in the Criminal Courts making the Hyderabad district number one in the non execution of NBWs. The prosecution must take immediate effective steps to serve the notices and execution of NBWs against the accused for speedy disposal of cases.

Crime is, now a days, organized overseas and on corporate lines with the help of modern technological innovations. Even the conventional and traditional crime is also committed in a sophisticated way. Trial of these offences demands the lawyers on criminal side and Bench for the acquisition of working knowledge in some other subjects like economics and sociology and Cyber laws, besides forensic science and forensic medicine.

Unless the tendency to crime in society is taken care of and arrested, any amount of stress we lay on the disposal of cases, may not yield full results. That is the reason why we have given equal importance to Legal literacy and Lok Adalats and Fast-Track Courts. Legal literacy camps are aimed at educating the people over the pros and cons of litigation or to impress upon them the vagaries of crime, whereas the organization of Lok Adalats and establishment of Fast-Track Courts is aimed at clearing the arrears of cases.

In Andhra Pradesh, the prisoners' strength is more than thirteen thousand out of which nearly six thousand are undertrials. The Legal Services Centre at Central Prison, Hyderabad inaugurated by me aims at providing free legal aid to the prisoners.

No discussion on the judicial system is ever complete without deliberating upon the significance of the relationship between the Bench and the Bar. This is so because the judicial system gets complete not with the Bench alone or with the Bar alone, but it acquires fullness only with both the Bench and the Bar. So it is inevitable that where the judicial system comes to be discussed, the relationship between the Bench and the Bar figures as an important subject. This happens because of the realisation that, if the judicial system has to remain healthy that will be possible only when the relationship between the Bench and the Bar is also healthy. The Judges and the lawyers function in Courts to safeguard and promote the cause of justice for which millions of litigants at enormous cost and sufferings come to the Courts every day. A lawyer should be true to the ethics, requirements and parameters of his legal profession and this must get reflected through his conduct towards the Bench. He must know, what are his limits which he cannot cross. Likewise, a Judge must never forget his limits. He must not forget that while sitting on the Bench, he is representing the sacred cause of justice and he must give expression not to his personal whims, but to his judicious sense while hearing and deciding cases. The principle applies to the lawyers also while in Courts they represent the cause of their litigants and therefore, by their conduct and their thorough preparation of the cases and their presentation before Courts in a systematic manner, they must demonstrate that they are in Courts to do their best to safeguard the legal interests of their litigant clients. The rules of good behaviour and etiquette expected of a lawyer must be strictly observed by him and if he does not do so or appears to be doing a poor job while preparing his litigant's case, he should have no grudge but try to learn when he gets the Court's adverse comments. I wish to emphasise that as a younger member of the family, it is morally incumbent upon a lawyer to show respect to the elder brother who is the judge. He should not be offensive and ill-mannered towards the Judge.

In the Bar Association of the Criminal Courts, there are many young lawyers. The Judge being the elder brother, has to be the large hearted, and must overlook sometimes the small lapses on the part of the young lawyers who are still in the process of learning. Such young lawyers particularly need encouragement and moral support from the Bench more so because these days, it is a tough struggle for the young lawyers to come up in the profession.

At the end, I would ask all members of the Bar as well as the Bench to take a pledge that they will fulfil their duties sincerely and work towards the effective and speedy disposed of cases.

ಲ ಲ ಲ

POLICE – ANSWERABLE TO LAW

Training has an important role to play for police personnel in framing attitudinal change. The role of police is constantly undergoing change to keep consonance with the aspirations of the people. The training becomes important not only for the police department but for the society as a whole. The Gore Committee had come out with the most comprehensive document on police training in the country. Training aids and methods are also being used, in accordance with the recommendations of the Gore Committee. The recommendations of the Gore Committee relating to the instructional staff, have been considered as model and further steps have been initiated towards full implementation of these recommendations. The trainees are being exposed to social science and effort is being made to familiarize the trainees to the latest research in criminology, human behaviour, management, police community relations and other similar subjects.

The endeavour is to make efforts towards shaping the police to attain the goals such as protection of life and property; prevention of crime; enforcement of laws; detection and apprehension of offenders; education about justiciable of law; promotion of respect for law and police; maintenance of social order; provision for security and service to the citizens; and, ensuring protection of weaker sections of society.

There can be no doubt about the importance of the police. In theory, citizens safety and liberty, depend upon the laws and the Constitution, but in practice, the decisions of Parliament, legislatures and the Courts would count for very little if the police were not there to enforce them.

In this country, development of the police has always been conditioned by two conflicting needs. One, to maintain order and protect people, the other to ensure that they themselves do not act oppressively. For this reason, the police have always remained answerable to the general law. They have no special immunities. A policeman who breaks the law is prosecuted and punished just like anyone else. The only power they possess is the power to bring people before the Courts, and even then they are at risk, if they use that power improperly or unfairly. It is truer to say that a policeman discharges responsibilities than that

---

Speech delivered to the R.P.S. Probationers, organised by Rajasthan Police Academy, Jaipur.

226

he exercises powers. These responsibilities have, during recent years, grown-wider and more complicated.

Every law enforcement officer must be thoroughly conversant with fundamental rights guaranteed under the Constitution of India. Our Constitution prohibits discrimination against any citizen on ground of religion, race, caste, sex or place of birth; it provides for the protection of the interest of linguistic, cultural and religious minorities and their right to establish and administer their educational institutions; it guarantees freedom of conscience and the right to profess, practise and propagate religion freely, subject only to public order, morality, health and some other essential provisions; and it guarantees freedom; of speech and expression, to assemble peacefully and without arms, to form associations or unions, to move freely throughout India and to reside and settle in any part of India, to acquire, hold and dispose of properties and to practise any profession, trade or business. Another important provision in the Constitution is that no person shall be detained in custody without being informed of, as soon as may be, the grounds for such arrest nor shall he be denied the right to consult and be defended by a legal practitioner of his choice. Every person arrested or detained in custody shall be produced before the nearest Magistrate within a period of twenty-four hours. These provisions do not apply to enemy alien or persons arrested and detained under any law of preventive detention.

It is the responsibility of every law enforcement officer to protect each citizen against any invasion of fundamental rights. Law enforcement officers must know what legal tools are available and when to use them. Emphasis must be placed on the importance of enforcing the law in a fair, impartial and equitable manner irrespective of who and what may be involved. They must know their authority and its limits.

Police, by the very nature of their responsibilities, have always been a handy scapegoat for those who resent law and order and those who seek public sympathy on controversial issues. As a frontline representative of government, police often bear the brunt of criticism – just or unjust – levelled at the constituted authority.

Admittedly, police have their shortcomings as do all professions. Contrary to some viewpoints, however, they are not responsible for the grievances with which they are charged. Our society is doomed unless the laws are enforced without fear or favour, and the police are ineffective unless their efforts to maintain peace and protect life and property are supported by the government and the people. In face of destructive rampage, arson, violence and lawlessness, no amount of force in tackling them can be called excessive, as they threaten the very survival and security of democracy.

The police are charged with the lawful duty to enforce the law, preserve the peace, protect lives and property, and detect and arrest offenders. Failure to perform these statutory duties make them answerable to the law.

Police are finding difficulty to enforce the law firmly due to leniency meted out to the offenders by the Courts. Some Courts show no concern for the main issues of guilt and innocence but seem bent on searching for misconduct or neglect by the Investigating Police Officers. Policemen, confronted with partisan interference, long hours, inadequate pay, inadequate staff, lack of more sophisticated equipment, inadequate funds, false "police brutality" charges, rising physical assaults when walking their beats or making arrests, and public apathy, together with the narrowing judicial rulings, must necessarily face each day with a great deal of perplexity.

The Government should no longer hesitate to spend heavily on the police; it should recognize that to do so would save immeasurable friction and money in future years. Police are too essential and too significant a responsibility of government, Central and State alike for half-measures to be tolerated.

Though, since after independence, in many areas, political reasons have been allowed to govern in the direction and management of the force especially in matter of appointments, promotions, punishments, transfers, and assignments, and the evil has injured the efficiency of the force.

Frequent complaints are received from citizens that policemen use vulgar, indecent and profane language; they are maltreated, insulted or driven away when they go to police stations with a just complaint or for reasonable information. In the interest of discipline, the officers on the top must be earnest and they themselves must set the example. Lack of courtesy is among the most frequent charges by citizens against the police, and contrasts to their disadvantage in this respect with similar bodies in foreign countries is often made. There are many policemen who are models in courtesy, kindness, and humanity, but the other elements bring the whole force into disrepute.

However, if our nation has to march forward, it is essential to have good scientists, technologists, philosophers, jurists, doctors, lawyers, judges and teachers; and, above all, a well-disciplined police force.

ಬುಬುಬು

PART IX

ALTERNATIVE DISPUTE RESOLUTION & SPEEDY JUSTICE

ACCESS TO JUSTICE

The Constitution of India guarantees to all its citizens right to life and personal liberty, right to equality, right to freedom etc. Apart from these public rights, there are various private rights arising from Torts And Contracts and also the various social welfare legislations such as Contract Labour (Regulation and Abolition) Act, 1976; Equal Remuneration Act; Minimum Wages Act and so on. But these rights are of no avail if an individual has no means to get them enforced. Rule of law envisages that all men are equal before law. All have equal rights but unfortunately all cannot enjoy the rights equally. The enforcement of the rights has to be through the Courts, but judicial procedure is very complex, costly and dilatory putting the poor persons at a distance.

The Constitution of India through Article 14 guarantees equality before law and equal protection of laws. It follows from this that equal opportunity must also be afforded for access to justice. It is not sufficient that law treats all persons equally, irrespective of the prevalent inequalities. But law must function in such a way that all the people have access to justice inspite of the economic disparities. The words 'access to justice' focus on two basic purposes of the legal system.

1. the system must be equally accessible to all

2. it must lead to results that are individually and socially just.

Traditional concept of "access to justice" as understood by common man is access to Courts of law. For a common man, a Court is the place where justice is meted out. But the Courts have become inaccessible due to various barriers such as poverty, social and political backwardness, illiteracy and ignorance etc.

To get justice through Courts, one must go through the complex and costly procedures of litigation. One has to bear the costs of litigation including court fee, stamp duties etc. and also the lawyers fees. Apart from these, the litigant loses much more in financial terms such as loss of income arising from attending the Court hearings. A poor litigant, who is barely able to feed himself will never be able to get justice or obtaining redress for a wrong done to him through courts. Further, a large part of the population in India is illiterate and live in abject poverty. Therefore, they are totally ignorant about the court procedures and will

Speech delivered at Dr. G.R. Damodaran College of Science, Coimbatore on 'Access to Justice – Present Day Scenario' on 2nd March, 2002.

be terrified and confused when faced with the judicial machinery. Thus, most of the citizens of India are not in a position to enforce their rights, constitutional or legal, which in effect generates inequality contrary to the guarantees of Part III of the Constitution.

The State in contemporary scenario is welfare oriented. It is one of the most important duty of a welfare State to provide judicial and non-judicial dispute resolution mechanisms to which all citizens have equal access on equal basis, for resolution of their legal disputes and enforcement of their constitutionally guaranteed fundamental rights. Poverty, ignorance, inertia or social inequalities should not become barriers to it. The Maneka Gandhi principle as enunciated by the Indian Supreme Court that fundamental rights do not constitute separate islands into themselves but constitute a continent had ushered in what Krishna Iyer, J. terms jurisprudence of access. He said:

> "We should expand the jurisprudence of access to justice and examine the constitutionalism of court fee levy as a facet of human rights highlighted in our Nation's Constitution. If the State itself should travesty this basic principle in the teeth of Articles 14 and 39A, where an indigent widow is involved, a second look at its policy is overdue. The Court must give the benefit of doubt the levy of a price to enter the temple of justice until one day the whole issue of the validity of profit making through sale of civil justice, disguised as Court fee is fully reviewed by this court". [**State of Haryana** v. **Darshan Devi**, AIR 1979 SC 855: (1979) 2 SCC 236].

Article 39A provides, equal justice and free legal aid. The said Article obligates the State to promote justice on the basis of equal opportunity and shall in particular, provide free legal aid by suitable legislation of schemes or in any other way, to ensure that opportunities for securing justice are not denied to any citizen by reason of economic or other disabilities. Article 39A puts stress upon legal justice put simply the directive requires the State to provide free legal aid to deserving people so that justice is not denied to any one merely because of economic disability. The Supreme Court has emphasised that legal assistance to poor or indigent accused, who is arrested and put in jeopardy of his life or personal liberty is a constitutional imperative mandated not only by Article 39A but also by Articles 14 and 21. In the absence of legal assistance, injustice may result. Every act of injustice corrodes the foundation of democracy [*Sheela Barse* v. *State of Maharashtra*, AIR 1983 SC 378: (1983) 2 SCC 96]. Article 39A makes it clear that the social objective of equal justice and free legal aid has to be implemented by suitable legislation or by formulating schemes for free legal aid.

The judiciary of its own is playing a significant role in providing justice to the under privileged, indigent and hapless individuals through public interest litigation.

Though Article 39A was introduced in 1976, its objective of providing access to justice could never have been fulfilled but for the majestic role played by the Supreme Court in Public Interest Litigation Movement. This is a movement whereby any public spirited person can move the Court for remedying any wrong affecting the public. This is a significant step by the Supreme Court in giving access to justice for the people belonging to the lowest strata of society and the constitutionally guaranteed rights. Further, it was only through cases filed in public interest only that the Supreme Court was able to encourage legal aid service to poor and indigent persons. Through public interest litigation the Courts were able to deal with people suffering from injustice and exploitation such as bonded labour, dalits, women, children, physically challenged, mentally challenged and so on.

The Lok Adalats, Nyaya Panchayats and Legal Services Authorities are also part of the campaign to take justice to the people and ensure that all people have equal access to justice inspite of various barriers like social and economic backwardness.

The legal aid network is staking firm roots and legal services functionaries are actively engaged in fulfilling the Constitutional promise of equality before the law. The provision of legal aid of eligible persons, the speedy settlement of their legal disputes by counseling and conciliation and failing that, Lok Adalats rank high on the agenda of legal services functionaries, as high as running legal education awareness programmes. Of course, we have miles to go before we can claim that the realm of equal justice for all has become a reality. Former Chief Justice of India, Dr. A.S. Anand has wished that the next century would not be a century of litigation but a century of negotiation, conciliation and arbitration. It is now our turn to make this dream of our judicial patriarch a reality. The need for establishment of permanent forum in settling disputes both pending in Courts as well at pre-litigative stage need not be over emphasized. In the present set up, where there is a huge pendency of cases, the only panacea is setting up of permanent Lok Adalats where the expertise of the Judicial Officer both in service and retired could be effectively utilized in resolution of matters by re-conciliation. A large number of consumers in our country feel handicapped in getting justice due to poverty, illiteracy, social backwardness and also geographical barriers. Permanent Lok Adalats help to follow up already settled cases that may sometimes end up in discordant notes and keep a continued vigil on the quality of the legal services rendered. Apart from setting up daily Adalats, it is advisable to establish permanent Lok Adalats in Government Departments and statutory bodies for settlement of disputes. The enactment of the Legal Service Authorities which aims at providing a protective umbrella to the weaker and poorer sections of the society against all injustices is a major step towards the fulfilment of the Constitutional goals of socio-economic justice. The efforts undertaken by the National Legal Services Authority to protect the rights of prisoners in custody and establishment of permanent statutory forums to the litigants for amicable settlement of disputes deserve economium.

Large population, more litigation and lack of adequate infrastructure are the major factors that hamper our justice system. Regular adjudication procedures through the constant efforts of Legal Services Authorities will act as catalysts in curing these maladies of our system.

Earlier in India, disputes were settled by a council of village elders known as a Panchayat. The decisions of the Panchayat were accepted and treated as binding. In 1982, in Junagarh in the State of Gujarat, a forum of Alternative Disputes Resolution was created in the form of Lok Adalat (People's Court). Looking to the usefulness of Lok Adalats, the Government of India set up a Committee under the Chairmanship of Mr. Justice P.N. Bhagwati and this Committee functioned until the Parliament enacted the Legal Service Authorities Act, 1987 in view of the mandates of Article 39A of the Constitution of India. The Legal Services Authorities Act, 1987 implemented in its true impact recognized the popularity and utility of Lok Adalats for speedy resolution of disputes. The awards passed by the Lok Adalats are executable like decree of Civil Courts and the same are non-appealable. Thus, the litigation, comes to an end.

The philosophy for setting up permanent and continuous Lok Adalat is that in our country, the litigant public has not so far been provided any statutory forum for counselling and conciliation counsellors and as such, these Lok Adalats may take upon themselves the role of counsellors as well as conciliators. After a *lis* is filed in the Court containing allegations, part of which may be untrue even, the attitudes of the parties get hardened and thereafter the efforts to bring about conciliation are usually scoffed at. Moreover, the Judicial Officers before the matters come up for hearing, are already reeling under the burden of heavy pendency and as such, they are seldom in a position to spare sufficient time for bringing about conciliatory settlement between the parties. Many times the Judicial Officers dealing with the matters feel hesitant to make suggestions for conciliation to the parties because they apprehend that one of the other party may misunderstand their effort. Permanent and Continuous Lok Adalats established in every District Courts Complex provide a statutory forum to the litigants where they may go themselves before litigation and the Courts may also refer to it pending cases for counseling and conciliation. These permanent and continuous Lok Adalats would be certainly in a better position to try conciliatory settlements in more complicated cases arising out of matrimonial, landlord-tenant disputes, property and commercial disputes etc., where repeated sittings are required for persuading and motivating the parties to settle their disputes in an atmosphere of give and take.

The disposal of legal disputes at pre-litigative stage by the Permanent and Continuous Lok Adalats would be providing expense free justice to the citizens of this country. It is also saving the Courts from additional and avoidable burden of petty cases enabling them to divert their Court time to more contentious and old matters.

The philosophy of permanent and continuous Lok Adalats sprouts from the seeds of compassion and concern for the poor and downtrodden in the country and deserves support from us all to make it grow as a tree giving fruit, fragrance and shade to all.

It is for the legal aid functionaries to achieve the goals set out in the Legal Services Authorities Act, which is the main feature and theme of Article 39A of the Constitution of India.

I firmly believe, that the legal literacy and legal awareness are the principal means to achieve the objective for ensuring equality before law for the citizens of our country. All efforts should be made to achieve the object setforth in the Act and make the legal aid programmes meaningful and purposeful. Needless to state that no objective can be achieved unless there is a will to implement with all sincerity and dedication.

Legal profession of the country is more than two centuries old. We can legitimately expect that the future of this profession ought to be very bright, particularly in the context of the enormous strides our country is making in various fields and human rights awareness. Legal profession shall not be equated with working in a factory or in Government office. It is a public service based on ethics, values and principles which assume significance in the context of the social order envisaged under the Constitution. Public interest has to be its motto and service in the cause of justice its creed. One shall keep in mind, the services rendered to humanity by great world leaders who themselves were lawyers. Mahatma Gandhi was a Barrister who practised law without compromising upon truth. Abraham Lincoln always considered legal profession as divine avocation. Lincoln's perception of legal profession in his own words is a pointer to you all.

> *"Discourage litigation, persuade your neighbours to compromise whenever you can. Point out to them how the nominal winner is often a real loser-in-fees, expenses and waste of time".*

In the words of Justice V.R. Krishna Iyer:

> *"The law is a profession and a profession is a learned calling in the spirit of public service, means of livelihood being a lessor consideration".*

Legal aid without legal literacy is less meaningful and purposeful. So, it would be highly useful, if some important legal topics are included as compulsory subject in school curriculum. Such legal education would enable the people to settle several of their disputes outside the Courts at the grass-root level without seeking help from legal experts who are generally expensive. This extremely important aspects seems to be forgotten by those who publicise free legal aid and conduct *neeti-melas* occasionally.

There are some proposals to introduce mobile Courts to move from village to village to settle disputes right there, without the presence of lawyers.

Unless the masses are aware of their legal rights and duties, such programmes would do more harm than any service, especially when unscrupulous elements are capable of exploiting such situations.

Some important legal topics such as certain basic fundamental provisions of the Constitution; family law relating to marriage, maintenance, adoption etc., laws relating to contract, property, motor vehicles, powers and duties of police, criminal and civil laws; general working of our legal system etc., should be included as a compulsory subject in the school curriculum of education.

The 'Legal Awareness' is totally alien to the basic requirement of a living citizen. He deems it unnecessary to be aware of anything legal, for it does not seem worth his time and effort.

I would point out as ultimate tribute to the growing legal awareness, the enactment of the Consumer Protection Act, 1986. Consumer is the king has been acknowledged in no mean terms in ushering in a forum for easy, inexpensive and speedy justice without the attendant rigours of law.

A stark reality that stares at our face is the fact that more than 70% of the people of this country are illiterate. The noble objective flowing from the Preamble of the Constitution and the earnest wish and hopes expressed in the Directive Principles shall remain on paper unless the people in this country are educated.

Time has come to think of providing a forum for the poor and needy people who approached the law Courts to redress their grievance speedily. However, the delay in disposal of cases in law Court, for whatever reason it may be, has really defeated the purpose for which the people approach the Courts for their redressal. Justice delayed is justice denied and at the same time justice hurried will make the justice buried. So, one has to find out a via media between these two to render social justice to the poor and needy who wants to seek their grievance redressed through Law Courts.

Before formation of Law Courts in India, people were settling the matters of dispute by themselves or by mediation.

Alternate Dispute Resolution in Modern India

Judicial Approach to ADR in India:

Labour Law: The first avenue where the Conciliation has been effectively introduced and recognized by law was in Labour Law, namely Industrial Disputes Act, 1947. Conciliation has been statutorily recognized as an effective method of dispute resolution in relation to disputes between workers and the management. The provision in the I.D. Act makes it attractive for disputing parties to settle disputes by negotiation and failing that through conciliation by an officer of the Government, before resorting to litigation.

The only field where the Courts in India have recognized ADR is in the field of arbitration. The arbitration was originally governed by the provisions of the Indian Arbitration Act, 1940. The Courts were very much concerned over the supervision of Arbitral Tribunal and they were very keen to see whether the arbitrator has exceeded his jurisdiction while deciding the issue which has been referred to him for arbitration.

There was much delay in settlement of disputes between the parties in Law Courts which prevented investment of money in India, by other countries. Further, there was no provision in the Indian Arbitration Act, 1940 to resolve a dispute between an Indian and non-Indian as the law relating to contract between the parties were different which caused difficulties to refer such matter for arbitration. In order to avoid such a difficulty, India has undertaken major reforms in its arbitration law in the recent year as part of economic reforms initiated in 1991.

Family Law: The other area Alternative Dispute Resolution is recognized in India is in Family Law.

Section 5 of the Family Courts Act provides provision for the Government to require the association of Social Welfare Organisations to help the Family Court to arrive at a settlement. Section 6 of the Act provides for appointment of permanent counsellors to effect settlement in the family matters. Further section 9 of the Act imposes an obligation on the Court to make effort for settlement before taking evidence in the case.

To this extent, the alternate dispute resolution has got much recognition in the matter of settlement of family disputes. Similar provision has been made in Order XXXIIA of CPC which deals with family matters.

Legal Services Authorities Act: The other legislation which has given more emphasis on the alternate dispute resolution is the Legal Services Authority Act, 1985. Though settlements were effected by conducting *Lok Nyayalayas* prior to this Act, the same has not given any statutory recognition. Matters settled in the *Nyayalayas* earlier were made decree by the Court in which the case was filed on the basis of settlement arrived at between the parties. But under the new Act, a settlement arrived at in the Lok Adalats has been given the force of a decree which can be executed through Court as if it is a decree passed by a Competent Court.

Further provision has been made in the Act for settling pre-litigation cases through such Adalats. Power has been given to the Lok Adalats constituted under the Act to decide the dispute referred to them, to effect settlement by mediation and if settlement is arrived at between the parties to draw a decree on the basis of a compromise and the same will be signed by the members of the Adalat which consists of a Judicial Officer working or retired, a lawyer and a person of social welfare association, preferably women and a copy of the same will be given to the parties, free of costs. This has really reduced delay in getting copy of the decree by the parties. Lok Adalats have acquired wide acceptance and no appeal will lie against the award passed in a Lok Adalat.

Advantages of Alternative Dispute Resolution:

(1) It is less expensive.

(2) It is less time consuming.

(3) It is free from technicalities as in the case of conducting cases in law Courts.

(4) The parties are free to discuss their difference of opinion without any fear of disclosure of this fact before any law Courts.

(5) The last but not the least is the fact that parties are having the feeling that there is no losing or winning feeling among the parties but at the same time they are having the feeling that their grievance is redressed and the relationship between the parties is restored.

With the advent of the Alternate Dispute Resolution, there is a new avenue for the people to settle their disputes. The settlement of disputes in Lok Adalat quickly has acquired good popularity among the public and this has really given raise to a new force to alternate dispute resolution and this will no doubt reduce the pendency in law Courts. Further, this will give a new avenue for lawyers to form Alternate Dispute Resolution Centres to settle the case out of Court as is being done in countries like Australia, England etc. Alternate Dispute Resolution will really achieve the goal of rendering social justice to the parties to the dispute which is really the goal of the successful judicial system.

Another right and welcome step taken was the enactment of the Consumer Protection Act, 1986 for the settlement of consumer disputes and for matters connected therewith.

The aim of the Consumer Protection Act is to provide for an effective, inexpensive, simple and speedy redressal to consumer grievances, which the Civil Courts are not able to provide. This Act is nothing, but an alternate arrangement for the effective adjudication of consumer disputes. The protection as envisaged by Consumer Protection Act provides for setting up of Three Tier Fora that is, District Forum, State Commission and National Commission for redressal of grievances of consumers. The unique Three Tier Quasi Judicial machinery and speedy consumer dispute redressal mechanism envisaged and established thereunder have significantly increased the chances dispensing consumer justice to a maximum number of people.

Large number of consumers are approaching these Fora to seek quick redressal for their grievances. There has also been a spurt in social action litigation on behalf of the consumers, by Consumer Activists, Voluntary Consumer Organisations and other Social Action Groups.

Since it is benevolent piece of socio-economic legislation, no stamp duties are required to be paid on consumer disputes; nor is there any Advocate necessary to pursue a case of consumer dispute and for the reason, the system of adjudication under Consumer Protection Act is simple and quick. No *batta* is required to be paid by the parties for sending the notices etc., and as such, there is no revenue to the Government. Being a welfare State, the Government have to meet the entire expenditure in this regard, besides payment of salaries to the President, Members and the entire staff of the Fora.

The Family Courts Act, 1984 (Central Act No. 766 of 1984) – (for short 'FC Act') had been enacted to provide for the establishment of FAMILY COURTS with a view to promote conciliation in, and secure speedy settlement of, disputes relating to marriage and Family affairs and for matters connected therewith. It received the assent of the President on 14th September, 1984 and published in the Gazette of India, Extraordinary to Part II, Section 1 dated 14th September, 1984 at pages 1 to 8.

The Law Commission, in its 59th Report (1974) had also stressed that in dealing with disputes, concerning the family, different from that adopted in ordinary civil proceedings and that it should make reasonable efforts at settlement before the commencement of the trial.

In selecting persons for appointment as Judges, every endeavour shall be made to ensure that persons committed to the need to protect and preserve the institution of marriage and to promote the welfare of children and qualified by reason of their experience and expertise to promote the settlement of disputes by conciliation and counselling are selected.

Social welfare agencies also are associated with FAMILY COURTS in effecting conciliation and settlement of disputes.

It is the duty of the FAMILY COURT to make all efforts for settlement. Permissible it is for FAMILY COURT to lay down its own procedure with a view to arrive at a settlement in respect of the subject-matter of the suit or proceeding or at the truth of the facts alleged by one party and denied by the other.

Justice in all its facets – social, economic and political – is to be rendered to the masses of this country without any further loss of time – the need of the hour. In such a situation, one must find out the ways and means of a solution to save the system and the country. The new found strategy consists of dispute resolution by conciliation, mediation and negotiation through Lok Adalats. The feat of resolution of disputes by conciliation, mediation and negotiation through 'Lok Adalat' had since been evolved without a statutory flavour. The time has now come to give statutory flavour for resolution of disputes by such method through Lok Adalats by enactment of LESA Act. As already indicated, the said Act in its entirety has come into force in certain States only. Excepting Chapter III, the rest of the said Act had been notified and made applicable in all the States. The need of the hour is that LESA Act as a whole has to be notified and made applicable in the Indian context. The salient provisions are adumbrated in the said Act to see that the pending disputes from the lowest to the highest Court of the land are capable of being resolved by reference to Lok Adalats. In such process, people of India may fervently hope for the delivery of quicker and cheaper justice to the masses of this country at their door-steps.

There is a ray of hope that the innovative team of the Hon'ble Judges of the Apex Court headed by the Hon'ble Chief Justice of India – a dynamic personality – is certainly to burn the orthodoxies of the past and bury them fathom deep and take invigorative steps to activate the salient provisions adumbrated in the LESA Act in such a way as to make the mechanism of Lok Adalat, serving not only as a just dispute resolution forum or a contrivance introduced to reduce the Court arrears but a people's movement for orderly progress through rule of law and participate in self government in the cause of social justice.

Conclusions

The Constitutional promise of securing to all its citizens justice – social, economic and political as promised in the Preamble of the Constitution cannot be realised unless the three organs of the State *i.e.* legislature, executive and judiciary join together to find ways and means for providing to the Indian poor equal access to its justice system.

The judiciary has tried to do this through Public Interest Litigation movement, but this movement has now lost much of its momentum. The executive is balking at enforcing the Courts orders in Public Interest Litigation cases. The persons undertaking PIL cases are misusing the opportunity provided or they are not able to fully utilise the opportunity.

The legislature has enacted the Legal Services Authorities Act, 1987 and thus provided for free legal aid to indigents. For the effective implementation of this scheme, much more diligence on the part of the legislature and the executive is needed.

An institutionalised legal aid will discourage frivolous litigation and instead lay emphasis on public interest actions and protection of unorganised sections such as consumers, women, weaker sections of society. Absence of tort litigation has left manufactures, medical practitioners as well as administrative authorities free to ride rough shod over the interests of consumers and citizens. The small man can rarely fight against the electric company which makes extravagant bills and threatens to cut-off the current if they are not paid. Telephone users in cities are used to being required to pay the telephone rents even when their telephones are dead for long periods. Municipal Corporations are indifferent to the plight of the rate payers suffering bad roads. Unfortunately, no single person takes recourse to law and the authorities think themselves to be unaccountable. In such areas, the legal aid organisations must take up the cudgels on behalf of the small men. Many agencies working on rural or urban development are in need of legal assistance. They need public interest litigation to protect the interests of the hutmen dwellers. They also need assistance in forming schemes of development and for avoiding future trouble. Women are in perpetual need of legal aid.

In India, where public interest litigation has to rescue the common people through the Court process, we must insist on a procedural blended brew, an activist judicial role and a dynamic legal aid project to enliven Article 39A and Article 14. Even, new para-judicial institutions with informal business methods and stress on conciliation, like Family Courts, Juvenile Courts, Settlement Tribunals and Mediation Committees must be fabricated with new social perceptions and processual innovations.

The dynamics of processual justice to the people, the economics of litigative prolixity and the sociology of access to justice, especially community justice, desiderata substantial changes in procedure including Court structure, appellate system and adversarial practice. Equally significant is the need to abolish Court fee which, in our country, is an obnoxious hurdle to people's justice. No where in the World is such heavy Court fee levied as an entrance cess.

The increase in Lok Adalats, Nyaya Panchayats and Alternative Dispute Resolution Mechanisms will help access to justice. A thorough revision of the Court fee structure to suit the indigents is necessary for bridging the gap between the ideal and the real besides lawyers willingness and commitment to this shared value in the contemporary scenario.

ಬಬಬ

ARBITRATION

Arbitration and Conciliation Act, 1996, is based on the United Nations Commission of International Trade Law (UNCITRAL) adopted in 1985, the Model Law on International Commercial Arbitration. In fact, the General Assembly of the United Nations had commended to all countries to give due consideration to the said Model Law on International Commercial Arbitration so that there could be uniformity of Law, Arbitral Procedures and Practices. The rule framed by the United Nations Commission on International Trade Law has been recommended by the General Assembly of the United Nations for the use of the Rules in case disputes arise in international commercial transactions and parties seek settlement of such disputes by resorting to conciliation. Model Law on International Commercial Arbitration and Rules regulate International Commercial Arbitration and Conciliation. The Arbitration and Conciliation Act, 1996, really consolidates and commends law relating to domestic arbitrations, international commercial arbitrations and enforcement of foreign arbitral awards. Settlement of disputes through Arbitration by inserting the Arbitration clause in all commercial transactions is a welcome step for the modern international transactions are not only complicated and complex but parties to the commercial transactions are also doubtful about the points of law and practices during commercial dealings.

Prior to the promulgation of the present Arbitration Act, the Law on Arbitration in India was governed by the Arbitration Act, 1940, Arbitration (Protocol and Conventions) Act, 1927 and the Foreign Awards (Recognition and Enforcement) Act, 1961. Since the Arbitration Act, 1940 became outdated, the new enactment came to be introduced. The provisions of the Arbitration Act, 1940 and the Arbitration Act, 1996, are totally different. The statement of "Objects and Reasons" appended to the Bill specifically says that the present Arbitration Act, 1996, seeks to consolidate and recommend law relating to domestic arbitrations, international commercial arbitrations, enforcement of all foreign Arbitration Awards and to define the Law relating to conciliation taking into account the said UNCITRAL model Law and Rules.

Inaugural Speech on the Ocassion of the 'Conference on Arbitration and Commercial Contracts', Chennai on 10th June, 2000.

The Apex Court had also taken the view that the provisions of the 1996 Arbitration Act should be interpreted by referring to the UNCITRAL model law rather than the Arbitration Act, 1940. It is also useful to refer to the decision of the Court of Appeal in the case of *Channel Tunnel Group Ltd.* v. *Balfour Beatty Construction Ltd.*, 1992 (2) All ER 609. In that case, the Court on appeal dealt with the jurisdiction of the Courts in England to grant interim injunction in cases where the parties have agreed that the dispute shall be settled by arbitration and the Court on appeal took the view that the High Court shall have, "for the purpose of and in relation to a reference, the same power of making orders in respect of interim injunctions or the appointment of a Receiver, as it has for the purpose of an action or matter in the High Court". The aforesaid decision of the Court of Appeal was referred to with approval with the Apex Court.

Under the 1996 Arbitration Act, the Courts have been vested with the jurisdiction and powers to grant interim relief with a view to strengthen the efficiency of the arbitration process. Grant of interim relief is absolutely necessary with a view to ensure that the Final Award can be enforced effectively. Under the provisions of the Arbitration Act, 1996, powers of the Court to interfere with the Award of the Arbitral Tribunal has been restricted to a great extent. This is absolutely essential in order to make success of the party to realise the fruits of the Award within a reasonable time. One of the salient features of the 1996 Act is that the Award is straightaway enforceable without having recourse to a Court of Law as if the Award is a Decree of the Court, unlike in the 1940 Act, where the legal requirement was to make the Award the Decree of Court so as to enforce the same. Thus, it could be seen that the Arbitral Forum is slowly gaining ground and acceptance as an alternative Judicial Redressal Forum.

The Southern India Chamber of Commerce and Industry is organising the Conference and I wish all success to this conference. This conference has got great relevance having regard to the fact that we have thrown open our doors to foreign investors to come to India and to take part in our business ventures apart from establishing their own industries. Though everyone would like to avoid disputes yet there is bound to be disputes in such international commercial transactions. Resort to ordinary course of law is time consuming and therefore, parties to international commercial transactions can consider the desirability of incorporating the Arbitration Clause in their commercial contracts. It is well settled that Arbitration is the Forum chosen by parties in place of ordinary Civil Courts. A study of history would reveal that the last decade of any Century has witnessed great changes. This decade in general and the last two years, in particular, have witnessed a great revolution in Computers. It is said that in the years to come "Citizens" would be replaced by "Netizens" and the world would become a Small Trade Circle irrespective of geographical barriers. This development coupled with the ongoing and ever expanding economic reforms and liberalisation creates a need for the parties in international commercial transaction to device ways and means to settle the disputes amicably, without resorting to Courts of Law which is not only time consuming but also expensive.

am sure, this Conference would seriously consider and debate the pros and cons of resorting to arbitral forum instead of ordinary Civil Courts.

I conclude by referring to the observations of the U.S. Supreme Court in the leading case of *Fireman* v. *Zapata off Shore Co.*, 407 US 1:

> "*A contractual provision, specifying in advance the forum in which disputes shall be litigated and the law to be applied is an almost indispensible precondition to achievement of the orderliness and predicability essential to any international business transactions.*"

I may also refer to the following observations in *Mitsubishi Motors Corpn.* v. *Chrysler-Plymouth Inc.*

> "*As in **Scherk** v. **Albert Culvert Co.**, 417 US 506, we conclude that concerns of international comity, respect for the capacities of foreign and transnational tribunals and sensitivity to the need of the international commercial system for predictability in the resolution of disputes require that we enforce the parties' agreement, even assuming that a contrary result would be forthcoming in a domestic context.*"

ಐಐಐ

JUSTICE IN FAST TRACK

In the State of Andhra Pradesh, 86 Fast Track Courts were contemplated as per the Scheme envisaged by the XI Finance Commission. In pursuance of Scheme proposed by the XI Finance Commission, the High Court prepared an Action plan for the establishment of the said 86 Fast Track Courts i.e. 73 Courts in the cadre of District and Sessions Judges and 13 Courts in the cadre of Senior Civil Judges were proposed at the places, duly identified with reference to pending work. Initially, 46 Fast Track Courts i.e. 43 in the cadre of District and Sessions Judges and 3 in the cadre of Senior Civil Judges were sanctioned by the Government of Andhra Pradesh, at those places where the accommodation is readily available.

Construction of buildings for all the 86 Fast Track Courts has been taken up in right earnest and the same has already been completed in respect of 39 Fast Track Courts.

The High Court has already addressed the Government of Andhra Pradesh for sanction of 18 Fast Track Courts, in respect of which buildings are now made ready, out of the remaining 40 Fast Track Courts to be established. Soon after the receipt of the orders from the Government sanctioning the said Courts, the Presiding Officers thereof will be posted by the High Court. The High Court has taken all the necessary steps to make functional all the 46 Fast Track Courts already sanctioned. Retired Judicial Officers who were found to be suitable were appointed to preside over 20 Fast Track Courts and in respect of the remaining 26 Fast Track Courts regular Judicial Officers were appointed by giving ad promotion. Necessary supporting staff as envisaged by the Fast Track Court scheme have also been recruited for the above 46 Fast Track Courts.

Regular Additional Public Prosecutors have been appointed by the Government of Andhra Pradesh for 21 Fast Track Courts only and for the remaining Courts, alternative incharge arrangements were made. The High Court has been insisting on the Government of Andhra Pradesh to appoint regular Additional Public Prosecutors in respect of the remaining Fast Track Courts also.

The Principal District Judges have been instructed by the High Court to extend all the necessary infrastructural facilities to the Fast Track Courts, so as to

Speech delivered at the inauguration of 'Fast Track Courts Buildings', Vijaywada on 21st September, 2002.

make their functioning real and effective. In pursuance of the directions contained in the judgment of the Supreme Court, the High Court addressed the Government of Andhra Pradesh to accord sanction for the creation of one more post of Junior Assistant and another post of Attender to all the 86 Fast Track Courts, so that the said Courts may not suffer for want of ministerial support.

The High Court has taken a decision to go in for direct recruitment from the members of the Bar, in respect of 24 Fast Track Courts out of the remaining 40 Fast Track Courts and the necessary draft notification has already been sent to the Government of Andhra Pradesh for issuance of the same. All the necessary steps are being taken by the High Court to complete the process of recruitment in quick time.

The High Court has issued instructions to all the Principal District Judges to propose transfer of old Sessions cases particularly, those in which undertrial Prisoners are involved besides, Criminal Appeals and Civil Appeals which are more than two years old to the Fast Track Courts, so that the backlog of old pendency can be substantially reduced. Thus, a total number of 12,271 cases of above categories have been transferred to the Fast Track Courts till now and out of them 4861 cases were disposed of by the end of July, 2002 leaving a balance of 7,410 cases.

A separate Committee of Hon'ble Judges, headed by me has been constituted to monitor all aspects pertaining to the establishment and functioning of the Fast Track Courts and the said Committee is meeting as often as required for the said purposes and keeping a close watch on the functioning of the Fast Track Courts in the State.

The speedy trial is guaranteed under Article 21 of the Constitution of India. Any delay in expeditious disposal of criminal trial infringes the right to life and liberty guaranteed under Article 21 of the Constitution of India. The debate on judicial arrears has thrown up number of ideas on how the judiciary can set its own house in order. Alarmed by the backlog of inordinate delay in disposal of cases, it has been decided to introduce Fast Track Courts. Thus, Fast Track Courts are to tackle the cases of undertrials first, as the graph of such persons in jail has gone high. It is high time to restore the confidence of people in judiciary by providing speedy justice, particularly to the undertrials.

Under the policy, infrastructure for the Fast Track Courts is to be provided by the State Government and the selection of the Judges is to be made by the High Court. The scheme includes; construction of new Court rooms, appointment of ad hoc judges, Public Prosecutors and supporting staff and arrangement for quick processors. It would be appropriate to have, our in-service Judicial Officers to be appointed in these Courts, after giving them promotions on purely temporary ad hoc basis initially for two years, extendable by another two years or till they are promoted on regular basis. These appointments shall be made as far as possible in Fast Track Courts. Their future regular promotion shall depend on their performance in these Courts. Those Officers who are not found fit to travel on fast track, shall be off-loaded and sent back to their regular cadre. It is a joint venture of the Central Government, State Government and the High Court to tackle the problem of undertrials on war footing. It is needless to say that realization of real justice needs co-operation of all the three wings of the Government with one single aim to reach out justice to individuals and thus, maintain rule of law. Interaction between the three wings of the Government is necessary to improve the justice delivery system and such co-operation should be seen in day-to-day dispensation of justice. Sessions trials in several Courts in the country are held-up because of unwanted adjournments on just asking either by the defence counsel or Public Prosecutor, not examining the witnesses within the scheduled time and the non-co-operation of the prosecuting agency. There is a general complaint that the Police has no sufficient time or force, to serve in time the summons to the witnesses and keep the undertrial prisoners present in the Court, at the time of trial. There are instances coming to light that the offenders are sentenced but sentences imposed are not executed because the convicts had already jumped bail and the police has no will and time to search them out. Thus, the Fast Track Courts system cannot pick up speed and deliver the much-awaited results without the co-operation of the Members of the Bar and the prosecuting agency.

The mandate of Legislature as contained in section 309 of the Code of Criminal Procedure is to proceed on day-to-day basis, as soon as the examination of the prosecution witnesses commences. A serious view will be taken of flouting the mandate of section 309 Cr. P.C. Recently, the Apex Court has held that inconvenience of an 'Advocate' is not a "Special Reason" for bypassing the mandate of section 309 Cr. P.C. the Court observed.

> *"If any Trial Court found that the day to day examination was not possible due to non co-operation by the accused or his counsel, the Court would remand the accused to custody or impose cost on the party asking for adjournment".*

It must be ensured by the presiding Judge that the witnesses are examined on the date fixed. The Apex Court has made a remark with respect to the plight of witnesses:

> *"Witnesses tremble on getting summons from the Courts in India not because they fear examination or cross examination but they fear that they might not be examined at all for several dates and on such dates, they will be nailed to precincts of the Courts".*

Regarding the investigation of a criminal case, there is a need of overhauling the State Investigating Machinery. The main reason of high percentage of acquittal is because of unskilled and poor investigation. Something is required to be done. The State must take up this issue on high priority.

However, all the Presiding Officers of the Fast Track Courts and the Staff Members, Lawyers and prosecuting agency should extend their unrestricted co-operation in achieving the goal and to clear backlog of pending cases.

It is not uncommon for any criminal case to drag on for years. During this time, the accused travels from the zone of "anguish" to the zone of "sympathy" The witnesses are either won over by muscle or money power or they become sympathetic to the accused. As a result, they turn hostile and prosecution fails.

In some cases, the recollection becomes fade or the witnesses die. Thus, long delay in Courts causes great hardship not only to the accused but even to the victim and the State. The accused, who is not let out on bail, may remain in jail for number of months or even years awaiting conclusion of the trial. Thus, effort is required to be made to improve the management of the prosecution in order to increase the certainty of conviction and punishment for most serious offenders. It is experienced that there is increasing laxity in the Court work by the police personnel, empowered to investigate the case.

Judiciary today is more deserving of public confidence than ever before. The judiciary has a special role to play in the task of achieving socio-economic goals enshrined in the Constitution while maintaining their aloofness and independence; the Judges have to be aware of the social changes in the task of achieving socio-economic justice for the people.

The Parliamentary Committee on empowerment of women made a recommendation, that the cases of women in detention may be entrusted to the Fast Track Courts for quick disposal. As such cases are not many in our State and being only 266, the High Court took a decision to entrust such cases to the respective Fast Track Courts in all the districts instead of, ear-marking separate Courts for that purpose.

The Fast Track Courts are functioning with meagre staff. The Supreme Court also took notice of the same while disposing off batch of writ petitions recently and directed *inter alia* that the State Government shall see that additional staff are provided to the Fast Track Courts. The High Court has already addressed the Government of Andhra Pradesh to sanction one post of Junior Assistant and one post of Attender to each of the Fast Track Court for their effective functioning. The orders of the Government in that regard are awaited. In the meanwhile, the High Court has taken a decision to instruct the Principal District Judges to provide the said additional Staff to the Fast Track Courts by drawing from the vacant Courts in their districts on a temporary basis, so that the work in the Fast Track Courts is not hampered on account of inadequacy of the staff.

Retired Judicial Officers presiding over the Fast Track Courts are required to dispose off not less than 14 cases per month as contemplated in the scheme and the regular Judicial Officers appointed to the Fast Track Courts by giving *ad hoc* promotion are instructed by the High Court to dispose of minimum of 10 units worth of cases every month. The High Court is regularly monitoring the progress of disposal of cases by the Fast Track Courts in order to ensure that the objective with which the Fast Track Courts are constituted is duly fulfiled. It is noticed that some of the Presiding Officers of the Fast Track Courts are fairing well but some are lagging behind and not reaching upto the norms prescribed by the High Court. Such of those Presiding Officers of the Fast Track Courts who are not coming upto the expectations of the High Court are being individually advised to improve their performance. Everyone associated with the justice delivery system shall endeavour to ensure, that the Fast Track Courts do function effectively and dispose off large number of old cases thereby reduce the pendency considerably.

I expect, the Judges of the Fast Track Courts and the Judicial Officers to:

    (i) maintain punctuality in Court;

   (ii) pronounce judgments within stipulated time;

  (iii) not to leave the headquarters without informing the District Judge or the Controlling Officer, as the case may be;

  (iv) decide the cases without fear or favour, affection or ill-will, apply for the leave at the appropriate stage; and

   (v) Work very hard and be honest and courteous to the litigants, witnesses and the members of the Bar and discharge your judicial functions with all humility at your command.

  (vi) the judicial officers should also make a habit to grasp the knowledge of law from out of the continued utility of their service in the profession.

Judiciary and People

For the members of the litigant public, I would like to say that every citizen in the country has a right to live with dignity; every citizen has a right to aspire for distinction. Availability of a large number of opportunities to resort, to just and fair means in order to attain that dignity and distinction, is what democracy is all about. That is what our Constitution says. And that is what makes life wholesome and worth living in a true and vibrant democracy.

The Indian legal system is committed to open justice. The Courts conduct their proceedings in public. The Courts provide a public service as a part of the function of deciding disputes, at almost no charge to litigants, who pay for their lawyers but not for the Judge and the court room. The role of judiciary continues to expand to cover the resolutions of all matter of disputes. Judges decide the scope and application of all matter of rights and duties with important consequences for individual and for society.

In a democratic and pluralistic society, increase in number of litigations due to growth in population and better and larger awareness of legal rights after a long period of deprivation is inevitable. Nevertheless, preventive and deterrent measures are likely to have their respective impact on the number by preventing vexatious litigations and deterring the litigation-fond section of the people. Such kind of people believe that by filing cases, they can take the benefit of laws delay to benefit themselves. Law's delay, though remains a matter of concern, has alienated the people from approaching the law courts for redressal of their grievance. All organs of justice delivery system must act in harmony, like the organs of a human body and work in close co-ordination so that the system would be healthy and effective.

Courts serve many purposes in the society, but the purpose with which they are most closely associated in the minds of the people is the resolution of disputes *i.e.*, to achieve the justice in each and every case without loss of much time. The courts must have a planned and organised process of managing the progress of each case to achieve it in a timely and economical manner. When the accumulation of cases reaches to an unmanageable stage, the judicial officers should try to detect the factors responsible and devise innovative techniques to clear off the arrears so as to reduce the burden. Several committees of Judges, Law Commission and other non-governmental organisations are engaged in suggesting the ways and means to meet the crisis.

The Court being an instrumentality of the State, under Art. 39A, *'shall secure that the operation of the legal system promotes justice on a basis of equal opportunity, and provide legal aid to ensure that opportunities for securing justice are not denied to any citizen by reason of economic or other disabilities'*. With a view to deliver speedy justice at the doorsteps at no or little cost is gathering momentum in the country, though the pace is very slow. The concept of parallel and alternative dispute resolution has been in vogue for quite some time now. It is one of the steps taken in the said direction.

With the active support from the judicial authorities, members of legal fraternity and officers of the prosecuting agencies, I am sure that Fast Track Courts in Andhra Pradesh will prove to be number one in the country in providing speedy justice to the undertrials, thereby making the constitutional mandate of social justice meaningful and effective.

ಬಿಬಿಬಿ

JUSTICE AT EASY REACH

I am extremely delighted to be a part of this great venture in Madurai. The esteemed presence of the judicial stalwart-Hon'ble the Chief Justice of India – Shri R.C. Lahoti, who has ushered in a revolution in the field of judicial system in this country, has added luster to this important function. His Lordship firmly believes that in any civilized society it is imperative that the rule of law must prevail.

A long cherished dream of the people of Madurai and southern Districts of Tamil Nadu, has been fulfilled today with the establishment of the High Court Bench here in Madurai, the Cultural Capital of Tamil Nadu. It is a moment of pride and elation both for the judiciary and the Executive when access to Justice is made more inexpensive and easier to the people here in Madurai. I had enjoyed the rare privilege of being the member of the Committee setup to identify and select the site for setting up he High Court Bench way back in 1995. Now at the very site, when I see this magnificent edifice of Justice, a rare sense of satisfaction and fulfillment crosses my heart.

The Indian Judicial system is constantly exposed to new challenges, new dimensions and new signals and has to survive in a world in which perhaps the only real certainty is that the circumstances of tomorrow will not be the same as those of today.

The need of the hour is to correct misconception about the Judiciary by making it more accessible and more explicit, by utilising the resources available to improve the service to the public, by reducing delays and making courts more efficient and less daunting.

Our Judiciary throughout the Union of India has earned a reputation for great integrity and independence. We are proud of it. We the members of the Judicial hierarchy have inherited the legacy of dedicated collective endeavour by the Bench and the Bar and establishing an unbroken tradition of high efficiency, perfect integrity and fearless independence. The true touchstone for measuring the success of a Judicial institution is the degree of confidence reposed in it by the public.

About 1000 million faceless citizens of this country are looking towards us with deep and abiding faith and high hopes. Our Justice delivery institutions, in spite of their innumerable drawbacks and failing still command high esteem.

I close with fervent hope that the great tradition of an efficient Judiciary, wholly dedicated to the cause of the people will be kept alive as was done in the past. I sincerely congratulate the Hon'ble Chief Justice of the Madras High Court – Shri B. Subhashan Reddy, Hon'ble Chief Minister of Tamil Nadu, Hon'ble Law Minister – Shri H.R. Bhardwaj and all other Hon'ble Judges, the Tamil Nadu Judiciary and the Bar, and the High Court staff and Government for their efforts to bring the temple of Justice at the doorstep of the people here in Madurai. I salute & pay tributes to all those who had strived this endeavour and making it a reality. May this temple of justice shine and reflect the soul of the famous temple of Madurai Meenakshi and render the divine task of justice forever.

ಬಂಬಂಬಂ

Delivered at the Inauguration of "The Madurai Bench" of the Madras High Court on 24th July, 2004.

ADR – A REAL REMEDY

lternative Dispute Resolution is a very important and stimulating theme of contemporary relevance. A dispute is *'lis inter partes'*. It is a dispute between two or more parties, where a right is asserted by one or more parties against the specified persons and those persons deny that right or claim either totally or partially. Litigation through the Courts and Tribunals established by the State, is one way of resolving the disputes. The Courts and Tribunals adjudicate and resolve the dispute through adversary method of dispute resolution. In this adversarial process, each party will be competing to get the decision in their favour. Obviously, litigation promotes game theory of justice and dispute resolution. Persons with good resources are likely to win the game. Litigation as a method of dispute resolution leads to a win-lose situation. Associated with this win-lose situation is growth of animosity between the parties, which is not congenial for a peaceful society.

Litigation involves lot of delay given the appeals/revision/review including the constitutional remedies. Once there is delay, obviously, the litigation process will become expensive. When I say expensive, it is not just the fee paid to the Advocates and Courts; it includes the cost of conveyance to the Courts, Advocates office, loss of mandays and the psychological trauma one goes through in sustaining the litigation. Ultimately, when the apex court finally decides on the dispute, invariably one of the parties to the litigation will not be happy because of losing the case, the other party though has won the case would have paid heavily for that.

In this background, comes the importance of Alternative Dispute Resolution (ADR) methods. Alternative Dispute Resolution is alternative to litigation as a method of dispute resolution. The ADR methods are – Negotiation, Mediation, Conciliation, Mini Trial, Arbitration and hybrid forms of these methods like Conciliation-cum-Arbitration, mediation settlements being converted to compromise decree etc. The term ADR has been used to describe various systems that attempt to resolve dispute through methods other than litigation in Courts or Tribunals. India has a very rich tradition of ADR methods, which were

---

Speech delivered on 'Alternative Disputes Resolution, Arbitration Lok Adalat and Mediation' at Judicial Colloquia, Pune on 12th February, 2005.

existent in the form of Panchayats. In fact, the Panchayat's decisions were respected by the Judiciary also. In *Sitanna v. Viranna*, AIR 1934 SC 105, the Privy Council affirmed the decision of the Panchayat in a family dispute. *Sir John Wallis* stated the law in the following words:

> *Reference to a village Panchayat is a time honoured method of deciding disputes of this kind and has advantages like – it is comparatively easy for the Panchayatdars to ascertain the true facts and that in this case it avoids protracted litigation which as observed by one of the witnesses might have proved ruinous to the estate. Looking at the evidence as a whole, their Lordships see no reason for doubting that the award was claimed based on both legal and moral grounds and therefore of the opinion that there is no ground for interfering with it.*

There is lot of flexibility in the use of ADR methods. The flexibility is available in the procedure as well as the way the solutions are found to the dispute. The solutions can be problem specific. The rigidity of precedent as used in adversarial method of dispute resolution will not come in the way finding solutions to the disputes in a creative way.

If the ADR method is successful, it brings about a satisfactory solution to the dispute and the parties will not only be satisfied, the ill-will that would have existed between them will also end. ADR methods, especially, Mediation and Conciliation not only address the dispute, they also address the emotions underlying the dispute. In fact, for ADR to be successful, first the emotions and ego existing between the parties will have to be addressed. Once the emotions and ego are effectively addressed, resolving the dispute becomes very easy. This requires wisdom and skill of counseling on the part of the Mediator or Conciliator.

The ADR method is participatory and there is scope for the parties to the dispute to participate in the solution finding process. As a result, they honour the solution with commitment. Above all these, the ADR methods work out to be cheaper and affordable by the poor people also. As of now, there are some aberrations, when it comes to the expenses incurred in arbitration. In course of time, when there are good number of quality arbitrators, the expenses of arbitration will also decrease. The promotion of institutional arbitration will go a long way in improving the quality of ADR services and making them really cheaper.

The development of ADR methods will provide access to many litigants. It helps in reducing the enormous work load that is imposed on the judiciary. Once the cases pending before the judiciary become manageable, the courts will be able to improve the quality of their decisions. All these will go a long way in improving not only the access to justice, but even the quality of justice.

A brief look at the international scenario reveals the popularity of the use of ADR methods for dispute resolution. In the Native American culture, peace-making is the primary method of problem solving. More conciliatory than mediation, peace making is concerned with sacred justice. Disputes are handled in a way which deals with underlying causes of conflict, and mends relationships. [Mediation Principles and Practice by Kimberlee K. Kovach, P.19,

West Publishing Co., 1994] Mediation was used in China and Japan as primary means of conflict resolution. Mediation was the first choice for dispute settlement. China's principle use of mediation was a direct result of the Confucian view of natural harmony and dispute resolution by morals rather than coercion. Chinese mediation boards or committees made up of several individuals from each local community resolve more than 80% of all civil disputes.

In Japan, Conciliation was historically the primary means of dispute resolution with village leaders serving as mediators. Current Japanese negotiation style still places an emphasis on the relationship and is often regarded as a purely conciliatory style. Informal dispute resolution was used in many other cultures as well. For example, India, Africa, Israeli Kibbutzim. The ADR or informal methods of dispute resolution placed emphasis on peace and harmony over conflict, litigation and victory.

In USA, Mediation as a method of dispute resolution was used in an *ad hoc* way since long time, though, litigation was the primary method of dispute resolution. In 1976, Pound conference was held to commemorate the 70th anniversary of Dean Rosco Pound's dissertation on the "Public dissatisfaction with the American legal system". This Conference took a close view as to the reasons as to why Americans were dissatisfied with the administration of justice by American Courts. One of the reasons why justice administration in America was criticized was because of the overcrowded and costly Court system. It was in 'Pounds Conference 1976'. The current ADR movement of America started. Now the ADR is so successful in America nearly 93% of the civil dispute are settled outside the courts.

The Indian scenario reveals that there are many legislations in India facilitating ADR and sometimes making it compulsory.

The Civil Procedure Code contains the following provisions: Order 23, Rule 3 provides for compromise of suit – where it is proved to the satisfaction of the Court that a suit has been adjusted wholly or in part by any lawful agreement or compromise, written and signed by the parties. The Court after satisfying itself about the settlement, it can convert the settlement into a judgment decree. Order 32A, Rule 3 requires the Courts to make efforts for settlement in case of family disputes. Section 80 of the Civil Procedure Code requires giving of 60 days mandatory notice in case of suits by or against the Government with a view to facilitate settlement of disputes amicably wherever possible.

Section 89 of the CPC introduced in 2002 read with Order 10 says that, where it appears to the Court that there exists elements of a settlement which may be acceptable to the parties, the court shall formulate the terms of settlement and give them to the parties for their observation and after receiving observation of the parties, the court may formulate the terms of a possible settlement and refer the same for (a) Arbitration; (b) Conciliation; (c) Judicial Settlement including settlement through Lok-Adalat; and (d) Mediation. In case of mediation, the Court shall affect a compromise between the parties and shall follow such procedure as may be prescribed.

Under Order XXXIIA, inserted by Amendment Act 104 of 1976, dealing with suits relating to matters concerning the family, an endeavour shall be made by the Court in the first instance, where it is possible to do so, consistent with the nature and circumstances of the case, to assist the parties in arriving at a settlement in respect of the subject matter of the suit.

Though such in-built mechanism are there, in the Code of Civil Procedure, for speedy disposal of cases by resorting to settlements, yet such provisions remain as law-inaction, in the sense of being a dead-letter. Such state of affairs should not be allowed to continue any longer. Every concerted effort is to be undertaken to make such salient provisions as law-in-action.

Section 9 of the Family Courts Act, 1984 provides for compulsory conciliation. The Industrial Disputes Act, 1947, provides for conciliation and Board of Conciliation. [Sections 4, 5, 12, 13 & 18]. The Family Courts Act, 1984 (Central Act No. 66 of 1984) had been enacted to provide for the establishment of Family Courts with a view to promote conciliation and secure speedy settlement of disputes relating to marriage and Family affairs and for matters connected therewith.

The Law Commission, in its 59th Report (1974) had also stressed that in dealing with disputes, concerning the family, the Courts ought to adopt an approach radically different from that adopted in ordinary civil proceedings and that it should make reasonable efforts at settlement before the commencement of the trial.

In selecting persons for appointment as Judges, every endeavour shall be made to ensure that persons committed to the need, to protect and preserve the institution of marriage and to promote the welfare of children and qualified by reason of their experience and expertise to promote the settlement of disputes by conciliation and counselling, are selected.

The Arbitration and Conciliation Act, 1996 facilitate the parties to resolve disputes either through conciliation or arbitration. The settlement reached in Conciliation or the Award of the Arbitrator, is a deemed decree. It will be enforced by the Courts as if it were a decree. The Lok Adalats organized under the Legal Services Authorities Act, 1987, facilitate between the parties. The settlement will have the status of a deemed decree. If pending disputes go before the Lok Adalat and are settled in the Lok Adalat, the court fee paid to the Court will be returned to the person who has filed the suit.

From the above description, the importance of ADR and how legislations are made to promote the same is very clear. The unfortunate thing is that we have not been able to develop a cadre of persons who will be able to use these ADR methods in dispensing justice. Lawyers by and large still believe that litigation is the way of resolving disputes. Litigants are also advised accordingly. The challenge that we are facing today is bringing about awareness among the people about the utility of ADR and simultaneously developing personnel who will be able to use ADR methods effectively with integrity. The International Centre for Alternative Dispute Resolution, I believe will be able to meaningfully address this issue.

Experiment of 'Lok Adalat' as an alternate mode of dispute settlement has come to be accepted in India, as a viable, economic, efficient and informal one.

Lok Adalat, as the very name suggests, means 'People's Court'. 'Lok' stands for 'people' and the vernacular meaning of the term 'Adalat', is 'Court'.

Generally speaking, it is not a 'COURT', as understood by the common people, though they may find the attributes of a COURT in it and may call it by this name. It hardly has anything in common with 'LAW COURT', except that both are tools in the legal system to deliver justice. A difference is that, a Law Court sits in its premises, where the litigants come with their lawyers and witnesses, to seek justice, whereas LOK ADALAT itself goes to the people to deliver justice at their door-steps. So, it is a kind of forum, provided by the people themselves or by interested parties, including social activists, legal aiders and public-spirited people, belonging to every walk of life.

LOK ADALAT is another alternative to JUDICIAL JUSTICE. This is a recent strategy for delivering informal, cheap and expeditious justice to the common man by way of settling disputes, which are pending in Courts and also those, which have not yet reached Courts, by negotiation, conciliation or by adopting persuasive, common sense and human approach to the problems of the disputants, with the assistance of specially trained and experienced Members of a Team of Conciliators.

Another right and welcome step taken was the enactment of the Consumer Protection Act, 1986 (Act No. 68 of 1986), for short "Consumer Protection Act" for the settlement of consumer disputes and for matters connected therewith.

The aim of Consumer Protection Act is to provide an effective, inexpensive, simple and speedy redressal to consumer grievances, which the Civil Courts are not able to provide. This Act is nothing, but an alternate arrangement for the effective adjudication of consumer disputes. The protection as envisaged by Consumer Protection Act is protection of consumers, as a class. Consumer Protection Act provides for setting up of Three Tire Fora that is, District Forum, State Commission and National Commission for redressal of grievances of consumers. The unique Three Tier Quasi-Judicial machinery and speedy consumer dispute redressal mechanism envisaged and established thereunder, have significantly increased the chances of dispensing consumer justice to a maximum number of people.

Arbitration is an alternative to litigation as a method of dispute resolution. Bernstein defines arbitration as a mechanism for the resolution of disputes which takes place usually in private, pursuant to an agreement between two or more parties, under which the parties agree to be bound by the decision that is to be given by the arbitrator according to law or, if so agreed, other considerations, after a fair hearing, such decision being enforceable at law. [Bernstein *Hand Book of Arbitration Practice*, 3rd Edn., 1998, p. 13] Arbitration is a process of dispute resolution between the parties through the arbitral tribunal appointed by the parties to the dispute or through the appointment made by the Chief Justice or the designate of the Chief Justice under section 11 of the Arbitration and Conciliation Act, 1996.

The parties have the option to go for *ad hoc* Arbitration or Institutional Arbitration depending on their convenience.

Ad hoc Arbitration

It refers to an arbitration conducted according to the procedure which will either be agreed by the parties or in default of agreement, procedure laid down by the arbitral tribunal at a preliminary meeting once the arbitral tribunal is constituted. *Ad hoc* arbitration is, therefore, an arbitration agreed to and arranged by the parties themselves without recourse to an arbitral institution. In *ad hoc* arbitration, if the parties are not able to agree as to who will be the arbitrator or one of the parties is reluctant to cooperate in appointing the arbitrator, the other party will have to use section 11 of the Arbitration and Conciliation Act, 1996 wherein the Chief Justice of a High Court or the Supreme Court or their designate will appoint the arbitrator. In case of domestic arbitration, it will be the Chief Justice of a High Court or his designate. In case of international commercial arbitration, it will be the Chief Justice of India or his designate. In *ad hoc* arbitration, the fees of the arbitrator will have to be agreed by the parties and the arbitrator. The present Indian experience is that the fee of the arbitrator is providing to be quite expensive in *ad hoc* arbitration.

Institutional Arbitration

It is an arbitration administered by an arbitral institution. The parties may stipulate in the arbitration agreement, to refer an arbitral dispute between them, for resolution to a particular institution. Some of the Indian institutions are; Indian Council of Arbitration (ICA), Federation of Indian Chamber of Commerce and Industry (FICCI), International Centre for Alternate Dispute Resolution (ICADR), Hyderabad. Some of the leading international institutions are; International Chamber of Commerce (ICC), Paris, London Court of International Arbitration (LCIA), American Arbitration Association (AAA), World Intellectual Property Organization (WIPO). All these institutions have rules, expressly formulated for conducting of arbitration. These formulated rules are based on experience, hence address all possible situation that may arise in the course of arbitration.

Why Institutional Arbitration

- In *ad hoc* arbitration, the procedures will have to be agreed by the parties and the Arbitrator. This needs cooperation between the parties. When a dispute is in existence, it is difficult to expect cooperation among the parties.

    In Institutional Arbitration, the rules are already there. There is no need to worry about formulating rules or spend time on making rules.

- In *ad hoc* arbitration, infrastructure facilities for conducting arbitration is a problem, so there is temptation to hire facilities of expensive hotels. In this process, arbitration costs will increase. Getting trained staff is difficult. Library facilities will be another problem for ready reference.

    In Institutional Arbitration, the arbitral institution will have infrastructure facilities to conduct arbitration, they will have trained secretarial and administrative staff. There will also be library facilities. There will be professionalism in conducting arbitration. The costs of arbitration should work out to be cheaper in institutional arbitration.

- In Institutional Arbitration, the institution will maintain a panel of arbitrators along with their profile. The parties can choose from the panel. It also provides for specialized arbitrators. While in *ad hoc* arbitration, these advantages are not available.

- In Institutional Arbitration, many arbitral institutions have an experienced committee to scrutinize the arbitral awards. For example, the ICC has this facility. Before the award is finalized and given to the parties, it is scrutinized by the experienced panel. So the possibilities of, the Court, setting aside the award is minimum. This facility is not available in *ad hoc* arbitration. Hence there will be higher risk of Court interference.

- In Institutional Arbitration, the Arbitrator's fee is fixed by the arbitral institution. The parties know before hand what will be the cost of arbitration. In *ad hoc* arbitration, the arbitrators fee is negotiated and agreed. The Indian experience shows that it is quite expensive.

- In Institutional Arbitration, the arbitrators are governed by the rules of the institution and they may be removed from the panel for not conducting the arbitration properly. Where as in *ad hoc* arbitration, there is no such fear.

- In case, for any reason, the arbitrator becomes incapable of continuing as arbitrator in institutional arbitration, it will not take much time to find substitutes. When a substitute is found, the procedure for arbitration remains the same. The proceedings can continue from where they were stopped. Whereas these facilities are not available in *ad hoc* arbitration.

- In Institutional Arbitration, as the secretarial and administrative staff are subject to the discipline of the institution, it is easy to maintain confidentiality of the proceedings. In *ad hoc* arbitration, it is difficult to expect professionalism from the secretarial staff.

When I was the Chief Justice of Andhra Pradesh, I had an occasion to work closely in the promotion of this ADR methods as the Chairman of the Advisory Council of ICADR. The first step I took as Chief Justice was to instruct all the District Judicial Officers to help ICADR to conduct workshops to apprise the Judicial Officers as well as the Advocates and other interested persons about the Arbitration & Conciliation Act of 1996 and also the techniques of Conciliation. The idea being, that those trained persons could be utilized to work as Mediators or Conciliators or Arbitrators as and when section 89 was invoked. The next step I took was the ICADR conducting P.G. Diploma Course in ADR. I encouraged the students by awarding Certificates to them and also presenting Gold Medal to the best candidate of ICADR. I also took initiative to enhance the Corpus Grant of ICADR with a view to provide income to it and facilitate the conduct of its programmes. I started a P.G. Certificate Course in Vijayawada where with great enthusiasm about 50 students participated, all of whom were Chartered Accountants, leading Advocates and business people. I helped ICADR to empanel the Diploma & Certificate Holders as Conciliators for Lok Adalat and also for the purpose of adoption of ADR methods for expeditious resolution of disputes in a peaceful and satisfactory manner. Unless these ADR methods are sincerely encouraged by the Judiciary, the Executive and the Advocate fraternity, the strives in the society will not end and the resort of people out of frustration to other unsocial elements which disturbs the peace and harmony in the society will not be put to an end. It is, therefore, a duty of the Judiciary and the executive to give maximum encouragement to ADR methods. We should endeavour to inspire the parties to settle disputes out of court by utilizing section 89 of CPC more and more. It is a very beneficial section. There may be some deficiencies in the New Arbitration & Conciliation Act of 1996 which is now on the anvil of amendments. One amendment that is immediately needed is to section 36 of the Arbitration and Conciliation Act of 1996. It is this section that confers on the Award, the status of a court decree. It becomes a deemed decree only when an application for setting aside the Award was not filed in a court and if filed not disposed of by the court. The courts in the Indian experience are taking enormous time for the disposal of these applications. In other words, till the disposal of these appeals the Award cannot be implemented which means that the filing of an appeal for setting aside an Award is operating as an inbuilt stay. It frustrates the very purpose of expeditious disposal of disputes. The Supreme Court recently has expressed its helplessness to interfere in these matters and expressed a desire to an early amendment to this section by making it obligatory on the courts for quick disposal of these applications.

The Governments both at the Centre and at the States as well as the Judges of the Supreme Court, High Courts and jurists are genuinely concerned to tackle this menace of legal delays, which turned out to be bane in the system. A Committee headed by Justice Mallimath called the "Arrears Committee" went deep into this question of arrears and suggested various measures to resolve disputes by laying emphasis on A.D.R. methods. Thereafter, series of meetings of the Law Ministers and Chief Ministers were held and a national consensus for judicial reforms was arrived, according to which Negotiation, Conciliation and Arbitration were considered the most viable alternative to Court litigation as they are considerably less expensive, more informal with procedural flexibilities and at the same time took lesser time for resolution. The result is the enactment of the Arbitration and Conciliation Act of 1996 for the purpose of providing more expeditious and less expensive way of settling disputes by recourse to Arbitration and Conciliation on the model of UNCITRAL (United Nations Commission on International Trade Laws). This beneficent piece of legislation applies not only to domestic litigation in all fields of legal relationships but also to international commercial arbitration. The Model Law gave maximum freedom and autonomy to the parties in the matter of choice of Arbitrators, applicable Law, procedures to be followed, the evidence to be led and time frame for the award.

The Supreme Court also recently observed:

> "We should make the law of arbitration simple, less technical and more responsible to the actual realities of the situations but must be responsive to the canons of justice and fair play and make the arbitrator adhere to such process and

norms which will create confidence, not only by doing justice between the parties, but by creating sense that justice appears to have been done."

The Hong Kong International Arbitration Centre, most probably the largest arbitration service center in Asia, has held the view that "arbitration as compared to litigation has become very popular for resolving the disputes. Similarly, conciliation and mediation find an increasing measure of support in future."

Lastly, I wish to recall what Abraham Lincoln said, more than a century ago:

"As a peace–maker, the lawyer has a superior opportunity of being a good person." (Notes for a Law Lecture – Home Book of American Quotations (by Dodd, Near) New York, 1967, p. 226).

ಬಲಬಲಬಲ

ARBITRATION FEE

I always feel that there must be a cordial relationship and atmosphere between the Bar and the Bench. There must be co-operation and co-ordination between the two. But for the co-operation of the Bar, the Judges would not be in a position to discharge their duties effectively, with the result, the ultimate sufferers would be the litigant public.

Lawyers, as a body, are also duty bound to discharge their duties to the Court, client and to their own fraternity. If they observe this principle, the Courts will be in a position to effectively function and dispose of cases quickly.

Lawyers must read the law journals so that they will be in a position to assist the Court in effectively disposing of cases by the Judges, which will in turn help the lawyers to have up-to-date knowledge of the legal position.

I would like to cite one instance where three over-ruled decisions were cited before the concerned trial court and the trial court, on the basis of those citations allowed the application for injunction, which was later reversed by me in the High Court at the revisional stage. For this, the Presiding Officer is not at all to be blamed. It is for the lawyers to read and cite the up-to-date case laws and also to see whether the judgments are still good law or over-ruled by the Courts. Anyhow, this mistake was brought to our notice and ultimately the order of the trial court was set aside and the matter was set at right.

Many Bar Associations do not have even the ordinary law books which are to be referred very frequently, and are also not in a position to contribute and purchase law journals.

Arbitration is nothing but a forum selected by the parties instead of going to the regular Courts. The Arbitration Act, 1940, is not an exhaustive code. No provision is found in the Act as to the procedure to be adopted by the Arbitrators while dealing with the resolutions of the dispute between the parties. There is no clear-cut answer to the question as to what is legal misconduct and as to how far the Arbitrator is bound by law. It is not an arbitrary method of settling the disputes. The Arbitration act contains enough provisions for referring the disputes to arbitration without the intervention of Court and with the intervention of Court. Any civil dispute between the parties can form the subject-matter of arbitration proceedings. One of the essential ingredients of the

Speech delivered at the Bar Association, Cuddalore, on 6th August, 1994.

submission to the arbitration is, that the parties should agree that the dispute intended to be referred should be determined in a quasi-judicial manner. The arbitration clauses in contracts is a collateral term as distinguished from the substantive terms. If the contract containing the arbitration clause is non-est in law or it was void *ab initio*, the arbitration clause cannot operate independently and the same is also void. There is no requirement that the arbitration clause should be expressed in any particular form. The only requirement is that there must be an agreement to submit/present future differences to arbitration and that the said agreement must be in writing. In other words, there cannot be any oral arbitration agreement. One of the main reasons for resorting to Arbitration procedure is to avoid undue delay in getting the disputes settled in normal Courts of law. But, the experience has been that even the arbitration procedure has been made as much cumbersome and time consuming. In many cases, one of the parties to the arbitration agreement will challenge the scope of the arbitration clauses and in particular, whether a particular matter will fall within the terms of the Arbitration Act. After the conclusion of the Arbitration proceedings, the person who is successful before the Arbitrator files an application for passing a decree in terms of the Award and the person who is unsuccessful files a petition to set aside the Award of the Arbitrator.

Since there is no definition as to what legal misconduct means, in each and every case, the Court has to decide this question on the facts and circumstances of that particular case. If, ultimately, the Court decides to grant a decree, the said decree is subject to further right of appeal, which is again time consuming. Hence, it is necessary that provisions have to be made, by amending the Arbitration Act, stipulating the time within which the Arbitration should be completed and the time within which the Court should dispose of the matters which come before them.

An Arbitration Agreement, whereunder the Arbitrator abrogates the powers of Magisterial Courts to decide whether or not the offence has been committed, is invalid. An agreement to refer a non-compoundable offence to Arbitration is opposed to public policy. Equally, the claim arising out of illegal actions cannot be referred to Arbitration because the contract itself is illegal and void. Likewise, matters relating to appointment of guardians to minor and questions relating to guardianship cannot be settled by reference to Arbitration.

I had an occasion to consider the amounts charged by the Arbitrators as their remuneration and I had opined that it is time the Central Government steps in and brings about the amendments to the Arbitration Act, stipulating the rates of fees payable to the Arbitrators. Arbitrators should not charge exorbitant fees.

It is not necessary that an Arbitrator should be named in an agreement. The Arbitration Agreement, unless a different intention has been expressed therein, shall be deemed to include the provision set out in the First Schedule to the Arbitration Act. It is better to choose an experienced person in the field of dispute as Arbitrators. The person selected as Arbitrator should not only be a specialist in the matter but should also have adequate knowledge of law.

Courts have also got power to appoint Arbitrator or Umpire. When the Court appoints the Arbitrator or Umpire, it is the duty of the Court to select a competent and impartial person. The Arbitration Act provides the circumstances under which the Arbitrator or Umpire can be removed by the Court and also the Court has the power to set aside the Awards of the Arbitrators.

It is gratifying to note that several questions arise *viz.*, whether checks should be put on the Arbitrators, whether necessary qualification is to be prescribed and whether the necessary provision should be made to make the award of the Arbitration appealable. If the decision of the Arbitrator is subjected to appeal provisions, there would be enormous delay in the disposal of the arbitration case. Moreover, the qualification of the Arbitrator is to depend on the facts and circumstances of each case.

In one meeting in which I participated, a suggestion was made that the disputes involving less than Rs. 25 lakhs should not be taken to Court, which may not be possible. If that suggestion is to be accepted then the entire Arbitration Act should be repealed and replaced by a new enactment.

It is true that the purpose of resorting to Arbitration Proceedings is to get expeditious and speedy remedy. For this purpose, Special Courts can be constituted for deciding the disputes arising out of the Arbitration Act.

The settled law is that an Arbitrator is not bound to give reasons for an Award and an unreasoned Award cannot be set aside merely on that ground. Necessary provision should be made in the Arbitration Clause or the contract that whenever the value of the claim exceeds a particular amount, the Arbitrator should be obliged to give reasons for making an Award.

ಐಐಐ

Part X

Human Resource and Dispute Resolution

SCOUTING

Founded by Lord Baden Powel, Scouting has now grown as the biggest uniformed organisation for young boys – an organisation that primarily channelises the interests and energies of the younger generation towards outside world & develops sociability as well as a sense of service and self-sacrifice among the boys. Scouting instils discipline, sacrificial mentality and patriotism while removing thoughts of selfishness and sectarianism from young blood. It helps to foster good relations and co-operation between different countries, in the true spirit of the adage 'World itself is a family (*Vasudhaiv Kutumbakam*).

The objectives of scouting are not unreal nor are they impractical. But instilling these noble ideals and objectives is the need of the hour to build up a better generation in whose hands the destiny of our country lies.

When we are stepping into the new millennium, we have to create a new outlook and image to the outside world. The need of the hour is that we have to rise as one, dedicated to the task of national re-construction on the sound foundation of truth and honesty. Organisations like Scouts and Guides can help prepare the younger generation to meet these challenges, and infuse in the younger blood, the spirit of self sacrifice for the sake of their motherland.

Gandhiji used to say that if one really wants to serve his country and its people, it is essential for him to concentrate on service that is to say he should think of service and service alone and not of any other gain or advantage for himself. True service can be performed only when a person is sincerely and single mindedly, devoted to the cause of service itself.

If we have to build a strong and vibrant new India, it is necessary for us to work in a spirit in which our collective skills are co-ordinated for national development. This reminded me of the words of Pandit Jawaharlal Nehru "Let's wipe every tear from every eye" "That may be beyond us but as long as there are tears and suffering, so long our work will not be over".

The lofty ideals reverberated in the qualities of idealism, unselfishness, universal brotherhood, enthusiasm, dutifulness-propagated by the Scouts

---

Speech delivered at the inaugural function of the Platinum Jubilee Celebration of Scouting in Cochin.

movement are echoed in the fundamental duties, under Art. 51A of our Constitution. Art. 51A enumerates the various fundamental duties to be performed by every citizen of India. These duties imply certain corresponding rights in every citizen, which are implied and justifiable. The idea behind these duties is attainment of social and economic justice consistent with the Rule of Law. However, attention is to be invited to some of these fundamental duties. Art. 51A(e) exhorts every citizen _"to promote harmony and the spirit of common brotherhood among all t'..: people of India, transcending religious, linguistic and regional or sectional diversities."_ While in Art. 51A(j) there is demand of _"the citizens to strive towards excellence in all spheres of individual and collective activity so that the nation consistently rises to higher levels of endeavour and achievement."_

For achieving excellence in all spheres of our activities, there should be understanding, unity and the earnestness to work hard. The mathematical equation for excellence in every sphere of life teaches us to

+ Add good friends
− Subtract bad qualities
x Multiply one's strength
÷ Divide the work
(d) Differentiate between right and wrong and
(s) Integrate personality

I wish the torch of lofty ideals of the Scout Movement will lead the younger generation in the right direction, towards their quest for national service and development.

ಬಿಬಿಬಿ

CAPITAL & LABOUR

Industrial law occupies a predominant place in the legal system of our country, not because it affects directly a large section of the population but because the economic growth and prosperity of any nation is determined by the high level of production which is not possible without joint efforts of Capital and Labour. Hence, it is essential that there should exist harmonious and cordial relations between the management and labour and that can be achieved only by industrial relation practices, healthy trade unionism and support of Labour Laws.

Though industrial law, in its present form, came into existence only in 1947, it has made great strides with the passages of time. Therefore, this branch of law occupies an important and prominent place in the legal system of our country.

What we learnt in the Law College that a contract ensues out of an offer, freely made and freely accepted and a contract, thus, made is final, binding and almost sacred, is still holding the field. Though heavy in-roads have been made in many directions but it is in the field of industrial law that the principles of contract law have almost been given a go-bye.

The Industrial Disputes Act, 1947, has been frequently referred to as "a piece of social legislation". This legislation seeks to ensure to the workmen, who have not the capacity to treat with capital on equal terms, fair returns for their labour and to prevent disputes between employer and employees so that production might not be adversely affected and the larger interest of the society may not suffer. Tribunals, administering industrial law are not trammeled, either by the contracts of parties or by the law of master and servant and that the industrial tribunal has a wide discretion in dealing with the disputes before it. It is, therefore, as Ludging Teller in his treatise on "Labour Disputes and Collective Bargaining, has said:

"Industrial arbitration may involve the extension of an existing agreement, or the making of a new one, or in general, the creation of new obligations or modifications of old ones".

Speech delivered on the occasion of Sri R. Venkataraman Endowment Lectures, conducted by Madras High Court Advocates Association, Madras on 16th March, 1996.

It is a matter of great satisfaction to note that late B.R. Dolia took out a Labour Law Journal and constituted an Endowment for the purpose of delivering lectures on Labour Laws so as to enlighten the members of the Bar and the Bench on Labour Laws and keep them abreast of the same.

It is said in our ancient Vedas that a man who has acquired knowledge commits a great sin if he does not partake his knowledge with others. It is necessary that erudite and eminent persons in the field of industrial Law should partake their knowledge with others.

I wish the endowment created in the name of Sri R. Venkataraman, former President of India, should organise many more lectures like this so as to benefit the members of the Bar and the Bench and all those connected with Industrial Relations.

The 'S. Viswanathan – B.R. Dolia Lecture Trust' is being inaugurated by Hon'ble Mr. Justice M.M. PUNCHHI with a corpus of Rs. 2.5 lakhs. I have been suggesting that a Trust should be created in the name of B.R. Dolia, who was a leading and able member of our Bar. His contribution to the Labour Law was immense. It is he who argued in the 1970's that Gymkhana Club was in 'industry' and that the appropriate Government has got power to refer an industrial dispute for adjudication, notwithstanding the fact that on earlier occasions it has declined to refer the dispute for adjudication and that the power of the Government is not exhausted merely by reason of such refusal. Recent decisions of the Apex Court have accepted the above contentions of late B.R. Dolia. He was not only a thorough gentleman to the tip of his fingers but also a philanthropist. He was generous and kind-hearted. So far as Mr. S. Viswanathan is concerned, he is a lawyer turned into a top class industrialist. He is closely associated with our former President of India, Sri R. Venkataraman, and both of them championed the cause of workers in the State of Tamil Nadu. I understand that Justice Mack used to characterise Mr. S. Viswanathan as 'Snake Charmer'. Such was his forensic abilities. He is the Chairman of Seshasayee Paper and Boards, Erode, Ponni Sugars and Chemicals and High Energy Batteries, Trichy. He is the man responsible for using 'baggasse' (a waste in sugar industry) as a raw material for making paper in the place of conventional raw material *viz.,* wood and forest produce. Thanks to his efforts, Tamil Nadu News Print is using baggasse as raw material instead of wood.

I desire that more endowments should be created so that the Lawyers association can organise lectures on different subjects in the field of law.

ಖಲಖಲಖ

DISCOVER FREEMASONRY

As observed by Mackey, in his Symbolism of Freemasonry "Wisdom of all the ancients that has come down to our hands is Symbolic". Street in his classical book "Symbolism of the Three degrees" has pointed out that a Freemason, who knows nothing of our symbolism, knows little of Freemasonry and that besides rendering the ritual perfectly, it is most desirable, that the Masonic symbolism is properly understood. The great Mason and Scholar Bro. Albert Pike has urged that "The Symbolism of Masonry is the soul of Masonry, Every symbol of a Lodge is a religious teacher, the mute teacher also of morals and philosophy. It is in its ancient symbols and in the knowledge of their true meanings that the prominence of freemasonry over all other orders consists". He has further added that "Science makes use of symbols; for its transmission language is also indispensable; wherefore the sages must sometimes speak. But, when they speak they do so, not to disclose or to explain, but to lead others to seek for and find the truth of science and the meaning of the symbols". Our ceremonies and symbols give an allegorical or symbolic representation of human existence not only here, but hereafter and point the way which leads to the greatest good, both in this life and in the life to come. It is only, when we reflect upon them in relation to this sublime allegory of human life, that we are enable to comprehend them in the fullness of their beauty and grandeur. We must therefore endeavour to understand that every sign, every symbol and every portion of the ceremony, in the first degree is designed to illustrate allegorically, some moral phase of human existence.

Let us now understand and analyse the symbolism of the distinguishing characteristics of a Freemason.

- After the blessing of the light of Freemasonry is revealed – to the initiate, he is instructed and shown the three great, though emblematic lights in Freemasonry, followed by an explanation of the three lesser lights and after entrustment and investiture, he is placed at the North Eastern portion of the Lodge, figuratively, to represent the foundation stone. Our ritual teaches that from the foundation laid in the evening of the initiation, the initiate is expected to raise a superstructure, perfect in its parts and

Speech delivered at the seminar on 'Discover Freemasonry', Warangal, Andhra Pradesh on 5th October, 2002.

honourable to the builder, with the aid of and with the assistance of all the moral virtues and the excellencies of character symbolically taught to him. The charge at the North East explains, in a solemn and dramatic manner, but symbolically, the crown of all virtues, which is the distinguishing characteristic of a Freemasons heart, namely CHARITY.

- I cannot adequately emphasise this aspect, than to quote Saint Peter. He has taught that, "Giving all diligence, add to your faith, virtue and to virtue, knowledge and to knowledge, temperance and to temperance, patience and to patience, godliness and to godliness, brotherly kindness and to brotherly kindness, charity". He has, thus, likened the formation of a perfect character to the erection of a seven storied house, in which the foundation is the faith and the coping stone or the pinnacle, Charity. The V.S.L. describes it as "a principle of prevailing love to God and Goodwill to men, which effectually inclines one endued with it to glorify God to do good to others, to be patient, slow to anger and ready to forgive wrongs, to show kindness to all and seek the good of others though with prejudice to himself. A person endued therewith does not interpret doubtful things to the worst sense, but the best; is sorry of the sins of others, but rejoices when anyone does well and is apt to bear with their failings and infirmities and lastly, this grace is never lost, but goes with us into another world and is exercised there. The following other passages from the V.S.L. are also enlightening.

(a) Knowledge puffeth up but charity edifieth, (b) Charity suffereth long and is kind, Charity, envieth not, (c) faith, hope and charity but the greatest of these is charity, (d) Follow after Charity and desire spiritual gifts, (e) Let all your things be done with Charity, (f) Have fervent Charity, for Charity shall cover sins (g) Greet ye one another with a kiss of Charity. All the V.S.Ls have eulogised charity. Bhagavad Gita, in Chapter 17, extols this virtue. The scriptures define charity as kindly state of mind, which renders the person full of goodwill and affectionate regard towards others. Charity is derived from the Latin Word "Caritas" and has been translated as Charity in the Holy Bible. Masonic Encyclopaedia describes it as the distinguishing grace of freemasonry. In the Masonic lectures, the following is mentioned, while describing Charity. "Lovely in itself, is the brightest ornament which can adorn our Masonic profession. It is the best test and surest proof of sincerity of our religion. Benevolence, rendered by Heaven born Charity, is an honour to the nation, whence it springs, is nourished and cherished. Happy is the man, who has sown in his breast, the seeds of benevolence; he envies not his neighbour, he believes not a tale reported to his prejudice, he forgives the injuries of men and endeavours to blot them from his recollection . . . . . . We are free and accepted masons, ever ready to listen to him who craves our assistance and from him who is in want, let us not withhold a liberal hand. So shall a heartfelt satisfaction reward our labours and the produce of love and Charity will most assuredly follow".

- Perhaps, it will be apposite at this stage to refer to an extract from an address in the Scottish ritual. "..... but true Masonry exists in the heart and is composed of brotherly love, relief and truth and that heavenly consummation of all virtues – Charity – so beautifully explained in the V.S.L. as bearing all things, hoping all things, believing all things, enduring all things and thinking no evil and it is to the practice of this virtue, that your Masonic efforts should ever tend, not only in its common acceptance of pecuniary relief, but as embracing true brotherly love to the full extent, inculcated in the sacred writings." In the Irish ritual the following is found, "Secondly, to remind, in the years to come, that at one time in your life you found yourself in the position of a person, who actually stood absolutely penniless in the midst of plenty, thereby enabling to visualise, more forcibly and intimately, the humiliation and suffering of those really so placed who might some day solicit your help. "The charge at the North Eastern teaches the Golden Rule, the duty of a man to his fellow in dire need in a manner never to be forgotten. It is not left to the imagination, since the initiate is actually placed in position of the man, who asks for his aid, making the duty more real and vivid. Amplifying that teaching, the initiate is exhorted to, in the explanation of the T.B., that freemasons' charity should have no bounds save those of prudence.

- In the explanation of the T.B., we are taught that the distinguishing characteristics of a good Freemason are Virtue, Honour and Mercy and that same should ever be found in a Freemason's breast. Let us, therefore, consider those distinguishing characteristics of a good freemason. Our ritual teaches us that Freemasons must imbibe all moral virtues as all of them constitute the staves of the Jacob's ladder. We are also taught that to the virtuous and just man, death has no terrors. In the history of ancient Rome, it is recorded that Consul Marcellus intended to erect a temple to be dedicated to Virtue and Honour. On account of opposition, he modified his plans and built two temples, contiguous to each other, but the only avenue to the temple of Honour was through the temple of virtue. The moral is explicit. That virtue is the only direct road to Honour. I cannot extol the virtue better than to quote, in extensor, the Masonic lecture dealing with Virtue. "*Virtue is the highest exercise of and improvement to reason; the integrity, harmony and just balance of affection; the health, strength and beauty of the soul. The perfection of the virtue is to give reason its full scope, obey the authority of conscience with alacrity, to exercise the defensive talents with fortitude, the public with justice, the private with temperance and all of them with prudence; that is in due proportion to each other with a clam and diffusive beneficence; to love and adore God with an unrivalled and disinterested affection and to acquiesce in the dispensations of Divine providence with a cheerful resignation. Every approach to this standard is a step towards perfection and happiness and any deviation therefrom has a tendency to vice and misery*". Every Freemason has to develop virtue as per the Masonic teaching and be more and more virtuous.

- The next distinguishing characteristic is Honour. We have sworn to preserve other brethren's' Honour and carefully preserve it as our own. It is, therefore, necessary to elucidate the attributes of Honour. Here again, I cannot do better than to quote from the Masonic lecture. *"Honour may justly be decided to be the spirit and supererogation of Virtue; the true foundation of mutual faith and credit and the real intercourse by which the business of life is transacted with safety and pleasure."* It implies the united sentiments of virtue, truth and justice, carried by a generous mind beyond those mere moral obligations, which the laws require or can punish the violation of True Honour though a different principle from religion, is that which produces the same effects; the lines of action, although drawn from different parts, terminate at the same point. Religion embraces virtue, as it is enjoined by the laws of God; Honour, as it is graceful and ornamental to human nature. The religious man fears, the man of Honour scorns, to do an ill action, the latter considers vice as something beneath him; the other as something which is offensive to the Divine being. A true man of Honour will not content himself with the literal discharge of the duties of a man and a citizen; he raises and dignifies them to magnanimity; he gives, when he may, with propriety, refuse and forgives, where he may with justice recent. The whole of his conduct is guided by the noblest sentiments of his own unvisited heart; a true moral rectitude is the uniform rule of his actions and a just praise and approbation of his due reward. A life well regulated as per the Masonic teaching certainly makes the brethren Honourable and that is the reason for our fraternity being known as Ancient and Honorable fraternity of Free and Accepted Masons.

- Let us now consider Mercy as it "is a refined virtue and when possessed by the monarch, adds a lustre to every gem that adorns his crown; if by the warrior, it give an unceasing freshness as to the wreath that shades his brow. It is the companion of true honour and the ameliorator of justice, on whose bench, when enthroned, it interposes a shield of defense on behalf of the victim, impenetrable to the sword. And as the vernal showers descend on the earth, to refresh and invigorate the whole vegetable creation. So, Mercy, acting on the heart, when the vital fluids are condensed by rancour and revenge, by its exhilarating warmth, returns nature to its source in purer streams. It is the peculiar attribute of the Deity on which the best and wisest of us must rest our hopes and dependence; for at the final day of retribution, when arranged at his bar and the actions of this mortal life are unveiled to view, though His Justice may demand the fiat, we hope and trust His mercy will avert the doom." Such is the divine virtue of Mercy, which like its sister Charity, blesses him, who gives as well as him, who receives.

- Having regard to the time needed for the presentation of all the papers, I have confined to some important aspects alone. Let, "Charity, Virtue, Honour and Mercy, ever distinguish us as men and as Freemasons. May the God Almighty of the Universe (kindly take the full form of his Abbre) bless us all with abundance of those virtues and dispose our hearts to succour the weakness and relieve the necessities of Brethren and fellowmen. Let us seek the solace of our own distress, by extending relief and consolation to the fellowmen in the hour of their affliction. That way each one of us will be enabled to lay up a crown of joy and rejoicing, which will endure when time, with us will be no more.

ജ്ഞാന

PERFUSIONISTS

Clinical Perfusionists deal with management of heart-lung machine which enable heart surgeons to temporarily stop heart and lungs, and maintain blood circulation in various body organs. Many enviable achievements and advancements have happened in this field in the past few decades which has made heart surgery very safe and enabled lasting results. Famous heart surgeon and scientist, Dr. John Gibbon of Philadelphia, performed the first successful heart surgery using a heart-lung machine on 6th May, 1953. Since that time, with ups and downs in research and inventions, the equipment went through remarkable improvement to reach the present stage. For the efficient management of heart-lung machine, better oxygen and carbon dioxide exchange, warming and cooling the patient's blood, etc., a group of paramedical personnel were deployed known, as Clinical Perfusionists. It is beyond any doubts, that they are as important, even more, at times, than the surgeon and anesthetists for the effective conduct of open heart surgeries.

In India, heart surgery became popular in the 1970's. Till recently, advanced cardiac care was confined to places like Chennai, Bombay, Delhi, etc. Sree Chirtra Institute of Medical Sciences, under the guidance of Dr. Valiyathan, has achieved great advancements in open heart surgery. The invention of a heart valve (Chitra valve) in this institute, the only artificial heartvalve manufactured in India, is the pride of India. Now there are many institutions in Kerala to cater the needs of our people with results as good as or even better than international standards.

The people of Kerala had to travel long distances, even crossing the border to obtain advanced cardiac care. However, now with the development of super specialty cardiac care in many centres in Kerala, the people do not need to travel to obtain this any more. Also it is extremely welcoming that the cost of advanced care in all hospitals of Kerala remains much cheaper than outside.

The support of clinical perfusionists in producing good results need not be emphasized and it is nice to learn that this is one of the few associations of Clinical Perfusionists in India. The organisers and members of this Association, supported by surgeons, need to be congratulated for this good organisation to enable professional and personnel communication and sharing. Open heart

---

Speech delivered in the annual conference of 'The Association of Clinical Perfusionists of Kerala', (an Org. of Heart-lung By-Pass specialists), Cochin on 2nd October, 1999.

surgery is a team work. Each and every member for this team is equally important. It is the duty of Surgeons and Anesthetists to guide the rest of the team to maintain the spirit which obviously is the basis of obtaining good results.

The training in Clinical perfusion is given in India in various centres like Sree Chitra Institute, Trivandrum, and Christian Medical College, Vellore. We have still scarcity of Perfusionists in India and it is important that more number of people should be trained to support new centres coming up. Besides the need for more personnel, the quality also needs to be closely monitored to ensure best possible results.

However, the current recommendation is that two Perfusionists are necessary to conduct one open heart procedure so that the safety of the procedure is ensured invariably. Since concentration and utmost agility make their job very stressful and chances for accidents are high, unless supported by adequate number of personnel. So, it should be borne in mind that Surgeons and Anesthetists should make sure that their working conditions are upto the mark. They should not be taxed beyond their limits to the advantage of the hospital or Surgeons concerned.

The scientific sessions that follow, would educate all on the current advancements in open heart surgery.

I, therefore, exhort the members of the Association to strive hard to maintain the public confidence in the medical system of our country. For this, one has to maintain a strong sense of identity, solidarity and commitment. A better public image can be built up through hard work and sense of values.

The challenge of the new millennium is the changing technological scenario. This will envelop the profession of Clinical Perfusionists also. They will have to keep pace with the fast developing technological arena.

ಬಿಬಿಬಿ

HIRE PURCHASE

On account of legal position contained in the Banking Regulation Act, 1949, Banks are not in a position to give direct financial assistance to the hirer under the hire purchase contracts. However, Banks are doing refinancing of hire purchase deals. Reserve Bank of India has allowed Banks to enter into the business of hire purchase subject to certain conditions. Hire purchase finance really provides a supplementary source of finance for purchase of automobiles and certain other consumer articles. Various Committees set up to study the working of Non Banking Companies have laid great stress on the need for encouraging hire purchase finance. Banking Law Committee, set up under the Chairmanship of Dr. P.V. Rajamannar, in its Report, has recognized, the vital role played by the hire purchase financiers and recommended draft legislation called Personal Property Security Act. The Report of the aforesaid Committee *inter alia* covers hire purchase contracts.

A hire purchase transaction consists of 'hire & purchase'. When a hire purchase financier lets out, on hire purchase, an article, control of bailment comes into existence. If the hirer pays all the installments duly and promptly as per the agreement, he can exercise his right to purchase the articles and if he decides to purchase the property, the title passes to him.

The Law Commission of India in its 20th Report has said as follows:

"A hire purchase agreement is a form of bailment, the hirer is given the right to purchase the goods on certain conditions. That, however is an option not an obligation to purchase. The hirer may elect to purchase the good and when he does so, after he fulfils all the conditions prescribed in the agreement, the title to the goods will pass to him. But he may elect not to do so, and in that event he is entitled to return the goods and terminate the agreement in the manner provided therein."

The twin nature of hire purchase agreement has been succinctly brought out by the Madras High Court in the case of *Dakshinamurthi* v. *General & Credit Corporation*, (AIR 1960 Mad 328) in the following words:

"It (hire purchase) is comparatively modern in origin and is designed to serve the need of credit buying while at the same time protecting the vendor from being

Speech delivered at the "Federation of All India Hire Purchase Financiers', Madras on 4th April, 1993.

caught in the meshes of law relating to sales stricto sensu. In effect, hire purchase is bailment with an option to purchase though it is sometimes used in a wider sense to include agreements when there is irrevocable agreement to buy in installment terms with the proviso that the title shall not pass until the installments are paid. A hire purchase agreement thus not only creates a bailment, but a bailment plus an option to purchase. The transaction is compounded of the element of both the hire and sale, and it would be clearly wrong to assimilate it to hypothecation of movable property".

A hire purchase transaction is not a lease. Unlike 'hire purchase', in the case of lease, no option is given to the lessee to purchase the goods. That brings out the essential distinction between a lease and hire purchase. Hire purchase agreements have been classified as

(1) Hire purchase finance agreement; and

(2) Hire purchase refinance agreement.

In the first classification, there exists a real hire purchase agreement and in the second type of cases, the intention is basically to give loan. Such agreements are regarded as secured loans.

The Hire Purchase Act, 1972 was enacted to define and regulate the rights and duties of parties to hire purchase agreements and for matters connected therewith or incidental threats.

The hire purchase transactions play a very crucial role in the financial market and occupy an important place in the economic development of the country.

ಬಾ ಬಾ ಬಾ

DISPUTES IN FLAT PROMOTION

O n account of the recent increase in the building construction activities in the recent years, many disputes have arisen between the owner of the land and the developer and also the prospective buyers. Most of the building contracts have in-built provisions for referring the dispute between the parties to the Arbitration and as to who is to be appointed as the Arbitrator. The Construction Industry is the second largest industry in the world, being next to agriculture. Thus, it has become necessary for the people who are engaged in the nation building activities like Engineers, Architects and Contractors, to know the essential legal provisions.

Arbitration is nothing but a forum selected by the parties instead of going to the regular Courts. The Arbitration Act, 1940, is not an exhaustive code. No provision is found in the Act as to the procedure to be adopted by the Arbitrators while dealing with the resolutions of the dispute between the parties. There is no clear cut answer to the question as to what is legal misconduct and as to how far the Arbitrator is bound by law. It is not an arbitrary method of settling the disputes. The Arbitration Act, 1948, contains enough provisions for referring the disputes to arbitration without the intervention of Court and with the intervention of Court. Any civil dispute between the parties can form the subject-matter of arbitration proceedings. One of the essential ingredients of the submission to the arbitration is, that the parties should agree that the dispute intended to be referred should be determined in a quasi-judicial manner. The arbitration clause in contracts is a collateral term as distinguished from the substantive terms. If the contract containing the arbitration clause is non-est in law or it was void *ab initio,* the arbitration clause cannot operate independently and the same is also void. There is no requirement that the arbitration clause should be expressed in any particular form. The only requirement is that there must be an agreement to submit/present future differences to arbitration and that the said agreement must be in writing. In other words, there cannot be any oral arbitration agreement. One of the main reasons for resorting to Arbitration procedure is to avoid undue delay in getting the disputes settled in normal Courts of Law. But, the experience has been that even the arbitration procedure

---

Speech delivered in the seminar on 'Disputes in Building Contracts and in Flat Promotion' at IIT Madras, on 25th June, 1994.

has been made as much cumbersome and time consuming. In many cases, one of the parties to the Arbitration Agreement will challenge the scope of the arbitration clauses and in particular, whether a particular matter will fall within the terms of the Arbitration Act. After the conclusion of the Arbitration proceedings, the person who was successful before the Arbitrator files an application for passing a decree in terms of the Award and the person who is unsuccessful files a petition to set aside the Award of the Arbitrator.

Since there is no definition as to what legal misconduct means, in each and every case, the Court has to decide this question on the facts and circumstances of that particular case. If ultimately the court decides to grant a decree, the said decree is subject to further right of appeal, which is again time – consuming. Hence, it is necessary that provisions, be made by amending the Arbitration Act, stipulating the time within which the arbitration should be completed and the time within which the Court should dispose of the matters which come before them.

An Arbitration Agreement, wherein the Arbitrator abrogates the powers of Magisterial Courts to decide whether or not the offence has been committed, is invalid. An agreement to refer a non-compoundable offence to the Arbitration is opposed to public policy. Equally, the claim arising out of illegal actions cannot be referred to Arbitration because the contract itself is illegal and void. Likewise, matters relating to appointment of guardians to minor and questions relating to guardianship cannot be settled by reference to Arbitration.

I had occasion to consider the amounts charged by the Arbitrators as their remuneration and I had opined that, it is time the Central Government steps in and bring about the amendments to the Arbitration Act, stipulating the rates of fees payable to the Arbitrators. Arbitrators should not charge exorbitant fees.

It is not necessary that an Arbitrator should be named in an agreement. The Arbitration Agreement, unless a different intention has been expressed therein, shall be deemed to include the provision set out in the First Schedule to the Arbitration Act. It is better to choose an experienced person in the field of dispute as Arbitrators. The person selected as Arbitrator should not only be a specialist in the matter but should also have adequate knowledge of law.

Courts have also got power to appoint Arbitrator or Umpire. When the Court appoints the Arbitrator or Umpire, it is the duty of the Court to select a competent and impartial person. The Arbitration Act provides the circumstances under which the Arbitrator or Umpire can be removed by the Court and also the Court has the power to set aside the Awards of the Arbitrators.

It is gratifying to note that one of the Speakers is going to touch upon the question as to whether checks should be put on the Arbitrators, whether necessary qualification are to be prescribed and whether the necessary provision should be made to make the award of the Arbitrator appealable. I am of the view that, if the decision of the Arbitrator is subjected to appeal provisions, there would be enormous delay in the disposal of the arbitration case. The qualification of the Arbitrator is to depend on the facts and circumstances of each case.

The settled law is that an Arbitrator is not bound to give reasons for an Award and an unreasoned award cannot be set aside merely on that ground. Necessary provisions should be made in the Arbitration Clause or the contract that whenever the value of the claim exceeds a particular amount, the Arbitrator should be obliged to give reasons for making an Award.

Some of the State Governments like Maharashtra, West Bengal, Gujarat, Karnataka, Uttar Pradesh and Delhi have enacted laws like Apartment Ownership Act or Ownership Flat Act. These laws vest the State Government with powers to intervene and settle disputes with the seller and buyer of apartments. Very often, the promoter does not disclose his title to the lands on which flats are constructed. Even the encumbrances over the lands are not disclosed. There are many cases where there is great deviation from the sanctioned plan of the Town Planning Authorities. After the sale of the flats, the promoter disappears from the scene and the purchasers are left alone to fight against the Town Planning Authorities, who threaten to demolish the building. Sales tax is collected by the promoters but the same is not remitted to the State and the Promoter goes to a Court of Law and gets stay of the order, demanding payment of sales tax. No doubt, the Consumer Protection Act provides some relief to the buyers of flats. However, the best course would be for the State Government to a take notice of the existing state of affairs and the helpless condition of the buyers of flats and bring about suitable legislations containing the Form of Contract entered by the buyers of flats and promoters, licensing of promotions, etc. This would go a long way in reducing the number of disputes between the flat promoters and buyers. Very often it is found that the promoters do not complete the construction on time or hand over the same to the buyers. The disputes in building contract and flat promotion is on the increase.

It is imperative to find suitable remedial measures to settle such disputes speedily and satisfactorily.

ಐಐಐ

SERVICE DISPUTES – EXCLUSIVE JURISDICTION OF ADMINISTRATIVE TRIBUNALS

Constitution of India and the Service Law

In the statement of Objectives and Reasons underlying the Administrative Tribunals Act, 1985, it was envisaged that the setting up of tribunals to deal exclusively with service disputes would go a long way in not only reducing the burden of various courts but also providing speedy relief to the persons covered by the tribunals. It must be remembered that this enactment was necessitated mainly to tackle the problem of backlog of cases in the High Courts.

Part XIV of the Indian Constitution deals with the services under the Union and the States which contains the Articles 308 to 323. Article 312A was inserted by the Constitution 28th Amendment Act, 1978 with effect from 27th August, 1972, enabling the Parliament to make law to vary or revoke conditions of Article 314 which was repealed in order to obviate controversies, arising out of the Constitutional protections of the special provisions of the members of the ICS and other civil servants appointed by the British crown who continued in the service of Government of India after the commencement of the Constitution.

Under Article 323A of the Constitution of India, the Parliament provided for the adjudication or trial, by administrative tribunals, of disputes and complaints with respect to recruitment and conditions of service of persons appointed to public services and posts in connection with the affairs of the Union or of any State or of any local or other authority within the territory of India or under the control of the Government of India or of any corporation owned or controlled by the Government.

The Constitutionality of the Rules made under Article 309 to regulate the recruitment and conditions of services of persons appointed to public services and posts in connection with the affairs of the Union or of any State is tested on the touch stone of Articles 14, 15, 16, 19, 20 and 21 of the Constitution of India. Where there are no statutory rules made under Article 309, Article 162 empowers the Executive to make non-statutory rules in exercise of its general executive power. The enforceability of the rules made under both the Articles or any other

Speech delivered at the National Seminar on Administrative Tribunals – Role, Problems and Perspectives, at Hyderabad on 9th March, 2002.

Articles depends upon the nature of the rules, *i.e.,* mandatory or recommendatory. Only the rules which are mandatory in nature are enforceable in Courts of law be it statutory or non-statutory. Apart from powers conferred under Articles 309 and 162, the rules can be made under Article 15(4) to make, special provision for advancement of any socially and educationally backward classes of citizens or for the SCs and STs under Article 148(5) to frame conditions of service of persons serving in the Indian Audit and Accounts Department, under Article 154(1) by the Governor of the State in exercise of residue of Government functions. Article 310 deals with the pleasure doctrine of President in regard to the tenure of the Civil/defence servants under the Union. The said doctrine is controlled by the fundamental rights. Service under the Government though originating in contract, is governed by the provisions of the Constitution and the rules made under Article 309.

The next important and foremost protective gear to the civil servants is Article 311 which mandates that no person mentioned therein shall be dismissed or removed by an authority, subordinate to that by which he was appointed except after an enquiry in which he has been informed of the charges against him and given a reasonable opportunity of being heard. The Chapter II of Part XIV is with regard to the Public Service Commissions, their constitution, and functions. Part XIVA containing the Articles 323A and 323B were inserted by the Constitutional Amendment Act, 1976. An attempt to omit this part by 45th amendment bill 1978 did not succeed due to opposition in Rajya Sabha. This part of the Constitution enabled establishment of Administrative Tribunals. These provisions came into effect by enactment of Administrative Tribunals Act, 1985 on 2nd October, 1985 and establishment of Central Administrative Tribunals. Accordingly with the said provisions, the A.T. Act, 1985 was enacted making a provision for appeal to Supreme Court only under Article 136, ousting the jurisdiction of all other Courts including High Court over the judgments of the Administrative Tribunals.

But the position is altered with the pronouncement of judgment in *Chandra Kumar* case by the Supreme Court in 1997. The Tribunals are competent to hear matters where the vires of statutory provisions are questioned. However, in discharging this duty, they cannot act as substitutes to the High Courts and the Supreme Court which have, under our constitutional setup, been specifically entrusted with such an obligation. Their function in this respect is only supplementary and all such decisions of the Tribunals will be subject to scrutiny before a Division Bench of the respective High Courts. The Tribunals will consequently also have the power to test the vires of subordinate legislations and rules.

Accordingly, in *Chandra Kumar's* case, the Apex Court held clause 2(d) of Article 323A and Clause 3(d) of Article 323B, to the extent they exclude the jurisdiction of the High Courts and the Supreme Court under Articles 226/227 and 32 of the Constitution, as unconstitutional.

Judicial Review of Administrative Action

The object and scope of judicial review of administrative action is different from that of appeal. The object of judicial review of administrative action by ordinary Courts is to keep the administrative authorities within the boundaries of their powers under the law. Appeal on the other hand, means that the superior Administrative Tribunals or Court to whom appeal lies under the law has the power to reconsider the decision of the inferior Tribunal on the merits. In all the modes of judicial review, the jurisdiction of the Court, whether in a declaratory action or in a writ proceedings is simply to set aside the unlawful order and not to substitute its own decision for that of the statutory authority. In exercising power of judicial review, the Court cannot enter into the merits of the conclusions arrived at by the authority or interfere with the decision as if in appeal and also cannot interfere with the policy laid down by the Government unless it appears to be plainly arbitrary or *mala fide* or violative of fundamental rights. The various aspects of judicial review are writs of judicial review *viz., locus standi* of the person seeking intervention of the Court, nature of litigation whether public or private, justiciability of the action relating to the matter, presumption of constitutionality of the administrative action, presumption of legality of official acts, presumption against *mala fides* or abuse of power, non-interference with the exercise of discretionary power and judicature satisfaction and policy.

Thus the administrative adjudication, which is quasi-judicial in nature, is the main function of Administrative Tribunals. In brief, the objective of the Administrative Tribunals is to provide for speedy and inexpensive justice to the litigants for which the procedure followed by Tribunal is made flexible and technically free from the Ordinary Courts.

The Role, Problems & Perspectives

It is well known that by design, judicial process is slow and tedious. The astronomical number of cases pending in different courts in itself is an indication of this facet of the judicial process in India. The number of times hearings are adjourned on one ground or the other and the time taken for ultimate disposal of cases is phenomenal.

Apart from formal Courts of Law created under the Constitution, in our legal system tribunals can be set up for different purposes. The underlying idea is that such tribunals can provide specialisation in different fields and also dispense justice speedily, if not at comparatively cheaper cost.

It is by now well settled that tribunals are not substitutes of the High Courts. Yet, most tribunals have the strapping of High Courts in the matter of procedures and technicalities. They follow the same procedure involving cause lists, voluminous paper books mentions, special-mentions, lengthy arguments and counter arguments, adjournments affidavits, certified copies of the orders and what not.

The definition of service matters, under the Act, is wide enough to deal with the service matters of the employees of the Central Government, State Governments, local bodies employees or other authorities employees within the territory of India and under the control of the Government of India or Corporation or society owned or controlled by the Government. Section 14 of the Act deals with the jurisdiction, powers and authority of Tribunals. It is specified clearly in sub-section 1 that the Central Administrative Tribunal shall exercise its jurisdiction, powers and authority in relation to service matters of the person belonging to All India Service or any civil service of the Union or any civil post under the Union or a Civilian appointed to any defence service or post connected with the Defence or any corporation or society owned and controlled by the Government. Sub-section 2 of the said section contemplates that the Central Government may, by notification, apply the provisions of sub-section 3 to the local or other authorities within the territory of India or controlled by Government. Under the said section, number of notifications were issued bringing various societies for example Kendriya Vidyalaya Sangathan, Navodaya Vidyalaya Samithi, Indian Council for Agricultural Research, Indian Council for Scientific Research etc., under the purview of Central Administrative Tribunals Still there are number of organisations and their employees which are corporations or the societies or other bodies owned and controlled by the Central Government which can be brought under the jurisdiction of the Administrative Tribunals by issuing Notifications. As far as Central Administrative Tribunals are concerned, there are about 21 Benches operating throughout India. In many of the Benches the number of cases being filed are very less and not commensurate with the infrastructure provided. The Bill introduced in the Parliament to bring the various nationalised banks etc., and their employees under the purview of the Central Administrative Tribunals is yet to be passed. The autonomous institutions like Universities, deemed Universities, research Institutes etc., should essentially be brought under the purview of the Administrative Tribunals for speedy justice to its employees.

Conclusions

The powers of the Tribunals, in exercising their jurisdiction in respect of the service disputes, is narrowed down to a great extent by judge-made law. Its power to interfere in the administrative decision in respect of transfer of employees, selection conducted by D.P.C. for promotion and appointments, quasi-judicial decisions in respect of the punishments imposed on the employees, proportionality of the punishments, sufficiency or otherwise of the evidence in departmental enquiries is practically nill. It is in this area only, the aggrieved employees approach the Tribunals seeking justice. We are currently passing through an era where the effectiveness of this institution is being questioned. In one sense this is the essence of democracy. Since the Tribunals are the Courts of first instance, as far as these service matters are concerned, they should be bestowed with the power to interfere in the above areas in order to do complete justice to the aggrieved persons.

There should be one guiding principle. In origin, many tribunal functions started within the administrative process. Tribunals were established because it was clear that the citizens needed an independent means of challenging possible mistakes and illegalities, which was faster, simpler and cheaper than recourse to the regular Courts. Tribunals will keep the confidence of users only insofar as they are seen to demonstrate similar qualities of independence.

ಬಬಬ

Part XI

Taxation

PART XI

TAXATION

TAXATION – AS OLD AS MANKIND

The theme of the National Tax Conference is Taxation in the New Milieu.

"Milieu" is an expression wider than "Millennium". Milieu is derived from the word "Middle" and means "Environment", "setting", "medium" or "element", while the word "Millennium" refers to Thousandth Anniversary or 1000 years after the Second coming of Christ. In fact, it is also understood as the coming of the Golden Age. The organisers have appropriately preferred "Milieu" to "Millennium", because what is relevant today is the "environment, setting and the medium" and not merely the time frame.

What is the relevance or necessity for a rethinking on the form of taxation that we should adopt in the new Milieu? How is the new Milieu different from what existed earlier? How best does taxation as an instrument of development become relevant in this context? These are some of the thoughts that come uppermost in your mind when you deliberate on the theme of this Conference.

Taxation is as old as Life. Even Vedic texts talk about the right of the king to raise revenue by taxation. Kautilya's 'Arth Shastra' has a Chapter on 'Taxation'. Taxation, as a revenue raising measure, has been adopted in the Anglo Saxon civilisation as well as in European countries.

The History of Indian Taxation starts with the first Income Tax Law, introduced in 1860, consequent to the financial difficulties arising from the Mutiny of 1857, which is known as the first struggle for independence. The tax was in force for a period of 5 years. This tax lapsed in 1865, but was revived in 1867 in the form of a Licence Tax on Trades and professions. In 1868, a new tax known as "Certificate tax", not materially different from the "Licence Tax" was introduced. While in the original tax, introduced in 1860, agricultural income from lands above a rental value of Rs. 600 per annum was included. Licence Tax and the Certificate Tax did not cover agricultural income. In 1869, Certificate Tax was converted into a general income tax, which included Agricultural income as well, in its purview. This Act was in force only for one year but for the subsequent 4 years, annual tax legislation was resorted to. With the improvement of financial position, 1873 witnessed the abolition of Income tax.

Speech delivered on Taxation on the New Milieu at the National Tax Conference held at Jodhpur.

This was not to last for long. The Great Famine 1876 to 1878 brought in the revival of Direct Taxation by the Act of 1877. This had the character of Licence Tax on trader and a cess on land. The tax was based on local conditions which stressed the fact that the power to tax should be based on the ability to bear the burden and was enforced through local Acts in the Presidency Towns of Bengal, Madras and Bombay, by way of Local Acts and Central Acts for the Northwest Frontier provinces and Punjab. This continued till 1886 with various amendments. Considering the number of amendments that the Income-Tax Act has undergone in recent times, it may be a matter of consolation that between 1880 and 1886, there were as many as Twenty-three Tax enactments.

The Act of 1886 was a fullfledged Tax Act which had great improvement over its predecessors and the basic structure laid therein has endured since then.

The next land mark in the history of Indian Taxation is the Income Tax Act of 1918, more than 30 years after the Act of 1886. This Act made substantial strides in the law relating to taxation in India. Close on the heels of the Act of 1918, there was change in policy relating to taxation and the administration of Income Tax till then carried on by the Provincial Governments was vested in the Central Government. Based on the recommendations of the All India Income Tax Committee, a new law was put on the anvil resulting in the Indian Income Tax Act, 1918. A major improvement was that instead of specifying the rates of taxation in the Schedules to the Act, it left the rates to be determined by the Annual Finance Act to give taxation structure greater flexibility and economic relevance. This feature has survived till today.

The Act of 1922 was substantially amended in stages; major amendments being in 1939 after an experience of almost 2 decades in the administration of the previous Act. Large scale amendments were introduced in 1939 which were based on the recommendations of the Expert Income Tax Committee appointed in 1935. After 1939, amendments were a regular feature.

The period subsequent to 1939 witnessed the Second World War which necessitated raising higher revenues on one hand and a closer monitoring on large incomes which were made by certain assessees because of the war conditions on the other. Two of the important amendments which require to be mentioned during the period 1939 to 1956 which saw as many as Twenty-nine Amending Acts, are the amendment, made pursuant to the recommendation of the Commissions appointed under the Taxation of Income (Investigation Commission) Act, 1947 and the Taxation Enquiry Commission, under the Chairmanship of Dr. John Mathai.

The Income Tax Act was thereafter referred to the Law Commission and a draft Bill was submitted in 1958. The Law Commission took almost two years to deliberate on and recommend a comprehensive law on Income Tax. Two areas which concerned the Government were (i) rationalisation of the Law to prevent inconvenience to assessees and (ii) prevention of evasion of income tax. Direct Tax Enquiry Committee, popularly known as Thyagi Committee considered both the angles and submitted a detailed report in 1959, resulting in the Income Tax Act of 1961 which holds the field today, though substantially changed by frequent amendments from 1961 till now.

Some of the Committees which deserve mention in the shaping of the Tax Law are (i) Boothalingam Committee Report, (ii) Vanchoo Committee Report, (iii) Raja Chelliah Committee Report, among others.

Almost about a quarter of a century after we became Republic and about 25 years before this millennium, in the Budget for the year 1976, the Finance Minister declared in the Budget Speech in Parliament that—

1. Realistic rates of taxation are preferable to condiscatory rates;

2. Social justice cannot be achieved in a poor country like India without economic growth and accent of tax should be on economic growth with social justice.

It cannot be gainsaid that taxation far from being a necessary evil, has to be recognised as a compensation for buying civilisation as stated by Justice Holmes. Sir Lesmoney of U.K. stated before the Royal Commission of Income Tax that taxation was the best expenditure he made. These eminent declarations regarding the nature of taxation can be achieved only by stability in tax rates, rationalisation of tax structure, easy procedures, simple laws and a practical and humanitarian approach of the tax administration.

The need for stability of tax was recognised for the first time in the White Paper published in 1986, declaring a long term Fiscal policy. In the last decade, taxation policy has witnessed sweeping changes starting with reduction of tax rates, repeal of uneconomic tax law and streamlining the system. Abolition of Estate duty, Repeal of Gift Tax, streamlining of the Wealth Tax Act are but a move in this direction. The earlier concept of integrated system of tax laws, propounded by Prof. Kaldor which provided for a tax when you earn income, a tax when you owned wealth, a tax when you gifted a property, and tax when you die leaving property, with the result that at the end of the day, you will be surrounded by taxes, is no longer the norm today. The system has undergone a change for the better. It is needless, hence, to say that if the system has to continue to be proactive, it necessarily calls for total cooperation on the part of the tax payer and a voluntary compliance. The stress now is on tax payer compliance and reducing the administrative discretion to the minimum.

The new millennium has witnessed changes all-around. The State as a custodian of the common good has pledged itself to economic growth, social development, environmental protection and simultaneously secured for India a place in the Global map. The old concept of taxation, as a tool to raise revenues is no longer existent. Taxing enactment can be the means to secure economic growth and social justice. The Income Tax Act contains provisions for economic growth by providing incentives to setting up industries in backward areas, incentives for exports, incentives for undertakings set up in Export Promote Zones and 100% export oriented units with a view to encourage industrialisation of the country, exemptions in respect of royalties for foreign enterprises, foreign remuneration to academicians, professional income from foreign sources and remuneration for services rendered outside India.

In order to encourage Information Technology and Computer related activities, deductions and allowances are provided to such businesses. With a view to secure infrastructure development, which improves the lot of the common man, section 80HHE and 80HHF provide for concessions in respect of infrastructure development. Concessions are given to Senior Citizens and women, rebates to encourage savings and investments and to promote thrift. The Income Tax Act recognises that development of society cannot be the sole responsibility of the State and Non-Governmental organisations contribute substantially to social development. In order to encourage such non-governmental organisations to work in conjunction with the Government to achieve the goal of social, educational and cultural development, tax concessions are allowed to Charitable Trusts which contribute substantially to developmental activities.

Environmental protection has been a major area which causes considerable concern. In order to secure these ends, provisions have been made in the Income Tax Act, section 54G providing incentive for shifting businesses from urban to non-urban areas with a view to reduce imbalances in the ecology. This provision has also a social objective namely, promoting jobs in non-urban areas and to prevent exodus of people from non-urban to urban areas.

The Rule of Taxation in the Millennium and in the new Milieu is thus not merely to raise revenues but to secure a balanced all round growth, an economic, social and cultural growth for the benefit of the common man.

ଓଓଓଓ

ROLE OF CHARTERED ACCOUNTANTS

We have reached the twilight zone of the new Millennium. The bright rays' of the dawn of the 21st century have already begun to shine. The birth of a new millennium will bring along new challenges and problems for us to face. Old systems will give way to new ideologies. The birth pangs of a new order and a bright tomorrow have already begun to be felt. The profession of chartered Accountants will have to cope up with the multitude challenges of the new millennium. The role of the Chartered Accountants in a changing society assumes much significance in the light of their contributions towards development. Chartered Accountants hold the key to the coffers of the nation. They play a pivotal role in the destiny of a country. They are the part of the machinery of economic upliftment of the nation. Hence, the Chartered Accountants will have to gear themselves up to face the challenges of the new millennium.

The challenges of the new millennium are multitude. One of the challenges is the erosion of values in the profession. The Chartered Accountants Act, 1949 has prescribed high standards in the profession and laid down the code of conduct to regulate and maintain the status and standard of the profession. A Chartered Accountant has to assume onerous responsibilities involved in the discharge of the public duties by securing maintenance of the requisite standard of discipline and conduct.

Another challenge of the new millennium is the changing technological scenario. This will envelop the profession of Chartered Accountants also. They will have to keep pace with 'the fast developing technological arena. There have been spectacular development in the fields of computers, micro-electronics and communication that have given rise to a wholly new age of humanity – the age of informatics. Chartered Accountants have to update themselves to utilise maximum use of computers and other electronic devices. Today, information can be stored electronically in computers and worked upon. This will lead to an enormous increase in efficiency as well as in the speed of processing.

Presidential Address on the occasion of the 'Conference of Institute of Chartered Accountants of India Branches', Cochin on 1st July, 1999.

Coupled with the technological advances, the impact of globalisation on trade and commerce will have its repercussions on the profession of Chartered Accountants. Liberalisation and free market policy will give rise to new problems and challenges in the area of trade and commerce.

The complicated tax structure and policies of the country and the plethora of judicial decisions on tax laws have given rise to uncertainty and confusion in the minds of the assessees. To add to these are the frequent amendments to law relating to Company and Public Sector Undertakings, Stock Exchanges, Income Tax, Financial Investments and allied laws. A Chartered Accountant, as a guide and ready reckoner to the fast changing tax laws, has to update and equip himself with all the necessary knowledge. Maintenance of a well equipped library and publication of books and periodicals on relevant subjects can in a way help one to update knowledge of law and tax policies. Continuing professional education through conferences, workshops and seminars is the need of the hour.

I exhort the members of the Chartered Accountant community to strive hard to maintain the public confidence in the economic system of our country. For this, one has to maintain a strong sense of identity, solidarity and commitment. A better public image can be built up through hard work and sense of values.

I conclude with an earnest hope that the Chartered Accountants will rise to the occasion and meet the challenges of the coming years with vigour and enthusiasm.

ಇಂಬಿಂಬ

CORPORATE GOVERNANCE – COMPANY SECRETARIES

I had very few occasions to interact with Company Secretaries but whenever I had an opportunity to interact with some of the Company Secretaries they incidentally also happened to be from the legal profession; I was convinced that Company Secretaries are competent professionals to discharge the responsibilities of senior managers in corporate organizations. I was given to understand that Company Secretaries of late have risen to the highest equalance of Management Director. That is positively a definite indicator of the competence of Company Secretary as a corporate professional.

As all of you are aware, the country is passing through a very crucial state. Gone were the days when industry was operating under various controls in the form of numerous legislations. The country is passing through a stage of deregulation, decontrol and liberalization. India has a very long history of business activity, dating back perhaps to civilization as such. The corporate form of management in India as elsewhere in the world is increasingly resorted to because of the obvious advantage that such form of organization has with it. Thanks to the brilliant judgment, delivered by the House of Lords in Solomon's case, today, I was told that a little over two lakhs and odd companies are at work with almost five companies being incorporated in the country everyday. Looking in retrospect, one would see that when corporate management was uncontrolled, unfettered, unsheppered, public money was at stake and protection of public interest was the casualty. To protect the public money possibly and also to protect the public interest regulations, a form of corporate legislations were enunciated. When controls through legislations were the order of the day, the industry and profession alike felt that too many controls had gone out of control. Control as a syndrome, in a way, to me, is a necessary adjunct of any judicial system, but possibly the rigour of the controls could be reduced. In a democratic and developing country like ours, some governmental controls in the form of legislations, in the form of administrative orders are inevitable for a healthy industrial atmosphere. The only point I would like to stress here is that the

Speech delivered at Silver Jubilee Celebration of 'Institute of Company Secretaries of India at Southern Region,' Chennai on 21st December, 1992.

controls as a concept are necessary. The control should be meaningful and more responsive. Today the country is passing through a phase of liberalization, a situation which was necessitated because of a variety of factors. Liberalization as a concept should not be understood in a lose form but should be construed as amounting to selective and strategic planning and purposive governmental intervention. Corporate governance, corporate management with which all of you are, day in and day out, connected in the context of liberalized environment, in the context of purposive controls, is thereafter, a specialized job, calling for professional acumen. Today a need has arisen to look into the various facets of corporate law and all other connected legislations with a view to appreciating the deficiencies if any and evolve strategies for growth oriented policies and legal framework. Quite sometime back, when I was handling company cases, I had an opportunity to look into the Companies Act and also other important corporate legislations. To me, the observations of Shri C.D. Deshmukh, who piloted the Companies Bill in 1956, are still relevant in understanding the Companies Act. Increasing the efficiency of corporate business as measured by expected standards, reconciling managerial efficiency with the legitimate rights of investors, safeguarding of the interest of various partners in the process of production and distribution and the attainment of the ultimate ends of the social policy continue to be the guiding principles and objectives on which our Companies Act is administered. In the very recent past, the country has witnessed a scenario where the average investor was put in a difficult situation. Some felt that the average investor was taken for a ride. While the end result of such consequences could be because of either systems failure or because of lacunae in the legislations or because of over-reaction to certain situations, yet as people concerned with study of law, we should understand that legislative lacunae has to be found out, well in advance and the government should be sounded of possible disastrous consequences. When the country went through the trauma of the Bhopal Gas Tragedy, my senior colleague Justice V.R. Krishna Iyer termed it as Bhopshima, equating the consequences of the disaster with the Hiroshima disaster. Such a consequence has later on resulted in enactment of legislations to protect the environment. Managers in the industry concerned with compliance of various laws, should have foreseen such disastrous consequences and as a professional body, you should have done well in representing to the government, a need for enactment of such a legislation before any tragedy struck the country. Similarly, though you may not directly be concerned with forewarning of sickness in the industry, I would like to call upon all the professionals to discharge their functions given to them by their respective legislations only then, the social objectives which the Constitution has envisaged could be achieved. An example that strikes to me immediately is that of the accounting profession which should be in a position to forewarn not only the management but also the shareholders and public at large, through their audit reports about any possible sickness creeping into the industry. The country expects every professional to do his duty to the people of the country, at large. The constitutional obligations, tempered by the needs of humanism galvanize the professionals, including the Company Secretaries to sharpen their tools and be amenable to public accountability and above all evolve philosophy in tune with the social moorse. The profession of Company Secretaries has changed from a modest company law secretary to a corporate secretary. The profile of a Corporate Secretary is changing in the vast canvass of corporate management. With new responsibilities being assigned to the company secretaries profession, I am sure this vibrant profession would meet the challenges of tomorrow. In today's context, what is required is a dynamic dialogue, with focus on the millions and not on the millionaires, a structural change in the profession which activates the new popular ethics and catalyses their community dedication a creative fall for higher vocation.

Everybody is vitally interested in the simplification of various corporate laws including the Companies Act, 1956. While the MRTP Act, 1969 has been amended to give effect to the liberalization, proposed in the new industrial policy approved by the Parliament in July, 1991, and amendments to the Foreign Exchange Regulation Act, 1973 are under way, what is important in my opinion is a total overhaul of the 640 and odd sections of the Companies Act, 1956. In my view, the Act is too long and most of the Sections are redundant in today's context and need to be taken off the statute. The exercise to recodify the Companies Act was taken up by the Government almost two years ago and the Government has assured the industry and the profession that about 200 and odd sections would be deleted or amended drastically to simplify and rationalise the Company law. I share the concern that the expectations of the industry and the profession have not yet been fulfilled.

I have been advised that the amendments have been proposed with a view to protect the investors interest and to give a fillip to self regulation. What is heartening to note is that the profession, namely members of your Institute, would be given more statutory recognition by being called upon to undertake Secretarial Audit in Companies above a particular size which need not statutorily employ qualified Company Secretaries. Further, it is good to note that returns certified by professionals will be accepted by the Registrar of Companies, without further scrutiny and that the records at the Registrar of Companies office will be computerized to enable quick collection of data and information by all those concerned.

All this would go a long way in ensuring appropriate legal compliance at the right time which is the hallmark of effective administration of any legislation. After all, legislations are for compliance and non compliance would render the legislation redundant. Not only that the increasing reliance on professionals would make the job of the Government also simpler and meaningful.

I have briefly outlined the role of professionals, generally and the Company Secretaries witnessed in particular in the context of ever changing socio economic legal scenario. With the tremendous growth, a glorious past and a bright future looking ahead for the profession of Company Secretaries, I have no hesitation to say that this vibrant profession of corporate managers would structurally alter its priorities, plan well ahead to meet the challenges in the years to come.

ಬುಬುಬು

IMPORTANCE OF TAXATION

I am glad to associate myself with this convention organised by the ever-active HINDUSTAN CHAMBER OF COMMERCE. The agenda is of tropical importance provoking intellectual curiosity, besides a desire to grapple with practical problems faced by Trade and Industry.

All tax experts and tax executives who, I am sure, would be diving deep into the ramifications of various tax issues and legislations, with particular emphasis on fiscal policy in a free economy which is the theme of this convention. I, on my part, would only like to generally touch upon certain broad areas and provoke a free and frank discussion. The present juncture throws up a lot of food for thought especially from the fiscal and economic stand points when we take into account the number of far-reaching changes and plans of the powers that be. Various committees like Rajah Chelliah Committee, Narasimham Committee to name a few, have already submitted their reports.

Realising the importance of taxation, the Govt. of India constituted Tax Reforms Committee with Dr. Rajah, J. Chealliah as its Chairman to review the existing structure of Direct and Indirect Taxes. The Committee under the able leadership of Dr.Chelliah has recommended many far reaching useful changes like lowering of tax for domestic and foreign companies, Taxation of agricultural income of non-farmers, gradual transformation of the present Excise Tax System to a genuine Value Added Tax (VAT) at the stage of manufacture, extension of MODVAT to more items, reformation of the existing duty regime for Textile Sector, abolition of Interest Tax and retention of the general rate of depreciation on Plant and Machinery at 25%. The Committee has made various other recommendations and structural reforms in Taxation with a view to make this country progressive.

This apart, tumultuous changes are taking place in the thinking process of various Governments and people, the world over. All of us must ask ourselves this question, namely, as to how to integrate INDIA into the global economy and how far the free markets and the opening up of the economy shall improve the resource availability at competitive costs and increase the efficiency of resource

---

Speech delivered on the occasion of '20th Convention of Tax Executive of Southern Region', Chennai on 28th November, 1992.

296

utilisation. Fiscal and monetary policies concern the very basic framework of the economy. A framework inevitably means some constraint. Nevertheless, all constraints are not always inevitable. Viewed from this angle and taking into account the distinguished panelists as well as the participants, I am sure, the deliberations would be of high order.

To achieve the above objectives, one of the important tools is thorough fiscal measures, which, of course, includes taxation aspect as well.

As regards taxes, two extreme positions are discernible over the years. One is that of Justice Holmes, who said, "taxes are the price we pay for civilised society; I like to pay taxes with them I buy civilsation" such delight in paying one's taxes is rather uncommon this is strictly off the record!). The other opinion is that of Haliburton, who said years ago that, "death and taxes are inevitable". Perhaps, the truth is what has been attributed to J.B. Colbert who seems to have said that the art of taxation consists in *"so plucking the goose as to obtain the largest amount of feathers with the least possible amount of hissing"*. All of you are sure to cover various aspects of direct and indirect taxation in your deliberations in a comprehensive and accurate manner.

It is of importance that you have to highlight not only the irritants but also come out with specific suggestions to the Government as to how to augment its resources which are so essential to a welfare state such as ours. The founding fathers of our Constitution have envisaged INDIA as a Sovereign, Socialist, Secular, Democratic Republic. Public opinion is a significant force in any Democracy. Chambers of Commerce and other Industrial and Trade Associations must cultivate it by organising conventions like this and earn the goodwill of the Government as well as the public at large.

As a Judge, I can only give a preliminary decree that the Report of the Taxation Reforms Committee headed by eminent economists Dr. J. Chelliah, is an excellent and useful one and I expect that the Government would consider and accept the same.

ಐ ಐ ಐ

TAX IS THE PRICE WE PAY FOR OUR CIVILISATION

Taxation is as old as life. Even Vedic texts talk about the right of the king to raise revenue by taxation. Kautilya's *'Arth Sashtra'* has a Chapter on "Taxation". Taxation, as a Revenue raising measure, has been adopted in the Anglo Saxon civilsation as well as European countries. The history of Indian Taxation starts with the first Income Tax Law, introduced in 1860 consequent to the financial difficulties arising from the Mutiny of 1857 which is known as the first struggle for Independence.

Kanga and Phalkhiwala in the 8th Edn., had an occasion to observe in the book "the Law and Practice of Income Tax" that "Taxes are the life-blood of any Government, but it cannot be over emphasised that the blood is taken from arteries of the tax payers and, therefore, transfusion has to be accomplished in accordance with the principles of justice and fair play.

Every Government has as a right to levy taxes. But no Government has the right, in the process of extracting tax, to cause misery and harassment to the tax payer and the gnawing feeling that he has been made the victim of palpable injustice.

"Taxation" said 'Oliver Wendell Homes Junior' is the price we pay for civilisation. This illuminating comment prompts the reflection that if the price is too high, civilisation will be threatened by corruption, if the price is too low, civilisation will be threatened by violence. What is therefore, required is striking a proper balance.

Some precepts of Hon'ble Dr. Justice A.S. Anand, former Chief Justice of India:

> Taxation is a fascinating branch of law, though highly complex and complicated to comprehend.

> Tax practice today needs much more specialisation within the legal province.

> Tax practice demand adequate knowledge of accountancy and economics, besides a fair knowledge of various commercial laws, personal laws, laws relating to property as also civil and criminal laws.

Inaugural Speech delivered at the State Level one day seminar on 'Direct Taxes', Hyderabad on 16th February, 2002.

The statutes imposing direct taxes on income or wealth are intricate, cast in language which is difficult to comprehend without concentrated effort.

Some of the sections of the Income Tax Act run into pages, comprised of sub sections, sub clauses, provisos and explanations not forgetting the amendments.

To the original Act have been made almost 3500 amendments till date.

For a common man, it is quite difficult to appreciate frequent changes brought about in the Act.

It is a tragedy that millions of main-hours of tax gatherers, tax payers and tax advisors are squandered away in grappling with the torrential spirit of such amendments.

There is an urgent need to appreciate that fiscal policy must attempt at simplification of direct tax laws.

The ambiguity in the enactment of tax laws, therefore, needs to be avoided to reduce the zone of uncertainty in tax administration as also to ensure uniform application of laws, which in the ultimate analysis, lead to reduction in litigation.

Increased litigation because of ambiguity of legislation is counter productive and fails to achieve the object of the legislation.

Further:

(1) The administration of Income Tax in India leaves much to be desired.

(2) An Income Tax System can be said to be functioning properly only if it leaves no arrears of assessment at the end of the year – collects the determined taxes in time, without causing undue hardship to the tax payers and provides for an efficient machinery to look into the grievances of taxpayers and quick disposal of cases in appeal and claims for refund.

(3) Indeed, it is necessary that taxpayers must change their attitude towards their tax obligations through greater compliance, but the tax administrators must also ensure that no undue harassment is caused to the taxpayers.

(4) While the tax evaders must be dealt with strictly in accordance with the law, the honest taxpayers should also receive the desired help in fulfilling their tax obligations.

It is very often quoted and said that:

(a) Tax evasion results in an increase of tax burden on the honest taxpayers and therefore, every attempt to prevent tax evasion is laudable as being in public interest.

(b) Tax evasion has, however to be distinguished from tax planning or legitimate tax avoidance not resorted to, through any colourable device.

(c) A taxpayer is indeed entitled to so arrange his affairs as not to attract tax liability.

(d) The success of any tax system does not depend only upon how it has been formulated but also upon how it is administered.

(e) This, in turn, depends, among other things, on simplified procedure and rendering of smooth administrative processes.

(f) Laws which define fiscal liabilities should be precise and unambiguous.

(g) An excellent and ideally just system, if incapable of enforcement, may not only lead to public irritation and ill feeling but even defeat its own aim.

(h) The citizens should have the satisfaction that the taxes paid by them have been properly utilised for advancing the nation towards prosperity and have not been dissipated in activities, not in public interest nor for public benefit.

(i) The concept of a welfare State and the purpose of taxation must be kept in view not merely by the Government in formulation of its fiscal policy, but also by the judiciary in interpretation of the tax laws and should be so understood by the taxpayers for discharge of their tax burden.

(j) It is the cumulative effect of the manner in which all the three functions, govern proper and effective formulation as well as implementation of the nation's economic policy.

It would be apt if I quote Lord Macnaughtan that "Income tax, if I may be pardoned for saying so, is a tax on income".

The taxpayer as well as the tax gatherer must be not only diligent, but also must exercise abundant care and caution in ascertaining what is the real income that is eligible to tax and what would be the tax that becomes payable on the real income. Therefore, it is not the case that every income of the taxpayer is liable to tax in as much as, "it is not the case that the tax collected by the Government is entirely in respect of the income that is liable to tax. There may be certain deeming provisions that would creep in, making certain incomes taxable though apparently on the face of it they would not be income in the hands of tax payer but become so for the purpose of tax, as a consequence of such deeming provisions, provided by the Act, as for example the provisions of section 69 etc., that it is only the 'real income' that is to be taxed. Thus, the obvious statement of Lord Macnaughtan, as mentioned above is not without significance since, any amount of tax in excess of tax due from the taxpayer can be insisted only on the ground that income tax is a tax on income and nothing more or nothing less.

In a federation like ours if it were not tax on income, it may not be within the taxing powers of the Parliament adding a new dimension to the concept. However, in the Indian Constitution entry No. 47 in list I of the Schedule VII gives wide power to impose tax on items which are really not income. That was how Wealth Tax on agricultural lands was upheld in *Union of India* v. *Harbhajan Singh Dhillon*, AIR 1972 SC 1061: (1971) 2 SCC 779: (1972) 1 SCR 33: (1972) SCJ 379: (1972) 83 ITR 582 as reported at p. 582 of 83 ITR by the Supreme Court of India.

The theory of 'real income' based upon the fundamental concepts has come to the help of the tax payer where the tax payer is unable to find in the maze of tax laws any other shelter, which spells out exemption from liability or any deduction. It is true that this concept cannot come to the aid of the tax payers merely because he claims something as not his income. Also when the Act deems certain items as income, the theory of real income will be of no avail.

Historically, tax policies have been developed primarily to address domestic, economic and social concerns.

The forms and levels of taxation were established on the basis of desired level of publicly provided goods. Regard is also taken to the allocation, stabilizing and redistributing aims that are appropriate for a country. The decision to have a high rate of tax and high level of Government spending or low taxes and limited public outlays, the mix of direct and indirect taxes and the use of tax incentives were all the matters which were decided primarily on the basis of domestic concerns and principally domestic tax systems. The accelerating process of global trade and investment has fundamentally changed the relationship among domestic tax system.

Globalisation has:

(i) Driving force behind tax reforms, focussed on broadening base and rate reductions thereby minimizing tax induced distortions.

(ii) Encouraged countries to assess continually tax systems and public expenditure with a view to making adjustments when appropriate to improve the fiscal climate investment.

(iii) Promoted the development of capital and financial markets.

(iv) Encouraged countries to reduce tax barriers to capital flows and modernised their tax systems to reflect those developments.

Another challenge of the new millennium is the erosion of values in the profession. The Advocates Act, 1961 has prescribed high standards in the profession and laid down Code of conduct to regulate and maintain the status and standard of the profession. An Advocate has to assume onerous responsibilities, involved in the discharge of the public duties by securing maintenance of the requisite standard of discipline and conduct.

ಜಜಜ

SALES TAX

Revenue from sales tax collections of most of the State Governments is the main stay in the budget, particularly after the enforcement of prohibition. In Tamil Nadu, collection from sales-tax amounts to a very substantial portion of the receipts in the budget. No doubt, therefore, it is referred to as the "*Kamadhenu*".

It was Mr. C. Rajagopalachariar who introduced sales tax for the first time in the State of Tamil Nadu. It was started at a very modest rate and has now grown to great heights. The rate of sales tax now ranges from 1% to even as high as 50%. Commodities are chosen, depending on whether they are goods of necessities or luxury goods or goods that are injurious to the health of the citizens. Based on this, rates of sales tax are imposed.

Not only the rate of sales tax has increased but also the base for taxation has been widened. After the advent of the 46th Amendment to the Constitution of India, ushering in certain changes, the concept of "Sale of Goods" has acquired new dimension of vast amplitude. What was traditionally considered not to be sale of goods are now, by a fiction of law, deemed to be sale of goods so as to come within the mischief of the levy of sales tax. Thus, not only the manner of incidence as to the rate of sales tax but also in the matter of persons who come within the ambit of sales tax, laws have been broadened.

Recently, the Government of Tamil Nadu set up a High Power Committee under the Chairmanship of Mr. B. Vijayaraghavan, I.A.S., to suggest necessary changes that are called for to improve upon the Tamil Nadu General Sales Tax Act, 1959. We understand that the High Power Committee has submitted its report to the Government of Tamil Nadu. However, the contents of the said report have not been made public by the Government of Tamil Nadu.

In the recent budget of the State of Tamil Nadu for 1993-94, lots of changes have been brought about, evidently taking note of the recommendation of the said High Power Committee. It is significant to note that the budgetary changes disclose an across the board changes in the rate of sales tax and the first Schedule to the Tamil Nadu General Sales Tax Act, 1959, which has been thoroughly recast. The commodities are grouped rate-wise under various categories and the multi-point rate of sales tax which was done away with earlier is wholly discarded. After doing away with the multi-point levy, section 3(1) of the Tamil

---

Inaugural Address delivered on the occasion of 'Executive Training Programme on Sales Tax,' Madras on 24th June, 1993.

Nadu General Sales Tax Act, 1959, was earlier retained with a single point levy. The budgetary changes dropped section 3(1) thereby, making it obvious that only a single point levy is imposed. A residuary entry is introduced in the First Schedule itself to take care of commodities that are not specifically listed elsewhere in the said Schedule.

Keeping in mind the suggestions of the High Court of Madras with reference to the levy of sales tax on works contracts, the Amendment Act, introduced pursuant to the budget, and passed, has brought about statutory changes.

On the levy of tax on transfer of right to use goods also, changes have been effected. In the matter of levy of penalty, perhaps based on the High Power Committee's recommendations, the scheme and the quantum of penalty have been redone. All these and other aspects require an in-depth study.

It is not known why the change for a value added system of taxation, which was in the air, is not considered and implemented. Perhaps, it is one of the areas which has to be explored to find out whether V.A.T. as the system of taxation can conveniently replace the present system of levy of sales tax.

I had a glance through the monthly journal of Hindustan Chamber Review and it contains useful and current information on each and every aspect of trade and industry. For the benefit of its members, the Chamber also has a library, containing reference books on Sales Tax, Income-tax, Central Excise, Import and Export, Labour Laws, etc.

By conducting Executive Training Programmes at regular intervals, the executives of the public and private sector organizations are greatly benefited. In order to run an organization on sound economic lines, the executives should have a thorough up-to-date knowledge of Central Excise, Foreign Exchange, Company and Taxation Laws. It will not be possible for a single individual to be abreast with all laws. Therefore, lawyers have started specializing in different branches of law. By requesting the specialists in each branch of law, the Executives get an opportunity to know the current legal position of different branches of law.

The training programme on sales tax provides yet another opportunity to the executives to know the intricacies of sales tax laws. Unless a person knows the rudiments of Central Acts, Sale of Goods Act, Constitutional Law of India, etc., it would be impossible to practice in this branch of law. By virtue of the powers conferred by the Constitution, the States exert their taxing power in an important area of social and economic life of the community. It is necessary that extent and width of such power should be known by the executives of trade and commercial organization.

I am happy to note that the Chamber of Commerce is represented on almost all important public bodies and that, as a liaison body between the members and the Government, it is playing a significant role through its representation in several public bodies and through the various seminars, study groups, conventions, etc., at which representatives of Government and public and private sector undertakings, tax officers etc., come together for discussion and exchange of views.

ಐ೨ಐ೨ಐ೨

MERGERS AND AMALGAMATIONS

Madras Chamber is more than hundred years old and during these hundred and odd years, the Chamber has been rendering useful service to its Members, to the Government and to the society at large. I understand that the representations made by the Madras Chamber to the Central and State Governments are given the utmost attention they deserve and in the legislative policy of the Governments, the representations of the Madras Chamber are being taken into serious consideration.

Our country has been passing through an economic transition in such a manner as was never witnessed before. The last four years from June 1991 have seen economic reforms being ushered in a very significant measure, affecting the various segments of economy. World is becoming shorter and shorter day by day and perhaps is moving towards the dream of the famous historian, Toynbee who wanted a World Government to come into existence. If not World Government, we are moving towards establishing a common world economic order. The signing of GATT by India along with several countries of the world is a pointer towards globalization of Indian economy. Liberalization and globalization no doubt, have raised doubts and suspicions as to whether the reform would benefit the common man or only the rich in this country.

India is a Sovereign, Socialistic, Secular, Democratic Republic and the People of India have give unto themselves a Constitution to secure to all its citizens social, economic and political justice and equality of status and opportunity. There can, therefore, be no doubt that economic reforms initiated and pursued by the Government will have certainly as its destination, the ultimate goal to secure to all its citizens economic and social justice. While there can be genuine and valid differences of opinion in approach or in details or even in the speed at which reforms should continue, all of us have accepted that the economic reforms are a must for the on-going increase should continue in the interest of our own economic survival in a fast changing global environment.

Citizens of the world have realized that political and economic changes have become an imperative necessity for mankind to progress further and further.

Speech delivered at the seminar on 'Tax and Legal Dimensions involved in Mergers Demergers and Amalgamations' conducted by the Madras Chamber of Commerce and Industry, Chennai on 24th February, 1995.

Economic reforms are the result of the political and social changes that are taking place all over the world.

The industry has been freed from the so-called Licence Permit Raj and one is free to set up any industry that one wants anywhere in the country. The only requirement being, to comply with the pollution and environmental laws in order to preserve the ecology of the country and the health of the people. Having realized the imperativeness of economic reforms, we should concentrate on the type of reforms that are necessary and desirable in today's world context. While small is beautiful, it does not necessarily mean that small is always good. Bigness has its own inherent strengths and advantages and there is nothing wrong to aspire to become big. Corporations can perform much better if they are bigger. Mergers and amalgamations will make Corporations bigger in size and volume so that they can play better and more effective role in increasing production of goods and services, lowering costs of production and ensuring quality of goods and services which will also go towards meeting the requirements of common man ultimately. By becoming much more productive, employment opportunities will be generated and more jobs are bound to be created, despite automation and computerization. In a country like India, where labour is available in abundant quantity and at low cost, opportunities are being availed of by multinational Corporations which are competing to enter Indian market in which they see a large consumer market for their goods and services.

Indian Industry has, therefore, to face competition from the giant multi-nationals and they cannot successfully do so if they remain small in size. Wherever opportunities exist, mergers and amalgamations should be encouraged to take place. Our Companies Act, 1956, is modeled on English Company Law and many of the provisions of the English Companies Act have been copied and/ or modified in the Indian Companies Act. Compared to the Company Law in the West, especially in U.S., the English and Indian Laws are rather more regulatory and between the two, Indian Law takes the cake. The relevant provisions are contained in Chapter V of the Companies Act, 1956, especially in sections 391, 392, 393 and 394. The other provisions in the Chapter will also facilitate de-mergers. These provisions, if looked at comprehensively, would tell us that the Board of Directors and the shareholders have to decide and approve any proposal regarding merger or demerger. When once their approvals to the requisite levels are secured, then, the Court looks into it from the creditor's angle and public interest angle and then gives its seal of approval before the merger can be given effect to.

Before proceeding further, I would like to distinguish between an amalgamation and a merger. Amalgamation is a union of corporations so as to form a homogeneous whole or new body. Merger is a fusion or absorption of one corporation into another. An amalgamation of two corporations, pursuant to statutory provisions, in which one of the corporations survives and the other disappears is generally called the merger. The absorption of one company by another, the former losing its legal identity and the latter retaining its own name and identity and acquiring assets and liabilities, franchise and powers of former, and the absorbed company ceasing to exist as separate business entity is called merger. Amalgamation differs from merger, in the sense, that amalgamation is a consolidation wherein all, the corporations terminate their existence and become parties to a new one.

In the U.S., there are anti-trust laws to control monopolies and discourage the acquisition of market power. Historically, mergers have provided an important route to positions of market dominance. Here lies the reason why the Legislators thought it fit to vest certain powers in the Judiciary so that the Courts could objectively look into such proposals and sanction the same, if they are not against public interest or if they do not affect vitally the interests of any one party involved.

We have seen vertical mergers, horizontal merger and conglomerate mergers. A pure conglomerate merger occurs when the two merging firms operate in unrelated markets having no functional economic relationship. A *defacto* merger is a transaction that has the economic effect of a statutory merger but is cast in the form of an acquisition of assets or an acquisition of voting stock and is treated by a Court as if it were a statutory merger. The merger of a parent corporation into its subsidiary is called down stream merger. Merger between business competitors such as manufacturers of the same type of products or distributors, selling competing products in the same market area is horizontal merger. A merger of a subsidiary corporation into its parent is called upstream merger. A vertical merger is a union with corporate customer or supplier.

Our Company Law requires a notice to be sent to the Central Government in respect of all amalgamations and the Courts are expected to take into consideration the representations, if any, made to it, by the Central Government before passing any order more often the Central Government files affidavits alleging certain irregularities or contraventions of law on the part of either the transferor company or the transferee company. These irregularities and contraventions are obviously based upon the findings from the statutory records maintained at the office of the Registrar of Companies which are required to be maintained under the Companies Act. The experience of Courts is that these alleged irregularities and contraventions are not such that they are strong enough to urge the Court not to order amalgamations as prayed for in the Company Petitions.

In *Ucal Fuel Systems Limited and another (in re:),* (1992) 73 Comp. Cas. 63 (Mad), I have held that the approval of the Ministry of Industry for transfer of the Letter of Intent, standing in the name of the transferor company to the transferee company does not warrant the Ministry of Industry to be made a party to the proceedings for sanction of the scheme of amalgamation. I have also held that the fact that the scheme envisaged, paying back the shareholder of the transferor company was a matter of indoor management and a decision taken by the shareholders of their own volition. Unless it was affirmatively shown that the scheme was patently unfair, the Court would not interfere in the proceedings under section 391 of the Companies Act. There was no reason to doubt the *bona fide* recommendation made by the Board of Directors of the two companies.

In a Division Bench judgment delivered in August 1991, the Bombay High Court; Bharatiya Kamgar Sena v. Geoffrey Manner & Co. Ltd., (1992) 73 Comp. Cas. 122 (Bom) held that where workmen are likely to be adversely affected, the companies could put the matter to vote by workmen and if more than 80% of workmen opted to join the transferee company, the scheme has to proceed and those not joining are to be given retrenchment benefits as formulated under the aegis of Court. If more than 20% of workmen declined, the scheme has to be given up.

In *Cetex Petrochemicals Limited (in re:)*, (1992) 73 Comp. Cas. 298 (Mad), I had an occasion to consider whether the opposition by a share-holder *inter alia* on the grounds that the scheme was against the interest of the share-holders and the public and was only for the benefit of a particular group which had a controlling interest in both the companies in order to reduce the shareholding of the financial institutions in the petitioner company and that a public issue of a petitioner company had been made, stating that the benefit of section 80CC of the Income-tax Act, 1961, would be available but the share exchange involved in the proposed amalgamation would amount to a transfer, disentitling the shareholders to the benefit of section 80CC. An objection was raised on behalf of the Central Government that, as the petitioner company had not refunded the excess share application money within the statutory time limit, section 73 of the Companies Act was violated and any dissolution of the petitioner company without winding up would effectively nullify the penal proceedings which might be taken by the Central Government against the company. After a very careful consideration of the objections, I dismissed the same and sanctioned the scheme holding—

1. that it was for the shareholders of the company to decide whether the company should be merged with another undertaking and so long as such decision has been taken in accordance with the provisions of the Companies Act, the Court could not decline to confirm the scheme;

2. that the financial institutions were not objecting to the scheme of amalgamation;

3. that none of the creditors has come forward to oppose the scheme;

4. that it was not for the Court to see whether the particular scheme of amalgamation is beneficial or not, or to launch into the commercial merits or demerits of the scheme;

5. that it was not necessary for the Court to postpone the scheme till penal proceedings under section 73 of the Companies Act were completed as the interest of the Central Government would be safeguarded if liberty was reserved for the Central Government to initiate proceedings against the company for any alleged violation of law; and

6. that the allotment of shares in exchange was neither an exchange nor a relinquishment, particularly when no question of any transfer of property from one to another arose and therefore, the grievance that the benefit of section 80CC of the Income-tax Act, 1961, would not be available did not survive.

In another case *Asian Investments Limited (in re:),* (1992) 73 Comp. Cas. 517 (Mad) reported in the same volume of Company Cases at page 517, I had held that the provisions of reduction of capital, contained in section 100 of the Act are not attracted in a scheme of amalgamation as the provisions of law relating to amalgamation are a separate code in themselves and in a scheme of amalgamation, the entire assets and liabilities of the transferor company are vested in the transferee company and there is no release of any assets and consequently the interests of the creditors are not affected.

In *Coimbatore Cotton Mills (in re:),* (1980) 50 Comp. Cas. 623) Justice S. Padmanabhan was of the view that before the Court sanctions a scheme under sections 391 and 394 of the Companies Act, 1956, it should normally be satisfied of four matters:

1. The resolutions are passed by the statutory majority in value and in number in accordance with law. The Court should not usurp the right of the members or the creditors to decide whether they approve the scheme or not.

2. Those who took part in the meeting are fairly representative of the class and the statutory meeting does not coerce the minority in order to promote the adverse interest of those of the class whom they purport to represent.

3. In exercising discretion, the Court is not merely acting as a rubber stamp. The Court should see that the scheme as a whole is a reasonable one and a fair one. The Court may refuse to confirm the scheme if it is of the opinion that the objection is such that any reasonable man would say that he would not approve of it.

4. There should not be any lack of good faith on the part of the majority. It was also held that it was impossible to calculate the real value of any shares with mathematical accuracy. The value of a share is the price which a buyer will pay for it and that price will depend on the number of shares offered by sellers and sought by buyers at any particular time.

The Madras High Court has been following the principles, laid down in the above case and has generally been confirming the scheme of amalgamation petitioned for. While it is not the function of the Court to assume the role of a businessman or a commercial manager, the Courts will certainly look into the reasonableness and fairness of the scheme and whether any reasonable man would approve of the scheme in the circumstances in which the shareholders of both the transferor and transferee companies have approved the same. Amalgamation decision is basically a commercial and business decision and the role of judiciary is only to ensure that there is no fraud or unfairness in the scheme and in the method by which the approval of statutory majority is prescribed under the Companies Act has been secured.

I would certainly like to refer to my judgment, delivered in regard to a trade mark case, only to emphasize the expectations of multinational corporations when they enter India and to debate as to whether such expectations are reasonable or not. In the case, I have dealt with in a very detailed manner, the provisions of law on trademarks and particularly on passing off. My conclusions in that case were:

> *In a passing off action, the plaintiff must establish goodwill and reputation in the geographical area where passing off is alleged and that the reputation of the plaintiff elsewhere is irrelevant. Our Courts and the Courts in other countries have consistently taken only this view as could be seen from the twenty two judgments cited by the respondents.*

I am only referring to these judgments to point out that the local industry's claims should not be affected by a claim of a multi-national corporation under the pretext of protecting their own trade marks. The law on trademarks, right now, is undergoing a change after signing of the GATT. We have, therefore, to evolve a law and a procedure, acceptable to persons in India and abroad in the course of time.

ಬುಬುಬು

PART XII

SPIRITUALISM

THE LANGUAGE OF GOD

The word *"Sanskrit"* overwhelms me spontaneously because this is the language which not only reflects the Indian lifestyle but also touches the deepest core of our heart. It is considered as the *"Devavani"* or the language of God. It is made up of the primordial sounds, and is developed systematically to include the natural progressions of sounds as created in the human mouth. Sanskrit is a language which is amazingly rich, efflorescent, full of luxuriant growth of all kinds, and yet precise and strictly keeping with the frame-work of grammar, which Panini laid down two thousand years ago. The Panini grammar reflects the wonderous capacity of the human bran, which till today no other country has been able to produce except India.

Sanskrit (meaning "cultured or refined"), the classical language of Hinduism, is the oldest and the most systematic language in the world. The vastness and versatility, and its power of expression can be appreciated by various factors. The Sanskrit language is of wonderful structure, more perfect than the Greek, more copious than the Latin and more exquisitely refined than either of the two.

Sri Aurobindo, India's great sage and seer, declared long back, "Sanskrit" is the mother of all languages and it could become the unifying language of India, apart from English, which is spoken only by a tiny minority. Sanskrit ought still to have a future as the language of the learned and it will not be a good day for India when the ancient tongues cease entirely to be written or spoken". It is said that Sanskrit is a dead language and that it is impossible to revive it. I do not agree. We have many scholars in our midst. Let the scholars begin to revive and modernise the Sanskrit language now and it would be a sure sign of the drawing of the Renaissance of India.

The usefulness of Sanskrit literature for modern times can be demonstrated in two ways. Firstly, by unravelling the basic knowledge of wisdom, new theories and paradigms of knowledge can be built on the basis of the principles laid down in Sanskrit literature. There is a widespread fear amongst people that Sanskrit is a difficult language. In order to eliminate this negative attitude, we should:

Speech delivered on the occasion of 'Sanskrit Day' State Level Celebration Programme at Jaipur, on 4th August, 2001.

(a) encourage basic research on the linkages that exist between Sanskrit and Science, and launch innovative activities to bridge the gap between Sanskrit and the modern world.

(b) Encourage research and debate on the application of Sanskrit in the development of Computer Software for language processing (NASA and others have been looking at Sanskrit as a possible computer language since its syntax is perfect and leaves little room for error).

(c) Produce documentaries and T.V. Serials in simple Sanskrit for telecast (T.V. Serials like; The Mahabharata, the Ramayana etc. have made a number of Sanskrit based words, such as; "Bhratashri", "Matashri", "Pitashri", "Taatshri", "Mamashri" quite popular among masses)

(d) Change the teaching methodology and launch innovative schemes for teaching Sanskrit conversation.

(e) Set up computer based networking among Sanskrit institutions and Sanskrit manuscript libraries for improving the communications among Sanskrit scholars and Researchers.

The concept of "Indian Culture is unimaginable without Sanskrit. Our sacred sacraments, right from birth to death, and which considerably affect our life, are all performed in Sanskrit language.

Linguistically strong, which makes human life socially and culturally strong.

Sanskrit is recognised as the only language that can keep the country united. Most of the South Indian languages such as; Malayalam, Kannada, Telgu etc. have their origin in Sanskrit. One can easily find ample examples of Sanskrit based words in these languages. Bangla words "Aamar-Tomar" are derivatives of Sanskrit words, namely; "Ashmakam-Yushmakam". On the question of "one language" for this country, speakers of various regional languages have their own view-points. However, no one has ever disputed Sanskrit as the only unifying language for the whole nation. I would, therefore, urge the citizens in general and the scholars of Sanskrit in particular, to pay greater emphasis for promoting Hindi and other Indian languages to the maximum possible extent.

Sanskrit is, no doubt, such a unique treasure of ours which has the potential of reinstating us as the *Vishva Guru*. All we need to do today is to take up intensive research and the outcome, I am sure, would cater to not only India but the whole world also.

All languages, and Sanskrit in particular, are the gifts of the Goddess of Learning. Every language has its own excellence and has contributed to make the well being of human beings. There is no harm in learning as many languages as we can. Learning other language will strengthen and enrich the learning of one's own language. By learning other languages, one can contribute more to the growth of one's own language. We can gain more knowledge in other spheres by learning more and more languages.

It is good to know that the Government of Rajasthan has understood the importance of this language and proved its utility for the common man. Rajasthan is the only State in the country, which has a separate Directorate of

Sanskrit Education, established way back in the year 1958. Government of India has resolved to celebrate the festival of "Raksha-Bandhan" as the "Sanskrit Day", every year. It is a matter of great pleasure to note that the Government of India has issued directions to celebrate from now onwards "Sanskrit Week", every year. The Directorate of Sanskrit Education is playing a leading role in it, setting an example for other States to follow.

ಜಜಜ

NARAYANEEYAM

The temple of Sree Krishna at Guruvayoor, Kerala, is one of the most noted ancient temples in India. The image of the temple is said to be not of earthly origin. Originally, Mahavishnu gave this image made of a material called 'Patalasila' to Brahma. Brahma gave it to a Rishi named Sutapas, he to Kasyapa Prajapati and Kasyapa Prajapathi to Vasudeva, the father of Sree Krishna. From his father Vasudeva, Sree Krishna got it and it was installed and worshipped at his Capital, Dwaraka. Before the divine accent of Sree Krishna and the inundation of his Capital City of Dwaraka. He instructed his devotee and Minister, Uddhava that this image would come floating after the sea engulfed Dwaraka. Uddhava was asked to communicate this to the Guru of the Gods, Brihaspati and request him to instal it in a suitable place so as to serve as a means for the spiritual upliftment and salvation of man in Kaliyug. As instructed by Uddhavar, Brihaspati, the Deva Guru got possession of the image, with the Sea-God Varuna, and along with Vayu, the Wind-God, installed it at a place in a coastal region of Kerala. As the image was installed by Guru and Vayu together, the place came to be known as Guru – Vayur. As the image installed had its origin in Vaikunta, the devotees began to look upon the temple of Guruvayur as a heaven on earth.

When the devotees reach the temple, they find themselves surrounded on all sides by the Holy name, Na – ra – ya – na, and their ears are regaled by the sacred name of Narayana, uttered by numberless devotees inside and outside. The moment they enter the Gopuram or the ornamental pyramidal entrance, an indescrible bliss bursts upon them, as infinite joy wells up in them. At the very first darsan or sight itself of the Lord in the Sanctum-Sanctorum, they get a new life, a new Arogya or health and a new happiness. In the general atmosphere of joy and happiness, there is no place at Guruvayur for sorrow. Those who come to the temple sobbing go back always smiling. The procession of humanity that comes to the temple to obtain the grace of the Lord, swells day to day.

No temple in Kerala can claim such a long line of saints and devotees, reflecting and adding its Mahatwa by their life and works. Many great saintly

---

Speech delivered on the occasion of the inauguration of 'The Cultural Meeting in Connection with 412th Narayaneeyam Day', at Guruvayur on 14th December, 1998.

devotees who lived in the 16th and 17th centuries, the accounts of whose life and mystic experiences, woven round the Deity at Guruvayur, began to evoke the faith and adoration of an increasing number of worshippers. Of all these, Melppathur Narayana Bhattathiri, by his great poetical Hymn, the 'Narayaneeyam' and his remarkable recovery from a crippling paralysis, has immortalised the temple and spread its reputation as a great centre of worship. He resolved to get rid of his rheumatism by Bhajan. Accordingly, he decided to compose a hymn, in praise of the Lord, giving an account of all His Leelavataras (incarnations). His plan was to identify the Lord of Guruvayur with Mahavishnu and present the various incarnations, as narrated in the Shreemad Bhagavatha, in a series of Dasakas or groups of ten slokas, composing a Dasaka every day in the presence of the Lord. So sitting in the precincts of the temple, he started composing the Narayaneeyam.

In the first verse and the succeeding verses of the Narayaneeyam, the principle behind the worship of the Divine Image is stated. The Vigraha in the temple (the Divine Image for worship) is considered as an incarnation or descent of the Deity out of His abundant mercy for men, so that He might be accessible to every one, endowed with faith for worship and communion.

So, in the whole of the Narayaneeyam, the Vigraha is addressed as the Divine Person, identified with Krishna. In the Narayaneeyam, Bhattathiri describes in the last dasaka, in lyrical language, how did he actually behold the living spiritual presence of Krishna in the Vigraha at the temple of Guruvayur. With a genius to get at the heart of the subject, he completed his work in one hundred Dasakas.

Bhattathiri is the author of many works, numbering about forty major and minor. But his most noteworthy contribution which has gained him immortality is the Sanskrit hymnology (Stotras or devotional hymns). He lived a long life rich in devotion, rich in literary creation, rich in honours and rich in admirers and disciples.

The Narayaneeyam is indoubtedly the major work of Melppathur Narayana Bhattathiri for which he is remembered, today, by scholars as well as devotees. It is a work consisting of 1036 verses in various Sanskrit *mantras*, divided into 100 Dasakas of approximately ten verses each. It is a unique work in the Sanskrit language, insofar, as it combines in itself three distinct features (a) it is a literary masterpiece, a great poetical work (Kavya), (b) it is a hymn of rare devotional fervor, and (c) it is an exposition of Veds with a dominance of devotional teachings. The matter dealt with, in the Bhagavata, in eighteen thousand verses is optomized and recast in the Narayaneeyam into 1036 verses, brought into a hymn of praise, wherein almost every verse is directly addressed to the Lord of Guruvayur as a fervent prayer and as an exposition of His divine glory and excellence. The depiction of the Sree Krishna Incarnation, especially the portion dealt with in the Dasakas thirty-seven to seventy-six, constitutes the most artistic care of the work, and the reader is led to feel, sometimes, that this abridged instatement of the Narayaneeyam is not in any way inferior to the Bhagavatha, itself, in its poetic effect and devotional impact. As already stated,

Narayaneeyam is a summary of the Bhagavatha Purana and its reading as a religious routine confers the same merit as the reading of the Bhagavatha Purana. To people, hard pressed for time, the Narayaneeyam is a boon. Further, as almost every Dasaka ends with a prayer to the Lord of Guruvayur, it brings also the benefit of a pilgrimage, with the mind, if not with the body also, to this abode of bliss on earth.

The Narayaneeyam serves also as an effective faith cure. The belief is that as the author, Bhattathiri attained 'longevity, health and happiness' through its composition, so will a person, reading it with faith and devotion, attain those highly coveted wealths and have the grace and protection of the Lord of Guruvayur in all difficult situations of life. It is after Bhattathiri's cure that Guruvayur became a healing centre. The Narayaneeyam identifies the Lord of Guruvayur with the central figure of the Bhagavatha and offers to a devote Mahavishnu Himself to be seen and worshipped. No work of this magnitude and thematic brilliance has been ever seen in any other temple in India. As such, Narayaneeyam is a valuable treasure to the Guruvayur Devaswom.

ഇരിരിരി

BEACON LIGHT OF SPIRITUALISM

I consider it a rare privilege to preside over this unique function of the Centenarian Trust, formed to spread the Indian heritage, at the behest of the Centenarian Mahaswami of Kanchi. It is very noteworthy that the unique body has Hon'ble Shri R. Venkataraman, Former President of India, as the Chief Patron and Dr. K. Venkatasubramanian as the President.

The Centenarian Awards are really unique in themselves because a top level Committee selects people of real merit and one more appreciable feature of the Award is that the Trust never charges or takes any donation from the Awardees. This marks the Centenarian Trust as different from other bodies giving Awards.

Regarding Kanchi Mahaswami, the late Centenarian Paramacharya, Sri Sri Sri Chandrasekharendra Saraswati Sawmigal, I have intimate knowledge I had gone to Kanchi, several times, to have a darshan of this great Saint.

His conquest over the mind, body and the senses was so complete that people saw in him a glow of fire rather than a body or person. He radiated light, exuded benevolence and taught us the path without teaching. If ever we saw divinity in human form, it was in the Mahaswami of Kanchi. In his presence, the affluent and underprivileged, the robust and the weak, the scholar and the illiterate, the saint and the sinner, Hindus and other religionists felt elevated and ennobled and, subconsciously, realized the place of finer instincts in the human frame.

The Mahaswami had, by his austerity and devotion, acquired a mastery of the Vedas – scriptures. He was often found in discussions, indepth, with pandits and scholars from all over India. He held a large number of 'Sadas' where eminent scholars participated in analyzing the esoteries of our ancient scriptures. He was regarded as the greatest Jnani of his times.

Apart from the scriptures, the Mahaswami was a master of other arts and sciences like archaeology, temple architecture, numismatics, sculptures, music, dance, folk arts etc. He used to hold Conferences and Workshops on all these items and honour experts in each field. His discussions with great philosophers, astute politicians, erudite scientists and a number of intellectuals from India and abroad, impressed every one of them and they were amazed at this knowledge

---

Speech delivered at the award function of the Centenary Trust at Chennai on 3rd February, 2002.

and approach to the problems. They always felt greatly enlightened and benefited by these talks. Nothing is more illustrative than the remark that Gandhiji made after his talks with the Paramacharya that the conversation with the Sage was more than a feast and he did not want any other food.

Like Adi Sankara, the Mahaswami was a true advaitin in thought, word and deed. He saw the spark of 'Atman' in every being and perceived the Supreme being in every living being. As stated in Iso Upanisad,

"He who sees all beings in his own self.

And sees his own self in all beings.

He does not hate any one thereafter".

He, once, told his disciples who wanted to kill a scorpion which dropped near the Saint that it was also another jivan (life) and should not be disturbed. He saw 'aatman' in every being, human or other.

For decades, he travelled on foot to distant places and remote villages, exhorting the people to observe the path of Dharma. He told them that if each one observed, the righteous conduct, there would be peace and harmony in society and the world.

He appealed to all religionists to follow the tenets of their religion honestly, faithfully and diligently since each and every religion preached kindness, compassion, love, charity and morality. People following the different religions used to throng to hear him, to receive his blessings and his benevolent grace. The stream of people—Hindus, Muslims, Christians, nuns, priests, the less privileged sections—who passed in queue to pay their last reverence to the Mahaswami was an unforgettable sight. Once a Muslim poet wanted to read some verses he had composed before the Mahaswami. When his wish was granted, he chanted the verses with emotion and tears filled his eyes. He said that he saw 'Allah' in the Sage.

Likewise Albert Franklin, former Counsel of America, in Madras, said that he saw 'Jesus' in the Paramacharya.

The Kanchi Kamakoti Peetham is the most ancient institution, started by Adi Sankara himself. There has been an unbroken chain of 70 Acharyas in the Peetham since its inception. Eminent scholars and sages have, in the past, shed light and lusture on the Peetham. The 68th Acharya, the Mahaswami Sri Chandrasekhara Saraswati Swamigal was the brightest diadem in the lustrous chain of Peethadipatis. He was believed to be in a reincarnation of Adi Sankara and was regarded, all over the world, as a living divinity. People used to pour into his compassionate ears all their problems from petty admission to schools to profound problems of life and death and would feel that they would get relief by his grace.

The spirit of Mahaswami pervades the Kanchi Mutt. Even today, people pray for relief at the Brindavan as if the Mahaswami still sits there. May the grace of Mahaswami ever abide with us.

The Centenarian Trust is doing a signal service to spread the message of love of the Centenarian Mahaswami and I place, on record, my deep sense of admiration of their seminal work.

ಲುಲುಲು

KRISHNA JAYANTHI

Lord Krishna was born in a prison cell, belonging to a tyrannical monarch in the august presence of Kansa, who was none else than his maternal uncle. Vasudeva, father of Krishna, crossed the river Yamuna and exchanged his son, Krishna, for the infant daughter of Yasoda. Thus, Kansa was informed that only a baby girl was born to his beloved sister, Devaki. The queen mother, Yasoda, was unaware of the exchange of babies and brought up Krishna with all love and affection.

On getting complaints from friends of Krishna that Krishna was eating mud, his mother Yasoda asked him to open his mouth and to her astonishment and wonder, she saw the whole universe in the tiny mouth. On his becoming a well grown youth, Krishna manifest his divinity to Brahma. Krishna was the teacher of all teachers and embodiment of all knowledge. When we think of Lord Krishna, we are reminded of Gita, one of the most attractive sources of Hindu Doctrinal Ethics. Gita begins with the agitation in the mind of Arjuna in the battle field and the speeches of Krishna to Arjuna. Throughout Gita, Krishna speaks as God Himself.

The teachings of Gita is of universal validity and it helped solve Arjuna's problems and doubts. There are about 700 slokas in all in Gita. The very fact that Bhagwat Gita has been translated into different languages bears testimony to its universal applicability and relevance and validity, irrespective of caste, creed and religion. It is also said that knowing that the Lord of the Universe had assumed the form of Sri Krishna, Brahma and Siva descended from heaven to pay homage to Lord Krishna at Dwaraka and sang in praise of Lord Krishna and requested the Lord to return to his eternal abode to protect and guide them for ever. Lord Krishna agreed to their request and told them that he had determined to leave the earth since he had fulfilled the mission of incarnation. Knowing that Lord Krishna had decided to leave the earth and return to its heavenly abode, Uddhava, who was ever devoted to the Lord, prostrated before Krishna and addressed him reverently and raised many queries. The teachings of Lord to Uddhava reflect the wisdom of God.

Presidential speech delivered on the occasion of 'Sri Krishna Jayanti Celebration/Annual Day' of Sri Gaudiya Mutt, Madras on 18th August, 1995.

In one of his answers, Lord Krishna tells Uddhava "those who do not follow the path of love, knowledge or work, as taught by Lord, but pursue the path of the worldly and seek to gratify their selfish desires will be born again and again. Those who are steeped in worldly desires and try to gratify their senses are blinded by the ignorance of the true nature of the immortal soul".

As a matter of fact, the teachings of Lord Krishna to Uddhava are more appealing than the teachings of Lord to Arjuna in the battle field. After finding that the teachings of Lord Krishna were difficult to follow, Uddhava requested him to teach him, the simplest way to attain the highest end and Lord Krishna taught him the spiritual practices which were easy to follow. It is said that Uddhava followed the teachings of Lord Krishna and enshrined him in the inner sanctuary of his heart and attained oneness with Lord.

Bhagwad Gita is accepted by great religious teachers as 'mines of knowledge'. The incarnation of Lord Krishna is with a view to dispel darkness of our mind and make us all enlightened souls.

Though it is very difficult in the modern world to practice the teachings of Lord Krishna, yet, it should be our endeavour to follow and practice Dharma and reach the highest goal of human life, that is, to join the universal goal.

I am really happy to notice that Sri Gaudiya Mutt, Madras, is one of the several branches of Sri Chaitanya Mutt, the holy birthplace of Lord Sri Chaitanya Maha Prabhu, situated at Sri Mayapur in West Bengal. The Mutt has got a glorious history of preaching the message of love and peace for the mankind, under the divine guidance of Lord Sir Chaitanya Maha Prabhu and all the savants of the country, whether it was the politics or religious and philosophy, closely associated themselves with this institution.

The Mutt has a single name in the field of religion and it celebrates Sri Krishna Jayanti as the Annual Day function of the Mutt.

ಐಐ

SPIRITUAL LIFE IS THE GENESIS OF INDIA

Spiritual life is the true genesis of India. Those who make the greatest appeal to the Indian mind are not the military conquerors nor the rich merchants or the great diplomats, but the holy sages, *rishis* who embody spirituality at its finest and purest. India's pride is that almost in every part of the country, from the time of recorded history, it has produced these holy men who embody for her all that the country holds most dear and sacred. By their lives, they teach us that pride and power, wealth and glory are nothing in comparison with the power of spirit.

Today, our nation is facing various problems, both within and outside the country. The years of post-Independence witnessed a plethora of changes, affecting all variables of human life and existence. The problems that challenge the world of today, are relatively new; at least physically as years or decades before they occurred. But great sons of India like Swami Vivekanda, Mahatma Gandhi, Jawaharlal Nehru had professed solutions to the then anticipatory situations. Swami Vivekanda stressed on man himself and said that for the right kind of man, no problem need be daunting. Despite the fact that 55 years have passed since we attained Independence, the country has not been able to fulfil the hopes and aspirations of the people. The talents of many of the citizens are required to be tapped and utilized for the betterment of the country. The potential of the masses at the grass roots is yet to be fully encouraged. No country can progress without genuinely enlightened and educated citizensy.

Proper education is the solution for all the ills that our country has been suffering from. Need of right kind of education cannot be over emphasized. Enlightenment of the citizens through right kind of education is the cry of the day. Education should be used even for the working classes who had been neglected so that they may mend themselves.

Every parent, while sending his child to the school, wishes that the child should be so educated that he/she is able to earn a very honourable living. No one can deny the truth of economic needs of man. It is the economic self-sufficiency of a person, which makes him a worthy and contributing citizen. Education should prepare students for a useful life and useful occupation.

Speech delivered at 2nd Annivesary of Vivekananda Institute of Human Excellence at Ramakrishna Mutt, Hyderabad on 8th September, 2002.

Numerous aims have been given at various times in various countries by various thinkers of education. That means, education cannot be a single aim activity. It must aim at developing the multi-sided personality of the individual, in the context of social setting. Only then the interests of both the individual and the society can be best served.

There can be no second opinion regarding knowledge as one of the most important aims of education. *"Knowledge is power by which things are done"*, said Socrates. Knowledge must be based on truths, and courage alone can lead towards truthfulness. It is, therefore, said that some educators very strongly advocate that the aim of education should be the acquisition of knowledge. True knowledge consists in possessing "Ideas of universal validity". They should be functional and valuable. Knowledge must be relevant to the situations of life. Without character, no one can even utilize the knowledge gathered by him. Man is essentially a moral being and his education consists in the cultivation of certain human values, development of attitudes and formation of ethical conduct and habits. Character is a mental quality. Man is not mind alone. He is body as well as mind. To impart character, education is a crucial problem. Teachers must set a stage for such education. If they are to understand and influence young people, they must be persons not only of superior character themselves but intelligent, gifted, capable and creative. Such persons can teach excellence in the best way through the example of what they themselves are. Merely asking the students to become moral beings carries no weight. It can better be done through activities like morning assemblies, mass prayers, meditation and talks by eminent persons and by actually living in the situation. Above all, parents also need moral education. With the active cooperation of different agencies like this institution, we can save the society and the nation from mass moral degeneration. In our institution, presently, the intellectual aspect is dominant, physical aspect plays second and the moral aspect is totally neglected. Education, in the fullest sense of the term, must take care of all-round development *i.e.*, physical, intellectual and moral development of the individual. Moral life cannot grow in a vacuum. Morality has social reference.

As Vivekananda rightly said, *"We want the education by which character is formed, strength of mind is increased, the intellect is expanded and by which one can stand on one's own.*

Swami Vivekananda, in his lecture delivered in Sanfransisco on 28th March, 1900, quipped that education is not filling the mind with a lot of facts, perfecting the instrument and getting the complete mastery of mind. The modern science of education recognizes that the important need in education is to relate to the life needs and aspirations of the people and thereby, make it a powerful instrument of social, economic and cultural transformation necessary for the realisation of national goals. For this purpose, education should be developed so as to increase productivity, achieve social and national integration, accelerate the process of modernization and cultivate social, moral and spiritual values.

Today's child is tomorrow's citizen. What is essentially needed is to produce good citizens. Patriotism is the only key which can make one's country a great one. We should take examples from China and Japan apart from United States of America and United Kingdom which have developed within a short time. To be a patriot, one must have a disciplined mind. Discipline, character and love for the motherland are the main pillars of patriotism. We have inherited a good culture. All endeavours of ours should be to preserve the same and not destroy it.

If India dies, according to Swamiji, *"then from the world all spirituality will be extinct, all moral perfection will be extinct, all sweet souled sympathy for religion will be extinct, all ideality will be extinct."*

It is heartening to note that the Vivekananda Institute of Human Excellence is aiming at emphasizing, professing and practising spiritual education for a better valued life, thus, putting an end to the injustice that the human-kind is now subjected to and as a result of that, peace is sought to be restored to every one. Spirituality is one of the intricate and inseparable aspects of Yoga, a science which purifies the body and soul. In common parlance, we understand the meaning of spirituality as a way of discipline in life and that discipline could only be achieved by controlling the five evil forces operating in the body, viz., *Lust, Greed, Ego, Anger* and *Hatred*. They always crave for achieving materialistic outlook and such a principle would cause a cancerous disorder, making the human being fall prey to these evil forces.

According to Swami Vivekananda, education should not be restricted merely to book learning and clearing examinations. Education, to him, was not information but man making, life giving and character-building. It was a chain of ideas and skills to be churned into productive and efficient practice.

Even under dire conditions, in a situation that may seem hopeless, there are examples of how human spirit is capable of bringing forth a ray of hope. Self-awareness, ethics, insight, responsibility characterise all human beings. The principal characters of spirituality have to be imbibed by one and all. In the present day, pluralistic society comprised of different linguistic, ethinic and religious denominations, deep sense of tolerance for others' view points, their religious practices, cultural pursuits and language is the most important requirement in the society. Virtues of peace, cooperation, love, sacrifice, contentment, humility, tolerance and truthfulness are the natural traits of a human being and they form integral part of spiritualism.

The manifestation of dignity in the human being is nothing but a spiritual embodiment. We need a core system of values which combine the twin demands of excellence and social equality, which celebrates India's diversity, which recognises the role of peaceful resolution of social, economic and political tensions and conflicts and which are built into the body politic of a poor country trying to modernise itself. Right to liberty and the right to equality are the most important fundamental rights, enshrined in the Constitution. In all these rights, the golden thread of spirituality passes through. To make these rights meaningful and effective, they should be interpreted with a spiritual theme.

With the hope that if India can produce a few thousand human beings who would be men of character, it should be second to none in the world, let us pray for a better India tomorrow.

According to Mahatma Gandhiji, quoting in his own words:

"I would try to develop courage, strength, virtue, the ability to forget oneself in working towards great aims.

I should feel that if we succeed in building the character of the individual, society will take care of itself".

Be it the relations between the countries or the relations between the individuals of a family, these values play a very vital role. We all know and understand that these values are very much needed but still all of us have our own weaknesses in implementing them in our practical life. So, mere education and awareness of values are not enough. The actual need of the hour is not just the awareness of values, but the empowerment of individuals for adopting these values which they too wish to implement. The Institutions like these are very much aware that a very secular and non-controversial system of training is needed, which can really help in the overall development and empowerment.

Before concluding, I must mention that we must have self restraint and code of conduct, prescribed by ourselves, in order to add to our contribution in the making of a welfare society. It is exactly for the said causes that the institutions like this can render services. The values in the living system is the craving need of the hour throughout the world.

There is a need for such environment where the present generation and coming generations can adopt these values in their lives.

Therefore, whatever be the branch of knowledge of study you are persuing, your education should help you to achieve the Upanishad goal—

Asathoma Sadgamaya
Tamasoma Jyothirgamaya
Mruthyorma Amruthangamaya

That is,

O God!

Lead us from the unreal to the real,
Lead us from darkness to light,
Lead us from death to eternity.

ಬ‌ುಬ‌ುಬ‌ು

SPIRITUAL EMPOWERMENT OF JUDICIARY

It is said that prayer is speaking to GOD and meditation is listening to GOD. Rajyoga takes us on a spiritual journey through meditation, where we start experiencing God Consciousness. Successful are those who can first manage themselves. The topic of Self Management may lead the mind into a plane where it can efficiently manage all its emotions with inner stability. We all are aware that all the physical relationships are temporary and there is no other relation which can constantly be with us except the eternal true relationship with GOD, but we still get involved into the attachment of physical relationships. The topic of "Developing a deep personal relationship with God" may enlighten us as to how we have to experience, maintain and develop a true relationship with GOD.

It is the leadership, which really counts when we want to measure the development or the progress. The one who can properly lead himself is the one who can lead the world. The topic of inculcating "Leadership Abilities" will focus on developing the inner leadership qualities. Even the leadership depends on the inner strength of an individual. So, the topic of "Developing Inner Powers through Rajyoga" will help us to fill ourselves with the divine strengths.

It is said that every action has an equal and opposite reaction, it exactly suits the actions of our day to day life also, which is well defined in the Karma Philosophy, as we sow-so shall we reap. The present day world needs much deeper understanding of this philosophy. One has to understand these secrets, so that the topic of "Deep Secrets of Karma Philosophy" may enlighten us to understand the eternal laws of action in deeper perspective.

Life is an opportunity to serve and to experience the pleasure of knowledge and understanding. Life is for satisfaction and not for mere pleasures. Though stress and pressures are also a part of life, one has to learn the art of living by acquiring the abilities to face the hardest of the hard situations with lightness and spirit. The topic of "Stress-Free Living" would be very helpful for all, in the present context, as stress has become the most common ailment of the modern world.

Delivered at Academy for A Better World, Gyan Sarovar, Mt. Abu, Rajasthan on 30th September, 2003.

Brahma Baba, the founding father of this institution was a great visionary, his dedication towards the service of the humanity at an age when all retire is a great example. We are looking at the vast branches of this institution, where Baba worked in the background. An old man who untiringly worked for this cause, upto an age of 93 years, to bring about a global transformation is the source of inspiration for this whole movement. Brahma Baba has not confined his spiritual experiences to himself, he did not rest, till he made everyone experience the same. When Baba experienced GOD face to face, the transformation which took place in him, led to an intense penance which he continued for 14 full years, but not alone, he inspired around 400 small children to undergo the same tapasya along with him. Today we see Dadiji's before us, who were part of those 400 small Yoginis and Yogis who dedicated themselves for bringing a new world order of Satyuga with purity, peace and prosperity. Now, that small movement which started its services from one of the remote corners like Abu, has spread its service throughout the world with 7000 branches in 90 countries, with thousands of voluntarily dedicated Sisters and Brothers and lakhs of spiritual students. The whole Abu vibrates with the vibrations of the penance performed by these children of God. Hearing the real life stories of these saints will be a wonderful experience and a great inspiration. Hope that the respected Dadis will enlighten us with such experiences through the "History of the Institution".

Spirituality is the most important strength of any individual, going deep into the consciousness we awaken the dormant divine being to act for the welfare of the self and the humanity. Spirituality gives us the strength and the wisdom. It also gives us the vision of a better world. It opens the hidden dark spots of our soul and illuminates us with the divine light; thus all the negative darkness disappears from us. Spirituality makes us transparent, open and fearless in accepting the truth. It is said that self-realisation leads to God Realisation. We have to realize ourselves and also the purpose of our existence. Especially to the Legal Fraternity, Spirituality works as a shield of protection to the inner self, from getting influenced by the negativities.

దుదుదు

SPIRITUAL EMPOWERMENT FOR JURISTS

Empowerment of the jurists, is the need of the day, to rejuvenant them to fulfil the expectations of the society and repose faith and confidence in the justice delivery system.

Law enforcement or sustenance of law and order is becoming a prime issue day-by-day. The quantum of piling of the cases in the Courts and the cumulative growth in its rate is giving us an indication that there is a need of deep concern in this matter, worldwide. Merely increasing the number of courts and the number of Judicial authorities may not be the solution for this. There is a need for an attitudinal change and overall structural change in the society, which should be brought about in all walks of life of the community. The increase in the number of people, approaching the Judiciary for proper justice shows their confidence of getting proper justice from the Judiciary but the matter of concern is that this increase is proving to us that there is a constant increase of injustice, outside, in the society.

The basic spirit of our Constitution is to provide each and every person of the nation irrespective of race, religion, caste, community and social status with equal opportunity and the structure of the Constitution is built with the bricks of moral and ethical values, which have really made the whole nation stand inspite of facing so many adverse situations.

Though the Judiciary is only one of the three organs of the State, it plays a very responsible role in building up the confidence and integrity of the nation. It is like the foundation of the nation. This is the reason, which make the jurists of the country to think about the future of the nation. Is it not the time to think about some permanent solutions for these problems? Is it not the time to bring about a change in the attitudes of the people? Is it not the time to make them realize more about their responsibilities along with their rights? It is said that "Prevention is Better than Cure". Doctors deal with the problems of physical and mental health of the patients. It is said that the social health is also an important factor. However, the jurists are those doctors who take care of the overall social health of the society at large. Only when there is a problem in the social health,

---

Speech delivered at inaugural session of 'National Dialogue on Spiritual Empowerment for Jurists', Mt. Abu.

a person approaches a jurist – doctor of social health spending so much of our time and resources to find out some suggestions for preventive measures. Yes, Prevention is Better than Cure in many ways. The punishment and sentence, we give, is in principle to bring about a change in the behaviour of a person or criminal. The very spirit is to make him realize the mistake and change his behaviour. Any effort in bringing about this realization before breaking the law is highly appreciable and is in act, strengthening the law and order of the nation. The value system of the culture of our nation is in fact protecting the structure of justice. There is a need to strengthen this value system. Values like; truthfulness, non-violence, self-less services, honesty, tolerance, sincerity etc., when inculcated with dedication will solve so many present day problems. It will promote a natural law abiding culture. It is wonderful to note that the basic spirit of spiritual education of any religion is primarily based on inculcating such values as universal brotherhood. It means to see every human being as a child of God and as his own brother. Then he shares his resources with his brothers who are in need of it. Spirituality teaches selfless service and having a feeling of global family. When spirituality is inculcated in practical life, a person becomes a natural embodiment of moral and ethical values.

The nation should, now, give birth to a new generation with tremendous strength of moral values and with an uncompromising Will towards the spirity of truth, justice and non-violence. This is possible only when the older generation sets an example before them.

The spirit of our profession is not calculative by arguments for winning over the case, but is for the protection of justice.

Legal profession has a vital role to play in the administration of justice, not merely as representing one of the parties to the litigation but as officers of the courts. The Profession is a commitment to the people to protect their legal and fundamental rights, but unfortunately over the years it appears to have put its true purpose on a back burner and allowed aggressive materialism to overtake it. Moral values and professional ethics have suffered in the bargain. The bar and the bench have to act collectively to retrieve the image of the profession by taking stringent steps against malpractices and their practitioners.

For discharging the judicial obligations, many challenges have to be met in order to provide inexpensive, speedy and unpolluted justice to the people. We should respond to the hope and aspirations of the citizens.

Unless the justice delivery system functions smoothly, cordially & effectively and maintains balance between love and law, it will loose its vibrancy in delivering the justice. The Function of judiciary is to administer justice, according to law and in doing so the system must respond to the hopes and aspirations of the people who have reposed confidence in the judiciary to secure Justice. The progress of society depends upon proper application of law to the needy in achieving the constitutional goal *i.e.*, justice, liberty, equality, peace, purity and happiness. We believe that once upon a time *Satyuga* – (Paradise – the age of Truth) existed on this earth. But presently we are living in a World of fear, insecurity, distrust, intolerance, hatred, violence and injustice. We are living in a world where human, moral and spiritual values stand at a distantce. Consequently, happiness, which is the birth right of every human being, has become an elusive dream. The man is suffering from hopelessness, carelessness and depression. Material progress is like a squeezed sugarcane, devoid of its juice and sweetness. The route cause of the global injustice is because of sex, anger, greed, attachment, arrogance, alcoholism, obscene literature, peacelessness etc. The evils like eve-teasing, rape, abduction, prostitution, use of filthy and abusive language, obscenity in art and literature as well as on screen and stage, exhibition of some human nude pictures in commercial advertisements, instances of divorce and the suicide and various kinds are all attributable to sex and lust. Renunciation of this vice of sex will lead to establishment of a healthy society. Similarly, if the vice of anger, hate and malice are eschewed, for establishment of peace in the globe, we would establish peace within us. Self-transformation leads to the universal transformation.

The present day society requires only those quintessential, fundamental principles, whether within history, philosophy, ethics, culture, jurisprudence or other disciplines, which ennoble attitudes and behaviours and which improve human understanding and the quality of life. It is the need of the day to introduce value based education in legal system and in law colleges. Create men and women of character, based on the values and integrity.

The message to the jurists is that the jurists must be fair, righteous, upright in their work or profession and in all other walks of life. Jurists shall work together in achieving the goal of the jurisprudence and spiritual prudence in promoting the culture of peace, justice and harmony. One must devote some time, daily, on introspection, meditation, silence and study for our spiritual and moral development. One shall endeavour in affirming the brotherhood of all human beings for achieving the spiritual values and divine qualities. "Be good and do good'. *Sarvey Jana Sukhino Bhawantu* (Universal Love and Benediction) as is being imparted by this spiritual organization. We shall endeavour at all stages of life in rendering positive and substantial justice to all, more specially to the poorer and under privileged section of the society, with affordable cost and quicker pace for achieving a purified and holistic world.

ಜಿಜಿಜಿ

TOWARDS BETTER LIFE

I heartfully appreciate the attempt of this noble organization for extending a divine opportunity.

The basic spirit of our Constitution is to provide each and every person of the nation irrespective of race, religion, caste, community and social status with equal opportunity and the structure of the Constitution is built with the bricks of moral and ethical values, which have really made the whole nation stand inspite of facing so many adverse situations.

The nation should now give birth to a new generation with tremendous strength of moral values and with an uncompromising will towards the spirit of truth, justice and non-violence. This is possible only when the older generation sets an example before them.

We are living in a World where human, moral and spiritual values stand at a distance. Consequently, happiness which is the birth right of every human being has become an elusive dream. The man is suffering from hopelessness, carelessness and depression. Material progress is like a squeezed sugarcane devoid of its juice and sweetness. If the vices of anger, hate and malice are to be eschewed for establishment of peace in the globe, we should establish peace within us.

The present day society requires only those quintessential, fundamental principles that can be found within history, philosophy, ethics, culture, jurisprudence or other disciplines, which ennoble attitudes and behaviours and which improve human understanding and the quality of life. It is the need of the day to introduce value-based education in legal system and in law colleges. Create men and women of character, based on the values and integrity.

At this hour, we need a:

1. World without War.

2. Economic Justice.

3. A fair Judiciary.

4. Reformation of Culture.

Delivered at the Conference on "Towards Better Life & Society" on 6th October, 2004 at Vigyan Bhawan New Delhi.

5. Living under the Guidance of Intellectuals.

6. Respecting Womanhood and giving them Full Equal Rights.

7. Living in tune with the law of Nature.

8. Food and Water to be available for each person of the World.

9. Universal Agreement on one Truth (God) to bring about true realization of God and self.

If we were to put it briefly, spiritual power comes from, and in the form of, five main achievements:

(i) Purity and Divine Virtues.

(ii) Spiritual Meditation, based on soul-consciousness.

(iii) Tyaga and Vairagya (spirit of Renunciation or Dispassion and Detachment).

(iv) Seva (service with a spirit of dedication) and good wishes for all.

(v) Surrender to God and leading life as His instrument or as a Trustee.

Purity and Divine Virtues enable the soul to stabilize its original nature and stature. Purity and Divinity are the essence of Spirituality. They give immense power to the soul. The soul now has self-respect. The soul is no longer slave to its senses, nor does it yield to material or wordly temptations. Purity comes when (a) one realizes fully the consequences of sinful actions and tendencies such as anger, hatred, arrogance, etc., (b) then observes self-restraint and inculcation of divine qualities as against each vice, (c) avoids bad company and bad reading or visual material, (d) does not take intoxicating drugs, and (e) food by killing animals and birds. Spiritual Meditation gives one the experience of withdrawal from the body, peace and bliss and these, naturally, make the foundations and the edifice of Purity and Divine qualities strong.

It is through Meditation that one's spiritual battery is charged and one gets guidance and help from God. Meditation also builds the spirit of renunciation, dispassion etc. and creates and sustains the attitude of good wishes and service. "Smriti is Samarthi" (Remembrance of God brings power). Seva enables one to get the blessings of all. But, spiritual knowledge, revealed by God Himself, is essential for all these spiritual achievements and for the practice of Meditation, one has to make efforts to understand this knowledge, inculcate divine qualities and vicelessness and practice soul-consciousness and Meditation, have good wishes for all and do seva through mind, speech and action and the rest will be done by the almighty and Merciful God. The knowledge, as given by God, is easy to grasp and the Meditation; He teaches, is also easy. One does not take long to experience the self and God if one sincerely practice what God has revealed and asked us to practice.

As part of its efforts towards promoting spiritual empowerment, the Brahma Kumaris have been offering to people of all walks of life around the world a very simple, accessible and effective education in self-awareness, spiritual principles and values.

ಬಿಬಿಬಿ

LIFE IN HARMONY WITH NATURE

Earth is the only planet in the universe which has an environment for life. Environment normally means its surroundings. We, Indians, are proud of our culture and heritage. Our culture demands that we should start our day by taking a bath. For water, we need to preserve the natural resources like river, pond, and other water sourses etc. Taking a dip in river is considered as holy for the reason that it flows and is a gift of God. Going to the temple to pray to God for allowing us to use the earth re-iterates our duty to protect the nature. Walking around the temple (pradikshana) is an exercise to our body, and we do it in a clockwise direction for the reason that we want to run our life in a smooth manner like the clock. We bow to the bull in temple as a respect to the animal kingdom. Bull is considered as a useful animal without which ploughing of fields is not possible. If agricultural properties are properly preserved, there will not be any scarcity of food. We treat the Banyan tree as God, because it gives more oxygen than any other tree. As we cannot keep a tree as a symbol of respect in every house, we keep a "tulsi" plant in our house to mark our respect to all the plants. Since time immemorial, natural objects like rivers enjoy a high respect from the society. They are considered as Goddesses having not only the purifying capacity but also self purifying ability. Fouling of the water of a river was considered as a sin and it attracted punishments. The earth also equally had the same importance, and the ancient literature provided the means to purify the polluted soil. Everyone is careful to maintain his own residence in a best environment. But at the same time, he forgets the fact that surrounding areas are also important. The public should feel that they have also got a duty to preserve the environment in the best interest of themselves. I had the occasion to deliver a judgment, when I was the judge of the Kerala High Court, banning smoking in public places. The smokers in public places not only harm themselves, but also adversely affect the persons standing nearby.

The beginning of the Environment Law culminated from the United Nations Conference on Human Environment, held at Stockholm in 1972, where India was a participant. The foundation for environmental protection and control legislations were incorporated into the Constitution of India by the Forty-Second Amendment Act of 1976. Art. 48A was added to the Directive Principles of State

Speech delivered at the Karnataka State Intellectual's Conference at Ambedkar Bhavan, Millers Road, Bangalore on 1st August, 2004.

Policy. It declares *"The State shall endeavor to protect and improve the environment and to safeguard the forests and wild life of the country."* An additional fundamental duty was imposed on every citizen to protect and improve the natural environment including forests, lakes, rivers and wild life, and to have compassion for living creatures by incorporating Art. 51A to the Constitution. This constitutional amendment is the foundation of the legislations for environment protection. The allocation of legislative authority is an important one. Some environmental problems such as sanitation and waste disposal can be best tackled at the municipal level. Protection of air, water and wild life are better regulated by uniform national laws. The 42nd amendment also moved the subject "forests " from State list to Central list. Thereafter, several legislations were enacted so as to preserve the environment.

The Indian judiciary, for protecting and preserving the environment, has given a wider interpretation to the fundamental right conferred by Art. 21 of the Constitution. While giving a broader meaning to the term "right to life", Hon'ble Mr. Justice Bhagwati, speaking for the Supreme Court, has stated that: *"We think that the right to life includes the right to live with human dignity and all that goes along with it, namely, the bare necessaries of life such as adequate nutrition, clothing, shelter over the head and facilities for reading, writing and expressing oneself in diverse forms, freely moving about and mixing and commingling with fellow human beings"*. The right to life is a fundamental right and it includes the right to enjoyment of pollution free water and air, for full enjoyment of life.

Being a developing country, economic progress is essential. At the same time, care has to be taken of the environment. It cannot be disputed that no development is possible without some adverse effect on the ecology and environment. It has become necessary to sacrifice certain ecological resources, to meet the needs of human necessities. Rising poverty and unemployment have increased pressure on environmental resources as more people have been forced to rely more, directly upon them. There should be balance between development and environment. The basic approach should be sustainable development, a development in harmony with environment. Sustainable development is essentially a policy and strategy for continued economic and social development, without detriment to the environment and natural resources on the quality of which continued activity and further development depend. The richness of the earth's biodiversity should be conserved for future generations. Being a developing country, economic progress is essential; at the same time, care has to be taken to preserve environment. Therefore, while thinking of the developmental measures, the needs of the present and the ability of the future to meet its own needs and requirements, have to be kept in view. While thinking of the present, the future should not be forgotten. We owe a duty to future generations and for a bright today, bleak tomorrow cannot be countenanced. We must learn from our experiences of past to make both the present and the future brighter. We should learn from our experiences, mistakes of the past, so that they can be rectified for a better future. The United Nations Conference and Development held at Rio, 1992, proclaimed 27 principles, the first of which, *inter alia*, is thus:

"Human beings are at the centre of concerns for sustainable development. They are entitled to a healthy and productive life in harmony with nature."

It cannot be lost sight of that while today is yesterday's tomorrow, it is tomorrow's yesterday. There is a day after tomorrow which the future requires.

The greenery of India should not be allowed to be perished, to be replaced by deserts. Euthopia, which at a point of time was considered to be one of the greenest countries, is virtually a vast desert today. We have learnt much from the Bhopal tragedy, which has led to a lot of environmental legislations. The non-availability of drinking water in many States have lead to severe problems. The over exploitation of ground water, has damaged the traditional drinking water resources like, wells, ponds, streams, etc. Improper management and disposal of wastes has lead to severe pollution. The depletion of forests has lead to climatic changes. Uncontrolled mining has resulted in depletion of natural resources. Fishery resources has adversely affected the exports. The indiscriminate construction of buildings in violation of Building Rules and Town Planning Regulations have made life miserable. The level of flood and drought has started increasing. Shortage of agricultural commodities have led to famine. Several persons are dying due to diarrhoeal diseases related to unsafe drinking water and malnutrition. Similar phenomena are emerging on a global scale, such as global warming, and loss of ozone. A safe, environmentally sound, and economically viable energy pathway that will sustain human progress into the distant future is clearly imperative. New dimensions of political will and institutional co-operation is required to achieve it. New technologies, which offer promise of higher productivity, increased efficiency and decreased pollution should be encouraged. Dumping of hazardous wastes should be totally prohibited. Multinational companies can play an important role in sustainable development, especially as developing countries have come to rely more on foreign equity capital. If these companies are to have positive influence on development, the negotiating capacity of developing countries must be strengthened so that they can secure terms that respect their environment concerns.

Striking a balance between protection of the environment and sustainable development is an onerous and delicate task. Supreme Court had the occasion to consider several issues relating to environment. The technical hurdles in approaching the Courts have been relaxed by means of public interest litigations. *Locus standi* has been widened. Even letters and telegrams are converted as writ petitions. Court had stepped in where there is no law and laws are interpreted for the preservation of the natural resources. For the protection of the forests, several conditions were laid down. In the process, directions were given to ensure that degradation does not take place. Noise pollution, in the name of religious activities, disturbs the old and infirm persons whose sleeps are adversely affected. Supreme Court, in *Church of God (Full Gospel) in India* v. *K.K.R. Majestic Colony Welfare Association,* (2000) 7 SCC 282: (2000) 3 LRI 1034 recognizing the right to sleep of the persons, came to their rescue and honoured their right. In *Murli. S. Deora* v. *Union of India,* (2001) 8 SCC 765: AIR 2002 SC 40 the Supreme Court gave utmost importance to the health of the public affected by smoking in public places. For controlling the vehicular pollution several directions were issued. The city of Delhi was one of most polluting city in the world. It is due to the intervention of the Supreme Court that the air quality in the National Capital region has improved. For protecting monuments like Taj Mahal, directions were issued. Rain water harvesting and linking of rivers have become a necessity. Environment education has been made compulsory in all schools. Building Rules and Town Planning violations have been strictly dealt. For the proper management of wastes, directions were issued.

Preservation of the global environment is a vital priority that must be borne in mind by all. A good coffee is a gift from the sun and the earth, and one born only under the right environmental conditions, in the coffee plantations. India indeed was once a land of plenty with its mountains covered with luxuriant forests, and the fertile land yielded the basic needs of its people. If such a land is today in shambles, its mountain slopes devastated, forest cover removed, its pure waters, not excluding even the sacred Ganga, converted into glorified sewers and the free air surrounding us poisoned with noxious gases, we only have ourselves and the modern ways, we have adopted, to blame, ignoring the wisdom and teachings of our forefathers. Open spaces, land for a home, clean air to breathe and clean water to drink, which are to be considered as our birthright, have started diminishing. The tradition of religious bath and tree worship which has deep rooted historicity is a general feature of India's religious life. Lord Krishna's acceptance in Bhagavad Geeta himself as the pipal tree, Lord Buddha's enlightenment symbol, the relation of all the Jaina Trithankaras with vivid trees shows that love for nature is not only a Brahmanical concept but it is the genetic character of our land. When we waste water, we face escalating crisis, even of biblical proportions. In Ecclesiastes, I recall the passage:

One generation passeth away, another generation come:

But the earth abideth always ....

All rivers runneth to the sea, yet the sea is not full............

Rig veda praises the beauty of dawn and worships nature in all its glory. A holy dip in Ganga and Yamuna was capable of washing all the sins. Man has overdrawn from nature for satisfaction of his multifarious needs, desires and ambitions. Nature has lost its capacity for self-stabilisation and started retreating. In the last century, a great German materialist philosopher warned the mankind:

"Let us not, however, flatter ourselves over much on account of our human victories over nature. For each such victory, nature takes its revenge on us."

Environmental initiatives extend beyond legal compliance and include energy conservation, environmental preservation, recycling, waste management, water conservation and using of eco-friendly products. Preservation of environment raises difficult and complex issues. The fundamental question before the world today is whether we can allow this destruction of the environment to continue. We are proud of our culture and heritage. We have been taught to worship nature. We acknowledge our dependence on the environment. Our religion enshrines respect for nature, environmental harmony and conservation. Trees, animals, hills, mountains, rivers are worshipped as symbols of representatives of nature. Since vedic times, the main motto of social life was to live in harmony with nature. The following hymn is found in *Rigveda*:

> *"The Sky is like Father, The Earth is like Mother, and The Space is as their son; The Universe consisting of the Three, is like a Family, and any kind of damage done to any one of the three, throws the Universe out of balance. "*

Though in ancient times, there was no scientific methodology for the preservation of environment, we cannot deny the fact that our forefathers took proper care in handling environment. They were well acquainted with some of the natural things. The leaves of Neem were kept between the pages and holy books, like the great epics, were wrapped in red cloth, explicit that there was preservative sensibility among people of the period. It is now well known that burning of Deodar, Amra (Mango), Chandan (Sandal) and other woods not only fulfilled sanctitious purpose but also purified the environment.

More than any political, civil, social, cultural or economic right, it is the right to life which Islam regards as the supreme right. "By means of water we give life to everything" – Koran 21:30

Rivers are our brothers, they quench our thirst and feed our children. Our future depends on the preservation of environment. As observed by Albert Einstein. *"Environment is everything that is not me"*.

৪৪৪৪

MAKE A DIFFERENCE

This is a world full of imbalances, injustices and inequalities. We witness undeserving successes and unfortunate failures, unbelievable ups and downs around us. Good times and bad times are beyond our control. But is that all destiny? Do we not have a role to act and achieve heights of excellence and set examples? Do we not have the opportunities to react positively to the situations we are in? Don't we have a role to make life better, rewarding and self satisfying? Yes, certainly we have a great role to play in carving not only our future but also the destiny of the society and the generations to follow. But it needs real positive thinking and confidence in yourself to **assume roles that make a difference**. Whoever you might be and whatever be the position you hold, you can make a difference and that is what matters ultimately. The point I am trying to drive home is that anyone, whatever be the position and the situation in which he or she is can make a difference, provided he has the will power to do so and a commitment to the society, at large.

History is dotted with names of many such great personalities who have been instrumental in carving out the destiny of the era, they lived in, and the society of which they were a part. They have made the world better for the posterity by acting and reacting against tides and currents that were detrimental for survival of the mankind. They were men of vision and concerned for the humanity at large. Many of them rose from depths of penury, poverty and neglect. But they all managed to **make a difference** through their sheer will power, commitment and positive thinking. They fought the odds and swarm against adverse currents to make this world much better. I would like you to recall the contributions of **Mahatma Gandhi, Swami Vivekananda, Albert Einstein, Louise Pastor and Mother Teresa** (to mention a few) who, with their selfless services, set excellent examples and have made this world a better place to live. The core of Gandhi's religion was faith in God, in himself as an instrument of God and in non-violence as the way to God in heaven, and to peace and happiness on earth. Swami Vivekananda lived on this earthly sphere for thirty-nine and a half years, of which nearly ten years alone were devoted to works of public significance. He took the world by storm at the Parliament of

Speech delivered at the Inauguration of "Rotary District Conference of the Rotary International District 3190" on the Theme "Making a Difference" on 18th December, 2004 at Bangalore.

339

Religions at Chicago, and since then spent himself, unsparingly, in spreading the message of Vedanta among mankind. Was this meteoric career only a passing fanfare, or did it leave any abiding results – a legacy to India and the world at large?

At the very outset, it has to be pointed out that Swamiji's life and work have a two-fold significance. On the one hand, he was the first great leader, spearheading the modern Indian resurgence and giving the clarion call to his people to rouse themselves up from the slumber of slavery, and to work for the nation's upliftment. He was, on the other hand, an Acharya, a preacher of the Vedanta, whose message of salvation from the cycle of recurring births and deaths is of world-wide import and makes no distinction of country or nation or religion. The legacy which Swamiji has left pertains to both these fields – service and salvation of the soul.

Albert Einstein, the only American citizen to have ever offered the presidency of another nation, died at Princeton at the age of 76, still seeking the answers to more secrets of time and space. *The possibility of failure never disturbed him.* He knew that man can never learn everything and that "the most beautiful thing we can experience is the mysterious". Louise Pastor, though he was in frail health, his head buzzed with plans. As disease knows no international boundaries, he and his men would attack sickness anywhere, and no wonder, Louise Pastor has been called "a legend in the annals of humanity" and so too is the institute he founded.

Mother Teresa thought profoundly on matters of life and death. Unlike many of us, in her value system there was no gap between words and action. They were all of one piece. Her power came from an integrated personality. If she criticized abortion, she did not stop at just attacking abortion as 'a terrible sin'. She would go to the dustbins, retrieve the abandoned infants and struggle for their survival. If her mission was to serve 'the poorest of the poor', she was equally concerned about the rich westerners. One could see it in her eyes as she talked to the tourists. If the poor feel unwanted, so do the affluent. The loneliness of the Westerners touched her as much as that of the dying destitutes on the streets of Calcutta. Hers was a conscience, finely tuned to the world's suffering. 'Loneliness', she once observed, 'is worse than poverty.' Most of the personalities I have mentioned to you just now were unassuming, who chose tracks which many feared to tread and left their marks in history. Let me quote a few lines from Frost here which I think are appropriate: "....... **Two roads diverged in a wood, and I took the one less traveled by, and that has made all the difference.**" (the Road Not Taken 1916). In my opinion, we must display enough courage to break open new paths in our journey towards progress rather than mechanically following the beaten track. Fortunately, our country has no dearth of personalities who added value to our culture, enriched our heritage and moulded our psyche. Nehru, Rajaji, Vinoba Bhave, K.M. Munshi, the queen of music M.S. Subbulakshmi etc., were all born in this very land of ours and made a difference.

I am proud to note that the **Indian judiciary** was also fortunate to have many such great men who took on their shoulders the task of ensuring a life of dignity for the suffering millions of this country, upheld their rights and privileges and strengthened the democratic foundations of our polity. Many of our great judges set the tones of judicial activism, acted right in time to check intrusion into the basic rights of the individual by the executive thereby, setting invaluable examples. I would like to recall a few names whose judicial contributions had a remarkable impact in the society at large. **Justice Tarkunde**, who died in the early part of the year 2004, was a rare breed of judges whose rationalist beliefs did not inhibit him to defend the rights of religious denominations. But he rallied the forces of secularism amidst communal hatred. His was the voice of sanity which guided activists to confront the communal forces in the anti-sikh riots in 1984.

Justice V.R. Krishna Iyer is a living legend who, by his landmark, verdicts in the Apex Court, humanized the law, including the judicial struggle against death sentence, whereas **Justice H.R. Khanna** in deciding the Habeas Corpus case played a pivotal role at the most critical juncture in our history. Posterity will admire his classic dissenting judgment, as a brilliant example of judicial integrity and courage, and cherish it for the abiding values it embodies.

Nani Palkhiwala combined eloquence with wisdom, sincerity with versatility, vision with achievement. He had an impressive record of public service and known for his passionate advocacy of constitutional public causes and prolific authorship. He was a colossus among lawyers and a giant among men who succeeded **in making a difference**. When India was confronted in international legal forums with Pakistan's claim to territory, in Kutch, and its claim to overflight rights over India, it was Palkhiwala, the defender of the people, who became the Indian Government's champion. All arguments before the World Court, at The Hague, were read from written briefs; since every word matters and there is not a moment to waste. The solitary exception was Palkhiwala, who argued orally, brilliantly, and successfully **and with a difference**.

I am proud to recall that, in my own humble way, I could also make a few crucial judicial decisions leaving indelible impressions on the sands of time. When the Division Bench of the Kerala High Court, comprising of myself and my learned colleague Justice K. Narayana Kurup, pronounced the judgment banning smoking in public places, we were targeting at a menace which was eating into the very roots of public health. Thanks to the valuable research and studies made on the adverse impact of smoking, we could pronounce this landmark verdict which has been hailed by the international community as a unique contribution by the Indian judiciary to protect human rights to health. For the first time, smokers were booked by police in public places and fined. We were glad that the apex court also agreed with our observations and States after States started banning smoking in public places. The verdict banning smoking in public places has been a signal contribution to protect the environment from the vicious tobacco vapour and as a sequel, protecting millions of innocent and unsuspecting passive smokers from the scourge of **Environmental Tobacco Smoke (ETS)** or second hand smoke. It was the startling revelations of ETS which made us pronounce this first ever judicial initiative in the world against the scourge of passive smoking. It was heartening that the judgment served as an eye opener and trend-setter not only for India but for the entire humanity.

The Kerala High Court was the origin of many such path breaking judicial initiatives. It goes to the credit of my learned colleague Justice Kurup for his crucial decision from banning five species of animals—Lion, Tiger, Panther, Bear and Monkey – being trained and displayed in circuses throughout India. A Division Bench comprising Justice Kurup and Justice K.V. Sankaranarayanan which pronounced the judgment, rightly observed that it is not only our fundamental duty to show compassion to our animal friends but also to recognize and protect their rights. **While ruling that animals have right to dignity akin to human beings**, the Kerala High Court, striking an entirely different note, showed once more that it is prepared to go beyond the letter of the law to reinterpret or even extend it, in the light of evolving public consciousness.

The Court also took up the cause of public transportation, which was the monopoly of the State – run corporation, in the capital city of Trivandrum. Taking due account of a **media survey** conducted, as ordered by the Court, to determine an issue pending before it – really a unique one in the annals of judicial history- the ruling allowed private buses to operate in the city, breaking the decades old monopoly of State – owned transport corporation in the nationalised routes.

In *Bareilly Development Authority* v. *Vrinda Gujarati & Ors.*, (2004) 4 SCC 606: JT 2004 (3) SC 83 (a bench of three Hon'ble Judges), the Development Authority demanded for enhanced price after the allotment which was disputed by the allottees. Allotment letter indicated that the price of the flats was still an estimate and that the final costing would be done after completion on the basis of actual cost. Consequent to increase in the built-in area, the demand was made on the allottees for payment of enhanced cost. Speaking for the Bench, I have held that the enhancement in the cost was due to actual increase in the cost of the flat and such an enhancement was in accordance with clauses 2 and 15 of the brochure and the said enhancement was also in accordance with clause 2 of the allotment letters, issued to various applicants. The allottees after undertaking to pay the enhanced amount, and after taking possession of the flats on that ground cannot be allowed to raise frivolous contentions to avoid payment to the appellant. The Supreme Court directed the allottees to pay the enhanced price of the flats in six monthly equal instalments.

In *The Commissioner of Police & Ors.* v. *Acharya Jagdishwarananda Avadhuta & Anr.*, JT 2004 (3) SC 224 (a bench of three Hon'ble Judges) an interesting question came up before the Supreme Court with regard to Tandava dance which was introduced by Ananda Margis in Calcutta and other places, requiring it to be performed by the Ananda Margis as one of their religious rites. Hon'ble Rajendra Babu and Hon'ble G.P. Mathur, JJ. took the view that the practice of Tandava dance in public streets is not an essential part of Ananda Margis and, therefore, they have no right to perform Tandava dance in public streets of Calcutta, as ordered by the Commissioner of Police. Mine was a dissenting judgment. I said that Article 25(1) of the Constitution of India guarantees to every person freedom of conscience and the right to freely profess, practice and propagate any religion and this right is not confined to citizens alone but covers all persons residing in India. Therefore, I said that the Ananda Margis have a right to take procession in public places after obtaining necessary permission from the concerned authorities and they are also entitled to carry trishul or trident, conch or skull so long as such procession is peaceful and does not offend the religious sentiments of other people who equally enjoy the fundamental right to exercise their religious freedom. I also said that every religious right is subject to public order and the State has got ample powers to regulate the secular activities associated with religious practices.

In *Mukand Ltd.* v. *Mukand Staff & Officers Association* [JT 2004 (3) SC 474] another interesting question came up before the Supreme Court, under the provisions of the Industrial Disputes Act, 1947 and the jurisdiction of the Tribunal to decide whether disputes relating to employees who were not workmen could be adjudicated by the Tribunal. The High Court held that the Industrial Tribunal has jurisdiction to decide the disputes relating to both workmen and non-workmen. The judgment of the Bombay High Court was set aside by the Supreme Court. Speaking for the Bench, I have held that it was not open to the High Court, in exercise of writ jurisdiction, to modify the award which had its very basis flawed as it lacked proper application of the fundamentals of wage adjudication. We also held that the Tribunal has exceeded its jurisdiction and has embarked upon an inquiry against non-workmen and, therefore, the decision of the Tribunal is a non-compliance of the provisions of the Industrial Disputes Act.

In *Goa Plast (P) Ltd.* v. *Chico Ursula D'Souza*, (2004) 2 SCC 235 the party issued as many as 40 cheques. When only one cheque was presented, instructions of stop payment was given. A complaint, under Sections 138 and 139 of the Negotiable Instruments Act, was filed against the person who issued the cheque. Speaking for the Bench, I have held as under:

> It is essential that to issue stop payment instructions, there must be funds in the accounts in the first place. On this aspect, the courts below have failed to see whether, as on the date of signing of the cheque dated 20th July, 1992, the date of presentation of the cheque dated 10th January, 1993, the date of writing of letter dated 12th February, 1993 and the date on which stop payment instructions were issued to the bank, the respondent has sufficient funds in the account. The respondent was otherwise admitting the liability when the cheques were being issued. This was sufficient evidence to prove that there was a liability and as per the presumption under section 139 of the Act, the cheques issued, therefore, were towards the liability even as per the version of the respondent.

> In the instant case, the cheque issued by the respondent has been stopped for payment on his instructions and the cheque was returned to the appellant, unpaid. On the consideration of the facts and circumstances of the case and the law on the subject, we hold that the respondent shall be deemed to have committed an offence.

In *Tamil Nadu Kalyana Mandapam Assn.* v. *Union of India and Ors.*, JT 2004 (4) SC 568: (2004) 5 SCC 632 extension of the levy to services, provided by the kalyan mandap keepers was in question. The constitutional validity of the relevant provisions were challenged before the High Court by the Tamil Nadu Kalyana Mandapam Association. The challenge was in regard to the extension of service tax in respect of services provided by the kalyan mandap keepers. The High Court of Madras dismissed the writ petitions. The matter was taken up to the Supreme Court. Speaking for the Bench, I have held that the levy of service tax, on mandap keepers is constitutionally valid and the Supreme Court also held as follows:

> Making available premises for marriages does not involve transfer of moveable property but is an act of providing services and cannot be classified as any other kind of legal concept and the services cannot be termed as hire purchase agreement of a right to use goods or property. The service provided by the mandap keepers are essentially professional services. The tax is, in pith and substance, a tax on services and not a tax on sale of goods or on hire purchase activities. Therefore the service tax levied, under an enactment made by the Parliament, cannot be considered to be unconstitutional.

In *Gayatri De* v. *Mousumi Co-operative Housing Society Ltd. and Ors.*, JT 2004 (3) SC 83: (2004) 5 SCC 90 (a bench of three Hon'ble Judges) Speaking for the Bench, I have held that the heirs of the deceased persons are entitled to inherit the flat allotted to the deceased.

The appellant, being one of the heirs of the deceased member, in our opinion, is entitled to succeed to the estate of the deceased and that being so, the right, title and interest of the deceased member in the apartment of the society devolves upon his heirs and the aforesaid section 85(3) and Rule 135(3) cannot have any application in the instant case.

In *Ganesh Santa Ram Sirur* v. *State Bank of India & Anr.*, 2004 (9) SCALE 449 the matter relates to the granting of a loan by a branch manager of a nationalized bank to his wife. Departmental proceedings were initiated against him and ultimately bank manager realized the mistake and tried to salvage the same by not encashing the draft issued in the maiden name of his wife though the draft was issued but not encashed. The Supreme Court held that the relevant rules of the bank prohibits the bank manager to sanction the loan to his wife or relative or to any partner and the said rule 34(3)(1) is a rule of integrity and, therefore, the respondent bank cannot afford to have the appellant as bank manager and the punishment of removal of service awarded by the bank was confirmed.

In *Saurabh Chaudhary* v. *Union of India*, JT 2003 (8) SC 96: (2004) 5 SCC 618 (a Constitution Bench of five Hon'ble Judges) the core question involved in the said case was about the constitutional validity of reservation whether passed on domicile or institution in the matter of admission into PG courses in Government run medical colleges. While concurring with the other Hon'ble Judges, I wrote a separate judgment, highlighting entry qualification, unplanned growth of institutions, fee structure, certificates hassles, etc. I said, the higher the level of the speciality, the lesser the role of reservations and at the level of super-specialities the role of equal chance for equal marks dominates. As regards the scope of reservation of seats in educational institutions, affiliated and recognized by the State Universities, the Constitutional prescription of reservation of 50% of the available seats has to be respected and enforced. In conclusion, I said:

Before parting with this case, I am of the opinion that the younger generation in our society, nurturing fond hopes and aspiration for their future professional careers, should feel it as a pleasurable experience to explore the available options in higher education. They should be spared from the mental torture due to hassles and unsavoury experiences in getting to the first base. To the extent possible, they should be made to feel that they are part of one nation. Tensions and frustrations, at their impressionable age, will surely result in a society with distorted and negative values, damaging the foundations of a healthy society. The policies and procedures for admission should be viewed from the larger impact on the future of India.

I also recall another of my widely debated judgment on the right of the Government employees to go on **strike**. Though the decision of the Bench was attacked from all sides, even the bitterest critics agree with my observations relating to the grave inconveniences, the strikes cause to the public.

Banning of bandhs was some of the other decisions the Kerala High Court took, despite angry reactions from vested interests.

Another question came up before the Kerala High Court when I was the Acting Chief Justice of the said Court that whether the Consumer Disputes Redressal Forum, constituted under the Consumer Protection Act, 1986, has jurisdiction to entertain the complaint made by an individual/subscriber with regard to the disconnection of his telephone. The matter came up before me and another learned Judge. The Division Bench held that the dispute regarding payment of telephone bills is to be dealt with under the provisions of arbitration clause, contained in the Indian Telegraph Act and is not in derogation of any other law for the time being in force. We also held that in disputes regarding disconnection of telephone for non-payment of bills, the Consumer Disputes Redressal Forum lacks jurisdiction to entertain the complaint. The correctness of our above judgment was doubted by another Division Bench of the Kerala High Court in Writ Appeal No. 535 of 2002. According to the Division Bench, our judgment requires reconsideration by a larger Bench of the High Court. The matter was, thereafter, placed before the three Judge Bench. The Full Bench was of the opinion that our judgment reported in 2002 KLT 195 does not contain the correct statement of law and does not promote the declared objective of better protection and consequently our decision was over-ruled.

Aggrieved by the decision of the Full Bench of the Kerala High Court, the General Manager, Telecom, BSNL, Kozhikode preferred special leave petition before the Supreme Court of India, questioning the correctness of the order passed by the Full Bench of the Kerala High Court, over-ruling our Division Bench Judgment of the High Court, reported in 2002 KLT 195.

I am happy to say that the Supreme Court, by order dated 29th Novermber, 2004, granted leave to appeal against the Full Bench decision of the

Kerala High Court and have also granted stay of the operation of the Full Bench judgment in Civil Appeal No. 7687 of 2004 (*G.M. Telecom* v. *M. Krishnan & Anr*). In view of granting of leave and of staying the order of the Full Bench of the Kerala High Court, the parties/subscribers cannot now move the Consumer Disputes Redressal Forum and that the only forum now to redress their grievance is the arbitration proceedings, provided under section 7B of the Indian Telegraph Act.

I have also held, in another decision, that section 94 of the Motor Vehicles Act bars the jurisdiction of the Civil Courts to entertain any question relating to the grant of permit and fare stages like timings and grant of permit. The Bench was of the opinion that any grievance regarding anomalies in the fixation of fare stages have to be first raised before the Regional Transport authority and then, by way of revision, before the State Transport Appellate Authority and the Consumer Disputes Redressal Forum has no jurisdiction to decide the same. We said that the fixation of fares under the Motor Vehicles Act is a legislative function. The fixation of fares of a stage carriage bus is purely administrative and either way judicial scrutiny into such acts, as repeatedly held by this Court, is extremely limited in scope. We said that the passenger in a bus is not a consumer for the purpose of Consumer Protection Act; nor is the Regional Transport Authority, a statutory functionary under the Motor Vehicles Act, a provider of any service, the quality of which can be complained of by the bus passenger. This judgment is reported in 1999 (2) KLT 898.

These are a few examples of how judges could also **make a difference** by responding positively to anomalous and bewildering situations, public sentiments and the felt necessities of time.

I was only trying to point out a few examples from the Indian judiciary of which I have been a part for decades. From these situations, one can say without fear of contradictions, that the judges also could **make a difference**, if they have a Will to do so, changing the life of millions.

I would like to wind up this talk, reminding this impressive gathering that each one of you could **make a difference**, whoever you are or wherever you are. It is only a question of opening your eyes wide open and realizing your capabilities and opportunities. Yes, you all could also **make a difference** and make life better for yourself and the posterity.

A great American judge **Oliver Wendell Holmes**, once said, that the intensity with which one does one's work was vital. He said an hour's intensity was more productive than many days of dragging work. Let us have that intensity and I am sure we could **make a difference**.

In the end, I would like to quote a moving poem by Emily Dickinson

"If I can stop one heart from breaking
I shall not live in vain.
If I can ease one life the aching or cool one pain
Or help one fainting robin into its nest again
I shall not live in vain".

ೞೞೞ

PART XIII

ACADEMIC ENLIGHTENMENT

AN UNENDING PURSUIT

In our country, one of the most poignant circumstances to my mind, is the existence of certain short-comings in our educational system, in so far as the universities are concerned. We hear of batches and batches of students who achieve scholastic standards of the University, year by year, but are unable to get proper employment inspite of their high education and attainments. We hear also of the advice that University education should be job-oriented. The problem is two-fold. It is not only a question of job orienting our education. It is a question of having jobs ready for the job oriented people. There is a plethora of students who are good only for clerical or such other employment. There is also a disinclination on the part of students to acquire new knowledge, additional to the curriculum and do not continue further studies to keep abreast of advancements in their own fields.

A University is a place, not merely, for courses of varied teachings but one for imparting education. University education to be true to itself should have a purpose and it should make the mind productive. It is really a growth of the consciousness of the mind. Education does not begin and end with learning the contents of a few books, but is directed to the mind and its development. It leads to the building up of character and finally to social adjustability. The student who undergoes true education is not only well-read but also well-bred. He shares in the continuity and growth of knowledge and contributes to it. An American Educator, Alexander Flexner, in his book titled Universities says:

"Without ideals, without effort, without scholarship, without philosophical continuity, there is no such thing as education."

We have yet to define the aim of university education in the context of population, job availability, unemployment and earning power. It is to be noted that these are all inter-related matters and the solution must be viewed and determined from all these angle. It is not sufficient to open the doors of universities and provide different courses of teaching. We must know how the entrants will be required, in future, to use the knowledge and whether there will be any opportunity for those who leave the universities.

Convocation Address at University Campus, Ajmer, Rajasthan on 4th March, 2001.

I do not think that any University has created an employment bureau where the student, desiring university education can get information about job openings and where he can register his name. I do not think that our universities maintain a dialogue with offices of government, with industrial houses and other employers on the subject of their requirement. The Universities think that their task is over after they have prescribed courses of study, employed teacher and held examinations. Upto a point this is the fundamental duty of the university. But I feel that, in the circumstances which exist today in our country, the universities must go a step or two farther and try to procure for their students, information as to how their degrees and qualifications could be put to use in earning a livelihood. Our universities owe it to their alumni, a certain measure of aid in solving the vital problem of unemployment. Education is not merely the acquisition of knowledge of a certain kind. It is intended to be an asset to face the problems of living which crop no sooner the student leaves the portals of the university. Our constitution confers on the citizen, the right to receive education and also the right to work. The State should not feel satisfied at the thought that there are universities which would, leave the student to fend for himself. Both State and the universities must work together to help the student in his search for occupation.

If our nation has to march forward, it is absolutely essential to have good Scientists, Technologists, Philosophers, Jurists, Doctors, Lawyers, Judges and Teachers. It is also my duty to remind that the students should not forget their teachers. It is their duty to set apart a portion of their earning for the education of the underprivileged. I would suggest that a trust could be founded by the old students who, by contributing according to their might to a common fund, would help for the education of economically poorer sections of the society.

A teacher removes and dispels the darkness in the students mind. It is the teacher who enlightens the student and moulds his future. Therefore, they are entitled to great respect and reverence. It is disheartening to find that lately there is a growing tendency among the teachers to organize themselves collectively and adopt agitational methods to coerce the persons in authority to concede to their demands. My request to the respected teaching class is to set a good example for the students to emulate.

> *Don't do all things which your teachers do. Whatever blameless acts they do, follow them but not others."*

Unfortunately, the subject of education has become a great pasture of litigation in the Court of law. Students and management of unrecognised educational institutions enter the law courts instead of spending their time usefully in the class rooms. It is also true that some unscrupulous persons who do not really evince any interest in the cause of education, are converting the educational institutions into money spinners. What I mean is that people open educational institutions without even obtaining necessary recognition from the Government and the University concerned. It is the duty of every one of us to prevent such exploitation by money spinners in the field of education.

It was Albert Einstein who said:

> "We owe a lot to the Indians who taught us how to count without which no worthwhile scientific discovery could have been made."

> Mark Twain had written "India is the cradle of the human race, the birth place of human speech, the mother of history, the grand mother of legend and the great grand mother of tradition. Our most valuable and most instructive in the history of man are treasured in India only".

The Conference of Vice-Chancellors, organised by the University Grants Commission and the 66th Annual Meeting of the Association of Indian Universities, held at Thiruvanathpuram have talked openly and boldly, for the first time, about the cancer that is eating into the vitals of the university education system in this country. The real cure for the malady is to give the universities complete autonomy. Look at the academic bodies of any University in the West. You will find only academicians in these bodies, nobody else. With greater university autonomy, our institutions would be blossoming and radiating fragrance throughout the length and breadth of our country.

The greatest cankers that eat upon the system of higher education are ragging and politicisation of campus. Terrorising and harassing innocent victims under the name of ragging has greatly affected our system of higher education. Inspite of legislations banning ragging, the menace still continues with impunity.

ಜಜಜ

READING MAKETH A FULL MAN

Books play an important part in a man's life. It is the means of knowing the world. Books have become part of one's cultural, emotional and even quotadian life.

In this age of speedy and stressful life, people find little time for reading and recreation. Younger generation spends most of its free time before Television Sets. Busy parents find little time to care for their offsprings. The aftermath is apathy, sloth and lethargy among school children. It is high time we encourage reading habits and creative instincts in our younger generation in a more profitable manner.

Sloth, lethargy, extravagance and ostentation, coupled with deceit, arrogance and corruption have stained out national character and affected our national performance. We have to help, prepare the younger generation to meet these challenges and infuse in the younger blood the spirit of self sacrifice, noble ideals and objectives so as to build up a better generation in whose hands the destiny of our country lies.

For achieving excellence in all spheres of activities, there should be understanding, unity and earnestness to work hard. Notwithstanding the significant progress we have made in so many fields, our country still continues to be poor and illiterate, 30% of our people live below poverty line and 268.4 million above the age of seven are illiterate (1997). The literacy level even at the end of 1997 is only 62% while all the South East Asian Countries, barring Pakistan, Bangladesh and Nepal have attained the state of Universal Education. Children constitute one fourth of Indian humanity. Child care and integrated child development should be placed at the priority level in our national agenda.

Our children should be trained to appreciate our cultural heritage, to develop their talents and capacities by which they would become useful members of the society, to practice virtues and graces that will make them eventually stable individuals and enable them to live in peace and harmony.

In a multilingual country like India, it is regrettable that the wealth of literature available in various languages are not read by majority of the

Inaugural speech delivered at International Book Festival, Cochin.

population. Most of the outstanding books, in vernacular languages, are inaccessible because of the language barriers. Often translations do not inculcate the real spirit in the book and are sometimes faulty. The themes which mean much to the readers in the original language may not excite the readers who read translated versions. So the outside world is unaware of the wealth of literature India possesses.

School libraries and public libraries often offer a rather dismal picture. The inflow into libraries is decreasing day by day due to pre-occupation of children with other media forms, like T.V. and the Internet. It is high time libraries are updated and children are coaxed to visit them, daily so as to improve their reading habits.

ಬಿ ಬಿ ಬಿ

EDUCATION – A MIDAS TOUCH

The G R G & Sons Charities is a Public Charitable Trust created on 15th September, 1958, it is the living proof of the success of the trusteeship concept, expounded by Gandhiji.

Now popular as GRG & Sons Charities, it is an edifice of G R G's Greatness, as a man; as an eminent educationalist, as an agriculturist; as an industrialist; as a seasoned co-operator and philonthropist and as an architect of South Indian Economy.

Born on 20th January, 1919 and until his demise on 1st April, 1986, G R G was an institution by himself. He dreamt of many lofty things in life and achieved them by sheer meticulous planning. People admired him as "Midas", as whatever he touched, flourished. He had many glowing facets like a diamond. He was an able administrator. His stewardship of P S G Charities contributed to the growth of many Educational Institutions, besides the mills. I am very well aware that G R G Trust has been rendering yeomen service for the cause of education in general and women's education in particular.

The success of any institution, depends on the way the objectives of the institutions are realised and sustained. It is a matter of great mental satisfaction that the institutions started under the dynamic guard and patronage of Thiru G R G, the then founder, are still run by dynamic Smt. Chandrakanthi, his wife and her sons and daughters-in-law, with the same zeal and with the same spirit of service.

It is said. This is a rightful attribute so far as Thiru G R G was concerned because Smt. G. Chandrakanthi, is the woman, who was behind her husband in all his successful endeavours. It is said often that behind every successful man there is a lady. But the converse is true in the case of G R G.

Holding the hand of the beloved husband

Helping him in all his endeavours

We (women) shall also grow good and magnificent things.

Speech delivered at the Founder's Day at Krishnammal College, Coimbatore on 20th January, 1996.

354

Smt. G. Chandrakanthi had lent her hand in all his endeavours and she continues to fulfil his great ambitions even today and holds the family torch high.

Though women constitute almost half of the world population, their importance as individuals have never been felt in the social, economic scenario. Traditional women had been confined to the four walls of the house, children, household and family rituals and remained 'invisible'. As early as in 1982, I.L.O. had reported that 'Women are fifty per cent of the world population and they do 2/3 of the world's work hours and receive 10 per cent of the world's income and own less than 1 per cent of the world's property, all because of sheer accident of birth".

But, these are the things of past. Things are changing, changing for the better as far as women are concerned, thanks to the services of G R G's to the cause of women's education.

I am indeed overwhelmed to mention that of all the acts of charities, imparting knowledge to the poor is the most glorious. In the words of Mahakavi Subramania Bharathi:

It is better to educate a poor man

Instead of building a thousand

Choultries and temples in more numbers.

The G R G Charities is the embodiment of the above stanza.

I am deeply impressed by the involvement of G R G Centres in the cause of education of women. I find a list of one dozen institutions which perform glorious service for the cause of education in general and women's education in particular. What surprised me is the ratio of staff members to the number of students. In G R G Polytechnic for women, the ratio between teachers and students is 1:5. In G R G School of Applied Computer Technology it is 1:6. In preparatory Schools and Children School there is one teacher for every 30 students. This shows the quality of the education being imparted in these institutions. No doubt, these institutions, have to their credit high academic achievement and excellent performance in extra-curricular activities.

The net thrust given to this process of economic development of the country has an all round enthusiasm and the new slogan of "March towards the 21st Century" has a lot of popularity. In this context, the participation of women in the economic activities gains more thrust. G R G Polytechnic for women, which is the first of its kind, started by private management in the south, has an unique duty of active and meaningful participation in the social, economic and cultural development of women in the country.

The educational institutions of G R G Charities, starting from Nursery to Post Graduation and Polytechnic for Women, apart from rating high degree in performance, have the special distinction of catering to the population of backward area. These certainly will bring transformation in the life of thousands of women.

A healthy body is the foundation for a healthy mind. I am glad to know that the GRG Institutions have earned the name, not only for achievements in the curriculum but also in extra-curricular activities, especially in the field of physical education, sports and arts.

The story of G R G family is a saga of initiative and of enlightened imagination. This is the tribe that the country is in short supply of today.

I am indeed happy to know that G R G School of Management Studies, for MBA Course and G R G School of Applied Computer Technology, for MCA programme were started recently and the management has spent Rs. 1.5 crores for building and Rs. 50 lakhs, in addition to the endowment of Rs. 25 lakhs exclusively for the MBA and MCA courses. I am extremely happy to know that these courses are the first of its kind in the South, exclusively for women, *run without capitation fee or donation* whatsoever, which is the rarest of rare things now-a-days.

G R G Trust, in general, and Mrs. Chandrakanthi Govindarajulu, in particular, have totally dedicated themselves for the cause of education and that too for women's education. She is an embodiment of simplicity and great achievements. Had *Mahakavi Bharathi* been alive, he would be gratified to find *"PUDHUMAIPENN"* in Mrs. Chandrakanthi Govindarajulu. The exemplary way in which she is running all the institutions run by G R G Trust would really attract anybody towards her and the institutions. She is not carrying on her work for the sake of publicity. Her deep sense of involvement in women's education has no parallel. I am told that even today she visits all the educational institutions run by the Trust, every day in the morning and takes care of even minute details. P.A. Krishnammal Women's College, which occupies an unique place in the field of women's education is the standing example of Mrs. Chandrakanthi's indefatigable energy and foresighted vision. It is my earnest desire and appeal to Mrs. Chandrakanthi Govindarajulu to start many more educational institutions and, in particular, a private law college which would cater exclusively to women students. I pray to Almighty to give her strength, energy, good health, peace of mind and long life to carry on her useful services to the society. We find a lot of variance in the present day Indian traditions. It is my humble opinion that, on account of lack of moral value this drifting is taking place. I am gratified to note that in the institutions run by Mrs. Chandrakanthi Govindarajulu, a special scheme has been introduced to cultivate and develop moral values like love, humility, patience, intelligence, initiative, modesty etc. In short, Mrs. Chandrakanthi Govindarajulu is not only running educational institutions, but running temples of education to make women useful citizens of the Society.

I wish all success to Mrs. Chandrakanthi Govindarajulu in all the endeavours. I am reminded of the words of Mahakavi Bharathiyar who said "God has put in enormous wisdom into the minds of women". Let this woman's wisdom glow for ever to enlighten her fellow women.

Cଓ8ଠ8ଠ

LEGAL CURRICULUM IN PRIMARY EDUCATION

"Ignorantia facit excusat –
Ignorantia juris non-excusat lex"

The Common Law phrase means "a mistake of fact is excusable, but a mistake of law is never a defense in law, whether civil or criminal." Every man is presumed to know the law of his land. But it is a notorious fact that even professional lawyers and legislators are sometimes at war as to what the law is. One can never be a 'walking encyclopaedia' of all laws. But laws and legislative enactments are not copyrights of the legislature. They are meant for the people and all persons, whether citizens or foreigners, are bound by them.

In a democratic setup, where rule of law prevails, it is essential that the citizen knows at least the rudiments of the law which governs him. 'Social Justice', under the Preamble of the Constitution, casts a duty on the State to secure that the operation of the legal system provides justice on the basis of equal opportunity through legislation as well as welfare and development schemes. State is duty bound to ensure that opportunities for securing justice are not denied to any citizen by reason of economic or other disabilities. But due to the vastness of the problem, these become ineffective. Hence, unless people themselves are made conscious of the importance of the problem and make the measures towards social justice, effective, the future of democracy will be in jeopardy'.

A stark reality that stares at our face is the fact that more than 70% of the people of this country are illiterate. The noble objectives flowing from the Preamble of the Constitution and the earnest wish and hopes, expressed in the Directive Principles shall remain on paper unless the people in this country are educated. It is only education that equips citizens to participate in achieving the objectives, enshrined in the Preamble. Tamil Poet, Thiru Valluvar, whose *'Thirukkural'* will surpass all ages and transcend all religions, said of education:

> "Learning is excellence of wealth that none destroy: to man what else affords reality of joy" (*J.P. Unnikrishnan* v. *State of Andhra Pradesh*, AIR 1993 SC 2178: (1993) 1 SCC 645).

> *"That is education which leads to liberation - liberation from ignorance which shrouds the mind; liberation from superstition which paralyses effort; liberation from prejudices which blind the vision of the truth".*

> *"Victories are gained, peace is preserved, progress is achieved, civilization is built up and history is made not on the battlefields where ghastly murders are committed in the name of patriotism, not in the council chambers where insipid speeches are spun out in the name of debate, not even in factories where are manufactured novel instruments to strangle life, but in educational institutions which are the seed beds of culture, where children, whose hands quiver the destinies of the future, are trained".*

(per Mohan, J. in *J.P. Unnikrishnan* v. *State of A.P.*)

A true democracy is where education is universal, where people understand what is good for them and the nation and know how to govern themselves. In the context of a democratic form of Government, which depends for its sustenance upon the enlightenment of the populace, education is at once a social and political necessity. It is only education that equips a citizen to participate in achieving the objectives, enshrined in the Preamble. It is primarily the education which brings forth the dignity of the State to respect and protect the same. The fundamental rights, guaranteed under the Constitution cannot be appreciated and fully enjoyed unless a citizen is educated and is conscious of his individualist dignity.

The state is under a constitutional mandate to provide educational institutions at all levels for the benefit of the citizens. Apart from basic educational inputs, the need to create awareness in the people of their rights, duties and laws of the land need not be specifically mentioned since it is also a part of the fundamental duty of the State. In this land of ours, where majority of the people are striken with superstition, poverty, illiteracy and exploitation, the only panacea is creation of awareness, through education. The explosion in population, the vast changes brought about by scientific, technological and other developments and the all round enlarged field of human activity, reflected in the modern society and the consequent increase in litigation in courts also are factors that point towards the need for legal awareness at a primary stage of education. The need for a continuing and well organised legal education is absolutely essential, reckoning the new trends in the world order, to meet the ever growing challenges. Legal education and literacy will also help curb atrocities against women by making them aware of their rights and equip them to fight for their rights, wherever necessary. Legal education curriculum should not be confined to existing rights but should include both the potential and limitation of law as well as the interaction between law and prevalent social conditions.

ಬಬಬಬ

EDUCATION – A TOOL TO DRAW
OUT IGNORANCE

It is in the fitness of things that I, at this stage, should pause and think about the several problems, confronting education and its dissemination. Although there is nothing that prevents me from provoking one to reflect on certain aspects of education which I, as a dutiful citizen and a close observer of men and matters, have been concerned about. I wish to share some of my thoughts on the following subjects:

1. The pattern of education, obtained is our country from the primary level to the university level.

2. The degree of control, the Government exercises over the Universities and correspondingly the degree of autonomy, enjoyed by the academic world.

3. The problems that confront the nation in the matter of educating its citizens who range from the child to the adult, the rich to the poor, the haves to the have notes, and the restrictions imposed by our Constitution.

4. Finally, the problems that generally affect every citizen of our country, in the matter of acquisition of knowledge.

Broadly speaking, education is a must for all the citizens of the country. It must be universal. Of this, there can be no dispute. It is easy to proclaim that all the citizens of the country shall have education. The problem arises only when we think of what it implies, particularly in a country of the size of India. When Aristotle was asked how far educated men were superior to the uneducated, his quick reply was: "As much as the living are to the dead". That is why I said the problem is a very complex one. The Government at the Centre is endeavouring to solve it by fixing targets for each State to eradicate illiteracy. The Mass Literacy Campaign, such as the one that Annamalai University had conducted, is an example. Literacy has now been taken to many remote villages and to many, living below the poverty line. Again, the seats of learning cannot be expected to

Speech delivered at Fifty-seventh Founder's Day Commemoration, Annanmalai University, on 7th December, 1991.

accommodate all who seek to enter their portals. In order to solve this problem, Governments have directed the Universities to start correspondence courses in various disciplines. Distance Education seeks to disseminate knowledge, but there are constraints, inherent in the process in that it cannot serve the needs of those who desire to have knowledge of Science and Technology whose rudiments cannot be comprehended without the use of laboratories, machinery etc. Also, Correspondence Courses lack one vital thing *viz.* the personal touch between the teacher and the taught.

The system has, necessarily, to suffer due to its inherent limitations. I have touched upon these shortcomings only to show how vast and complex the problem is, and what stupendous endeavours need to be made by the Government to attain its objectives. I do not want to probe further into the question for the simple reason that it does not involve consideration of the first theme, enumerated by me.

Now to repeat; my first theme is the pattern of education obtained in our country and the degree of its utility and usefulness to meet the needs of the country. Right from the beginning of this century, and particularly during the post-independence era, educationists of eminence have uniformly held the view that the pattern of education, obtained in our country is wholly unsuited to our genius, nor does it cater to the needs of our society to ultimately bring about progress on all fronts. Commissions after commissions have laid bare the maladies in our educational system, but nobody, till date, has propounded a new scheme to serve as a pattern for development. While I say so, I should not be thought of minimising the difficulties, faced in the matter of securing a new scheme to serve the needs of our country. The reports of the commissions reveal that the state of affairs is no better. Educationists and men of stature, like Gandhiji, exercised their thoughts and sought to remedy the situation by the introduction of vocational education. Zakhir Hussain, one of our learned Presidents, was the architect of basic education, and he strongly felt that such a scheme of education would be useful and serve the needs of the country. There was criticism of the scheme of vocational education, in that it totally dissociates itself from the ongoing development of arts and culture. They said that man does not live by bread alone, and that education should not be exclusively for the purpose of serving the utilitarian needs of the society. They proclaimed that greater ideals than mere learning of the arts were necessary to develop a culture of its own, suited to its genius. Etymologically, the word education comes from the Latin World "EDUCERE", the primary meaning of which according to Fowler's Modern English Usage is "to draw out". It is also used in the sense of "to rear"; Fowler notes: " those who like to remind their audiences on school speech days that education is a drawing out and not a putting in are not quite right in their etymology". Thus, etymologically, real education is not merely drawing out from an individual, but also putting into that individual thought processes. Education, meaning drawing out, is what is generally known as the Socratic Method. Socrates, in his scheme of thought, presumed that an individual knows an answer to a query, and the answer can be obtained by a series of questions put to him. Embedded in this theory is the concept of instilling in the minds of students a spirit of enquiry. It is at inculcating such a spirit of enquiry into the minds of the students that the teacher should aim. It in well known that the greatest scientists of the world have discovered many of the theories relating to time, space, sound, electromagnetism, and biological sciences, impelled by a spirit of enquiry. This should be the aim of education, in the ultimate analysis.

The questions now to be asked are that are the teachers instilling in the minds of their students that spirit of enquiry and again, are they inspiring them to pursue knowledge by provoking their thought instincts to greater heights? This is a question, very complex in nature, asked not in India only but all over the world, Given the context of our teachers and students, it may be some what difficult to answer this question squarely. What I mean is that our students and teachers much endeavour to inherit the Socratean spirit of enquiry even from the school level. Both our teachers and students should do whatever is possible to achieve this great ideal of education.

One of the very urgent needs of our society is to educate people of the backward, most backward classes, scheduled castes, and scheduled tribes. The Constitution, with all its appropriate provisions for the upliftment of scheduled castes and scheduled tribes by grant of concessions is a meaningful inspiration for the educationists of today.

The authors of the Constitution, honestly, believed that, within a time limit of ten years, the problem of educating the underprivileged would have been solved. But the problem has assumed greater proportions than what it was to start with, creating, in its wake, disharmony among the various castes, communal frenzy, casteism, and the like. However, it is in the hands of our educationists to find a solution to the problem of educating the downtrodden.

ಖಖಖ

LINGUA FRANCA – LANGUAGE THAT UNITES

Hindi is the official language of the Union, though, English continues to be an Associate Official Language. Many a time the non-Hindi speaking people have been assured that English will continue to be an Associate Official Languages so long as the non-Hindi speaking people require it. *Dakshina Bharat Hindi Prachar Sabha*, can take legitimate pride in popularising Hindi language in non-Hindi speaking areas. It has made very significant contribution in popularising Hindi in the Southern belt.

The Constitution of India provides that the Official Language of the Union shall be Hindi. The Parliament has enacted Official Language Act, 1963 which has extended the usage of English in addition to Hindi for official purposes of the Union. The ultimate aim of the Constitution is to spread and develop Hindi Language for the purpose of enrichment of the composite culture of our nation. Article 351(1) of the Constitution of India was held to be justifiable. When pension was sanctioned to anti-Hindi agitators in the State of Tamil Nadu, the Supreme Court annulled the grant of pension by placing reliance upon Article 351. No Educational Institution can be compelled to impart Hindi education.

Hindi Language is relevant to modern conditions. The Constitution of India itself recognises the prevalence of regional languages. It is needless to emphasize that, in our country with so many languages there should be one official language. The existence of different regional languages, have not divided citizens. All of us take pride in identifying ourselves as Indian Citizens. There is unity in diversity. On the contrary, we find that in many western countries English is the only national language. Nevertheless, the people are divided and fight with each other, notwithstanding the fact that they speak in one language.

One need not be swayed by provincial consideration for learning one more language. In modern times, we find people learning German, Japanese and French, in addition to the regional language. By learning more and more languages, the horizons of knowledge are widened and we come to know of the rich tradition and culture of people, who speak other languages. Language is the only medium of expression. There would be national unity and integration by

---

Convocation address delivered in first State Level Convocation of "Dakshina Bharat Hindi Prachar Sabha", Tamil Nadu held at Trichy on 3rd November, 1996.

adoption of one official language as it plays a major role in communicating one's thoughts and ideas to others.

Mere fact that we learnt other languages as well, does not mean that our love and affinity for our regional language will, in any way, get diminished. When we want to exchange our cultural traditions with others, it becomes necessary to know other languages. The hoary tradition of Tamil Language, cannot be made known to the other parts of India or the World unless there is a common language, through which it can be made known to others. We have to build a united and progressive India and for this purpose there should be a change in our attitude and outlook. We must develop the spirit of understanding harmony.

We know the case of one English Language separating England from America, Canada from Australia. They all talk one language but they are not members of any one Nation. They are divided by one Language and they are united by one language but in India we are united by different languages.

If one is anxious to know the culture of others, one should not be averse to learning other languages. It would be possible to establish unity by coming to know of other languages. *Dakshina Bharat Hindi Prachar Sabha*, which is popularising Hindi Language, is making us to raise the quality of Tamil Nadu people.

Nobody can claim to be familiar with all the 22 languages of our country. Our country has been multi-lingual from the beginning and each one of our languages has produced great literatures. The main object of language is to bring people, races, cultures etc., nearer and dearer to each other. The process of national integration can also be quickened by learning Hindi, which is the language spoken by the majority. There could be national unity and integration through literary media and stories of different languages. We can present a picture of one India, if all of us try to know the official language, without forsaking our regional language.

"LEARNING and MASTERING ONE'S OWN MOTHER TONGUE is laudable and praiseworthy and that will not suffice".

All languages are the gifts of the Goddess of Learning. Every language has its own excellence and has contributed to make the well being of human beings. There is no harm in learning as many languages as we can. Learning other languages will strengthen and enrich the learning of one's own languages. By learning other languages, one can contribute more to the growth of one's own language. We can gain more knowledge in other spheres by learning more and more languages. Nevertheless, we should avoid the tendency to import words of other languages to our own language, either in conversation or in writing.

It is a matter of very great satisfaction to note that the Father of Our Nation who founded this institution, was Life President of *Dakshina Bharat Hindi Prachar Sabha* and continued to be so till his death. It has celebrated the Silver Jubilee under the Presidentship of Late Mahatma Gandhi. It has also celebrated the Platinum Jubilee in 1994.

ಲಲಲ

A UNIVERSITY STANDS FOR HUMANISM

The realistic evaluation of higher education, through the portals of the Universities, has to be viewed in the backdrop of the objectives that we had set for ourselves in our Constitution in terms of constituting India into a Sovereign Socialist, Secular, Democratic Republic and to secure to all its citizens Justice, Liberty, Equality and Fraternity. It has always been felt that education plays a vital role in the achievement of these objectives. The national policy on Education evolved in 1986 has rightly stated that "Education revives sensitivities and perceptions that contribute to national cohesion, a scientific temper and independence of mind and spirit, thus furthering the goals, enshrined in our Constitution". It goes on to add that "in our culturally plural society, education should foster universal and eternal values oriented towards the unity and integration of our people". Such value on education should help eliminate obscurantism, religious fanaticism, violence, superstition and fatalism. On higher education, the policy document says, "Higher education provides with an opportunity to reflect on the critical, social, economic, cultural, moral and spiritual issues facing humanity. It contributes to national development through dissemination of specialized knowledge and skills. It is, therefore, a crucial factor for survival. Being at the apex of the educational pyramid, it also plays a key role in producing teachers for the educational system".

Our present system of higher education has indeed made significant contribution to the development of our country since independence. The most spectacular element of the system has been the building up of a large and highly trained pool of scientific and technical manpower which has helped the country to modernize and strengthen its industrial base, achieve self-sufficiency in agricultural production, improve health care, enhance irrigation and power potential and take great strides in the fields of nuclear sciences, satellite communication and oil exploration. Higher education has also spread reasonably amongst women in rural areas and also amongst weaker sections of the society. It has thus provided vertical mobility for several suppressed and oppressed groups and has created a new kind of workers and intelligentsia and a new type of leadership, which did not exist before. It has also made significant contribution

10th Convocation Address at Periyar Maniammai College of Technology for Women, Vallam, Thanjavur, on 18th March, 2003.

to the strengthening of democracy and to the more efficient administration of this vast and complex society. It has promoted Indian languages and helped in the growth of several social, political and economic forces which have enriched the quality of our national life.

There can be no doubt whatsoever, that higher education plays a vital role in the progress and the development of the nation. Keeping in view the needs of other crucial sectors of the nation, it has to be seen, as to how the essential requirements of the educational sector can be met. Hard decisions will have to be taken on the questions of ill conceived proliferation of colleges and growing trend of commercialization. There is always the problem of consolidation and quality, *vis-à-vis* expansion and dilution of standards. Equally, it is mandatory that the Governments, on their part, meet the essential requirements of educational institutions that are well established and ensure regular flow of requisite funds.

I feel it imperative that we make it a living reality, by setting ourselves as examples, to make the words of the former Prime Minister – Pandit Jawaharlal Nehru come true: "A University stands for humanism, for tolerance, for reason, for the adventure of inquisition and search for truth. It stands for the onward march of the human race towards higher objectives. If the university is discharging its duties adequately, then it is well with the nation and the people".

As Thanthai Periyar said,

"Our people should learn and understand the various scientific advancements going on in the World"

"A vocational guidance or a craft should be taught along with academic education".

I appeal to you, affectionately, to look upon education as an unending pursuit. As a Judge, I am tempted to bring to your notice the story of a ninety-year old retired Judge whom President Roosevelt once visited, Roosevelt found the Judge reading Plato and asked him why he was reading Plato at that ripe old age. The nonagenarian replied placidly "To improve my mind, Mr. President". It is this spirit of enquiry, this yearning for truth that should pervade the younger generation. For achieving this great objective, universities must really be liberal in structure and character.

The Conference of Vice-Chancellors, organized by the University Grants Commission and the 66th Annual Meeting of the Association of Indian Universities, held at Thiruvananthapuram, recently, have talked openly and boldly, for the first time, about the cancer that is eating into the vitals of the university education system in this country. The real cure for the malady is to give the universities complete autonomy. With greater university autonomy, you will see our institutions, blossoming and radiating fragrance throughout the length and breadth of our country.

I am sure that the Degree holders of this great institution would contribute to the growth of material and moral wealth of our nation. It is hardwork and total dedication which bring success. I am sure that all of you would turn out to be good and useful citizens. If our nation has to march forward, it is absolutely essential to have good Scientists, Technologists, Philosophers, Jurists, Doctors, Lawyers, Judges and Teachers. I have no doubt, in my mind, that the students of this magnificent institution would achieve great things in their life and I wish them all, success in all their endeavours. It is also my duty to remind that the students should not forget their teachers. It is their duty to set apart a portion of their earning for the education of the underprivileged. I would suggest that a trust could be founded by the old students of this great College, who by contributing according to their might to a common fund would help for the education of the economically poorer section of the society.

A teacher removes and dispels the darkness of the student's mind. It is the teacher, who enlightens the students and moulds their future. Therefore, they are entitled to great respect and reverence. It is disheartening to find that, of late, there is a growing tendency among the teachers to organize themselves collectively and adopt agitational methods to coerce the persons in authority to concede to their demands. I would appeal to the respected teaching class to set a good example for the students to emulate. It is also the responsibility of the University and persons in authority to endeavour to keep the teachers above wants.

Unfortunately, the subject of education has become a great pasture of litigation in Court of law. Students and managements of unrecognized educational institutions are after the law Courts instead of spending their time usefully in the class rooms. It is also true that some unscrupulous people who do not really evince any interest in the cause of education, are making the educational institutions money spinners. What I mean is that the people start the educational institutions without obtaining necessary recognition from the Government and the University concerned. It is the duty of every one of us to prevent such exploitation by money spinners in the field of education.

Our great nation is yet to achieve literacy and complete success in the field of education. I am confident that the teachers and students of the College will play a vital role in the building up of our nation as a prosperous one.

ಜಾಜಾಜಾ

LAW AS TAUGHT AND LAW AS PRACTICED

It is a historically accepted fact that even as back as during the Vedic times, India had an intricate and comprehensive legal system. In India, a step was taken in the direction of imparting formal legal education in the country in the year 1857. Three Universities, set up in the cities of Calcutta, Madras and Bombay, formally introduced legal education as a subject for teaching. This was the beginning of legal education in India. Initially, the study of the law was not exclusive and could be coupled with the study of arts. The system of legal education, which was introduced, was simple in nature and hardly any standards or test of aptitude. The importance of the study of law as a discipline came to be recognized soon after the British re-affirmed their sovereignty after the revolt of 1857, and India began enacting statutes. Except in the field of personal laws, pertaining to varied religious denominations, the British introduced laws along the pattern of laws in the United Kingdom. These laws were in English and the proceedings of all the courts, right from the lowest to the highest, were also in English. Since more than 80% of Indian people lived in villages and were largely illiterate, they came across certain difficulties in responding to the law courts. Even people living in urban areas could not grasp the confusing work of the law and the courts with the result that, besides the system becoming expensive, a need was felt to equip a class of individuals, with the knowledge of law, who could in turn facilitate the access of the public to the courts. Thus, simply speaking, the need to have advocates was felt and along with it came the responsibility to have specific institutions to impart requisite professional skill. The gap between the people who were unacquainted with legal proceedings and the justice delivery system could be bridged by engaging a person qualified to practice law as the advocate.

With the march of time, new demands emerge, which sometimes make the existing system outdated or non functional, requiring it to be replaced by a new one. Law should also respond to the demands of the society. In India, a change in the legal climate has never been so desired as it has been for the last few years. This may be due to worldwide demands of gender justice, expedient administration of justice, respect for human rights and in coming of the era of e-Courts, proposed by the then Chief Justice of India – Hon'ble Sri B.N. Kirpal.

Delivered at the Banaras Hindu University at Varanasi on 5th November, 2004.

We are a nation of Constitutional governance ruled by law. We believe in the saying – "Be you ever so high, the law is above you". In the modern era, ours is a welfare democratic State, which has adhered to the principles of equality of opportunity and equality of justice. Perhaps that is the reason why our Constitution gives primacy to the common man. Karl Marx said that "Men make Constitutions and Constitutions do not make men". Our Constitution, therefore, rightly recognizes the man as the component in the great wheel of progress towards prosperity.

We may take it, as part of Indian jurisprudence, that effective mechanism of legal services is part of Rule of Law and every citizen has a right for services of a trained legal counsel at the stage of arrest, investigation, interrogation and trial, and in every civil litigation involving vindication of common law right.

Equality of law and equal protection of law; guaranteed under the Constitution, cannot achieve the purpose unless protection by the Courts is afforded to the poorest among the poor. The Courts of law are temples of justice where justice is to be dispensed without any fear or favour without any distinction between the rich and the poor, the advanced and down trodden, protected and unprotected. The idea of providing justice to every person in need cannot be realized fully until such time as legal assistance is made available to the more indigent section of our society.

The right of true legal aid and speedy trial are guaranteed rights under Art. 21. Art. 39A mandates that the State shall provide free legal aid, by suitable legislation or scheme or in any other way, to ensure that opportunities for securing justice are not denied to any citizen by reason of economic or other disabilities. In Law Colleges, where no legal aid clinics are functioning, students may be involved in the work of the local legal aid committee. The task of ensuring good practical training to a law student is to be greatly shared by the law teacher, as the law teacher is the model point of all education.

Legal Education of highest standard revitalizes administration of justice, which at present is passing through a unique phase of being faced with peculiar challenges. Docket explosion, falling standards in professional excellence and inadequate funds are but a few such challenges. The almost successful efforts by Foreign Legal firms to set up their Offices are sure to send signals which cannot be ignored. Already there is a rumour that international arbitrations are dominated by Foreign lawyers and in such cases, Indian Lawyers play secondary role. The situation can be avoided, and can be prevented by changing and concentrating on policy options in all legal fields. But the beginning should be made at Law Colleges, from where all of us come.

To promote the advocacy skills and love for the profession among the new entrants, the Moot Court competitions are very essential for the law students. At these competitions, the students get benefit greatly in the development of their skills of study, research & analysis of presentation. The trial conducted in the moot courts offer immense opportunities to a law student to expand his knowledge and develop the power of articulation, analysis and legal reasoning. In the practice of legal profession, 50% work is oral. Hence fluency in language and power of argumentation are very important aspects. In the words of Glancille Williams:

> *"Mooting not only gives practice in court procedure but also helps to develop the aplomb (self confidence) that every advocate should possess."*

As a part of the legal curriculaum, there should be regular conduct of moot Courts and mock trials. The observations of the Gajendra Gadkar Committee on the Reorganisation of Legal Education in the University of Delhi are very relevant in this context. According to the Committee, "the aims of Legal Education would be to make the students of law good lawyers who have absorbed and mastered the theory of law, its philosophy, its functions and its role in a democratic society."

Many may join the Bar after enrolling as members of the legal profession. There has been a wide spread talk that of late the standards of lawyers, both in respect of efficiency as well as the ideas, have deteriorated.

Advocates are as much devoted to justice and fair-play as the Judges. I say this because the Advocate, today is the Judge of tomorrow and if a lawyer is not devoted to justice and fair-play, it is impossible to make good the same by crossing over from Bar to the Bench. Judges dispense justice in Courts with the help and assistance of Advocates. If there is decline in the efficiency of the Bar, it will be reflected in the caliber of the Bench. The Bar should be fearless in order to serve the end. Confidence in the administration of justice is unshaken and is increasing day by day as can be seen from the increasing number of litigants who approach the portals of Courts, seeking Justice.

The difference between law as taught and law as practiced is familiar. If I may be excused, I would say that in law as taught, the facts are clear and the law uncertain; whereas in law as practiced, the law is clear and the facts uncertain.

Every law student is primarily concerned in acquiring legal knowledge and skill, needed for his career and, therefore, he is selfish. On the other hand, a legal practitioner is essentially selfless, for, all his endeavours are bent towards doing the best he can for his client. An advocate should fearlessly uphold the interest of his client and he must comfort himself in a manner benefiting his status as an Officer of the Court, a privileged member of the community and a gentleman. The standards of professional conduct and etiquette are set out by the Bar Council of India, in the rules framed, in the exercise of its powers, under Advocates Act.

Justice Frank Furter said, *"It is the quality of justice which will establish the Court in the confidence of people and it is the confidence of the people which is the ultimate reliance of the Court."* I am sure, that the Indian Judiciary is trying to live up to the speech made by Justice Frank Furter.

A good judgment reflects the assistance which a Judge received from the Bar on either side. A great Bar, endowed with ability, integrity and independence, is necessary to keep the stream of Justice – pure and unsullied.

I would also appeal to the authorities, concerned to publish a Law College Magazine, containing the text of lectures delivered by academicians and also important and milestone judgments, which would be of immense help to the students.

Judiciary has a very vital role to play in protecting and preserving human rights and fundamental rights. Law school and Law teachers are the backbone of law.

A model law school, on the lines of American Law Schools, *i.e.*, the National Law School at Bangalore was constituted, which became operative in 1988. A decade later, two other law schools, modelled on the National Law School, have been set up at Bhopal and Hyderabad.

When I was the Chief Justice of the Rajasthan High Court, I started a National Law School of Rajasthan with the help of the then Rajasthan Government.

With their limited intake of students and ample resources, they are catering to the needs of a section of the society. Nevertheless, it is easy to experiment and implement any new change, desired to be introduced in the legal education at these institutes because they are not a part of the University system, which with its manifold problems, does afflict the legal education as well.

Conclusion

If legal education has to be salvaged, a fundamental change is required in pedagogy. It is generally stated that your efforts are only as good as the workers who operate a system. It means that no amount of attempts to transform the curriculum to be futuristic and challenge based will go too far without pedagogic transformation. All this requires all out innovation and committed teachers, who should be willing to modernize their curriculum, experimenting with new methods of teaching, creating the spirit of innovation and inculcating analytical approach towards the problems among the students, according to the need of the time and making it socially relevant. The basic responsibility remains that of the BCI which continues to be bound by the statutes for taking meaningful steps in making legal education worth facing the new challenges. The UGC and the Universities must, however, not shirk their responsibilities just by shifting the whole burden to the BCI.

అంజురీ

LEGAL LITERACY

L egislature is the main source of law. This includes the Parliament and State Assemblies. Numerous laws are enacted every day. In addition to these, the rulings of the courts and the executive orders having the force of law are also binding on the citizens. Law is a complex subject. Legal experts often disagree in its interpretation. While discussing the law, even the judges sometimes disagree and give different versions.

Laws are published in the form of bare acts, text books and commentaries and through law journals. These are within the reach of a group of persons or professionals.

But, there are many who cannot afford to buy law books which are generally dear. Besides, there are many illiterate persons in our society. There is no proper system or facility by which common men are informed of the various laws applicable in their day-to-day affairs. Still, ignorance of law is not an excuse.

Legal aid without legal literacy is less meaningful and purposeful. So, it would be highly useful, if some important legal topics are included as compulsory subjects in school curriculum. Such legal education would enable the people to settle several of their disputes outside the courts at the grass-root level without seeking help from legal experts who are generally expensive. This extremely important aspect seems to be forgotten by those who publicize free legal aid and conduct *neeti-melas* occasionally.

There are some proposals to introduce mobile courts to move from village to village to settle disputes, right there, without the presence of lawyers.

Unless the masses are aware of their legal rights and duties, such programmes would do more harm than any service, especially, when unscrupulous elements are capable of exploiting such situations.

All these would have to be presented in a lucid and interesting manner to capture the attention of young minds. However, the modality would have to be worked out carefully in consultation with educational agencies such as National Council for Educational Research and Training (NCERT) and the National Institute of Educational Planning and Administration, eminent law teachers and social workers.

Inaugural speech delivered in the seminar on 'Legal Literacy through Schools and Adult Education Schemes', Cochin on 1st August, 1998.

Similarly, these legal topics can be included in the non-formal education of adults through adult education schemes. In this case voluntary organizations and law students can play a vital role. Law students could be assigned this job as field work. Various social, cultural and voluntary organizations, mass media, law students and teachers should be motivated to render their services for this noble job.

The 'Legal Awareness' is totally alien to the basic requirement of a living citizen. He deems it unnecessary to be aware of anything legal, for it does not seem worth his time and effort.

Law, by itself, is difficult to define. It may be a simple term seemingly perceivable. But definitions galore have been offered, but have all fallen short of an absolute and to put it in layman's terms. I would say, "Law means all rules and regulations that are laid down for the maintenance of social order and humane living".

One has to understand that legal awareness would not suffice. There should be such awareness and consciousness on the part of the citizens to assert their rights and also vindicate their rights.

I would point out as ultimate tribute to the growing legal awareness, the enactment of the Consumer Protection Act, 1986. Consumer is the king has been acknowledged in no mean terms in ushering in a forum for easy, inexpensive and speedy justice without the attendant rigours of law.

Apart from collective consciousness of society even at the micro-level of an individual, legal awareness is incumbent lest he suffers immeasurably.

Being aware is always an advantage; Being legally aware is more so.

A stark reality that stares at our face is the fact that more than 70% of the people of this country are illiterate. The noble objectives flowing from the Preamble of the Constitution and the earnest wish and hopes expressed in the Directive Principles shall remain on paper unless the people in this country are educated.

It is only education that equips citizens to participate in achieving the objectives enshrined in the preamble. Poet Valluvar, whose, 'Thirukkural' will surpass all ages and transcend all religions, said of education:

> *"Learning is excellence of wealth that none destroy: To man what else affords reality of joy."* [*J.P. Unnikrishnan* v. *State of A.P.*, AIR 1993 SC 2178: (1993) 1 SCC 645].

> *"That is education which leads to liberation − liberation from ignorance which shrouds the mind; liberation from superstition which paralyses effort; liberation from prejudices which blind the vision of the truth."*

The State is under a constitutional mandate to provide educational institutions at all levels for the benefit of the citizens. Apart from basic educational inputs, the need to create awareness in the people of their rights, duties and laws of the land, need not be specifically mentioned since it is also a part of the fundamental duty of the State. In this land of ours, where majority of people are stricken with superstition, poverty, illiteracy and exploitation, the only panacea is creation of awareness, through education. The explosion in population, the vast changes brought about by scientific, technological and other developments, and the all round enlarged field of human activity reflected in modern society and the consequent increase in litigation in courts also are factors that point towards the need for legal awareness at a primary stage of education.

Legal education and literacy will also help, curb to the atrocities against women by making them aware of their rights and equip them to fight for their rights wherever necessary. Legal education curriculum in primary schools will be a welcome measure if introduced by the State towards fulfilment of its goal. The curriculum should not be confined to existing rights but should include both the potential and limitations of law as well as the interaction between law and prevalent social conditions.

It is high time, the Government authorities both at the Centre and the States considered the question of including some important legal topics in secondary school curriculum. Indeed, it will make our democracy more meaningful and purposeful.

NATIONAL LAW UNIVERSITY – JODHPUR

About the Act

The National Law University Act, 1999 (Act No. 22 of 1999) was enacted and received the assent of the Governor on 8th October, 1999. The object of the Act is to provide for establishment and incorporation of a National Law University at Jodhpur for the purposes of advancement of cause of learning teaching and research and diffusion of knowledge in the field of law as also to cater to the needs of the society by developing professional skills of persons, intending to take up advocacy, judicial services, posts of Law officers/managers and legislative drafting as their profession and matters incidental thereto.

University Profile

The National Law University is the fifth National University for Legal Education in the country following the institutions at Bangalore, Hyderabad, Bhopal and Calcutta. A University in ideal conditions draws its human resources, at the levels of both faculty and student community, from the entire world. National law universities, only answer intention to do the same from the entire country following the traditions of Indian Institute of Technology (IIT) in technology education, Indian Institute of (IIM) in the management education and All India Institute of Medical Science (AIIMS) in medical education. However, unlike IIT, IIM, and AIIMS, legal education is patronized not by the Union Government but by the State Governments. From that point of view, National Law Universities differ in origin and experiment. Presently, these sister universities have only mutual understanding and co-operation on non-formal basis.

National Law University, Jodhpur is a bold experiment in the sense that it is truly multidisciplinary. Legal education, unlike many other streams of professional education like technology, medicine, or finance, is a multidisciplinary education. Legal professional skills can be used by any other knowledge system. As for example, in the present growing complex world, a substantive legal education is very closely linked with knowledge in technology and science. As it is, legal profession is based on the premise of certain social

---

Inaugural Speech delivered at National Law University, Jodhpur inaugurating the 'First Degree and Post-Graduate Courses, on 15th July, 2001.

values that are built up in hundreds of years of sociological practices and ethos. The enormity of literature of interaction between law and medicine shows how intricately knowledge of law and medicine can be intertwined. This university shall endeavour to make a holistic effort to develop legal professional skills in all trans-border knowledge contexts.

Keeping this objective of multidisciplinary total education in view and the growing needs of legal profession in the global context, various undergraduate, postgraduate, continuing legal education for various groups of interests, training courses and research programs would be designed in this university.

This university shall, therefore, develop several schools of excellence in various branches of knowledge and shall try to indicate the legal principles and legal skills for the attainment of a just, fair and reasonable society.

The cost of education, in spite of making best efforts, to be affordable by lower middle class, cannot but be reasonable and obviously comparable to educational expenses at centers of excellence like IITs, IIMs and National level law schools. It is, therefore, necessary that leaders of the profession and eminent citizens come forward to make such educational investment possible and aid meritorious students from poor families under the annual scheme of *Each one reach one*, which shall provide adequate scholarships for able students. Our motto should be that no student, selected on the basis of national competitive examination, be deprived of this excellent education because of financial inability.

Autonomy

The University must get full autonomy and independence in its working, like the national institutions and other four-sister law schools of Bangalore, Bhopal, Hyderabad and Calcutta to fulfil its objectives. The State Government is required to allot the land, enact the Act and provide a capital grant. The Government has already enacted the Act and published *vide* Gazette Notification No. F.2(28) Vidhi/2/99, Jaipur, dated October 8, 1999 and allotted nearly 50 acres of land at Mandore, and is providing in due course the capital grant of 5 crores within the span of 3 to 4 years. Jodhpur is producing the highest number of C.As. in the country and now it must produce corporate lawyers, keeping in view the future requirements.

This university shall not put any financial burden on the State Government in the form of maintenance grant. It would rather help the Government by the way of research studies on various issues of public importance. The various schools buildings can be built by way of endowments from business groups, individuals, corporate houses, MP and MLA funds under local area development schemes.

The Institute must be a "Stamp of Excellence" in the field of legal education. Keeping in view the changing scenario various subjects like "Law and Poverty", "Army Law", "Military Trust Law" Comparative Jurisprudence, SEBI Laws etc. must be taken up. Presently "SUPW", Socially Useful and Productive Workforce is the most importance component. The various schools can be developed by way of endowments.

Since the University will be a national institution, the provisions of the Act and its operation shall be at par with other similar legal and other national institutions. Hence the Act and the Schedule under it require immediate amendment and for that purpose, a committee has been already constituted.

Since it is a national university there shall only be reservation of 15% seats for S.C. and 7.5% for S.T. and there shall be no discrimination on basis of geographical boundaries.

This University in the vision statement of Professor Mitra in the prospectus, 2001, aims at that integration to the optimum level. He has already introduced integration of social science with law; physical and life sciences with law and management sciences with law. Having the opportunity, he perhaps would also go for technology with law and medicine with law. So the University is going to create a space of knowledge for all disciplines with the domain of legal education. Law and justice are all encompassing. Therefore, all types of knowledge are relevant for law and justice. Whether we would land up with the problem of under-utilization of human resources as was faced by IITs, is another matter? We wanted also to solve the problem in similar manner. But presently, we have all high hopes of higher plain of curriculum design and training. With the dedication it is bound to produce higher skill and better understanding and appreciation of physical phenomena in the context of a social goal. With the development of various schools in the University, students will certainly have the opportunity of designing their own career by appropriate mix of learning from several courses, run by different schools.

The University is also planning to establish a school of judicial administration, which shall also be the judicial academy of the State. This is the first Judicial Academy of the country in which the legal scholars and the judiciary shall work hand in glove.

A long cherished desire of the people of Jodhpur is soon going to be fructified. But that is not the end in itself. This is just the beginning! This University shall try to achieve the best in quick time. As such, it is necessary that we also become active partners of this institution of excellence by contributing our time, talent and treasure. The faculty, under the leadership of Professor Mitra, is completely committed to attain self-financing and not to put further burden on the State.

Moreover, the faculty also decided that there should be only a minimum number of public holidays in the University. If there is any public holiday in a week, the University shall function in full on the weekly holiday. I am yet to know whether any faculty by any other University has taken this type of decision! During 2000, the University shall have teaching for 240 days in two semesters. From the next academic year, the University shall work for more than 270 days. Each student shall also spend six to eight weeks in placement with government organization; non-government organization, law-firms; companies; legislative departments; UN bodies and leading lawyers every year. That shall make the learning down to the earth. Students shall also be conscious about their environment and social conditions.

A teacher removes and dispels the darkness in the students' mind. It is the teacher who enlightens the students and moulds their future. Therefore, they are entitled to great respect and reverence.

I am confident that the teachers and the students of this University will play a vital role in the building up of our nation as a prosperous one.

ಬಬಬ

LOOK INTO JUDGE'S EYES AND SPEAK INTO HIS EARS

Mr. T.P. Kelu Nambiar, in short 'Mr. TPKN' , joined the Madras Law College and took B.L. degree in 1953. He enrolled himself as an advocate in the Madras High Court in 1954 and started his career as a junior to a leading lawyer on the civil side, the late Mr. A. Achuthan Nambiar, who later became his father-in-law too. On the re-organisation of the States in 1956, he shifted his practice to the High Court of Kerala. Finally, he took the M.L. degree from the Madras University in 1958. He was a part-time Law Lecturer at the Government Law College, Ernakulam during 1961-66. As a 27 born pushing 77 (to borrow his expression), he has rich and varied experience of the Madras High Court and the Kerala High Court.

Mr. TPKN was a member of the Board of Studies, Faculty of Law, worked as a Chief Examiner of Law in Kerala and M.G. Universities, and as an Examiner in Law in the Andhra University. He was appointed as a Lecturer by the Bar Council of Kerala for the Law Apprentices and by the High Court of Kerala for Trainee Munsifs and Magistrates. He was the Chairman of the Staff Selection Committees of some colleges as appointed by the High Court of Kerala. He was the President of the Kerala High Court Advocates' Association in 1983-84. He held many high positions as Standing Counsel for the Kerala Public Service Commission, Legal Advisor of the Goa Public Service Commission, standing counsel to the University of Kerala and the M.G. University, standing counsel for the Cashew Development Corporation, State Bank of India, United India Insurance Company and Fishermen's Welfare Board etc. etc. He was also a senior counsel for the Reserve Bank of India and other prestigious institutions. He has also functioned as the Advisor to the Government of Kerala on the Kavery Water dispute.

While he sharply criticizes levity and vanity, he has been striving for excellence in the profession and in every sphere of life. Because of his intellectual integrity and unflinching professional rectitude, he had been the Chairman of the Disciplinary Committee of the Bar Council of Kerala for about 20 years.

Delivered at the Golden Jubilee Celebrations of Sri T.P. Kelu Nambiar's Law Practice at Cochin on 25th September, 2004.

For over 40 years, he has been writing articles and comments in Kerala Law Times, Kerala Law Journal, The Hindu, The Indian Express etc. The earliest article that I could see is *"Limitation on Limitation"*. He has written very many articles and reviews, attended seminars and councils, featured in interviews by TV and other media. Some articles appear in *"Nambiar Miscellancy"* (1996). I pray that further books appear from and about him.

Mr. TPKN firmly believes in the importance of the English language and literature as a powerful tool in the armoury of every lawyer and as an essential vehicle of expression in the profession and outside. Mr. TPKN's flair for the English language, his knowledge of English literature, his firm style and the love for alliteration are clear from his writings.

I may at once advert to the Discipline of Law by Lord Denning (1979), where he says:

> *"To succeed in the profession of law, you must seek to cultivate command of language. Words are the lawyer's tools of trade. When you are called upon to address a Judge, it is your words which count most. It is by them that you will hope to persuade the Judge of the rightness of your cause."*

In his article *"The Art of Advocacy"* [2004 (1) KLT JI 9], he said,

> *"Please remember, English is the tongue for your survival; and custodian of your future. Therefore, be thorough with the Macaulay-imported diction".*

All along he has been a champion of the Bar; for the excellence, independence and integrity of the profession; and for a full opportunity for a lawyer to make relevant oral submissions in full, though briefly and logically. When one lacks in depth one tries to make up in length, is a universal truth applicable to lawyers too.

I have known him as a lawyer of brevity. In view of the docket explosion, the felt necessity of the times is limitation of oral arguments which will quicken the pace of justice and solve the problem of docket explosion. Therefore, brevity is a must. Delay in judicial process is a threat to the delivery of justice to the masses.

Now-a-days, the complaint of lawyers is not that oral arguments are lengthy, but they do not get time for making full and effective submissions. In *"Advocacy, Crippled and Stifled* [2003 (1) KLT JI 34], quoting Crompton J in *R. v. O`Connel* he said:

> *"This Court in which we sit is a temple of justice; and the Advocate at the Bar as well as the Judge upon the Bench, are equally ministers in that temple. The object of all equally should be the attainment of justice."*

He felt that now-a-days many of the Judges do not consider the Bar as an essential adjunct of the Judiciary. He quoted M.C. Chagla from *"Roses in December"*:

> *"I believe that the administration of justice is a cooperative effort between the Judge and the lawyer. It should not become a one-sided affair. There are judges who think that lawyers are superfluous...But grave injustice can be caused if such an approach were followed."*

He lamented,

> "I see a tendency in recent times in certain Judges to do exactly what Chagla despised. They even go to the extent of framing questions at home, and asking lawyers to answer in Court even at the start of the case, forgetting that advocacy is not a quiz programme and a Judge should not act as a quizzical quizzer........"

He always took pride of being a lawyer. In *"The Importance of Being a Lawyer"* [1995 (2) KLT JI 43], he said,

> "The legal profession is admirable. Ours is said to be a learned profession. We learn the law from law books but we cannot learn men from books or briefs. It is said that silence is learnt from the talkative, toleration from the intolerant; kindness from the unkind. And learning is most requisite which unlearns evil....Therefore, a lawyer of today should learn a lot, apart from law books. He should be a man of multiple excellencies".

He ended up with an exhortation to young lawyers:

> "Let us never forget our high vocations as Ministers of justice and interpreters of the law. The lawyer holds a prominent place. Every lawyer should try to be a Hortensius, who of all the advocates of antiquity, said Cicero, had given himself up most exclusively to that profession. Try to become an able lawyer. But do not carry negative baggage. Adjust your performance before the different Courts, as you do with grass court, hard court, or clay court."

He has always been a good reader of not only the books but of Judges too. His writings have taught the younger lawyers the essence of advocacy:

> "Read the facts in the trial Court; read the law in the appellate Court; read the Judge in the High Court and the Supreme Court."

Mr. TPKN felt that there is no sufficient comity and co-operation between the Bench and the Bar. In *Bar, Bench and the Gap* [2002 (1) KLT JI 39], he lamented about the fall in the standards of the profession and consequentially of the Judiciary itself. He said:

"The attitude of the present day lawyer is potentially interesting. He seems to say:

> "I do not get a lot of respect but I make of a lot of money. Lawyers seem to be innocent of advocacy. The profession has lost its lodestone. There is a massive conspiracy to harm the profession. There seems to be paddock parade in the legal profession, forgetting the great principle that advocacy has not element of road show; and advocacy should never be showcased. Publicity is no the oxygen for the legal profession; nor is the lawyer's bank account its heartbeat......The legal profession is the most faithful offspring of the western system of justice delivery. We have yet to see an Indian `Justenian' among our statesmen/politicians".

Many lawyers in the High Court of Kerala know him only as a senior lawyer. The younger generation probably does not know that he was a hard worker in his early days. I am told that he differed from the rest. He had shown tremendous interest in his professional work. He had an uncompromising approach at the Bar and was acclaimed as a fighter in Court, and a formidable adversary. In my experience, he has never spoken a word to placate a Judge or bent his back to get favour from any Court. He was a champion of his client's cause, a champion of the profession and a champion of himself. The only blot that any one could point out to me is his egoism. I do not think that it is a blot at all. I recall the Chinese proverb:

He who knows not he knows not, is a fool; shun him.
He who knows he knows not, is a student; teach him.
He who knows not he knows, is asleep; wake him.
He who knows he knows, is a prophet; follow him.

I would urge the younger generation to follow him. Mr. TPKN's motto is:

"Look not to the right, look not to the left, look straight into the eyes of the Judge, and pour your client's cause into his ears."

The sphere of law is highly uncertain and requires an alert intellect and sharp equipment to keep oneself up and up-to-date. "Law is law – and, as in such, and so forth, and hereby, and aforesaid, provided always, nevertheless, notwithstanding. Law is like a blistering plaster – it is a great irritator in cases of great extremity."(Book of Miscellany, 1856).

It is a matter of great pride and honour that he has become Legend in his own lifetime. He is a man who believes in maintaining the dignity of the legal profession and follows the tradition, handed down by the Legal giants of the yesteryears.

To say that Mr. TPKN was a lawyer par Excellence would be a gross understatement. He represents a generation which had lot of human values and traditions. He is humble. He is a *horacious* reader of books. He is absolutely independent and that kept him in good stead. It has rather a unique privilege to become a Legend in one's own lifetime and receive recognition for the same. His career in the legal profession is very eventful. In short, he has been additing lustre to the Kerala Bar. Though he is powerful and forceful in his Advocacy, he always maintains respect to the Bench. I feel that the Kerala Bar should feel proud of him.

Mr. TPKN is one of the top lawyers of the great Nation. He never believes in repeating arguments before Courts. He belongs to a School which believed in maintaining respect to the Bench and never offend the opponent or the Judge.

He is one of the unusual Senior Members of the Bar whose concern for the Junior Members is something unique. Whenever a Junior engages him, he would make it a point to ascertain whether he has been paid by the client or not. If the answer of the Junior is in the negative, he would immediately pay the Junior from the fees received by him.

Whatever office he occupies, he maintains the dignity and decorum of that office. He has got a distinctive style of his own. He is involved with a number of service organisations. He strongly believes that the noble legal profession should not be converted into a trade or business.

He has appeared in a number of important cases not only before me in Kerala High Court but other High Courts also. He is hale, healthy, active and vigorous. He has made a name for himself in a manner that no other lawyer of his times did.

I have derived lot of pleasure in hearing him in many cases. It is a pleasure to listen to his arguments.

Every thing should have a beginning, middle and an end. Let us wind up. His "tailpieces" are famous. Let me add my tailpiece from Shakespeare:

"The purest treasure mortal times afford
Is spotless reputation; that away,
Men are but gilded loam or painted clay."

He has reputation in abundant measure. God bless him.

I think that Mr. TPKN is a relentless fighter who will keep standing up for the cause of law in the times to come. He is a "Living Legend of Law" and is a glorifying example for others to follow.

ಬಬಬ

STAMP OF EXCELLENCE – NATIONAL LAW UNIVERSITY

Jodhpur has earned its reputation for producing and providing good number of brilliant Chartered Accountants and has now taken a leading role in the field of legal education to meet the future requirements of Corporate lawyers to provide legal support to the business and social life by establishing a National Law University, the first University of its own kind. Having heard Professor N.L. Mitra in the meeting of the General Council, Executive Council and Academic Council held on 12th May, 2001, vision statement of University, I am of the view that it is the first University of second vision of law. This could be possible only because of the dynamism and vision of Shri Ashok Gehlot, the then Chief Minister of Rajasthan. It appears to be a part of his dream vision to make the State of Rajasthan the most vibrant and prosperous State in the country.

The National Law University is the fifth National University for legal education in the country. A University, in ideal conditions, draws its human resources at the levels of both faculty and student community, from the entire world. National Law Universities only answer intention to do the same from the entire country following the traditions of IIT, IIM, and AIIMS. However, unlike IIT, IIM and AIIMS, legal education is patronized not by the Union Government but by the State Governments. From that point of view, National Law Universities differ in origin and experiment. Presently these sister Universities have only mutual understanding and co-operation on non-formal basis.

National Law University, Jodhpur is a bold experiment in the sense that it is truly multidisciplinary. This University shall endeavour to make a holistic effort to develop legal professional skills in all trans-border knowledge contexts. Keeping this objective of multidisciplinary total education in view and the growing needs of legal profession in the global context, various under-graduate, post-graduate, continuing legal education for various groups of interests training courses and research programmes would be designed in this University.

The cost of education, inspite of making best efforts, to be affordable by lower middle class, cannot but be reasonable and obviously comparable to

---

On occasion of The Foundation Laying Ceremony for National Law University, Mandore on 26th August, 2001.

educational expenses at centers of excellence like IITs, IIMs and national level Law Schools. It is, therefore, necessary that leaders of the profession and eminent citizens may come forward to make such educational investment possible and aid meritorious students from poor families under the annual scheme of "Each One Reach One" which shall provide adequate scholarships for able students. Our motto should be that no student, selected on the basis of national competitive examination be deprived of this excellent education because of financial inability. The various schools' buildings can be built by way of endowments from business groups, individuals, corporate houses, MP and MLA funds under local area development schemes.

The Institution must be a "Stamp of Excellence" in the field of legal education. Keeping in view the changing scenario, various subjects like "Law & Poverty", "Army Law", "Military Trust Law", Comparative Jurisprudence, SEBI Laws, etc. must be taken up. Presently, "SUPW"—Socially Useful and Productive Workforce is the most important component. The various schools can be developed by way of endowments.

The University is also planning to establish a School of Judicial Administration which shall also be the Judicial Academy of the State. This is the first Judicial Academy of the country in which the legal scholars and the Judiciary shall work hand in hand.

The globalisation of the world economy and the opening up of our own economy to invest from outside has thrown up challenges and many more opportunities to our legal community. The international community, at present has seen common surge towards linking each other economically and, as such, competition across the frontiers of the Nations, States among their economic enterprises have increased so much that international concepts such as sovereignty, independence and equality of Nations have been obliterated and virtually reduced to a fiction. As a matter of fact and law, the Nations are not only living in global village but are economically so inter-linked that no Nation can take independent decisions as a result of which the National Governments find it difficult to regulate their economies independently. Thus, the National Law University will prepare the tomorrow's lawyer who will be capable of countering the challenges of new international corporate life and law.

Today, the lawyers are not necessarily to be in the court-rooms. There is a growing concept of non-litigation lawyering. There is a growing need of Corporate Lawyers. The people are looking for holistic perspective under one roof. The approach of the clients has changed considerably. They don't want to be unnecessarily aggressive. They realize the dangers of litigation. They prefer certainty even if it comes at a cost. The profile of the clients has also undergone a change with more M.N.Cs seeking legal advice. These M.N.Cs are used to serve international standard of service and quality of advice and expect it in India too. To do such sort of things the client needs a lawyer who knows Science, Technology, Economics and can analyse and understand the market.

ಬಬಬ

FINDING NEW PATHS

The Council of Scientific and Industrial Research – CSIR, has spread like a banyan tree through the length and breadth of India in various disciplines of science and technology.

Today, CSIR is leading the country in the generation of intellectual property, and through its wonderful endeavours, in taking up the task of creating intellectual property, that knowledge is now recognised in the country and worldwide. Looking back at the history of CSIR, which is remarkable, it may not be an exaggeration to mention that the history of CSIR is the history of science in India. The talents of the scientists to research are closely interwoven with the need of the users in production through appropriate institutional mechanisms, so that science and technology work in tandem, rather than in parallel, for achieving the object of industrialisation.

The Council of Scientific and Industrial Research with its complement of 10,000 (ten thousand) highly qualified scientific and technical personnel is one of the largest research and development organisations in the world in the field of scientific and industrial research. Over the years, CSIR has contributed to many vital scientific, industrial, strategic and human resource development endeavours. In recent times, it has responded to the changing national and international economic trade and IPR regimes through appropriate organisational and management adjustments. This has now emboldened CSIR to set for itself higher goals coupled with the optimistic realisation of the increased international competition and its own desire to become substantially self-reliant. The belief that the prevailing environment in the country and within the CSIR is conducive, more than ever before, to engineer the transformation of CSIR, has influenced the enunciation of an ambitious vision of what CSIR could be in the coming years.

CECRI is one of the paramount branches of CSIR. as a student, as a lawyer and Government pleader and as a Judge I have been proud enough to witness the growth and development of this great Institution - CECRI, Karaikudi. Since my childhood, I have seen the growth of CECRI by leaps and bounds with many achievements to its credit and now it stands at a higher place in the field of

---

Speech delivered on occasion of Diamond Jubilee Celebrations of 'CSIR Foundation Day', orgnised by CECRI, Karaikudi on 26th September, 2002.

research and development in the country. I am told that 163 full-fledged scientific staff and 150 young research associates, project associates, project assistants are functioning for the growth of the CECRI in the field of research and development.

We can seek to invoke the wonders of science instead of its terrors. Through optimum utilisation of the science and technology, the country is already reaping the benefits of better and cheaper telecom and Internet services. But, we have seen the terrors of science in the devastation created by terrorists and the indiscriminate use of modern weapons by extremists. The problem has been created by the mind of man and from the same, a solution must emerge. Fruits of science and industry should be used in bailing out our teaming millions from poverty and ignorance. Election of Dr. APJ Abdul Kalam, President of India heralds the changing winds that strike us from the new horizons of intellectual world and throws open the doors of future India. His journey from Rameswaram, a small town in the State of Tamilnadu, to the Presidentship of this Country, speaks out, in unmistakable terms, that devotion and dedication towards motherland will never go unrewarded. It further proves that there are no inherent hurdles for a man to achieve the heights of fame, and it is the love for the country and its people that alone counts. Dr. Kalam's election as the President of India is the rarest felicitation made to the community of Scientists and every Scientist in the country can feel proud of his election.

The scientists at CECRI, working in this area are involved in developing luminescent materials, novel organic conducting polymers and oxide materials, efficient photovoltaic materials for both solid and liquid junction solar cells and supersonic conductors.

The Central Electrochemical Research Institute is one of the chains of forty national laboratories under the aegis of the Council of Scientific and Industrial Research (CSIR), New Delhi. During the last fifty years, CECRI has been recognised as the premier institution for R&D in the field of Electrochemical Science and Technology, not only in India but also in the South East Asia, with well-equipped personnel comprising scientists, engineers, technologists, skilled workers, administrative and other staff, with a combined laboratory space of four lakhs sq.ft. in a campus of 300 acres.

The programs are directed towards development of new processes of products or novel use of electrochemistry. The CECRI owns an excellent library, computer center, workshop, centralised characterisation and measurement laboratory.

CECRI also conducts short term refresher courses for the benefit of industry and educational institutions, brings out journals and runs a B.Tech program in Chemical and Electrochemical engineering of Madurai Kamaraj University. The institute is alive to the societal obligations and actively participates in the Rural Entrepreneurship Development (RED), and Swadeshi Science Movement (SSM), in collaboration with other agencies.

We have to formulate a series of research and development programmes which are related to specific socio-economic goals and which are integrated financially and institutionally into an overall strategy. We regard science as a powerful instrument of social change. Modernisation is not merely production through improved technology. It means changing the lives of individuals and of the nation. Science is as greatly concerned with distribution as with production. It implies the best use of material and human resources of equipment and social organisation, like CECRI have, therefore, a great responsibility to ensure a high pace of technological change and to undertake a succession of improvements and the substitution of scarce raw material or intermediates. Our laboratories should tackle the problems which confront industry and agriculture, etc. Industry must either do its own research and development or if it lacks the means and the competence, must transmit its problems to research laboratories.

In the long run, it is the ability of our scientists and technologists to develop the country's capability to absorb and improve technology which is relevant to economic growth. Industry must be encouraged to refer problems to our laboratories. These laboratories will then be better able to master new techniques and to innovate. The younger generation of scientists will work more readily on new techniques and new problems, and will have more basic orientation if they are encouraged to take up the problems of research which arise from the felt needs of industry. Such new orientation will enable our young scientists to gain experience much faster than the traditional method which confines the younger scientists to problems which are formulated by their superiors.

Life is not lived in compartments. Research and development are not the whole of science. Science cannot and must not be imprisoned in the laboratory, the modern industrial plants or educational institutions. It must be integrated in our thinking and be a part of our daily lives.

The future of our society & its development is vitally linked with the activities of our scientists and technologists. This is an occasion when scientists of all ages and different disciplines from universities, research institutions, industry and production sectors of the economy, meet and discuss one another's work. The scientific community is able to review its achievements and failures, and to search for new opportunities. To the young, it gives the great experience of making acquaintance with, and seeking inspiration from, distinguished scientists.

We, in India, must attempt to readopt technology and place man and his spirit at the centre of science. It is upto us to see that in the pursuit of the material necessities of life, we do not lose our human values or our distinctiveness as individuals and as a nation. Scientists should not live in their own world. They are an integral part of general society. It is for them to determine what is socially relevant and vital. A scientist's best reward is the excitement of working at the very frontiers of existing knowledge, the satisfaction of his intellectual curiosity and the joy of creative activity. We must never let problems overwhelm us. Rather, we should overwhelm the problems. India has always overcome the stiffest of challenges hurled at her. We have, especially, risen to the occasion whenever we have faced any challenge from outside. To find this new path is perhaps the greatest challenge to Indian scientists and technologists.

ಬಾ ಬಾ ಬಾ

INDELIBLE IMPRESSIONS ON
THE SANDS OF TIME

Mere literacy is not education; knowledge is not education; but, the real education is, that which makes a man grow in wisdom so as to acquire and develop the capacity to look upon the other objects, created by Almighty, with compassion. The education should make us look upon the other human beings as one who are kith and kin; education should help a person to develop purity of mind, purity of body and sanctity of spirit. The object of educational institutions should be to produce many good and civilized humans. If there is no civilization, the purpose of education would be rendered meaningless. The real education should train and develop the youth of this nation to be afraid of their own conscience instead of being afraid of people. Learning, which is part of education, cannot be done unless student lives a disciplined and strenuous life. It is the teacher who not only moulds the character of the student but also teaches him. The nation is built by good and dedicated teachers. A good educational institution like St. Joseph's College, undoubtedly, produces many graduates and post-graduates who hold very distinguished and important positions not only in this country but also in foreign countries. This institution can feel proud of having produced graduates, who occupy vital and strategic positions in life, and also living beyond petty provincial considerations. It is the unanimous view of every one that the Jesuit Fathers have carved out a special place in the field of education and in treating the poor and down-trodden people for different kinds of physical and mental ailments.

The Jesuit Fathers not only make the students civilized but also take special interest in each and every student and their family background. They make the students think that they are part and parcel of the family and thereby, create an emotional bond of love between the teacher and the taught. I appeal to the teachers of the present day to create and develop the emotional bond besides giving their part of knowledge. It is the duty of the students to set an example for the successors.

Delivered at the 160th College Day Celebrations of "ST. Joseph's College" at Tiruchirapalli on 5th March, 2004.

Education is very important and without education, there cannot be progress and growth. The real meaning of education is 'learning'. Thus learning is necessary for every one of us, without any distinction of caste or creed, in order to render useful service to the nation. The Founders of our Constitution have also laid great stress on education by providing, in Article 45, that the State should endeavour to provide within a period of ten years from the commencement of the Constitution, free and compulsory education for all children until they complete the age of 14 years. Though the idea of directive principles has been borrowed from the Irish Constitution, yet, they have very great relevance to our country. Dr. Ambedkar had said that failure to implement the directive principles would result in the party in power standing to lose. It cannot be gainsaid that the directive principles contained in Article 45 of the Constitution of India have not been fully implemented although many decades have elapsed since Independence.

I appeal to all, affectionately, to look upon education as an unending pursuit. As a Judge, I am tempted to bring to your notice the story of a ninety year old retired Judge whom President Roosevelt once visited. Roosevelt found the Judge reading Plato and asked him why he was reading Plato at that ripe old age. The nonagenarian replied placidly 'To improve my mind, Mr. President'. This is what our great tamil fact thiruvalluvar said, "tamil" it is this spirit of enquiry, this yearning for truth that should pervade the younger generation. For achieving this great objective, Colleges must really be liberal in structure and character.

The Conference of Vice-Chancellors organized by the University Grants Commission and the 66th Annual Meeting of the Association of Indian Universities held at Thiruvanathapuram, during 1992, talked openly and boldly, for the first time, about the cancer that is eating into the vitals of the University education system in this country. The real cure for the malady is to give the Universities complete autonomy. Look at the academic bodies of any University in the West, you will find only academics in these bodies, nobody else. With greater University autonomy, you will see our institutions blossoming and radiating fragrance throughout the length and breadth of our country.

It is also my duty to remind that the students should not forget their teachers. It is their duty to set apart a portion of their earning for the education of the underprivileged. I would suggest that a trust be founded by the old students of this great institution, who by contributing according to their might to a common fund, would help for the education of economically poorer sections of the society.

A teacher removes and dispels the darkness in the students' mind. It is the teacher who enlightens the students and moulds their future. Therefore, they are entitled to great respect and reverence. It is disheartening to note that, of late, there is a growing tendency among the teachers to organize themselves collectively and adopt agitational methods to coerce the persons in authority to concede to their demands. I would appeal to the respected teaching staff to set a good example for the students to emulate. It is also the responsibility of the Institution and persons in authority to endeavour to fulfil the teachers wants.

శుభశుభశు

PART XIV
MEN AND MATTERS

MAC – EPITOME OF ENTERPRENEURSHIP

The life of a man, it is said, can become a heroic poem, if only he becomes all that he was created capable of being. Dr. M.A. Chidambaram's multi-faceted career exemplifies the essence of this opinion. Endowed as he is with a 'do and dare' spirit, his mind has a fierce grasp of all higher thoughts and better things, of fancy and reflection, of art and culture together in a remarkable manner. It works with extraordinary freedom and candour. Dr. MAC's keen understanding of men and matters, his catholic outlook, his originality, his sense of discernment and, above all, his largeness of heart veritably mark him out as an illustrious son of a worthy father, Dr. Rajah Sir Annamalai Chettiar. Dr. MAC has nobly lived ever since his birth, inheriting, as he did, the fabulous name and fame of the Chettinad family, known for its many glorious benefactions and acts of noble public service. As a magnificent lover of sports and as a sportsman in his own right, Dr. MAC participated in various sports activities. Like his father, MAC too enlarged the scale of his operations and enhanced his usefulness in such a way as to win the grateful appreciation of the business community.

As a true scion of the Chettinad family known for its acute business instinct, Dr. MAC has taken onerous responsibilities as Chairman and Managing Director of several industrial establishments, organizations and enterprises. His way of handling financial and production problems testifies to his masterly comprehension of the complexities and intricacies of business and industry. He gave all his time and energy to SPIC, which has markedly grown in size and production capacity, thanks to his careful planning spurred by his sense of go-aheadeness. Dr. MAC looks upon hurdles as challenges to be surmounted with determination and courage. He attaches great value to open-mindedness. Dr. MAC is certainly a gifted "Organization Man" with a pioneering passion for innovativeness.

The game that most attracted him was Cricket. A giant among Cricket administrators and an industrial magnate, he had few parallels in both roles. In fact, the golden period of Indian Cricket was from 1960 to 1963 when Dr. MAC, who passed away on January 19, 2000 at the age of 81, was the Board President. His association with Cricket started in the early '40s, promoting Club Cricket with a fervour which surprised many. It was his passion and hunger for the game which culminated in his becoming the President of Madras Cricket Association.

Message delivered at the release of 'Commomerative Volume of Dr. M.A. Chidambaram.

His shrewd business mind was always open to new ideals. Dr. MAC's passion for horse racing is unequal.

Dr. MAC's time and resources were not confined to business and sports only. He had the glowing examples before him of the epoch-making contributions made to the promotion of education, Tamil Isai, Art and Culture by his highly eminent father whose qualities of head and heart, he has undoubtedly inherited. Dr. MAC's interest in the Tamil Isai Sangham and his participatory managerial role in the affairs of the Sangham at Madras is a known factor.

Dr. MAC had extensively travelled throughout the World. He had a cosmopolitan outlook and was conversant with the nuances of the varied cultures of the World. With his mental horizons widened, and his knowledge of the World around him deepened, he was gentle and soft-spoken, without the touch of theatrical.

"MAC", as he was popularly known, was connected with various industries like sugar, Steel, Automobile, Shipping, Fertilizer and others. He promoted the establishment of a fertilizer plant, popularly called "SPIC". Till the very end, he remained the Chairman of SPIC, which was the flagship of his family group of industries. As one who took deep interest in the welfare of the under-privileged, he established a home for destitute children which also provides them education and vocational training. He was the Managing Trustee of Voluntary Health Services and was largely responsible for its development and growth. He founded several institutions with humanitarian objectives. He established the MAC Public Charitable Trust to support deserving institutions in the field of education, medical and cultural activities. He had been the President of the Southern India Chamber of Commerce and Industry from 1951 to 1957 and was the builder of this premier chamber in the South. He was also the Honorary Consul General for the Philippines in Chennai. For nearly 50 years, he served as the Honorary Secretary of Tamil Isai Sangham and contributed, in no small measure, for its growth and development.

Noble men are made nobler by their thoughts and actions and such noble men are the sons of God. To that fraternity belongs the most respected Dr. M.A. Chidambaram. His illustrious son Dr. A.C. Muthiah, whose forte is benevolence and charity, has laid firmer foundations to achieve the motto of his father with courage and faith. My illustrious and revered Brother Dr. A.C. Muthiah, with his vast experience of men and matters, is now ordained to be the Chairman of the Institutions which were founded by Dr. M.A. Chidambaram. Dr. A.C. Muthiah, as a true son of a wise father, has always believed that if every man mends one, all around are mended. I have had the good fortune of having close acquaintance with Dr. M.A. Chidambaram and his son Dr. A.C. Muthiah. He always gave me the impression that his erudition and myriad activity have been fully injected into the system of working of the institutions, which is reflected by good people in the past and they are now being continued by Dr. A.C. Muthiah and it will continue to be a noble heritage in that family, for the chip of the old block Mr. Ashwin Muthiah has already shown and proved his mettle in progressing the ideals and ideologies with which the SPIC and other institutions are saturated. Let Providence shower its choicest blessings on everyone concerned with the future progress.

ಬಂಬಂಬ

IN MEMORY OF MUKUT BIHARI

I deem it my privilege to have secured an opportunity to pay my heartfelt tribute to Late Shri Mukut Bihari Lal Bhargava. Late Shri Mukut Bihari Lal Bhargava who was born on 3rd January, 1903 was a freedom fighter. While in Jail in connection with the Quit India Movement, 1942, he lost his eyesight completely. Despite blindness, he was elected as a Member of the Constituent Assembly and a Member of Parliament thrice, consecutively from 1952 to 1967. He was elected as Chairman of the Rajasthan Bar Council. He was designated as a Senior Advocate by the High Court of Rajasthan and by the Hon'ble Supreme Court. He was representative of different Bar Associations for number of years. He was felicitated by the Rajasthan Advocates' Association, at Jodhpur in 1976 on completion of 50 years practice as an Advocate. He has participated in many conferences, held abroad. The former Chief Justice of India, Hon'ble Shri A.N. Ray, named him as "moving Encyclopedia of law". Shri S.N. Bhargava, a worthy son of a worthy father, has retired as Chief Justice of Gauhati High Court and has also been was the Chairman of Human Rights Commission, Gauhati. Late Shri Mukut Bihari Lal Bhargava breathed his last on 18th December, 1980.

Nothing in my legal career has been a matter of great honour than the present one to preside over the function, organised by the Bar Council of Rajasthan in honour of Late Mukut Bihari Lal Bhargava who was, a phenomenally great forensic personage, colossus in the legal profession and a contemporary 'Bishmacharya' for the Lawyer community.

It is only in the fitness of things that such an impressive homage is paid by the Bar Council of Rajasthan. It is to the Rajasthan Bar that he contributed his services the Rajasthan most. It is from this Bar that he rendered his valuable services to the judicial function most.

The advice which he used to give to his juniors was "you may lose a dozen cases but never lose a Court". I am also told about his meticulous preparation of cases.

I have had no occasion to see the great soul, but I have learnt from others that late Shri M.B.L. Bhargava was exceptionally outstanding as a Lawyer and

---

Presidential Address at function organised by Bar Council of Rajasthan in memory of Late Mukut Bihari Lal Bhargava, Rajasthan on 14th October, 2000.

remarkably efficient as a counsel. His court craft was par excellence. He possessed penetrating intellect and infallible memory continuously. He used to marshal his arguments with relentless logic and powerful driving force. Mr. Bhargava was a true representative of the Bar. He has left a message to the younger generation to work hard to achieve success and not to rest till the goal is achieved. He created confidence among the masses and members of the Bar.

During his life time, he fought many battles in Court. His long life itself was a relentless effort; he fought it admirably. It is my duty to exhort all the members of the legal community to unfailingly continue the legal style and methods of late Shri Mukut Bihari Lal Bhargava of arguing cases in Courts and maintaining the traditions, which he safeguarded.

ಬಿಬಿಬಿ

HOMAGE TO SHRI R.C. GHIYA

This occasion gives me an opportunity to pay homage to the memory of Shri R.G. Ghiya, who was not only an expert Lawyer in tax matters, but who combined in himself qualities of an academician, a social worker and a philanthropist. I did not have occasion to meet Shri Ghiya personally, but those who knew him well talk of him with great affection and reverence and they remember him as a broad minded and hard working lawyer who lived a short life of just 47 years and left behind him a legacy of his noble deeds and thoughts. He was a dependable friend who had sympathy for the downtrodden and inner urge to do something for the have-nots.

Late Shri R.C. Ghiya's short, but purposeful life was an arduous journey from humble beginnings to high attainments. Born in 1941, in a respectable family of lawyers at Beawar, Shri Ghiya had carved out a prestigious position for himself. He was a thinker of great depth and frequently gave his observations on the economic and industrial trends, budget and taxation through his articles, research papers, symposia and seminars. As a Rotarian, Shri Ghiya was instrumental in promoting various service activities through the Rotary Club, Jaipur East. His area of service activities were not confined only to the corridors of Rotary but to other institutions as well. He was conferred many distinctions and honours during his hardly two decades of dedicated service in his own field. To name the few, he was the President of the Rajasthan Tax Consultant Association, Jaipur from 1986 to 1988 and Chairman of All India Taxation Seminar, organised by the Tax Consultants Association in the year 1986. He was a member of the Advisory Board "Tax World" monthly journal of Rajasthan Tax Consultants Association, Jaipur. Mr. Ghiya actively participated in many symposia and seminars and contributed several papers and articles in Sales Tax literature. He widely travelled throughout the world, several times.

On his demise, homage was paid to him by large number of his friends, admirers and dear ones who were shocked by his untimely death. Several Tax Bar Associations paid tribute to the departed soul. He had a magnetic personality and humanitarian out-look. He was a pride of Rajasthan in Taxation practice and

Presidential Address at the function organised in 'Memory of Late Shri R.C. Ghiya', Jaipur on 22nd September, 2001.

his untimely loss has caused a vacuum in the Rajasthan Tax Consultant's Association.

To narrate the forensic skill and texurity, which late Shri Ghiya displayed would be to replay a recorded cassette. It is my duty to exhort the successors of late Shri R.C. Ghiya's legacy to unfailingly continue the rhythm of his legal style on the methods which he pursued in presenting the cases in the courts and the traditions which he zealously safeguarded.

Shri R.C. Ghiya was exceptionally outstanding as a Tax Lawyer and remarkably efficient as a counsel.

I wish the young members of the legal fraternity to emulate the time example of Shri R.C. Ghiya.

ಬಬಬ

GRAND CHEVALIER JUSTICE JOSEPH VITHAYATHIL

Justice Vithayathil is a celebrity to be remembered and reverenced. His long chequered career and saga of success are the result of sheer dint of hardwork and intrinsic merit. As a Judge of the Travancore - Cochin High Court, he imbibed the faculties and qualities of a Judge set forth by Justice Felix Frankfurter thus:

> "The most relevant things about an appointee are his breadth of vision, his imagination, his capacity for disinterested judgment, his power to discover and to suppress his prejudice."

Justice Vithayathil substantially satisfied these requirements. He weighed things in the balance with supreme impartiality undaunted by any other combination except that of justice. His secular credentials reverberates the message of Christianity that is – universal brotherhood. He strived hard to bring unity among Christians, Muslims, Ezhavas and Nairs. But he never forgot his roots. His contribution towards the preservation of minority rights will be ever remembered by the present and the future. He was a true disciple of Lord Jesus Christ. The assumption of the office as a Judge of the High Court was one religious vow to him. I am quoting his own words said on 25th May, 1951 when he took oath as Judge of the High Court of Travancore - Cochin.

> "I do fully realize the significance of oath I have just taken. The solemnity of the ceremony has made me feel as if I were consecrated a priest of the sacred Temple of Justice and that I have made my religious vow".

Generally, Judges of the judicial hierarchy have worked with one common interest, that is to be fair between man and man, accurate to the best of their abilities in the application of the law, always alive to the fact that "the law is the key stone of the arch of liberty". Justice Vithayathil was no exception to this general rule. He held the scales evenly, not merely between all manner of men, but between the state and the citizen as well. To Justice Vithyathil, delivery of justice was a divine avocation.

Inaugural speech delivered at Centenary Celebrations of Grand Chevalier Justice Joseph Vithayathil, Kerela on 1st August, 1999.

Justice Vithayathil shone like a diamond in other fields of activities as well. He fought a crusade to safeguard and protect the rights of the minorities. Article 30(1) of the Constitution of India enshrines the fundamental right to minorities to establish, manage and administer educational institutions of their choice. These protection of rights are in consonance with the secular nature of democracy and the Directives in the Constitution itself. The rights of the minorities are protected with a view to advance excellence and perfection in the field of education. The minority institutions, especially Christian institutions, have contributed a great deal towards the spread of education thereby eradicating illiteracy, superstition, ignorance and oppression.

The Christian community has played a significant role in the nation's development. They have rendered valuable service in the cause of independence. But their contribution in the field of education, health care and alleviation of poverty has served the country by founding innumerable schools, colleges, hospitals and asylums. Though they constituted merely 3% of the total population, they have played a major role in eradicating illiteracy and misery. Through liberal education, they have instilled a sense of discipline and service in the younger generation of our country.

It was Justice Vithayathil who stressed the need for a Minority Commission to protect the interests of the minorities. His efforts did not go waste. The Central Government has now constituted a National Commission for Minorities under the National Commission for Minorities Act, 1992, with a view to protect and ensure the safety of the minorities from being oppressed by the majority.

The Centenary celebrations in memory of such a great personality will, no doubt, perpetuate his memory to the present and the future. Let these celebrations keep alive the tradition set forth by Justice Vithayathil - the tradition of selfless service to the cause of humanity.

ಜಜಜ

FELICITATIONS TO JUSTICE
V.R. KRISHNA IYER

Justice Krishna Iyer is an institution personified. Extolling Krishna Iyer is like singing hymns in praise of the Sun. Sun burns bright, giving light to the universe irrespective of any praise. Justice Krishna Iyer is a colossus who shines *sans praise* or flattery.

> "*For these high purposes, he was gifted by divine providence with endowments, rare in their separate excellence; wonderful in their combination; judgement; imagination, memory; wit; force and acuteness of reasoning, eloquence, copious and accurate; commanding and persuasive and suited from its splendour to the dignity of his mind and to the authority of his station.*"

These words said of *William Pitt the younger* are apt when applied to Justice Krishna Iyer.

I have had the good fortune of receiving Justice Krishna Iyer at the Cochin Airport when he first set his foot on the Kerala soil after receiving Padma Vibhushan from the President. I shall ever cherish my sweet encounters and meetings with a personality like Justice Krishna Iyer. Great men are born once in a while. I adore Justice Krishna Iyer because he belongs to the rarest of the rare.

ಞಞಞ

Speech delivered on the Occasion of Felicitations to Padma Vibhushan Justice V.R. Krishna Iyer on 21st May, 1999.

IN MEMORY OF SHRI M.C. BHANDARI

Late Shri M.C. Bhandari joined the chamber of his father, Shri B.C. Bhandarri, who was also a very eminent lawyer of his time. In a very short time Shri M.C. Bhandari made great impact and was in great demand. He was one of the very few lawyers in Rajasthan who was equally at ease with all types of cases – Civil, Criminal, Revenue and Constitutional. His mastery over principles of law, extremely quick grasp and extraordinary command over English language enabled him to handle even the most complicated matters, at a relatively very young age. He made it to the top in a comparatively very short period and stayed there till his sad demise on 1st June, 1990. His human touch and warmth were reflected in his concern for the welfare of others.

Shri Dalveer Bhandari, a worthy son of a worthy father, is adorning the Bench of the Delhi High Court.

It is only in the fitness of things that such an impressive homage be paid by people of Rajasthan. It is to this bar that he contributed his services the most.

I had no occasion to see the great son of the soil, but I have learnt from others that late Shri M.C. Bhandari was exceptionally outstanding as a Lawyer and remarkably efficient as a counsel. His Court craft was par excellence. Shri M.C. Bhandari was a true representative of the Bar. He has left a message to the younger generation to work hard to achieve success and not to rest till the goal is achieved. He created confidence among the masses and members of the Bar.

ಐ ಐ ಐ

Presidential Address delivered at the function organized in Memory of Late Shri M.C. Bhandari at Jodhpur on 25th August, 2001.

DR. M. CHENNA REDDY

There is a saying that service to people is service to God. This simple principle, Dr. Chenna Reddy followed throughout his life and served the people twice as Chief Minister of Andhra Pradesh and as Governor to four big States of our country *viz.*, Uttar Pradesh, Punjab, Rajasthan and my home State, Tamil Nadu. His political activity commenced with the non-violent struggle against the oppressive rule of the erstwhile Nizam Government in Hyderabad. While I was a Judge at Madras High Court, he was the Governor of Tamilnadu. His approach to the problems of the society is very significant and praiseworthy.

As agriculturist, Dr. Reddy was the founder of some of the youth organisations in 1930s and '40s. Dr. Reddy started his political career in 1950. He became a Member of the Hyderabad Legislative Assembly from 1951 to 1956 and the Andhra Pradesh Legislative Assembly from 1956 to 1962 and again from 1962 to 1967.

He was a widely traveled person and a seasoned political worker. Dr. Reddy led the Indian Delegation in the World Conference of Agriculturists held under the auspices of F.A.O. in 1953.

Dr. Reddy had a long and distinguished political career, starting with the political struggle in the then Hyderabad State. He was actively involved in State politics since the 1950s and held various important portfolios such as Minister of Agriculture and Food, Planning and Rehabilitation in the then Hyderabad Government. Subsequently, he was Minister for Finance, Education and Commercial Taxes in the Government of Andhra Pradesh.

Dr. Chenna Reddy became a Member of the Rajya Sabha in 1967 and held the important charge of the Union Minister for Steel and Mines in the Government of India during 1967-68. He was the Governor of Uttar Pradesh from 1974 to 1977 and Chief Minister of Andhra Pradesh from 1977 to 1980 and thereafter, during 1989-90.

He was a freedom fighter. He fought for the freedom of the people of Hyderabad. He was jailed a number of times. He became a Minister at a very

---

Presidential Address at 'Dr. M. Chenna Reddy Memorial Trust,' Madras on 2nd December, 2002.

young age. As a person, he had very strong views. He had strong likes and dislikes. Wherever he worked, he left his mark – whether at the Centre or at the State or as a Governor. As a politician, he was active in Centre and State politics for 50 years. He fought many battles and won them too. He fought with dignity. He fought for freedom. He was a freedom fighter. He was a good administrator. Every position which he held, he held with distinction. As a Parliamentarian, an administrator and a freedom fighter, his contributions cannot be forgotten.

Dr. Reddy took an active part in several public movements and played a notable role. In a broad sense, Dr. Reddy was a visionary. He was a born leader, good and true. He was a workaholic.

Dr. Reddy held the office of the Governor of Rajasthan in the year 1992. Even then, I heard about his administrative excellence. Rajasthan came under the President's Rule in December, 1992 after the dismissal of the Government, headed by Mr. Bhairon Singh Shekhawat. The reigns of the administration were takenup by Dr. Reddy till he left for Madras, as Governor, in May 1993. Dr. Reddy took up the reigns at the time when communal riots had put the law and order machinery on trial and posed a challenge to administration. He gave the highest priority to this aspect. Always, we could see humanism in his outlook. Dr. Reddy consoled the victims of the affected areas, but also went to the hospitals to meet the injured persons. During his tenure, the administration was responsive to the needs of the riot affected people and revised the norms of financial assistance, adopted by the previous Government. During the tenure of Dr. Reddy, the State administration was toned up and streamlined. Whatever could be accomplished was done immediately and that which could not be done, was conveyed to the people with reasons. No delay and no postponement were 'the watch words' then. I heard people saying *"Rajbhavan is Praja Bhavan"*.

Dr. Chenna Reddy has endeared himself to the devout of public by his remarkable service to the cause of people. He proved himself to be the most successful leader of our country. He was a philosopher, a great devotee and in a nutshell a *"Sthitha Prajya"* i.e. Omnipotent in all fields.

౩౦౩౦౩౦

IN HONOUR OF MR. JUSTICE B.P. BERI

Nothing in my legal career has been a matter of greater honour than to have felicitated a phenomenally great forensic personage – a colossus in the legal profession, a contemporary *Bhishmacharya* for the lawyer community.

To narrate the forensic skill and dexterity which Justice Beri displayed would be a replay of a recorded cassette. Though, I would keep up the tenor and tempo, the verve and gumption which Justice Beri assiduously maintained would be difficult to sustain. It is my duty to exhort you all, who are the successors of Justice Beri's legacy, to unfailingly continue the rhythm of his legal style and the methods which he pursued in presenting cases as a lawyer and deciding cases as a Judge in the Court and the traditions which he zealously safeguarded.

I have had no occasion to see the great soul functioning as a Judge/Chief Justice of this Court, but I have learnt from others that Justice Beri was exceptionally outstanding and remarkably efficient as the Chief Justice. His court craft, was par excellence.

Socrates said that four things make a great Judge; to hear courteously, to answer wisely, to consider soberly and to decide impartially. By example and percept, Justice Beri is known for his scrupulous adherence to this Socratic dictum.

Justice Beri's long chequered career and saga of success are the result of sheer dint of hard work and intrinsic merit.

Generally Judges of the judicial hierarchy have worked with one common interest, that is to be fair between man and man, accurate to the best of their abilities in the application of the law, always alive to the fact that "the law is the key stone of the arch of liberty". Justice Beri was no exception to this general rule. He held the scales evenly, not merely between all manner of men, but between the State and the citizen as well. To Justice Beri, delivery of justice was a divine avocation. He imbibed the faculties and qualities of a Judge, set-forth by Justice Felix Frank thus:

Presidential address delivered in the felicitation function to honour Hon'ble Justice B.P. Beri, former Chief Justice of Rajasthan High Court, Jaipur on 27th January, 2001.

Justice Beri substantially satisfied these requirements.

Justice Beri's life is his message to the future; his example and good deed remain with us as his legacy. Let us celebrate the saga of his life as a source of inspiration to all of us.

ಚಿಚಿಚಿ

IN PRAISE OF A BANKER – M.Ct.M.

The function is organised in memory of Sir M.Ct.M. Chidambaram Chettiar, the Founder of the school, who took over the management and assets and liabilities of what was then known as C.R.C. High School, subsequently named as Sir M.Ct.M. High School, on 23rd August, 1929. The school was formally opened by His Excellency The Lord Erskine and by the magnanimity and munificence of Mr. M.Ct.M. Chidambaram Chettiar, the Higher Secondary status was confered on it to note that the alumni of the school are shining both at the national and international levels in all spheres such as Business, Banking, Finance, Health, Engineering, Film World, etc.

Thiru M.Ct.M. Chidambaram Chettiar, not only inherited the vast estate of his father Sir M.Ct. Muthiah Chettiar but also the sagacity and soundness for which the family is known in business enterprise. The late 'Chidambaram' as he was affectionately known to his friends, began his childhood with Economics from his teachers. Then followed the unfolding of a full and varied life in public activity. He was, for years, a distinguished member of the Upper House of the Indian parliament then known as the Council of State. He was an active proponent of Chambers of Commerce an Industry. He was Steward of the Madras Race Club for many years. An unostentatious but generous philanthropist, his name has been associated with numerous educational institutions. He was a person of rare personal charm.

His greatest contribution has been in the field of insurance, banking and industry. I learnt from his life history that he made matchless contributions to the building up of the United India Life Assurance Company not only in India but also in countries abroad. He became the first to conceive the idea of a sky-scraper building, in the field of insurance in the whole of India, as early as in the year 1953.

By a stroke of the pen, the Life Insurance Corporation of India became the inheritors of the soundness and popularity that the name 'United India' carried.

He was also the New Guardian of India Life Insurance Company, which the late Sri Chidambaram Chettiar salvaged from the shock, that the failure of the Travancore National and Quilon Bank imparted to this company.

Presidential address delivered on occasion of Founder's Day in Memory of Sri M. Ct. M. Chidambaram Chettiar, Madras on 13th March, 1995.

Mr. M.Ct.M. Chidambaram Chettiar also founded the United India Fire and General Insurance Company in the year 1938, closely following the Indian Overseas Bank. Equally laudable is his contribution to Indian Banking, especially in the twin domains of exchange and overseas banking, which were largely the pre-dominant interest of Exchange Banks of India. When he was hardly 28 years old, he had the wisdom to found the first Indian Bank with the avowed object of doing, primarily, overseas and exchange banking. Indeed, he presided over the destinies of the Indian Overseas Bank with unique distinction and built it up, brick by brick. In fact, he lost his life in one of the missions for the Bank, which took him to Indonesia.

The Travancore Rayons Limited, conceived by Sri M.Ct.M. Chidambaram Chettiar, was the first major industrial venture in the line, not only in India, but in the Far East as well. The many undertakings that he founded and fostered in his all-too-brief but glorious span of life, have found the means of livelihood for some 10,000 people, directly associated with these economic pursuits.

In the field of education, late M.Ct.M. Chidamabram Chettiar addressed himself to the development to the Sir M.Ct.M. Muthiah Chettiar High School, started by his father and gave generously, in time and money boath, to make it a very useful institution in the City of Madras. Later, he started that Lady Muthiah Chettiar High School for Girls in memory of his mother. As pointed out by me, earlier Sri M.Ct.M. Chidambaram Chettiar started the school to honour and revere the memory of his father late M.Ct. Muthiah Chettiar and mother. His multifaceted genius found expression in a variety of pioneering activities which have contributed to national and social progress in an abundant measure.

Dr. Sarvapalli Radhakrishnan had said that 'Education is a second birth'. A really educated person is free from all prejudices and presuppositions and looks upon all as kith and kin. It is really a teacher who gives a second birth to student. Teachers have a vital role to play in the building up of the nation. They set the example for the students to follow. It is the duty of the teachers to ensure that students acquire better character, better conduct and better behaviour.

Mr. M.Ct. Muthiah Chettiar was always keen that the school children should be excellent not only in academics but also combine with it an insight into India's rich cultural heritage and proficiency in co-curricular activities, sports and games. It is a matter of gratification to find that this school provides best education for its pupils and inculcates integrity, honesty, trust, compassion and tolerance in the students, which is the Founder's dream.

ಐಐಐ

ILLUSTRIOUS SON OF A WORTHY FATHER

The life of a man, it is said, can become a heroic poem, if only he becomes all that he was created capable of being. M.CT.M. Chidambaram Chettiar's (MCt) multi-faceted career exemplifies the essence of this opinion. Endowed as he is with a 'do and dare' spirit, his mind has a fierce grasp of all higher thoughts and better things, of fancy and reflection, of art and culture together in a remarkable manner. It works with extraordinary freedom and candour. M.Ct's keen understanding of men and matters, his catholic outlook, his originality, his sense of discernment and, above all, his largeness of heart veritably mark him out as an illustrious son of a worthy father, Sir M.Ct. Muthiah Chettiar. MCt. has nobly lived ever since his birth, inheriting, as he did, the fabulous name and fame of the S.RM.M.Ct. family, known for its many glorious benefactions and acts of noble public service. Like his father, M.Ct. too enlarged the scale of his operations and enhanced his usefulness in such a way as to win the grateful appreciation of the business community.

As a true scion of the Chettinad family known for its acute business instinct, M.Ct. had to take over the reins of business as his father passed away in 1929, when he was only 21 years of age. He started and developed the following ventures – which bear ample testimony to his acumen, farsightedness and pioneering spirit, all of which were "firsts" by a Chettiar:

- Developed and established a life insurance company, the United India Life Assurance Co. Ltd., which was initiated by his father, Sir M.Ct. Muthiah Chettiar.
- Started a fire & general insurance company *viz.*, the United India Fire & General Insurance Co. Ltd.
- Started a bank (Indian Overseas Bank) with branches all over India and in South East Asia, specializing in foreign exchange, primarily to meet the needs of Indians living abroad.
- Started a large and complex manufacturing chemical industry, the Travancore Rayons Ltd., which was acclaimed as the first of its kind between the Suez Canal and Japan.

Delivered on release of Biography of M.Ct.M. Chidambaram Chettiyar at Chennai on 27th March, 2004.

- Held a major interest in Bombay when he took over the Elphinstone Mills in the 1940s.

His way of handling financial and production problems testifies to his masterly comprehension of the complexities and intricacies of business and industry. He gave all his time and energy to IOB, which has markedly grown in size, specializing in foreign exchange, thanks to his careful planning, spurred by his sense of go-aheadedness. M.Ct. looked upon hurdles as challenges to be surmounted with determination and courage. He attached great value to open-mindedness. M.Ct. was certainly a gifted "Organisation Man" with a pioneering passion for innovativeness.

M.Ct. was a Member of the Viceroy's Council of State, which was a nominated body, somewhat similar to the present Rajya Sabha, which helped the British Government in legislature and decision making, in the late 1930s when he was barely 29 years old.

M.Ct. accomplished the above and many more achievements during a short span of a little over two decades, while he was quite young; that too, more than 50 years ago when the socio-economic climate in India was not favourable for an Indian entrepreneur to spread his wings.

M.Ct's uncle, Dewan Bahadur S.Rm.M.Ct. Pethachi Chettiar, donated some of his lands in Trichy to National College and one of the blocks in that college bears his name.

Sir M.Ct. Muthiah Chettiar had cordial relations with the Maharaja of Mysore. To honour his memory, the Maharaja named the ophthalmic block of the hospital in Mysore after Sir M.Ct. Muthiah Chettiar.

This relationship continued to the next generation as well. H.H. Jaya Chamaraja Wadiyar was close to M.Ct.M. Chidambaram Chettiyar and the foundation stone of the present LIC building in Bangalore was laid by His Highness.

M.Ct's close relationship with the Mysore Royal family won him the friendship of the Dewan of Mysore, Sir Mirza Ismail. The depth of this friendship is borne out by the fact that, even though Sir Mirza had a daughter living in Madras, many a time he preferred to stay with M.Ct. when he visited Madras.

Sir M.Ct. Muthiah Chettiar and his brother, M.Ct. Pethachi Chettiar, Andipatti Zamindar, were regular guests of honour at the annual Dusserah festivities in Mysore.

M.Ct. thought big and built tall. His business ventures were far ahead of the times and they were all housed in tall, stately buildings.

The LIC building, standing proudly on the arterial Mount Road, is the tallest and the first sky-scraper of Madras. It was conceived and started by M.Ct. and is an all-time memorial to the great man.

M.Ct's time and resources were not confined to business only. He had the glowing examples before him of the epoch-making contributions made to the promotion of education, art and culture by his highly eminent father whose qualities of head and heart, he has undoubtedly inherited.

M.Ct. had extensively travelled throughout the world. He had a cosmopolitan outlook and was conversant with the nuances of the varied cultures of the world. With his mental horizons widened, and his knowledge of the world around him deepened, he was gentle and soft-spoken without the touch of theatrical. His vibrant life was terminated by an unfortunate aircrash at Singapore Airport on 13th March, 1954, when he was just in his mid forties.

Noble men are made nobler by their thoughts and actions and such noble men are the sons of God. To that fraternity belongs the most respected M.Ct. His illustrious sons are Mr. M.Ct. Muthiah Chettiar and Mr. M.Ct. Pethachi Chettiar, whose forte is benevolence and charity, has laid firmer foundations to achieve the motto of their father with courage and faith. My illustrious and revered brothers Mr. M.Ct. Muthiah Chettiar and Mr. M.Ct. Pethachi Chettiar with their vast experience of men and matters, are now ordained to be the Chairman of the institutions which were founded by M.Ct. Mr. M.Ct. Muthiah Chettiar and Mr. M.Ct. Pethachi Chettiar, as true sons of a wise father, have always believed that if everyman mends one, all around are mended. I have had the good fortune of having close acquaintance with these two brothers. They always gave me the impression that their erudition and myriad activity have been fully injected into the system of working of the institutions, which is reflected by its achievements. Good things have been done by good people in the past and they are now being continued by the sons and it will continue to be a noble heritage in that family.

M.Ct. was visionary, a person from a conservative merchant community, the Natukottai Chettiar, once renowned for trading, financing and banking who went on to beat a different path and play a pioneering role in modern industry in Southern India. Sadly, it is a story of a journey that ended long before it should have. I am happy to hear that Mr. M.Ct. Muthiah shared his thoughts with the researchers on numerous occasions and provided several photographs used in this book and Mr. M.Ct. Pethachi inspired the book titled the *Unfurnished Journey*, recalling vignettes of the past. There are host of others who are responsible for having made the unfinished journey possible.

For the sake of information to my dear readers, I state the following information:

Deep in the south of India's southernmost State, Tamil Nadu, is Chettinad, the land of the Chettiars. Once part of the ancient Pandya Kingdom, it is today spread around the town of Karaikudi, about 80 km east of Madurai, the capital of the ancient Pandyas, and about the same distance south of Thanjavur, the capital of the ancient Cholas. In this 600 sq. mile area were the 96 townships that the Chettiars founded. It was these settlements in a parched wilderness which earned them their preferred community name – **Nagarathar** – the townsfolk, or the sophisticated dwellers of anagrams or urban settlements in what is essentially a rural area in the middle of nowhere.

In their heyday, a glorious 150-year period, between 1800 and 1950, the Chettiars built their homes – fortress-like mansions, the cause for most others calling them **Nattukottai** (land-fort) **Chettiars** – and these they filled with the riches, earned from across the seas.

The ancient Nagarathar tradition of _mahimai_ was to open the annual account books by gifting a certain percentage of the previous year's profits to charity. It's a practice that has lapsed in modern times, but the habit of giving generously to charity has not wained. Religion and education, and healthcare to an extent, have all benefited from Chettiar generosity. And M.Ct.M. Chidambaram Chettyar did his part unobtrusively.

The schools he nurtured, the speeches and advice he gave on education, the Trusts he inspired, all leave those who knew M.Ct., well wondering what might he have not contributed to the field of education in Tamil Nadu if he had lived his full life and not been snatched away so tragically, so early.

M.Ct.M. Chidambaram Chettyar was a person who believed that people should always look their best. He believed in everything being neat and clean, tidy and orderly, everything in its place and everyone dressed just right for the occasion. Flamboyance had no place in his vocabulary. He himself was always immaculately dressed in what appeared the simplest of attire for the times.

The then Finance Minister, C.D. Deshmukh, inaugurated the LIC building, the South's first skyscraper, in 1959. It was to remain Madras's tallest building till the dawn of the 21st Century. Today, it may be the LIC's regional headquarters, but it was built according to the plans of a man who dreamt big and built tall. Still a landmark building in Chennai, it is a most fitting memorial to the man who ever had the big vision than any statue raised in his memory.

The good, it has often been repeated, die young. The tragedy in the case of M.Ct.M. Chidambaram Chettyar is that, when he died at 46, it was long before his dreams of establishing a conglomerate of all-India businesses could really take off, in an Independent India, that offered so many more opportunities than in the restrictive and discriminatory days of British rule. That he died less than seven years after the dawn of Independence, gave him hardly any time to establish his three major enterprises not only as all-India businesses but also as institutions to reckon with, in South and South-east Asian commercial circles. But saddest of all is perhaps the fact that he did not live long enough to face the unanticipated challenges posed by labour and Government to the M.Ct. Group's core businesses. He might not have been able to overcome either, but his dynamism would not have allowed himself to be brought to a stop by the circumstances of the times; instead, it would have spurred him on to tread new paths, establish new enterprises and even, in the view of many, find ways to work in partnership with Government on whole. What he might have done if he had lived twenty more years and seen the business scenario change in the country by Government and what he might have done in that changed scenario, those who knew his business acumen can only speculate on. But that he would have made a difference, all agree. And that is the saddest consequence of his dying, young, his journey unfinished.

He was a judicious combination of being approachable and yet distanced himself from those intruding on his valuable time. He set clear boundaries for himself, amongst which asking for favours was seen as being unacceptable.

He was that rare gentleman businessman – a visionary who combined the highest level of business acumen and entrepreneurial skill with a deep sense of idealism.

He was acutely conscious of the disruption that unthinking, unplanned and unimaginative industrialization could inflict on society. This sense of social consciousness and responsibility influenced many of his business decisions when he deliberately chose to subordinate profit to the overall social interest.

His investments were in people and personal relationships. In an era of restricted labour rights, he was perhaps one of the first, if not the only industrialist of his time, truly committed to nurturing good labour relations, a belief that he imbibed very early. He believed that a confrontationist stand was unproductive, that tensions were better resolved through dialogue, debate and discussion.

The *'Unfinished Journey'* attempts to cover the success story of a visionary within its 300 odd pages. But, the unfulfilled dreams of M.Ct. cannot be confined within space or time.

Let Providence shower its choicest blessings on everyone concerned with the future progress.

ಜಿಜಿಜಿ

WE SALUTE OUR FREEDOM FIGHTERS

Ours has been an eventful march on the path or progress towards the goal of establishing a welfare State. Our thoughts go out, in salutation to the torchbearers of freedom struggle and all those leaders and volunteers of the freedom movement whose supreme sacrifice led to the liberation of our motherland from the bonds of colonial rule.

It is appropriate to remember the freedom fighters of Andhra Pradesh who sacrificed their lives for the freedom movement.

We also salute those great men and women of eminence who contributed their qualities of head and heart for the growth of the Constitution, over the years and its effective functioning as an instrument of social change. Dr. B.R. Ambedkar, one of the Chief Architects of the Indian Constitution, declared in the Constituent Assembly that:

> "On the 26th January, 1950 India would be a democratic country *in the sense that India, from that date, would have a Government of the people, by the people and for the people*".

It is a Government 'Of the People' because citizens are both subjects and rulers and they are equally subjected to the Laws. It is *'For the People'* as it aims at establishing a welfare State wherein, maximum good to maximum number of people is sought to be secured. More importantly, it is a government *'By the People'* in as much as every adult citizen participates in the process of government through elected representatives. In other words, the people would have power to make or unmake the Government, irrespective of any distinction based on caste, creed, race, sex, religion etc.

The Preamble of our Constitution, the supreme law of our land, enshrines the solemn resolve of the people of India to constitute a Sovereign, Socialist, Secular Democratic Republic.

I am proud and happy that, even after 58 years of independence, India holds the highest position of the largest democracy in the world, even after the democratic system failed in most of our neighbouring countries. Though we are a little bit worried, for our country is now facing the threat of war at the borders, perpetrated by cross-border terrorism by our neighbouring country.

Speech delivered on the Eve of Republic Day at Hyderabad on 26th January, 2002.

414

The State of Andhra Pradesh must take the pride, in the fact, that the Indian tri-colour, which we have saluted today, was designed by Pingali Venkaiah, son of this soil.

On this glorious day, well over half a century ago, our tri-colour stood fluttering over a land that was overwhelmed by its historic deliverance from alien rule. Today is a day of silent, dispassionate, and, ruthless introspection. It is never difficult to be cynical. But one cannot help, feeling choked with unshed tears when one sees children, living in deplorable conditions, especially of lower strata and neglected in streets, who look as though they have come alone from the pages of Charles Dicken's novel – *Blighted lives*, in millions, whose dim, but fast fading light was made the stuff of the hopes and ideals of the by-gone generation, await a saviour in vain.

Today, our judiciary is over-stretched. It is a matter of concern for all of us that arrears in Courts have mounted up and scaled new peaks. The litigants are left out, high and dry. We may have to put our heads together to find out measures to overcome this menace. It is required to mention that, judicial activism has attained, perhaps its finest hour in recent times.

Today, the Judiciary in India is blamed for huge backlog of cases. It is time that the public is made aware that during the last fifty years of independence, little attention has been paid by the Government for improvement of the infrastructure of the judiciary. There is dearth of Courts and Judges and of buildings, both for Courts and Judges and Officers and Staff. In several cases, even minimum facilities have not been provided. The reason is that there is no planning and proper budgeting of the courts requirements, in consultation with the Judiciary as in done in other countries. Nor is there a long-range plan or at least a five-year plan. The result is that most of the Courts are over-burdened with cases on the civil side and criminal side. Delay results is a serious infraction of right to speedy trials and to violation of human rights in various cases. A stage has reached when the parties are thinking of taking the law into their hands. In the above scenario, it has become necessary to go into the subject of financial independence or financial support to the judiciary in India, at some length, on a comparative basis and also to consider the need for adequate provision for the judiciary as a planed subject. In a number of judgements of the Supreme Court, it has been laid down that independence of the judiciary is part of the basic structure of our Constitution. The independence has also other facets including, the institutional independence of the judiciary. One of the accepted facets of institutional independence is the one concerning financial resources and financial freedom or autonomy that is to be given to the judiciary. Today, this concept has been developed and accepted in most of the democracies, governed by the Rule of Law. The doctrine of separation of powers has been suitably modified and adjusted to achieve the above goal of financial autonomy and freedom of the judiciary. The principle of judicial independence is almost universally accepted. In my opinion, the judiciary as a whole should enjoy autonomy and collective independence *vis-a-vis* the executive. The central responsibility for judicial administration should preferably be vested in the Judiciary. It is the duty of the

State to provide adequate financial resources to allow for the due administration of justice. Court services should be adequately financed by the relevant Government. The position of the Judges, their Independence, their security and their adequate remuneration shall be prepared by a competent authority in collaboration with the judiciary. It is the duty of the State to provide adequate resources to enable the judiciary to properly perform its functions.

So far as financial independence or support is concerned, our present system is suffering from serious difficulties. It is these difficulties that causes for clogging of cases in the Subordinate Courts and in High Courts. It is true that, by means of Alternative Disputes Resolution Systems such as Lok Adalats, several lakhs of cases have been disposed of in the last more than a decade, but that, in the overal perspective, has not reduced the general congestion in the Subordinate Courts and the High Courts. Basically, lack of long range planning and lack of finances have been the main causes for the shortage of Courts and Judicial Officers in all parts of the country. Further, extreme bureaucratic procedures, requiring consultation with half a dozen departments, thwarted any progress.

Coming to figures of Judge - Population ratio, the conditions reflect a pathetic situation and a total governmental apathy. The Law Commission in its 120th Report on 'Management of Planning in Judiciary' stated that the State should immediately increase the present ratio from 10.5 Judges per million of Indian population to at least 50 Judges per million Indian Population within the next five years. It was further recommended that by the year 2000, India should commend at least 107 Judges per million of Indian population. This has not happened. Meanwhile, the population is galloping. The courts and Judges did not increase in number. The former Chief Justice of India in his address at the Bar Council of India on 10th October, 1998 stated that "in several European countries, the number of Judges per million population varies from 90 to 100. However, in India it was only 11 which was rather disappointing.

However, for independence and efficient functioning of judiciary, it should have full financial autonomy including preparation of its budget. The judiciary should have a final say in the matter of establishment of Courts and the paraphernalia, needed thereafter and that the recommendations of the judiciary should be binding on the executive.

The judiciary has a special role to play in the task of achieving socio-economic goals, enshrined in the Constitution. While maintaining their aloofness and independence, the Judges have to be aware of the social changes for the task of achieving socio-economic Justice for the people.

Our economy with its incredible resilience, is taking outlines of the dreams of our founding fathers. We have come closer to the dreadful realization that the enemy is within, as it is without. For we are our worst enemies. It is imperative that the members of the legal profession take a more prominent role in the matters of the nation.

History continues to happen all around us today, as technology makes rapid inroads into our lives. A computer revolution is now taking place. Today, Internet and E-mail are integral part in the day-to-day life of even common man in India. At present, millions have global access to all types of information, almost free of charge and instantaneously. Our hopes are brightened, as the 21st Century and third Millennium are brimming over with promises.

In the industrial sector, India has progressed much. In the field of technology and education also, tremendous are our achievements, compared to the other developing nations.

If we want India to become a great nation, substantial change is needed in the attitude of the people. Our society has to produce outstanding individuals who are cultured, educated, disciplined and filled with zeal to make India greater. It is the same society that produced leaders and social reformers of historic greatness. A happy and harmonious society, we will never be, until the vast majority of Indians start practicing ethical values.

I will take this opportunity to pay any respectful homage to the departed souls of the freedom fighters, but for whose sacrifice and selfless struggle for Independence, we would not be standing here today, as free citizens of the Sovereign and Democratic Republic of India.

The paramount need of the hour is to embark upon purposive action to restore confidence of people in the democratic institutions and re-establish the credibility of administration. There is an imminent need for the enlightened and educated citizenry. A few great men cannot make a nation great but the combined forces of entire populace can.

We are aware of the constant threat our country is facing from outside and the tension at the borders of our country. We should show our solidarity with our brave soldiers. In times of need, we shall shed internal squabbles and to show our unity irrespective of religion and caste he motto of every Indian should be what Mother Teresa had said. She summed up her mission in India, using Gandhiji's words, like this:

"Our goal is, to make a Hindu a better Hindu, a Muslim a better Muslim and a Christian a better Christian."

This should be the ideal of every citizen of this great country and the message of life is to be spread like this, amongst all Indians.

The future of our democracy depends on how best the democratic institutions are functioning and how far they are able to reflect the hopes and aspirations of the people and how sensitive and responsive they are to the grievances of the people. A vibrant and healthy democracy is sure to pave the way for establishing a Welfare State.

ಬಿ ಬಿ ಬಿ

PART XV

MODERN INDIA

INDIA – A LEADING MARITIME POWER

Men's adventures on water are as old as civilisation itself. Students of history believe that India was one of the earliest maritime nations known to man.

The finding of Indian teak in the ruins of the first Kingdom of Babylonia and the discovery of primitive craft in the ruins of Mohenjadaro suggest that India was a leading maritime power for more than 30 centuries.

This glorious heritage suffered a great deal with the ascendancy of the British Rule. But, our great pioneers like V.O. Chidambaram Pillai, Narotham Morarji, Walchand Hirachand and J.N. Tata struggled hard to revive our maritime glory, along with their fight for 'Swaraj'. In the year 1919, the aspirations of these heroes were crowned with success.

On 5th April, 1919, the first Indian Merchant Ship 'S.S. LOYALTY' owned by M/s. Scindia Steam Navigation Company Limited, ventured on a voyage from Bombay to United Kingdom. The National Welfare Board for Seafarers, a statutory body, constituted under the Merchant Shipping Act, 1958, under the Chairmanship of Union Ministry for Shipping and Transport, in its meeting, held at Madras on 11th January, 1964, recommended, that this day be celebration National Maritime Day.

Similar National Maritime Day is observed in certain other leading maritime countries such as U.S.A., Japan and West Germany. In U.S.A., 22nd May is celebrated as the National Maritime Day. On this day in 1819, the S.S. 'Savannah' sailed from New York to Liverpool, the first ocean crossing by an American steam vessels. In Japan, 20th July is celebrated as the National Maritime Day. It was on that day, in 1876, that the steamship, 'Meiji Maru' carrying the then Emperor Meiji, who had preferred a steamship for the first time for his inspection, entered the Yokohama Harbour.

The story of maritime trade goes as far back as the Rig Veda, which is estimated to be 3,000 to 5,000 years old. It narrates the story of voyages undertaken for commerce and other purposes.

The very objective of celebrating this day is to enable the public, not only to have a look at our glorious maritime past but to know more closely about the

Speech delivered on occasion of the 'National Maritime Day Celebrations', Madras on 5th April, 1994.

activities of Indian Shipping Industry so that they can understand how this salient trade, which operates far away from the humdrum of the life-on-hand, impinges every sector of our country's economy. Its role is vital for the prosperity of our nation and very essential, in times of war, as the second line of defence.

The mere thrill of knowing about the adventures of sea life and having a glimpse of the strenuous and risky lives of the tough and weather beaten sailors, who man our ships is sufficient, inducement enough for our younger generation to seek a career in Merchant Navy.

This day is also observed as the Merchant Navy Flag Day. The collections made out of the sale of flags are used for the welfare of seamen and their families, administered through the Seafarers Welfare Fund Society.

The Indian Seaman, whether an Officer or of any other rank, is resourceful, highly adaptable and can weather any climatic conditions. His efficiency, loyalty and dependability make him one of the finest seaman in the world. That is why several foreign shipping companies meet the manning requirements by employing Indian seamen.

Shipping is a highly capital intensive institution. The operational costs of ships are enormous. Shipping industry boosts up our country's economy by way of foreign exchange earnings by trading. Shipping has to be highly competent to match the modern technology and world wide competition. Ships personnel are also put through extensive training to gain knowledge on rapidly developing ship technology.

The seafarers lead a hard disciplined life & bear separation of their families, while sailing on the ships, to keep the Merchant Navy moving and earning valuable foreign exchange. 5th of April is remembered as the day of obligation to these men behind the Merchant Navy and we pay homage to those of them who have laid down their lives while on duty.

The National Welfare Board for Seafarers has implemented certain recommendations which include social security for seamen, formation of Welfare Fund Society for financing welfare measures, extension of medical facilities, construction of recreational facilities at the various ports and setting up of a benevolent fund for seamen.

The Merchant Shipping Act makes statutory provisions for seamen's welfare. It is a comprehensive legislative measure which ensures the safety of Merchant Navy Officers and Seamen, their congenial working conditions on board ships, fair employment prospects and regular payment of wages and dues. Seamen's welfare officers appointed by Govt. of India look after its implementation.

Maritime and related disputes exist in India by the thousands. Sadly, however, except in a handful, amongst the Bar and the Bench and some of the others involved in dealing with an adjudication of such disputes, specialised and deep-rooted knowledge of maritime and allied laws is generally found lacking in India.

For reasons which are not quite apparent, maritime law in India including commercial law germane to shipping practices, such as, some aspects of banking law, export trade laws, marine insurance laws, laws relating to sale and purchase of ships, contracts of carriage, admiralty laws and so on have not kept pace with the growth in the other fields of shipping.

The object of celebrating the National Maritime Day is to recognise the important role played by Merchant Navy in the country's economy. After independence, no time was lost in realising that utmost importance needs to be given for the development of our Navy as also the Merchant Navy, which was recognised as the second line of defence and the first thing we started doing, in that direction, is to write our own Merchant Shipping Act. The preamble of the Merchant Shipping Act is self explanatory which runs as follows:

> "An Act to foster the development and ensure the efficient maintenance of an Indian Mercantile Marine in a manner best suited to serve the national interests and for that purpose to establish a National Shipping Board and a Shipping Development Fund to provide for the registration of Indian Ships and generally to amend and consolidate the law relating to merchant shipping."

Pandit Jawaharlal Nehru at the time of inauguration of the National Shipping Board observed as follows:—

> *"Now, unfortunately, like other things in which we fell, we fell back in shipping and, almost you might say, that itself was a final indication of our decadence. And I am not, for a moment, laying stress on what foreign conquest did to India - of course it did – but I think we had fallen before that foreign conquest came, as a country inevitably does if it becomes static, becomes weak and loses its creative energy."*

The progress of Indian Shipping from 1949 is largely attributed to the efforts and inputs of the Government. Our shipping industry will have to compete with the shipping companies of the world on open competition basis. The infrastructure which the shipping industry needs is good communication facilities, simplifications of procedures, hinterland transport facilities, good ports and ship repair facilities.

The Government of India has already taken steps in formulating the policies for the multimodal/combined transport of goods by railways and roads.

The Government has taken a big step in removing the constraints in mortgaging the Indian ship to foreign financiers. Indian seafarer has proved that he is second to none in the world market. Indian officers are, today, manning the major portion of the foreign vessels. The foreign companies have employed our officers to manage their ships. India is, therefore, the world's envy in this field.

The Mercantile Marine Departments have also to play a big part in providing the right type of infrastructure in the context of globalisation of shipping.

ಬಿಬಿಬಿ

POLIO FREE INDIA

Year 2000 was the year of attaining the Universal objective of the eradication of polio. Better participation of the community is very important for the success of its eradication. As we all know, polio is a virus borne communicable disease and its virus attacks only human beings. It affects the nervous system of the child. This disease spreads through contaminated water and food and ordinarily targets the children of below the age of five years. In the beginning, the infected children complain of pain in the parts of body along with fever. The infected child is unable to move his hand or feet and the infected part of the body looms lose. It becomes paralysed. It is a disease which makes the child disabled for the rest of his life. Whichever family undergoes the black shadow of this annihilating disease is destined to suffer the agony of this incurable disease. This is one of the major cause of disability in our country.

The State Government of Rajasthan has vowed to eradicate this disease from the roots. The last five pulse polio immunization programmes have achieved glorious success by administering pulse polio-drops to all children, below the age of five years, with the active cooperation of the people and it deserves congratulations. If such an enthusiasm continues then I do hope that Rajasthan too would become polio free in the near future. But for the total eradication and destruction of polio, it is a must that not a single child should suffer from polio for three years in continuity. We have now arrived at the last stage of polio eradication but more caution and awareness is required for freedom from this disease.

The additional doses of polio would be administered on the days of pulse polio to children, irrespective of their having taken or not taken the polio-drops earlier. Since the wild polio virus can develop in the intestines of even such children who have been administered polio-drops during all the earlier stages and as such can infect the other children, it is absolutely necessary that all children be given the pulse-drops, at the same time. The basic purpose of administering the polio-drops to all the children at the same time, in each stage

---

Speech delivered at 'Pulse Polio Campaign' organised by Family Welfare Services, Rajasthan on 10th December, 2000.

of the campaign, is to totally destroy all places of growth of the virus so that all traces of this virus may be totally destroyed from the earth.

The basic objective of all the activities of the pulse polio campaign is to break the transmission chain of wild polio virus. As such, we must make every possible effort that no child is left behind. If we really wish to realize the dream of a polio-free country then we must provide due importance to each and every child, whether he is a Jhuggi dweller poor child or the one living in the distant, inaccessible and the terrible terrain of the state. Therefore, I appeal to the state authorities to give special attention to ensure that no child remains without taking the polio medicine. Even if a single child is left behind, total security circle will be eliminated.

As such participation and contribution of all the people in this programme is very necessary. One cannot safeguard one child alone by getting him polio-drops until and unless all the neighbourhood children of below the age of 5 years are also administered the polio-drops. Even a single un-immunised child can infect the other children. In such a situation, it is our moral obligation that we also undertake the responsibility of getting the polio drops administered to all the children of the neighbourhood and that of our relatives and acquaintances, alongwith our own children.

Therefore, appeal is to all the governmental and non-governmental institutions, religious, educational and social leaders, public representative and to all the citizens that, while expressing their love and affection towards all the children of the State, they must carry all the children below the age of 5 years to the nearest booth of this campaign, for the administration of polio-drops, to make this campaign also a successful one, as in the past, by their full co-operation in this national programme.

My dream is a "POLIO FREE INDIA".

ಬಲಬ

THE JEWELS OF SIKKIM

Earth is the only planet in the universe which has an environment for life. Environment normally means its surroundings. We, Indians, are proud of our culture and heritage. Our culture demands that we should start our day by taking a bath. For water we need to preserve the natural resources like river, pond, and other water sources etc . Taking a dip in river is considered as holy for the reason that it flows and is a gift of God. Going to the temple to pray to God for allowing us to use the earth re-iterates our duty to protect the nature. Walking around the temple (*pradikshana*) is an exercise to our body, and we do it in a clockwise direction for the reason that we want to run our life in a smooth manner like the clock. We bow to the bull in temple as a respect to the animal kingdom. Bull is considered as a useful animal without which ploughing of fields are not possible. If agricultural properties are properly preserved, there will not be any scarcity of food. We treat the Banyan tree as God, because it gives more oxygen than any other tree. As we can not keep a tree as a symbol of respecting it in every house, we keep a *"tulsi"* plant in our house to mark our respect to all the plants. Since time immemorial, natural objects like rivers enjoy a high respect from the society. They are considered as Goddesses having not only the purifying capacity but also self purifying ability. Fouling of the water of a river was considered as a sin and it attracted punishments. The earth also equally had the same importance, and the ancient literature provided the means to purify the polluted soil. Everyone is careful to maintain his own residence in a best environment. But at the same time, he forgets the fact that surrounding areas are also important. The public should feel that they have also got a duty to preserve the environment in the best interest of themselves. I had the occasion to deliver a judgment, when I was the judge of the Kerala High Court, banning smoking in public places. The smokers in public places not only harm themselves, but also adversely affect the persons standing nearby.

The beginning of the Environment Law culminated from the United Nations Conference on Human Environment, held at Stockholm in 1972, where India was a participant. The foundation for environmental protection and control legislations were incorporated into the Constitution of India by the Forty-Second Amendment Act of 1976. Art. 48A was added to the Directive Principles of State

---

Speech delivered at '2005 Sikkim' Intellectual's Conference', Gangtok on 29th May, 2005.

Policy. It declares *"The State shall endeavour to protect and improve the environment and to safeguard the forests and wild life of the country."* An additional fundamental duty was imposed on every citizen to protect and improve the natural environment including forests, lakes, rivers and wild life, and to have compassion for living creatures by incorporating Art. 51A to the Constitution. This constitutional amendment is the foundation of the legislations for environment protection. The allocation of legislative authority is an important one. Some environmental problems such as sanitation and waste disposal can be best tackled at the municipal level. Protection of air, water and wild life are better regulated by uniform national laws. The 42nd amendment also moved the subject "forests" from State list to Central list. Thereafter, several legislations were enacted to preserve the environment.

The Indian judiciary, for protecting and preserving the environment, has given a wider interpretation to the fundamental right conferred by Art. 21 of the Constitution. While giving a broader meaning to the term "right to life", Hon'ble Mr. Justice Bhagwati, speaking for the Supreme Court, has stated that: *"We think that the right to life includes the right to live with human dignity and all that goes along with it , namely, the bare necessaries of life such as adequate nutrition, clothing, shelter over the head and facilities for reading , writing and expressing oneself in diverse forms, freely moving about and mixing and commingling with fellow human beings"*. The right to life is a fundamental right and it includes the right to enjoyment of pollution free water and air, for full enjoyment of life.

Being a developing country, economic progress is essential. At the same time care has to be taken of the environment. It cannot be disputed that no development is possible without some adverse effect on the ecology and environment. It has become necessary to sacrifice certain ecological resources, to meet the needs of human necessities. Rising poverty and unemployment have increased pressure on environmental resources as more people have been forced to rely more, directly upon them. There should be balance between development and environment. The basic approach should be sustainable development, a development in harmony with environment. Sustainable development is essentially a policy and strategy for continued economic and social development, without detriment to the environment and natural resources on the quality of which continued activity and further development depend. The richness of the earth's biodiversity should be conserved for future generations. Therefore, while thinking of the developmental measures, the needs of the present and the ability of the future to meet its own needs and requirements, have to be kept in view. While thinking of the present, the future should not be forgotten. We owe a duty to future generations and for a bright today, bleak tomorrow cannot be countenanced. We must learn from our experiences of past to make both the present and the future brighter. We learn from our experiences, mistakes of the past, so that they can be rectified for a better future. The United Nations Conference and Development held at Rio, 1992, proclaimed 27 principles, the first of which, *inter alia* is thus:

> *"Human beings are at the centre of concerns for sustainable development. They are entitled to a healthy and productive life in harmony with nature."*

It cannot be lost sight of that while today is yesterday's tomorrow, it is tomorrow's yesterday. There is a day after tomorrow which the future requires.

The greenery of India should not be allowed to be perish, to be replaced by deserts. Euthopia, which at a point of time was considered to be one of the greenest countries, is virtually a vast desert today. We have learnt much from the Bhopal tragedy, which has led to a lot of environmental legislations. The non availability of drinking water in many States have lead to severe problems. The over exploitation of ground water, has damaged the traditional drinking water resources like, wells, ponds, streams, etc. Improper management and disposal of wastes has lead to severe pollution. The depletion of forests has lead to climatic changes. Uncontrolled mining has resulted in depletion of natural resources. Fishery resources has adversely affected the exports. The indiscriminate construction of buildings in violation of Building Rules and Town Planning Regulations have made life miserable. The level of flood and drought has started increasing. Shortage of agricultural commodities have led to famine. Several persons are dying due to diarrhoeal diseases related to unsafe drinking water and malnutrition. Similar phenomena are emerging on a global scale, such as global warming, and loss of ozone. A safe, environmentally sound, and economically viable energy pathway that will sustain human progress into the distant future is clearly imperative. New dimensions of political will and institutional co-operation is required to achieve it. New technologies, which offer promise of higher productivity, increased efficiency and decreased pollution should be encouraged. Dumping of hazardous wastes should be totally prohibited. Multinational companies can play an important role in sustainable development, especially as developing countries have come to rely more on foreign equity capital. If these companies are to have positive influence on development, the negotiating capacity of developing countries must be strengthened so that they can secure terms that respect their environment concerns.

Striking a balance between protection of the environment and sustainable development is an onerous and delicate task. Supreme Court had the occasion to consider several issues relating to environment. The technical hurdles in approaching the Courts have been relaxed by means of public interest litigations. *Locus standi* has been widened. Even letters and telegrams are converted as writ petitions. Court had stepped in where there is no law and laws are interpreted for the preservation of the natural resources. For the protection of the forests, several conditions were laid down. In the process, directions were given to ensure that degradation does not take place. Noise pollution,, in the name of religious activities, disturbs the old and infirm persons whose sleeps are adversely affected. Supreme Court, in *Church of God (Full Gospel) in India vs K.K.R.Majestic Colony Welfare Association*, (2000) 7 SCC 282 recognizing the right to sleep of the persons, has came to their rescue and honoured their right. In *Murli. S.Deora vs Union of India*, (2001) 8 SCC 765: AIR 2002 SC 40 the Supreme Court gave utmost importance to the health of the public affected by smoking in public places. For controlling the vehicular pollution several directions were issued. The city of Delhi was one of most polluting city in the world. It is due to the intervention of the Supreme Court that the air quality in the National Capital region has improved. For protecting monuments like Taj Mahal, directions were issued. Rain water harvesting and linking of rivers have become a necessity. Environment education has been made compulsory in all schools. Building Rules and Town Planning violations have been strictly dealt. For the proper management of wastes, directions were issued.

Preservation of the global environment is a vital priority that must be borne in mind by all. A good coffee is a gift from the sun and the earth, and one born only under the right environmental conditions, in the coffee plantations. India indeed was once a land of plenty with its mountains covered with luxuriant forests, and the fertile land yielded the basic needs of its people. If such a land is today in shambles, its mountain slopes devastated, forest cover removed, its pure waters, not excluding even the sacred Ganga, converted into glorified sewers and the free air surrounding us poisoned with noxious gases, we only have ourselves and the modern ways, we have adopted, to blame, ignoring the wisdom and teachings of our forefathers. Open spaces, land for a home, clean air to breathe and clean water to drink, which are to be considered as our birthright has started diminishing. The tradition of religious bath and tree worship which have deep rooted historicity is a general feature of India's religious life.

Environmental initiatives extend beyond legal compliance and include energy conservation, environmental preservation, recycling, waste management, water conservation and using of eco-friendly products. Preservation of environment raises difficult and complex issues. The fundamental question before the world today is whether we can allow this destruction of the environment to continue. We are proud of our culture and heritage. We have been taught to worship nature. We acknowledge our dependence on the environment. Our religion enshrines respect for nature, environmental harmony and conservation. Trees, animals, hills, mountains, rivers are worshipped as symbols of representatives of nature. Since vedic times, the main motto of social life was to live in harmony with nature. The following hymn is found in *Rigveda*:

> *"The Sky is like Father. The Earth is like Mother, and The Space is as their son; The Universe consisting of the Three, is like a Family, and any kind of damage done to any one of the three, throws the Universe out of balance. "*

Tiny Sikkim, the land of unspoilt and natural beauty is the Kingdom of Mountains, flowers and peace, with its majestic and gigantic guardian mount Khang-Chen-Dzo-Nga. Over the last three decades, one finds that the transformation from monarchy to democracy is always towards positive development of the State of Sikkim in order to project itself to be one of the best and model States of India. Law and development has taken place without affecting Sikkim's greens, environment, culture, traditions, langugages, style and way to life of the peace loving people. The main aim should be to achieve an eco-friendly sustainable development with stress on peace, national building, strong infrastructure, self-sufficiency, upliftment of the rural poor and unity among all people irrespective of their religions, communities, class, caste and creed to ensure a prosperous Sikkim in affluent India.

It is my earnest desire that in every sphere, intellectuals must adamantly play their dominant role in the all round development of Sikkim.

ಔಔಔಔ

PART XVI

MISCELLANEOUS

Part XVI

Miscellaneous

KALAKSHETRA

When one talks of Kalakshetra, one really talks about its Founder Smt. Rukmani Devi. It may not be an exaggeration to say that Smt. Rukmani Devi, the reasons for establishing Kalakshetra is, with the sole purpose of resuscitating in modern India, a recognition of the priceless artistic traditions of our country and of imparting to the young, the true spirit of the art devoid of vulgarity and commercialism. This great institution, Kalakshetra, stands as a monument to the life long devotion and total dedication of Smt. Rukmani Devi to the Indian cultural values in general and South Indian classical dances in particular.

During 1926, Smt. Rukmani Devi established this great institution as an Academy of Arts and started training young pupils in Bharathanatyam. Smt. Rukmani Devi, being an Indian Lady and belonging to a conservative family, broke the shackles of tradition and got married to Dr. G.S. Arundale. Later, she founded along with her husband, the Besant Theosophical High School. She also established Montessory School of Arundale for training teachers in association with Dr. Maria Montissory, who has invited Indians to train teachers from all over the country. Today, we find within the Kalakshetra Complex, Arts College, Besant Arundale English Secondary School, Craft, Education and Research Centre, cosisting of a Weaving Department, where traditional hand-woven sarees and dance costumes, silk and cotton, are woven and a unit for block printing and painting of textiles with vegetable dyes is set up.

The Kalakshetra theatre is again the brain child of Smt. Rukmani Arundale who constructed the same, based on the canons of Bharatha Natya Shastra and the fashions of the traditional Koothambalam, Kerala.

Smt. Rukmani Devi Arundale has also composed, choreographed, produced and staged many major dance dramas and plays as well as revival of a number of ancient dance drama forms.

When Smt. Rukmani Devi Arundale wanted to establish this great institution, she had no money, no land and no building. On account of her great efforts and perseverance, Kalakshetra was born and is situated in a sprawling

---

Speech delivered on occasion of the "Kalakshetrá Dance Festival" at Chennai on 21st October, 1994.

campus wherein, a full education in Arts is being imparted to young students. More than anything else, wearing of handloom sarees, for Mrs. Rukmani Devi was maintenance of cultural heritage. She found beauty in every aspect of life.

She brought out a hand-woven saree which is an admixture of cotton and silk. Kalakshetra Sarees are known for their deep colour and broad model with a traditional design. The saree is divided into three inner parts, the upper and the lower parts forming the borders. Smt. Rukmani Devi established the weaving centre in Kalakshetra to keep alive the cultural tradition of our land.

It is interesting to note that the sarees designed and collected by Smt. Rukmani Devi were exhibited by Kalakshetra in collaboration with co-optex in various cities in India. Today, Kalakshetra is taken over and run by the Government of India, having regard to the natural importance and value.

Shri K. Sankara Menon has been holding aloft traditions of Kalakshetra for all these years, despite his age. According to Smt. Rukmani Devi, there is no art which does not throw open the human emotions and without the human emotion, the art becomes cold and uninspiring. She wanted the revival of the spirit behind the arts and not merely the revival of art forms.

Dr. Besant did not want to have a statue or a memorial and she only wanted a monument in the form of boys and girls who would carry on the great message of the tradition of our country and who will also give to the new world a leadership which will bring happiness to men. This august institution had produced great musicians, dancers, painters, etc. It is also refreshing to note that Gurukula system is being followed here.

I am sure and confident that Kalakshetra is fulfilling the objects and purpose for which it was established *i.e.*, to produce good citizens who are proud of their motherland. The College of Fine Arts which has various disciplines, has grown from strength to strength.

Let the sounds of music, the rhythemic tinkle of ankle bells, the melodious ragas, the music of traditional instruments reverberate through the hallowed grounds of Kalakshetra in an atmosphere which is condusive to progress for all time to come and let not paucity of funds ever stifle this progress, dear to Smt. Rukmani Devi's heart.

Kalakshetra is progressing well and it shall be, in time, able to be much better, supported. In due course, this institution will be a memorial to the genius and vision of its founder and be a training ground such as she wished, for the young and highly talented youth of our country.

This institution has been recognised as one of national importance and accordingly it has been declared as an Institution of National Importance by the Parliament, under the Kalakshetra Foundation Act, 1993, and the Central Government has acquired all the assets and properties of Kalakshetra and established Kalakshetra Foundation to be administered by a Governing Body. This institution is an international institution which is primarily engaged in the promotion and development of Art and Culture in its pristine purity. Mrs. Rukmani Devi Arundale deserves all respect and admiration and this institution remains and will continue to remain as a permanent monument to her contribution for the development of Indian Arts and Culture. Her passionate quest of Arts and Culture has evoked international acclaim. My best wishes are for the future growth and development of this monumental institution.

Mr. R. Venkatraman, our former President, who incidentally happens to be my neighbour, is very active as ever. He is one of the Presidents who had to resolve many constitutional crisis. Many important decisions have been taken by him as the constitutional Head of the country. He is a man very faithful to the inner-voice of his conscience. He believes in parliamentary democracy. His decisions on the interpretation of Constitution are independent, impartial and above political parties. The industrial growth in this State is because of him.

He has faced many challenges and difficult times. He erased the wrong impression of some that the President of India is only is figure head. He held the office of President in a manner which elicited the esteem and approval of different political parties. I really look at him with great admiration and respect. The entire nation is indebted to him for his valuable service. I am confident that, as the Chairperson of this foundation, he will ensure that the institution will continue to grow from strength to strength. I wish the institution all success.

ಬಿಬಿಬಿ

CREDIT CARD SYSTEM

The modern Banker renders variety of services to its customers which were not in the contemplation of Sheldon or Dr. Hart when they defined a banker. During the course of centuries, the Banks have been catering to almost all the sanctions of the society. A modern Banker is the custodian of the monetary economics of the country. Introduction of credit card system is of recent origin and it really saves the customers from carrying money with them at great risk. Almost all the nationalized banks have introduced the credit card system. There cannot be two different opinions as to the usefulness of the credit card system. But, in my opinion the Banker has to be very cautious in fixing the credit limit for, an unscrupulous customer is likely to land the bank in litigation.

Under the credit card system, the bank grants credit to its credit card holders after satisfying itself about the credit worthiness of the customers. It is a novel method and it immensely helps the credit card holders and, they are saved from the botheration of carrying cash in hand.

I now learn that, of all the cards now in the market, CANCARD tops the list with 1,40,000 cards with over 10,000 member establishments. For any Card to be successful in the market, it is essential that there should be enough member establishments to accept and honour the Card. Canara Bank is successful in enlisting many member establishments and it has become a natural choice for many people to go in for Cancards. It is because of this advantage, several Bank have entered into tie-up arrangements with Canara Bank.

Indian Overseas Bank, one of the pioneering Banks in India is launching the Credit Card scheme today. They are going to market Cancard under their name. Because of their expertise in baking, I have no doubt whatever that they will be able to market Cancard very successfully.

The awareness about the Credit Card has already been created amongst people and soon IOB Credit Card will become part and parcel of everyone's life.

ಐ ಐ ಐ

Speech delivered at 'Inaugural Function of introducing Cancard – Credit Card System at Chennai on 2nd November, 1991.

RICH IN IDEAL – POOR IN REAL

In the last 55 years, ever since India became independent, we have witnessed tremendous changes in the status of women. Industrial Revolution opened up many avenues and opportunities for women. But due to casteism, illiteracy, and out-dated customs and tradition the full potential of Indian women could not be gauged.

Gender bias, injustice, violence and inequities towards women are a Universal phenomenon. In spite of multiple roles, she still belongs to a disadvantaged status in our society. She continues to be a sufferer of untold miseries and atrocities caused by a male dominated society. Condition of women in a developing country like India is still far from satisfactory.

Women account for 50% of the population in India. We cannot expect any sort of progress, enrichment or development by oppressing or suppressing half of our population. UNO Report (1980) points that Women constitute half the World's population, perform nearly two-thirds of work hours, receive one-tenth of World's income, but own less than 1% of World's property. UNDPs Human Development Report for 1995 further shows that 70% of world's poor are women. According to Common Wealth Human Rights Initiative, two-third of illiterate people in the World are women & 70% of dropouts from schools are girl children. Malnutrition and mortality rates are higher among girls. The figure regarding women's condition is more appalling in India. Rape takes place once in every 54 minutes, dowry deaths every 1000 minutes. The female – male ratio is in a descending pattern. In 1981, the figure was 933 Women per 1000 men. It descended to 929: 1000 in 1991. It has further descended in 2001. As per 1991 Census, female literacy rate was only 39.42% compared to male literacy rate of 63.86%. The figure has not improved much in 2001.

The representation of women has never gone beyond 8% in Parliament, 10% in State Assemblies and 13% in Council of Ministers. More disheartening figures indicate that 276 million women are still illiterate. In the total workforce, women representations do not exceed 23%. Women of India are the most unrepresented sections in the present political system. On the Executive side, only 5.8% of Senior management and administrative posts are occupied by women.

Delivered at Women Lawyers' Association, Chennai on 29th November, 2003.

In Judiciary, only 3% of the Judges are women. In the 12th Lok Sabha there were only 43 women MPs and 19 in Rajya Sabha. These figures are quite disheartening. Though Women's Reservation Bill, providing for 33% reservation for women in Legislature, was introduced, after much difficulty, the Bill could not be passed.

The National Policy for the Empowerment of Women was evolved in the year 2001. The Policy stresses the need for highlighting a gender perspective in the development process. The economic empowerment of women through poverty eradication, adverse impact of globalization and self-sufficiency for women was greatly emphasized in the policy. Social empowerment of women by addressing issues in various sectors such as education, health, nutrition, science and technology was also given primacy in the policy. While celebrating the 50th Anniversary of the Declaration of Human Rights, the United Nations Agencies had called for a global Campaign for the elimination of gender-based violence in 1998.

Coming to our women in India, we find plethora of laws and policies which are protective of women. Our very Constitution has shown deep concern for the upliftment of the womenfolk. The Preamble to the Constitution guarantees social Justice that ensures justice to women. The Constitution treats women as equal to men by virtue of Article 14 while they are considered special and more equal by virtue of Article 15(3). The Constitution prohibits any discrimination, solely based on ground of Sex in general, and in the matter of public employment. This is a fundamental right. Article 16 provides for equality of opportunity in public service. Directive Principles in Part IV, through Article 39(a), direct that the State shall endeavour to secure right to means of livelihood to all the citizens, irrespective of sex while Article 39(d) directs equal pay for equal work. Article 42 takes care of humane conditions of work and maternity relief. Above all, Article 51A(e) recognizes the fundamental duty of every citizen to renounce the practices, derogatory to the dignity of women. Statute Books over flow with protective laws for women. The Immoral Traffic Prevention Act, 1956 as amended in 1986, made drastic changes to curb the social evil of dowry harassment. The Indecent Representation of Women (Prohibition) Act, 1986; The Commission of Sati (Prevention) Act, 1987; The Medical Termination of Pregnancy Act, 1971, were all intended to curb the social depravity suffered by women.

The latest amendments to section 125, CPC have made the maintenance provisions more realistic and practical. Various other welfare laws include maternity benefits, prohibition of employment of women in dangerous activities and creche facilities for the children of the working women. A few attempts have already been made on the part of the Parliament to involve women in local governance. 74th Amendment of the Constitution (Panchayat Raj & Nagarpalika Amendment Acts) has reserved Seats for women in the local governments *vide* Article 243A to 243D and Articles 243P to 243ZG. Few seats are reserved for women to head Panchayats also. This is a progressive step towards women empowerment. National Commission for Women is an authority, constituted to supervise and implement the safeguards provided under the Constitution and other laws. The Commission is also empowered to monitor the socio-economic development of women in all spheres. But this Commission has not been given a Constitutional Status.

This Indian Judiciary has also not been lagging behind in its attempt to interpret and implement laws relating to women. By assuming a proactive role, the Supreme Court and the High Courts have been addressing the issues of women on a war footing.

Various decisions of the Supreme Court throw light on the role, assumed by the Judiciary in protecting the rights of women and upholding their dignity. In *Vishal Jeet* v. *Union of India*, AIR 1990 SC 1412: (1990) 2 SCR 861: (1990) 3 SCC 318 detailed guidelines were given to prevent trafficking in young girls, to be observed by the respective Governments. *Vishaka* v. *State of Rajasthan*, AIR 1997 SC 3011: (1997) 6 SCC 241 is a trendsetter that ensures full freedom and congenial atmosphere for working women at work places and prevent sexual harassment. In *Gita Hariharan* v. *Reserve Bank of India*, (1999) 2 SCC 228, the Supreme Court expressly placed a mother on an equal footing to that of a father as guardian of a child. In *Apparel Export Promotion Council* v. *A.K. Chopra*, 1999 SC 625: (1999) 1 SCC 759, the Apex Court has re-affirmed the rights of women *vis-à-vis Vishaka* guidelines, more precisely.

By taking recourse to purposive interpretation of Article 15(3), the Supreme Court had upheld a service rule that preferred women to the extent of 30% in Public Employment, in the famous case of *Government of Andhra Pradesh* v. *P.B. Vijayakumar*, AIR 1995 SC 1648: (1995) 4 SCC 520. The observation of the Court is relevant in this context *"To say that under Article 15(3), job opportunities for women cannot be created would be to cut at the very root of the underlying inspiration behind this Article. Making special provisions for women in respect of employment or posts under the State is an integral part of Article 15(3)"*.

Inspite of all the constitutional guarantees, protective laws and proactive role of the Judiciary, the sad plight of the Indian Women is far from being ameliorated. The goal of gender justice and equality can be achieved only by way of introspection and creating awareness, shedding male chauvinism and dominance. The class of working women needs social acceptability. Women, taking up employments are not favoured by the upper class. This is a social problem that negatives women empowerment. Our social system needs attitudinal transformation towards women's role and economic empowerment can be achieved only through collective consciousness. Similarly, women's political empowerment can bring forth a new vision oriented development wherein, there is poverty eradication, elimination of inequality in education, improvement of health care and over all development of the nation.

In Public Services especially the police, women are minimal. The role of the Judiciary regarding women and the law, leaves much to be desired. With male dominance at the higher judicial levels, role of the women in decision-making process is minimized. In this context, the Chinese legal system is highly appreciative. Today in China, where the number of lawyers are much less than ours, over 10,000 women Judges preside over the Courts. Of late, China has been laying greater stress on training women judges. The atmosphere in Courts can be changed to a large extent if women Judges are multiplied. If more and more women police are made to operate and if number of women Judges and legislators are increased so as to make and interpret Laws to meet the just demands of women, gender justice in law and in fact will be a reality.

We require adequate number of well-trained Mediators and Conciliators, functioning at all levels. The Retired Judges and Judicial Officers who are known to possess reasonable amount of patience and skill of persuasion, can be requested to function as Mediators and Conciliators. Apart from people with legal background, even persons of different disciplines and backgrounds can also be included in the panel.

A number of Judicial Officers and Advocates have been provided training to develop their skills in techniques of negotiation and conciliation. Such training programmes are conducted frequently for the benefit of judicial officers and members of the Bar.

It hardly needs to be emphasized that lawyers play an important role in the administration of justice. Judges cannot perform their task of dispensing justice effectively, without the support of lawyers. It is often said that judges and lawyers are the two sides of the same coin.

For any civil society, governed by Rule of Law, effective judicial system is a necessary concomitant. The Rule of Law reflects man's sense of order and justice. There can be no Government without order; there can be no order without law; and there can be no administration of law without lawyers.

In fact, Bar is the judge of Judges and, therefore, we need responsive, sensitive and an upright Bar. Once we justify the need for an effective Bar, justification for a strong and junior effective Bar is automatic.

The success and healthy development of any profession does not depend solely on the successful strata of that profession. The Junior members in any profession are the core and strength of that profession, as they are the seeds of tomorrow.

It is the solemn duty of Seniors in the profession to train and guide the junior members. Juniors are entitled to receive reasonable remuneration. It is equally the duty of the Courts to encourage the Juniors. The Government, the Bar Councils and Bar Associations have a very important and useful role to play as well.

No doubt, for creating strong Junior Bar, all the players *viz.* Senior Lawyers, Courts, Government, Bar Councils and Bar Associations have to play significant and meaningful role. As far as role of the Courts is concerned, it is emphasized in aforesaid remarks that it is their duty to encourage Juniors. In fact, a Judge can do much more than that.

By no means, it is suggested that a Judge should show undue favour to junior advocates or do something which law does not permit. Primarily, it is for the lawyer, whether Senior or Junior, to prepare his case thoroughly and do his home work in order to achieve results. However, the Court can create an atmosphere, ensuring that a junior advocate is able to exhibit the talent which he possesses. Shakespeare had said : *Some people are born sick, some acquire sickness and there are some upon whom sickness is thrusted.* I would give the statement a positive twist and say that some persons are born genius and some persons are helped to become genius. It is our responsibility to create genius of second category as far as junior Bar is concerned.

It is not only by giving such encouragement in Court proceedings that the Judge can help the junior Bar, there are many other ways available to the Court to encourage young advocates. Those junior advocates who are promising can be encouraged by appointing them as *amicus curiae* or as local Commissioners in the matter where such appointments is warranted. They can be encouraged in legal aid matters. On various occasions, particularly in PIL etc., committees of lawyers are appointed as fact-finding committees. In those committees, such young lawyers can be accommodated along with their senior colleagues as other members of the committee.

As a befitting epithet to women-hood, before finishing, I pay my respects to Indian Women by quoting SHERIDAN.

"Women govern us, let us try to render them perfect. The more they are enlightened so much more we shall be. On the cultivation of the minds of women, depends the wisdom of man".

ಬಬಬ

SUCCESS THROUGH A BALANCED APPROACH

On the occasion of the Golden Jubilee Celebrations of the Andhra Pradesh High Court, the Judges of the High Court and the Members of the Bar can be proud of the record of services and usefulness being rendered for all these years to the society at large.

We commemorate the occasions like Silver Jubilee Celebrations, Golden Jubilee Celebrations etc. to share our delightfulness with all the persons connected with the institution and recall the services of the persons who were instrumental for today's continued utility of the institution to the cause of the society through the passage of 50 years.

At the same time, on an occasions like this, we, both the Judges and the Members of the legal fraternity, should put ourselves to an accurate test and check ourselves as to whether we are discharging our pious duties, conferred on us, to the best of our ability and one's own satisfaction. Unless we do so, the purpose of such celebrations will be lost.

It is said that justice hurried is justice buried and at the same time justice delayed is justice denied. We have to read these two sayings with another important factor i.e., justice should not only be done, but should also manifestly appear to have been done. A perfect blend of these sayings strikes a nice balance between the quantitative and qualitative aspects of justice delivery system.

The consequences of judicial delays for ordinary litigants are immense, and in some cases even tragic. Judicial delays, whether in cases involving high-profile persons or those relating to ordinary litigants, are not justifiable, and so there is a dire need to alleviate their grievances. Any delay in expeditious disposal of criminal trial infringes on the right to life and liberty guaranteed under Article 21 of the Constitution of India. Therefore, a lawyer, being an Officer of the Court, should not seek adjournments for silly reasons and he owes a duty to assist the Court in speedy disposal of cases. Accordingly, the Officers also should not grant adjournments on mere asking. They must think judiciously to granting even a single adjournment. Otherwise, it will create mental agony for the parties. Especially in matrimonial cases, during the prime and blissful part of their age,

---

Speech delivered at the Golden Jubilee Celebrations of Andhra Pradesh High Court at Hyderabad on 5th November, 2005.

the parties round the corridors of the Courts, keeping immense faith in the administration of justice that their cases would be disposed of at the earliest point of time and that they could also live happily in the later part of their lives.

I have noticed that the Advocates have been boycotting the Courts very frequently for the reasons, not always justified. Frequent boycott of Courts by the Advocates, resulting in immense hardship to the litigant public, has been deprecated even by the Supreme Court on several occasions. A Bench of three Judges comprising of Hon'ble Mr. Justice S.N. Variava, myself and Hon'ble Mr. Justice S.H. Kapadia again reiterated the same in the case of Common Cause 'A' Registered Society etc. vs. Union of India & Ors. etc. pertaining to the Delhi Lawyers' Strike. On this occasion, I deem it necessary to appeal to the learned Members of the Bar to ponder on this aspect and avoid abstention from work by resorting to boycott of Courts for reasons unconnected with the administration of justice, and to discharge their professional obligation of assisting the Court in the pursuit of rendering justice to the litigant public. Hence, let all of us, connected with the administration of justice, pledge ourselves that we will put in all efforts for early disposal of such cases.

No discussion on the judicial system is ever complete without deliberating upon the significance of the relationship between the Bench and the Bar. This is so because the judicial system gets complete not with the Bench alone or with the Bar alone, but it acquires fullness only with both the Bench and the Bar. So it is inevitable that where the judicial system comes to be discussed, the relationship between the Bench and the Bar figures as an important subject. This happens because of the realization that if the judicial system has to remain healthy, the relationship between the Bench and the Bar should also be healthy. The Judges and the lawyers function in Courts to safeguard and promote the cause of justice for which millions of litigants at enormous cost and sufferings come to the Courts every day.

I will not be exaggerating if I were to say that in the course of 50 years of our Constitution, the best institution, of which we can be proud of, is our judiciary. Our judiciary has performed the task assigned to it under our Constitution in the best possible manner. Our Supreme Court is an institution which is comparable to the best in the world. Many jurists abroad mention that existence of a judiciary of this caliber, independence and eminence in a third world, is a rare thing. We are very proud of our Supreme Court.

What is sustaining this institution is public confidence. At times, it is said that the judiciary is exceeding its limits, or that the judiciary is not adhering to the principles of separation of powers. This criticism is not justified. The judiciary is doing something more than what the Constitution expected it to do, but that has been necessitated because the other wings of the State are not doing what is expected of them. The judiciary has to discharge its unpleasant, but nevertheless, fundamental duty, conferred on it under Article 32 of the Constitution.

From my experience, I am of the view that we do not need judges who are brilliant on the Bench of the Supreme Court or the High Courts. We need learned Judges. We need competent Judges, we need Judges who have patience and, above all, we need Judges of integrity.

My message to the jurists is that they must be fair, righteous, upright in their work or profession and in all other walks of life. Jurists should work together in achieving the goal of the jurisprudence and spiritual prudence in promoting the culture of peace, justice and harmony. We must devote some time daily on introspection, meditation, silence and study for our spiritual and moral development. We should endeavour in affirming the brotherhood of all human beings for achieving the spiritual values and divine qualities.

Every Judge in India bears faith in, and allegiance to the Constitution of India. This faith and allegiance have a meaning only if he truly shares the social, economic and political philosophy that forms the vital parts and the background of the Constitution and determines its thrust and its strategy of action. This philosophy and strategy are reflected, besides other parts of the Constitution, in its Preamble, Directive Principles of State Policy, Fundamental Rights, Fundamental Duties etc.

The Directive Principles of State Policy depict the ambitions and aspiration of the Fathers of the Constitution. These Directive Principles indicate the objects and goals of the Republic and also lay the strategy of action to achieve these. So, Judiciary which constitutes one of the four pillars of the State and is an important agency, empowered to work for realization of these goals, must interpret, apply and enforce the law in accord with the guide-lines provided by these Directive Principles.

"Every saint has a past; every sinner has a future;" It would, therefore, be wrong to think that a criminal was always a criminal and would always be a criminal. Let the judiciary and the law enforcing agencies, therefore, not snatch away from him his sense of individual dignity, his feeling of respect and let not his divine spark be attacked so hard as to give smoke instead of a shine. At the same time, your scales say that you have to strike a balance, there should not be a compromise in delivering the Justice. Steps towards transformation and realization are highly appreciable.

I must confess that this invitation had for me a special interest because it gave me an opportunity to renew my acquaintance with these familiar surroundings with which I have been so intimately connected for a long period as Chief Justice of this High Court. I am part and parcel of this legal fraternity and will always so remain wherever I am.

The High Court of Andhra Pradesh is an institution with a glorious history of about 50 years. It has produced ten Supreme Court Judges, innumerable High Court Judges, legal luminaries and Bureaucrats ; Justice K. Subba Rao, Justice Satyanarayana Raju, Justice Jagmohan Reddy, Justice Chinnappa Reddy, Justice K. Ramaswamy, Justice K. Jayachandra Reddy, Justice B.P. Jeevan Reddy, Justice M. Jagannatha Rao, Justice S.S.M. Quadri and Justice P.V. Reddi.

I am sure that the members of this great Court would contribute to the growth of material and moral wealth of our nation. It is hard work and total dedication which bring success.

I close with fervent hope that the great tradition of an efficient Judiciary, wholly dedicated to the cause of the people will be kept alive as was done in the past. I sincerely congratulate the Hon'ble Chief Justice of the Andhra Pradesh High Court – Shri Bilal Nazki, Hon'ble Chief Minister of Andhra Pradesh, and all other Hon'ble Judges, the Andhra Pradesh Judiciary and the Bar, and the High Court staff and Government for their efforts to bring the temple of Justice at the doorstep of the people here in Andhra Pradesh. I salute & pay tributes to all those who had strived for this endeavour, making it a reality.

On this memorable occasion of the Golden Jubilee Celebrations, let us once again take the oath that we will place all our efforts for the cause of justice to the people.

ಬಬಬ

SOCIAL RESPONSIBILITY OF LEGAL FRATERNITY

The Constitution of India, which according to Granville Austin is primarily a social document, encapsulates the aspirations and hopes of the people of this great nation and guarantees fundamental rights to every citizen.

India presents a mosaic of different cultures, a confluence of diverse religious and schools of philosophy and a synthesis of different ethnical and linguistic groups. However, the largest and greatest democracy in the entire world where all the global convergent influences, including Hinduism, Islam, Christianity, Sikhism, Jainism, Buddhism, Secularism, Liberalism, democracy, socialism, Gandhism run parallel it is extremely distressing to point out that all people do not have a level playing field.

The law which dictates as well as shapes the social behaviour of the population of any society is a close ally of liberty and constitutes important means of fostering personal freedom, safeguarding human rights and furthering broad social goals of equality and general well being. Law and life are symbiotic, law touches us at all points. It is an indubitable structure, organic and living and, in essence, nothing but synonym for fundamental principles of equity and fair play. The judges and lawyers have the undeniable duty to uphold and defend the law. Equal justice has to be delivered irrespective of caste, creed, religion, sex, place of birth, socio-economic status. This is also our Constitutional mandate.

Each country has its own socio-economic milleu and national ethos. In our social milleu, law is a social institution itself which has a great role to play in providing such an environment wherein, every inhabitant of the country can hold high their banner of rights fearlessly and with conviction. It is the task of jurisprudence to develop such a scheme whereby, maximum satisfaction of socially worthwhile purpose might be accomplished.

Fearlessness and service are part of our great Indian heritage. The judges who are the legal guardians and the lawyers who are officers of the Court and legally entitled spokesperson of the community have great social responsibilities. The real test of the independence of judiciary arises when times are abnormal, when the general atmosphere is surcharged with passion and emotion and when

---

Speech delivered at All India Seminar on Social Responsibility of Legal Fraternity, organised by Legal Assistance Forum at New Delhi on 11th November, 2005.

446

those in power attempt to superimpose their vested interests at the cost of common good. On day to day basis, the Courts undergo test as to whether they are efficiently and effectively able to dispose of cases with equal hands. The lawyers, as the general public, expects from them, should be thorough professionals of integrity and competence who uphold the cause of justice.

Lawyers must be men or women of substance, having full sense of their social responsibilities as social technicians and architects of the justicing process. They must have a grasp of the endless tradition and must be aware of the greatness of their task which shapes the categories through which life flows. They must put aside mere desire for material enhancement and be capable of humility in their exercise, being a servant of justice and the conscience of the community.

The vulnerable sections of the society who are marginalized, without actually participating in the true judicial, democratic and political process, have to be dealt with sensitively and carefully. Owing to their powerlessness, poverty, ignorance, they need assistance for empowerment with knowledge and capacity to uphold their own rights as being integral part of the society. Legal literacy campaign, paralegal training programmes, mobilization of public opinion against injustice and exploitation, out of Court settlement of disputes, legal advise etc. are some of the ways through which the poor and the underprivileged can be made to realize their rights and also learn about their own importance in shaping and rejuvenating this great nation.

This is where organizations like Legal Assistance Forum can render their service in both rural and urban areas through their multi-dimensional activities and be a great source of strength, support and inspiration to the oppressed and exploited sections of our country. I agree with the suggestion of Mr. Hansaria that senior lawyers must render free service to the poor and underprivileged for which the Bar Association must formulate a suitable mechanism. The Forum, by trying to conscientise the people of their social responsibility, has taken up a laudable task. I congratulate the entire Forum and wish them great success in this noble socially motivated venture.

ಬಬಬ

LAW & TERRORISM

Terrorism, a destructive phenomenon, is spreading rapidly with the virulence of an epidemic. The darkest chapters of the world history are full of violent tales of terror, differing only in form, time, names and communities. Today, terrorism has become part and parcel of world politics and has assumed alarming proportions. Almost every country is engulfed by some form or another of terrorism. The crisis has barely left any country unscathed. Amongst the nations most affected have been US, India, UK, France, Spain, Israel, Russia and Saudi Arabia. Though acts of terrorism are as old as human civilization, it has taken an unprecedented ugly turn over the last few years. Modern modes of creating terror stand on a different footing from those in the past because its victims are frequently innocent civilians who are picked at random. There is hardly a day when a dozen or more innocent persons do not fall to the bullets of terrorists, women raped, children starved, the elderly done to death and human beings kidnapped and made hostages. Terrorism has no ethics or conscience. It is being nurtured under the garb of religious training, manifested in fundamentalism.

To respond to the challenges passed by this problem, our government has time and again armed itself with stringent laws like TADA, POTA, Defence of India Rules, MISA, Armed Forces(Special Powers) Act, Terrorist Affected Areas (Special Courts) Act, 1984, Disturbed Areas (Special Courts) Act, 1976. However, experience has shown that these laws have not been completely effective in tackling the menace. The wings of terrorism keep spreading themselves to overawe the State. Sometimes it is Gujarat and sometimes it is Ayodhya. One day the merchants of terror attack the capital of the country, on another day they may choose some other commercial capital. The State of Jammu and Kashmir, once known for its picturesque landscape, has been reduced to a hub of terrorist activity. The rapture of bird song and murmur of gentile streams which were common place have been replaced by the misery of physical and psychic violence instigated in the name of religion. The number of leaders and activists who have fallen prey to terrorism is horrendous. No wonder, the issue has taken centre stage across the globe and has become a matter of concern, worldwide.

Speech delivered in the National Seminar on Law & Terrorism at Krishna Menon Bhawan, New Delhi organised by Indian Council of Jurists on 26th November, 2005.

Former Chief Justice of India, Hon'ble Shri M.N. Venkatachaliah, on writing a Foreword to the book authored by Mr. D.R. Kaarthikeyan has stated thus:

History is replete with instances of attempts to 'redraw national boundaries with blood'. Achievement of political ends by violent means has become increasingly attractive to those who do not trust legitimate means. Pursuit of political power is marked by a ruthlessness of the means. Democratic processes and alternatives are the only answer to the temptations to resort to violent means of political change. Fortunately, there has been in the last two decades a marked thrust towards democratic institutions. Some eighty one more countries in the world have opted for democratic systems in the last two decades. Thirty three of them earlier had military regimes. The number of countries that have ratified the two international covenants on Human Rights has gone up from 60 to 150 in the last decade alone.

The assassinations of Mahatma Gandhi, Indira Gandhi and Rajiv Gandhi profoundly influenced the course of political developments in the country and even altered, in a non-trivial sense, the course of contemporary history. These tragic events opened our eyes to the increasing vulnerability of Indian democracy.

Rajiv Gandhi's assassination, like other earlier assassinations, saddened and shocked the people of India. The entire world took anguished notice of the magnitude of this tragedy and its implications. There was a general demand for explanation and action. Mr. D.R. Kaarthikeyan, a police officer with vast experience and a reputation for integrity accepted the responsibility for investigation. It was an awesome responsibility at a time when the public image of the Indian police was not particularly high. Unlike President Kennedy's assassination, in which the Warren Commission found 'no evidence that either Lee Harvey Oswald or Jack Ruby was part of any conspiracy either domestic or foreign', Rajiv Gandhi's assassination was the clear outcome of a deep-seated conspiracy. In the Kennedy case, the speed of the investigation was, indeed, electric.

But the Rajiv Gandhi case had ramifications far too involved for complacence and needed skilled, dexterous, professional investigation."

It was a mammoth investigation with massive evidence and documentation. The judiciary not only upheld our investigation and findings but even applauded us.

The mounting incidents of terrorism called a unified approach and uncompromising measures to tackle it. It requires both domestic as well as international organizations. It has to be dealt with, in a concerted manner, by addressing all its dimensions, including smuggling and trafficking in drugs and arms. These ancillary activities constitute the backbone of organized crime through sponsorship. The paramount objective, after all is the security and integrity of a nation that believes in "live and let live".

ಬಲಬಲ